Processing XML documents with Oracle JDeveloper 11g

Creating, validating, and transforming XML documents with Oracle's IDE

Deepak Vohra

[PACKT] PUBLISHING

BIRMINGHAM - MUMBAI

Processing XML documents with Oracle JDeveloper 11g

First published: February 2009

Production Reference: 1190209

Published by Packt Publishing Ltd.
32 Lincoln Road
Olton
Birmingham, B27 6PA, UK.

ISBN 978-1-847196-66-8

www.packtpub.com

Cover Image by Vinayak Chittar (vinayak.chittar@gmail.com)

Credits

Author

Deepak Vohra

Reviewers

Avrom Roy-Faderman

Frank Nimphius

Acquisition Editor

James Lumsden

Technical Editor

Aditi Srivastava

Copy Editor

Sneha Kulkarni

Editorial Team Leader

Akshara Aware

Project Manager

Abhijeet Deobhakta

Project Coordinator

Lata Basantani

Indexer

Rekha Nair

Proofreader

Chris Smith

Production Coordinator

Aparna Bhagat

Cover Work

Aparna Bhagat

About the author

Deepak Vohra is a consultant and a principal member of the NuBean software company. Deepak is a Sun Certified Java Programmer and a Web Component Developer, and has worked in the fields of XML and Java programming and J2EE for over five years. Deepak is the author of the book *JDBC 4.0 and Oracle JDeveloper for J2EE Development* published by Packt Publishing.

About the reviewers

Avrom Roy-Faderman is a Java EE consultant, developer, and trainer, specializing in Oracle Application Development Framework. He's the co-author of two books with Paul Dorsey and Peter Koletzke: *Oracle9i JDeveloper Handbook* and *Oracle JDeveloper 10g Handbook*, both from Osborne/McGraw-Hill and Oracle Press. He's also the co-author, with PeterKoletzke and Duncan Mills, of a forthcoming book about Fusion web development with Oracle JDeveloper 11g.

Frank Nimphius has been a Principal Product Manager for application development tools at Oracle Corporation since 1999. Prior to this, he worked for Oracle Germany for more than three years in the Oracle Sales Consulting Orgnanization. Frank actively contributes to the development of Oracle JDeveloper and the Oracle Application Development Framework (ADF). As a conference speaker, Frank represents the Oracle J2EE development team at J2EE conferences worldwide, including various Oracle user groups and the Oracle Open World conference.

Table of Contents

Preface

While a number of books on XML are available, none covers XML support in Oracle JDeveloper. Welcome to *Processing XML documents with Oracle JDeveloper 11g*, a book that will teach you about using Oracle XML technologies in Oracle JDeveloper. XML is the standard medium of data exchange. Examples of data exchange using XML are web feeds, which include RSS feeds and Atom feeds, and XML messages in web services. Java is the language most commonly used to process XML. Among the IDEs, Oracle JDeveloper has the most XML features. Some of the graphical XML features in JDeveloper are an XML editor to create an XML document, an XML schema editor to model an XML schema, and an XPath explorer to process XPath expressions. JDeveloper also provides built-in support for JAXB compilation. JDeveloper includes an integrated application server — the WebLogic Server — for running XML-based applications. Oracle **XML Developer Kit** (**XDK**) provides a set of components, tools, and utilities for developing XML-based applications. The XDK 11g libraries are included with Oracle JDeveloper 11g.

The objective of this book is to discuss XML development in Oracle JDeveloper. We shall use JDeveloper 11g, the latest version of JDeveloper. As developers commonly use an IDE for processing XML and developing XML applications, the book covers all aspects of XML development, which include:

- Creating an XML document
- Validating an XML document with an XML schema
- Transforming an XML document
- Addressing elements/attributes in an XML document using XPath

We shall use the Oracle XDK 11g for Java to develop XML applications. We shall also discuss Oracle XML Publisher and Oracle Berkeley DB XML. By the end of this book, you should know everything there is to know about XML and JDeveloper.

What this book covers

Chapter 1: We discuss creating an XML document using Oracle's **XML Developer Kit (XDK)** 11g in Oracle JDeveloper. We also discuss parsing an XML document using SAX and DOM Java APIs, which are also included in XDK 11g.

Chapter 2: We create an XML schema in the XML schema editor of Oracle JDeveloper. An XML schema represents the structure of an XML document. Subsequently, we instantiate an XML document from the XML schema.

Chapter 3: We discuss validating an XML document with an XML schema using the built-in feature to validate the schema and the XDK 11g schema validation APIs. We discuss three different APIs for schema validation: the XSDValidator, the SAX parser, and the DOM parser.

Chapter 4: We discuss XPath, which is used to address nodes in an XML document. We use XPath in the XPath Search GUI tool in Oracle JDeveloper 11g. We also use the XPath Java API in XDK 11g.

Chapter 5: We transform an XML document using the **Transformation API** for **XML (TrAX)**, which is included in XDK 11g. We also discuss the XSLT extension functions.

Chapter 6: We parse and transform XML using the JSTL XML tag library in JDeveloper 11g.

Chapter 7: We load, save, and filter an XML document using the DOM 3.0 Load and Save APIs, which are provided in XDK 11g.

Chapter 8: We construct and validate an XML document using the DOM 3.0 Validation API, which is also included in XDK 11g.

Chapter 9: We discuss another built-in feature of JDeveloper 11g, the JAXB 2.0 compiler. We bind an XML schema to Java classes using the JAXB 2.0 compiler. Subsequently, we unmarshal an XML document and marshal an XML document using the compiled Java classes.

Chapter 10: We compare XML documents using the XMLDiff Java API included in XDK 11g.

Chapter 11: We convert an XML document to a PDF document using the Apache FOP Java API in JDeveloper.

Chapter 12: We create an MS Excel spreadsheet from an XML document in JDeveloper using the Apache POI Java API.

Chapter 13: We store an XML document in Oracle Berkeley DB XML, and subsequently query and update the XML document using both the Berkeley DB XML command shell and the Berkeley DB XML Java API. The Berkeley DB XML API is used in JDeveloper 11g.

Chapter 14: We create PDF reports in JDeveloper 11g using the Oracle XML Publisher Java API. We also merge PDF documents. We also create an XML report from a database table using the Data Engine API.

What you need for this book

The book is based on the Windows Install of Studio Edition of Oracle JDeveloper 11g. Therefore, you need to download and install JDeveloper 11g (`jdevstudio11110install.exe`) from `http://www.oracle.com/technology/software/products/jdev/htdocs/soft11.html`. The Windows Install requires Windows XP, 2003, or 2000. If you have Linux, the book may still be used (though it has not been tested with Linux) with slight modifications with the Linux Install. For example, the directory paths on Linux would be different than those of Windows used in the book. Other than Oracle JDeveloper 11g, you would need chapter-specific software. For example, for Chapter 11 you would need the Apache FOP binary distribution, for Chapter 12 you need to download the Apache POI HSSF API, for Chapter 13 you need to download Oracle Berkeley DB XML, and for Chapter 14 you need to download Oracle Database 10g or 11g and Oracle XML Publisher Enterprise 5.6.2.

Who is this book for?

The target audience of the book is XML application developers who want to learn about Oracle XML technologies and the XML features in Oracle JDeveloper 11g. Those who are already using Oracle XML technologies will learn about using the Oracle XML technologies in Oracle JDeveloper 11g. We won't be discussing the database-based XML technologies XSQL and XML SQL Utility, which were discussed in the book *JDBC 4.0 and Oracle JDeveloper for J2EE Development* (Packt Publishing). This book is suitable for professional XML developers. It is also suitable for an intermediate-level course in applied XML. The target audience is expected to have prior, albeit beginners', knowledge about XML such as: what an XML document is, what XSLT is, what XPath is, and what an XML schema is.

Conventions

In this book, you will find a number of styles of text that distinguish between different kinds of information. Here are some examples of these styles, and an explanation of their meaning.

Code words in text are shown as follows: "The XSDValidator class is used to validate an XML document that has been built into a DOM tree."

A block of code will be set as follows:

```
InputStream inputStream=new FileInputStream(new File("catalog.xsd"));
InputSource inputSource=new InputSource(inputStream);
XMLSchema schema =  builder.build(inputSource);
xsdValidator.setSchema(schema);
```

Any command-line input and output is written as follows:

```
dbxml>createContainer catalog.dbxml
```

New terms and **important words** are introduced in a bold-type font. Words that you see on the screen, in menus or dialog boxes for example, appear in our text like this: "In the **New Gallery** window select **Categories | General** and **Items | Generic Application.**"

[Warnings or important notes appear in a box like this.]

[Tips and tricks appear like this.]

Reader feedback

Feedback from our readers is always welcome. Let us know what you think about this book, what you liked or may have disliked. Reader feedback is important for us to develop titles that you really get the most out of.

To send us general feedback, simply drop an email to feedback@packtpub.com, making sure to mention the book title in the subject of your message.

If there is a book that you need and would like to see us publish, please send us a note in the **SUGGEST A TITLE** form on www.packtpub.com or email suggest@packtpub.com.

If there is a topic that you have expertise in and you are interested in either writing or contributing to a book, see our author guide on www.packtpub.com/authors.

Customer support

Now that you are the proud owner of a Packt book, we have a number of things to help you to get the most from your purchase.

Downloading the example code for the book

Visit http://www.packtpub.com/files/code/6668_Code.zip to directly download the example code.

The downloadable files contain instructions on how to use them.

Errata

Although we have taken every care to ensure the accuracy of our contents, mistakes do happen. If you find a mistake in one of our books—maybe a mistake in text or code—we would be grateful if you would report this to us. By doing this you can save other readers from frustration, and help to improve subsequent versions of this book. If you find any errata, report them by visiting http://www.packtpub.com/support, selecting your book, clicking on the **let us know** link, and entering the details of your errata. Once your errata are verified, your submission will be accepted and the errata added to the list of existing errata. The existing errata can be viewed by selecting your title from http://www.packtpub.com/support.

Piracy

Piracy of copyright material on the Internet is an ongoing problem across all media. At Packt, we take the protection of our copyright and licenses very seriously. If you come across any illegal copies of our works in any form on the Internet, please provide the location address or web site name immediately so we can pursue a remedy.

Please contact us at copyright@packtpub.com with a link to the suspected pirated material.

We appreciate your help in protecting our authors, and our ability to bring you valuable content.

Questions

You can contact us at questions@packtpub.com if you are having a problem with some aspect of the book, and we will do our best to address it.

Copyright credit

Some of the contents of this book were originally published by Oracle Technology Network. They are republished with the permission of Oracle.

1

Creating and Parsing an XML Document

One of the first programming exercises an XML developer wants to do is create and parse an XML document. The **Java API** for **XML Processing** (**JAXP**) includes an API to create and parse XML documents. Oracle XDK 11g provides an API in the `oracle.xml.parsers.v2` package that overrides some of the classes in the JAXP API. It also implements some additional interfaces such as `DocumentEditVAL`, `ElementEditVAL`, and `NSResolver`, which we shall discuss in later chapters. XDK also provides parser factory and parser classes in the `oracle.xml.jaxp` package that override the parser classes in the `javax.xml.parsers` package.

In this chapter we shall create an XML document, `catalog.xml`, and parse the XML document in JDeveloper.

The XML document that will be created and parsed is listed here:

```
<?xml version = '1.0' encoding = 'UTF-8'?>
<catalog>
    <journal:journal journal:title="Oracle Magazine"
    journal:publisher="Oracle Publishing" journal:edition=
    "March-April 2008" xmlns:journal=
    "http://xdk.com/catalog/journal">
      <journal:article journal:section="Oracle Developer">
      <journal:title>Declarative Data Filtering</journal:title>
          <journal:author>Steve Muench</journal:author>
      </journal:article>
    </journal:journal>
    <journal title="Oracle Magazine" publisher="Oracle
    Publishing" edition="September-October 2008 ">
      <article section="FEATURES">
          <title>Share 2.0</title>
```

```
            <author>Alan Joch</author>
        </article>
    </journal>
</catalog>
```

Some of the elements and attributes in the example XML document are in the namespace identified by URI http://xdk.com/catalog/journal, and namespace prefix journal. For example, the journal:journal element and the journal:edition attribute namespace nodes are included to demonstrate the creating and parsing of namespace nodes respectively.

The APIs of the oracle.xml.parsers.v2 and oracle.xml.jaxp packages are used to create and parse example XML documents. The oracle.xml.parsers.v2 package provides APIs for **DOM (Document Object Model)** and **SAX (Simple API for XML)** parsing. The oracle.xml.jaxp package provides APIs for obtaining parsers for DOM and SAX parsing.

Setting the environment

Download and install Oracle JDeveloper 11g Production. Create an application workspace in JDeveloper with **File | New**. In the **New Gallery** window select **Categories | General** and **Items | General Application**, and click on **OK**. The **Create Generic Application** wizard gets started. Specify an application name in the **Application Name** field and click on the **Next** button. In the **Name your Generic project** window, specify a project name in the **Project Name** field. From the **Project Technologies** list select **JSP and Servlets** and click on the **Finish** button. An application and a project get added to JDeveloper **Application Navigator**.

Next, we need to create applications for creating an XML document, parsing an XML document with the DOM API, and parsing an XML document with the SAX API. Select the **Projects** node in the **Application Navigator** and select **File | New.** In the **New Gallery** window select **Categories | General** and **Items | Java Class**, and click on the **OK** button. In the **Create Java Class** window specify a class name, CreateXMLDocument for example, in the **Name** field, a package name in the **Package** field, and click on the **OK** button. Similarly, add Java applications DOMParserApp and SAXParserApp to the JDeveloper project.

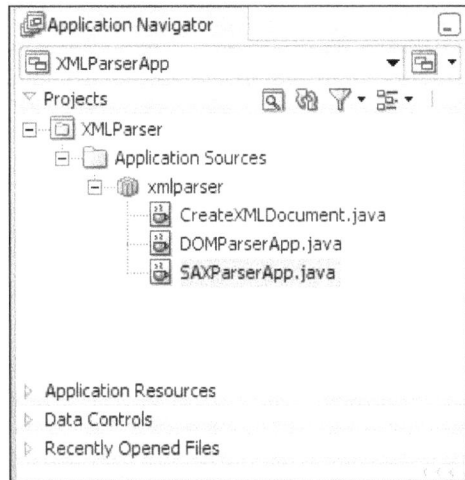

Next, we need to add XDK parser classes to the classpath of the XMLParser project. Select the project node in **Application Navigator** and select **Tools|Project Properties**. In the **Project Properties** window select **Libraries and Classpath**. Click on the **Add Library** button to add a library. In the **Add Library** window select **Oracle XML Parser v2** library and click on the **OK** button.

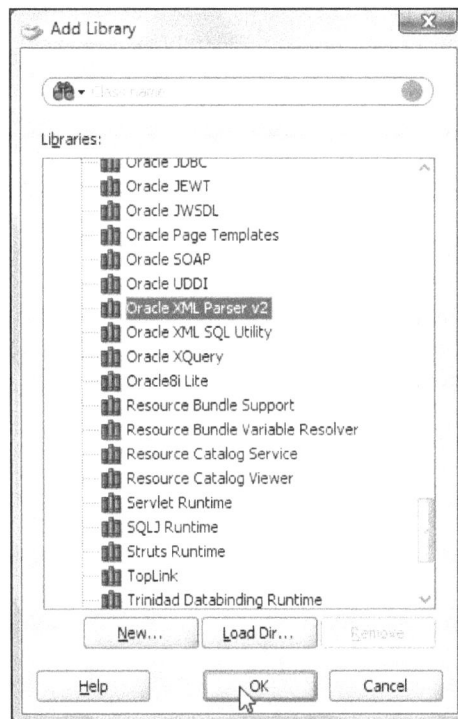

The **Oracle XML Parser v2** library gets added to the project libraries. Click on the **OK** button in the **Project Properties** window.

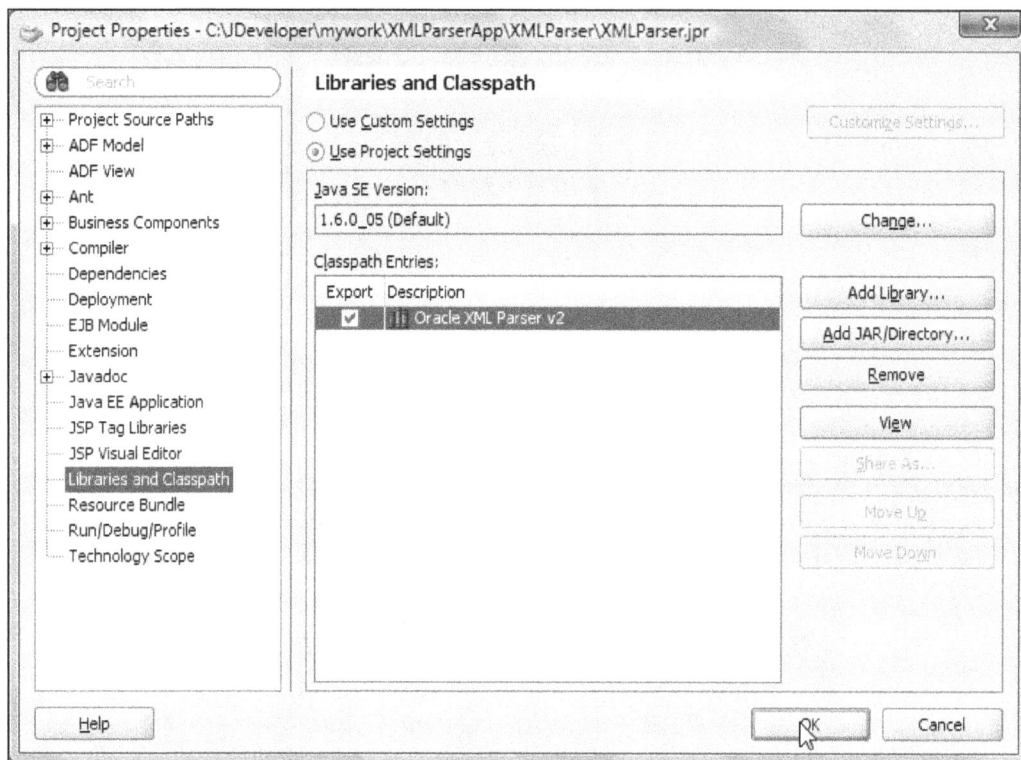

Generating an XML document

In this section we shall generate an XML document in JDeveloper. The example XML document in the introduction will be created by the `CreateXMLDocument.java` application. First, import the DOM and SAX parsing APIs package `oracle.xml.parser.v2`, and the DOM and SAX parsers package `oracle.xml.jaxp`:

```
import oracle.xml.jaxp.*;
import oracle.xml.parser.v2.*;
```

Creating the factory

Create a JXDocumentBuilderFactory object with the static method newInstance().
The factory object is used to obtain a parser that may be used to create a new DOM
object tree. The JXDocumentBuilderFactory class is the implementation class in
Oracle XDK 11g for the abstract class DocumentBuilderFactory:

```
JXDocumentBuilderFactory factory = (JXDocumentBuilderFactory)
        JXDocumentBuilderFactory.newInstance ();
```

The JXDocumentBuilderFactory class extends the DocumentBuilderFactory
class and provides some additional methods apart from providing some static fields
and constants. The constants are used in the setAttribute(java.lang.String
name, java.lang.Object value) method to set factory attribute values. The
attribute names are specified as a String object and attribute values are specified
as an object. The getAttribute(java.lang.String name) method may be used to
retrieve the value of an attribute. Some of these attributes are listed in the following
table; the attributes ERROR_STREAM and SHOW_WARNINGS will be used in the DOM
parsing section:

Attribute	Description
BASE_URL	Specifies the base URL to resolve external entities. The base URL is specified as a URL object. External entities are resolved using an EntityResolver, which is set on a DOMParser or a SAXParser using the setEntityResolver(EntityResolver) method.
DEBUG_MODE	Specifies the debug mode. The debug mode value is a Boolean and value may be set to Boolean.TRUE or Boolean.FALSE.
DTD_OBJECT	Specifies the DTD object to validate the XML document. The DTD object is set as an oracle.xml.parser. v2.DTD class object. As XML Schema is the preferred standard for validating an XML document, DTDs have become archaic.
ERROR_ENCODING	Specifies the text encoding for error reports in the error stream. Error encoding is specified as a string literal such as UTF-8. The ERROR_ENCODING attribute may be set only if the ERROR_STREAM attribute is set.
ERROR_STREAM	Specifies the error stream for reporting errors. The attribute value can be an OutputStream or a PrintWriter object. If ErrorHandler is set, ERROR_STREAM is not used and is ignored.

Attribute	Description
NODE_FACTORY	Specifies the `NodeFactory` object for custom nodes. The `NodeFactory` class provides methods, which may be overridden, to create nodes of the DOM tree built during parsing. These methods are different than the `XMLDocument` class methods in that they return an Oracle class object instead of a standard `org.w3c.dom` package class object. For example, the `createElement` method returns an `oracle.xml.parser.v2.XMLElement` object instead of an `org.w3c.dom.Element` object.
SCHEMA_LANGUAGE	Specifies the schema language to be used for validation. If its value is set to `http://www.w3.org/2001/XMLSchema` an XML Schema is used for validation. If Relax NG is used, set its value to `http://relaxng.org/ns/structure/1.0`. If DTD is used, set its value to `http://www.w3.org/TR/REC-xml`.
SCHEMA_OBJECT	Specifies the schema object to be used for validation. Schema object is an `oracle.xml.parser.schema.XMLSchema` class object.
SCHEMA_SOURCE	Specifies the XML Schema file to be used for validation. Its value may be set to one of the following: • `java.lang.String` • `java.io.InputStream` • `org.xml.sax.InputSource` • `java.io.File` • An array of `java.lang.Object` with contents as one the previously listed types
SHOW_WARNINGS	Specifies if warnings are to be shown during schema validation. Its value is a Boolean, which may be set to `Boolean.TRUE` or `Boolean.FALSE`.
USE_DTD_ONLY_FOR_VALIDATION	Specifies if the DTD object is to be used only for validation and not to be added to the DOM document. Its value is a Boolean, which can be set to `Boolean.TRUE` or `Boolean.FALSE`.

Creating the DOM document object

Create a `DocumentBuilder` object from the factory object with the `newDocumentBuilder()` method. The `DocumentBuilder` object is used to create a new instance of a DOM Document object or to obtain a DOM Document object from an XML document. The `JXDocumentBuilder class` extends the `DocumentBuilder` class, and is an implementation class in Oracle XDK 11g for the abstract `DocumentBuilder` class. Cast the `DocumentBuilder` object, returned by the `newDocumentBuilder()` method, to the `JXDocumentBuilder` class:

```
JXDocumentBuilder documentBuilder = (JXDocumentBuilder)
        factory.newDocumentBuilder();
```

Obtain a `Document` object from the `JXDocumentBuilder` object with the `newDocument()` method. The `XMLDocument` class implements the `Document` interface. Cast the `Document` object to `XMLDocument`:

```
XMLDocument xmlDocument = (XMLDocument)
      documentBuilder.newDocument();
```

In addition to the `Document` interface, the `XMLDocument` class implements `DocumentEditVAL`, `ElementEditVAL`, `DocumentEvent`, `DocumentTraversal`, `EventTarget`, and `NSResolver`. The `DocumentEditVAL` and `ElementEditVAL` interfaces are implemented for dynamic validation as specified in the DOM 3 Validation specification and will be discussed in Chapter 8. The `DocumentEvent` and `EventTarget` interfaces are implemented for event handling and will be discussed in Chapter 7. The `NSResolver` interface is used for selecting namespace nodes with XPath, and will be discussed in Chapter 4.

The `XMLDocument` class provides some additional methods not specified in any of the implemented interfaces. Some of these methods are discussed in the following table:

Method	Description
`addID(String, XMLElement)`	Adds an element associated with an ID to the document. An ID distinguishes an element from other elements and may be used to identify and retrieve an element. The String parameter specifies the ID and the `XMLElement` parameter specifies the element associated with the ID.
`getIDHashtable()`	Returns the ID hashtable associated with the DOM tree. If you know the ID of an element, the element may be retrieved by first obtaining the hashtable of all elements associated with an ID and subsequently retrieving the element for the known ID.

Method	Description
adoptNode (Node srcNodeArg)	Adopts a node from another document. The node is removed from the other document. If the node is to be kept in the source document, use the importNode method instead.
getEncoding()	Gets document character encoding. The document encoding is specified in the encoding parameter. For example, <?xml encoding="UTF8" version="1.0" ?>
setEncoding(String)	Sets document character encoding. The document encoding gets set as the "encoding" parameter in the XML declaration when the document is saved.
print (PrintDriver pd)	Prints the contents of the DOM tree using the specified PrintDriver. The print method is overloaded to take the output stream as an OutputStream, PrintWriter, or Writer object in addition to a PrintDriver object.
printExternalDTD (java. io.PrintWriter out)	Prints the contents of the external DTD using the specified PrintWriter. The method is overloaded to take the output stream as an OutputStream object.
setDoctype(java.lang. String rootname,java. lang.String sysid,java. lang.String pubid)	Sets the doctype for the document. When the DOM tree is saved, the <!DOCTYPE rootname PUBLIC publicid systemid> declaration gets added to the document.
getVersion()	Returns the XML version. The XML version is specified in the "version" parameter of the XML declaration, for example <?xml version="1.0" encoding="UTF8" ?>.
setVersion()	Sets XML version.
getSchema()	Returns the XMLSchema object corresponding to the XML Schema specified in the document. An XML Schema is specified in an XML document with the xsi:noNamespaceSchemaLocation attribute or the xsi:NamespaceSchemaLocation attribute in the root element of an XML document.
setSchema (XMLSchema)	Sets XMLSchema for validation. If an XML Schema is specified in the XML document and also set in the setSchema method, the XML Schema set using the setSchema method overrides the schema specified in the document.

Method	Description
setStandalone(String)	Sets the standalone parameter for the XML declaration. The value is "yes" or "no". A standalone document is a document that does not contain any external markup declarations. (A parameter entity is an example of an external markup declaration.) The standalone parameter is specified because markup declarations can affect the content of the document as transferred from the XML processor to the application.
getStandalone()	Gets the standalone parameter value for the XML declaration.
setLocale(java.util. Locale locale)	Sets the locale for error reporting. For example, for the UK you would create the Locale object as: new Locale(Locale. ENGLISH, Locale.UK).

Set the XML version of the DOM document object using the setVersion method, and the encoding of the DOM document using the setEncoding method:

```
xmlDocument.setVersion("1.0");
xmlDocument.setEncoding("UTF-8");
```

Creating the root element

Create the root element catalog with the createElement(String) method. Cast the Element object returned by the createElement() method to XMLElement:

```
XMLElement catalogElement = (XMLElement) (xmlDocument.createElement"
("catalog"));
```

The XMLElement class implements the Element interface. In addition to the Element interface, XMLElement implements the ElementEditVAL and NSResolver interfaces. The ElementEditVAL interface is used for DOM 3 Validation and the NSResolver interface is used for selecting namespace nodes with XPath, which will be discussed in Chapter 4. In addition to the validation methods from the ElementEditVAL interface, the XMLElement class has the overloaded validateContent() method to validate an element. The validation methods shall be discussed in Chapter 8.

Add the root element to the XMLDocument object using the appendChild method:

```
xmlDocument.appendChild(catalogElement);
```

Constructing the DOM document

Next, we shall create the DOM document tree:

1. Create the namespace element `journal:journal` with the `createElementNS(String, String)` method.

   ```
   XMLElement journalElement = (XMLElement)
   (xmlDocument.createElementNS("http://xdk.com/catalog/
   journal","journal:journal"));
   ```

2. Add the `journal` element to the root element using the `appendChild` method.

   ```
   catalogElement.appendChild(journalElement);
   ```

3. Add a namespace attribute `journal:title` with the `setAttributeNS(String, String, String)` method.

   ```
   journalElement.setAttributeNS("http://xdk.com/catalog/journal",
   "journal:title", "Oracle Magazine");
   ```

4. Similarly, add `journal:publisher` and `journal:author` attributes. Add `journal:article` and `journal:title` elements similar to the `journal:journal` element. Create an `XMLText` node, which represents a text node, to set the text of the `title` element using the `createTextNode(String)` method.

   ```
   XMLText title = (XMLText) xmlDocument.createTextNode
   ("Declarative Data Filtering");
   ```

5. Add the `XMLText` node to `journal:title` element using the `appendChild` method.

   ```
   titleElement.appendChild(title);
   ```

In the same way, add the other element and text nodes in the example XML document. The `XMLDocument` class provides additional methods than the `Document` interface methods to create XML document components other than those discussed in this section. Some of these methods are discussed in the following table:

Method Name	Description
`createCDATASection(java.lang.String data)`	Creates a CDATA section. A CDATA section is text that is not parsed by the parser. Special characters, which may need to be included in text data at times, generate a parser error. Text containing such data should be included in a CDATA section.
`createComment(java.lang.String data)`	Creates a comment. Comments are represented with `<!--    -->`. They are specified outside the markup and may also be specified within a document type definition, as permitted by the grammar. Comments are not included in a document's character data, but an XML processor may — though is not required to — retrieve the character data in a comment.
`createEntityReference(java.lang.String name)`	Creates an entity reference. An entity reference is a reference to an entity, which is data that is defined as an abbreviation or data that is found at an external location. Entity references are included to represent data that has multiple occurrences in a document.
`createProcessingInstruction(java.lang.String target, java.lang.String data)`	Creates a Processing Instruction. Processing Instructions are not included in a document's character data and are instructions for the application.

Outputting the DOM document

Output the DOM document object with the `XMLPrintDriver` class. Create an `OutputStream` object to output the XML document, and create an `XMLPrintDriver` using the `OutputStream`:

```
OutputStream output = new FileOutputStream(new File(
    "catalog.xml"));
XMLPrintDriver xmlPrintDriver = new XMLPrintDriver(new
    PrintWriter(output));
```

Output the XML document with the `printDocument(XMLDocument)` method. Flush the output stream using the `flush()` method and close the output stream using the `close()` method:

```
xmlPrintDriver.printDocument(xmlDocument);
xmlPrintDriver.flush();
xmlPrintDriver.close();
```

XMLPrintDriver may be used to print not only an XMLDocument node, but other nodes as well. The print methods in the XMLPrintDriver class are listed in the following table:

Print Method	Description
printAttribute(XMLAttr)	Prints an attribute node.
printAttributeNodes (XMLElement)	Prints attributes in an element node.
printCDATASection(XMLCDATA)	Prints a CDATA section node.
printChildNodes(XMLNode)	Prints child nodes for a node.
printComment(XMLComment)	Prints comment node.
printDoctype(DTD)	Prints DTD.
printDocument(XMLDocument)	Prints a document. We used this method in outputting the DOM document tree.
printDocumentFragment (XMLDocumentFragment)	Prints a document fragment. A document fragment represents a fragment of the document. Use this method if you only need to output a section of the document.
printElement(XMLElement)	Prints an element node.
printEntityReference (XMLEntityReference)	Prints an entity reference node.
printProcessingInstruction (XMLPI)	Prints a processing instruction node.
printTextNode(XMLText)	Prints a text node.

Running the Java application

To run the CreateXMLDocument.java application in JDeveloper, right-click on **CreateXMLDocument.java** in **Application Navigator** and select **Run**.

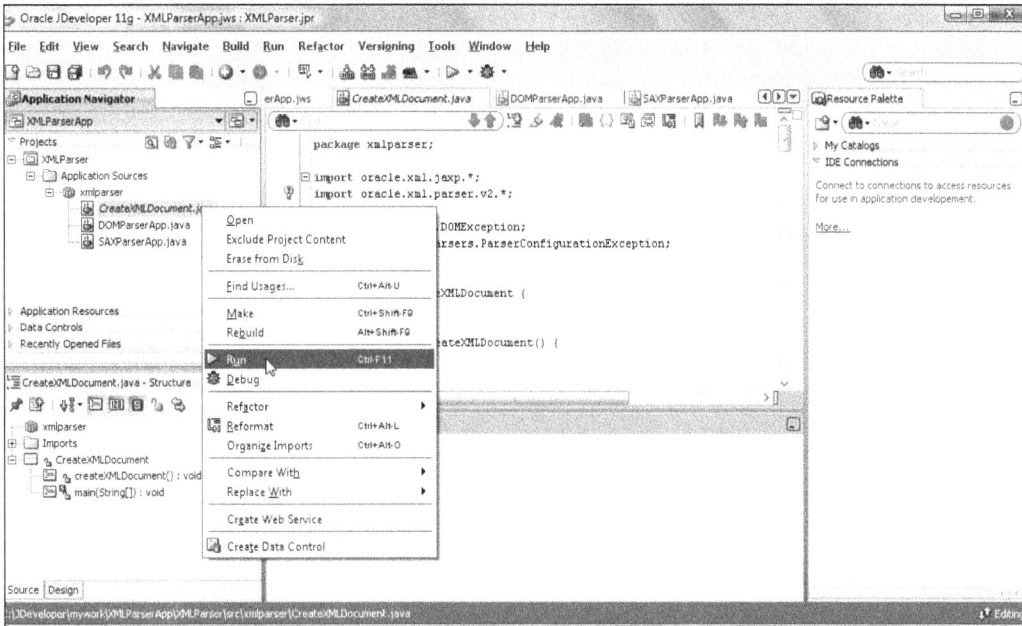

The XML document gets generated. Select **View | Refresh** to add the generated XML document, **catalog.xml**, to the **Application Navigator**.

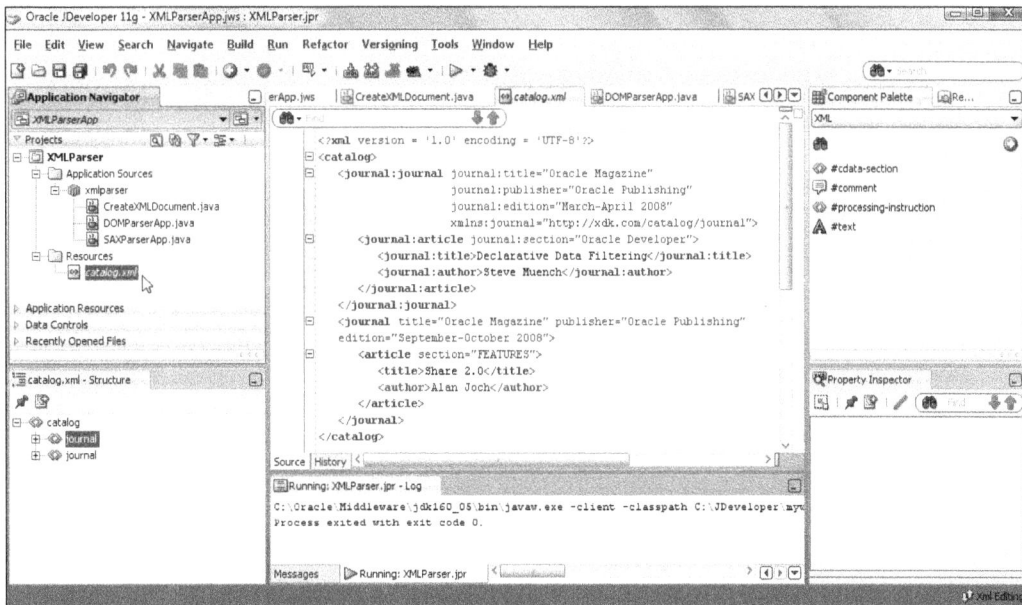

The complete **CreateXMLDocument.java** Java application is listed here with brief notes that explain the different sections of the application:

1. First, we declare the `package` statement and the `import` statements.

```
package xmlparser;
import oracle.xml.jaxp.*;
import oracle.xml.parser.v2.*;
import java.io.*;
import org.w3c.dom.DOMException;
import javax.xml.parsers.ParserConfigurationException;
```

2. Next, we define the Java class `CreateXMLDocument`.

```
public class CreateXMLDocument {
```

3. Now, we define the method to create an XML document.

```
    public void createXMLDocument() {
        try {
```

4. Next, we create the `XMLDocument` object.

```
JXDocumentBuilderFactory factory =
            (JXDocumentBuilderFactory)JXDocumentBuilderFactory.
newInstance();
JXDocumentBuilder documentBuilder =
(JXDocumentBuilder)factory.newDocumentBuilder();
XMLDocument xmlDocument = (XMLDocument)documentBuilder.
newDocument();
xmlDocument.setVersion("1.0");
xmlDocument.setEncoding("UTF-8");
```

5. Here, we create the root element `catalog` and the first subelement `journal`.

```
XMLElement catalogElement = (XMLElement) (xmlDocument.createElemen
t("catalog"));
xmlDocument.appendChild(catalogElement);
XMLElement journalElement = (XMLElement) (xmlDocument.
createElementNS("http://xdk.com/catalog/journal",
    "journal:journal"));
    catalogElement.appendChild(journalElement);
```

6. Next, we add namespace attributes `title`, `publisher`, and `edition` to the `journal` element.

```
        journalElement.setAttributeNS("http://xdk.com/catalog/
journal","journal:title", "Oracle Magazine");
        journalElement.setAttributeNS("http://xdk.com/catalog/
journal","journal:publisher", "Oracle Publishing");
        journalElement.setAttributeNS("http://xdk.com/catalog/
journal","journal:edition", "March-April 2008");
```

7. Now, we create the element, text, and attribute nodes in `catalog.xml`, the XML document.

```
XMLElement articleElement = (XMLElement) (xmlDocument.
createElementNS("http://xdk.com/catalog/journal","journal:
article"));
journalElement.appendChild(articleElement);

articleElement.setAttributeNS("http://xdk.com/catalog/
journal","journal:section", "Oracle Developer");

XMLElement titleElement = (XMLElement) (xmlDocument.
createElementNS("http://xdk.com/catalog/journal",
    "journal:title"));

articleElement.appendChild(titleElement);

XMLText title = (XMLText) xmlDocument.createTextNode
                ("Declarative Data Filtering");
titleElement.appendChild(title);
XMLElement authorElement = (XMLElement)  (xmlDocument.
createElementNS("http://xdk.com/catalog/journal",
                  "journal:author"));

articleElement.appendChild(authorElement);

XMLText author = (XMLText) xmlDocument.createTextNode(
                "Steve Muench");
authorElement.appendChild(author);

journalElement = (XMLElement) (xmlDocument.createElement
("journal"));

catalogElement.appendChild(journalElement);

journalElement.setAttribute("title", "Oracle Magazine");
journalElement.setAttribute("publisher", "Oracle Publishing");
journalElement.setAttribute("edition", " September-October 2008");

articleElement = (XMLElement)(xmlDocument.createElement("article")
);

journalElement.appendChild(articleElement);

articleElement.setAttribute("section", "FEATURES");

titleElement = (XMLElement) (xmlDocument.createElement("title"));

articleElement.appendChild(titleElement);

title = (XMLText) xmlDocument.createTextNode("Share 2.0");
titleElement.appendChild(title);
```

```
authorElement = (XMLElement)(xmlDocument.createElement("author"));
    articleElement.appendChild(authorElement);

author = (XMLText) xmlDocument.createTextNode("Alan Joch");
authorElement.appendChild(author);
```

8. Here, we output the XML document to the file `catalog.xml`.

```
        OutputStream output = new FileOutputStream(new
    File("catalog.xml"));
XMLPrintDriver xmlPrintDriver = new XMLPrintDriver(new
PrintWriter(output));
xmlPrintDriver.printDocument(xmlDocument);
xmlPrintDriver.flush();
xmlPrintDriver.close();
        } catch (DOMException e) {
            System.err.println(e.getMessage());
        } catch (IOException e) {
            System.err.println(e.getMessage());
        } catch (ParserConfigurationException e) {
            System.err.println(e.getMessage());
        }
    }
```

9. Finally, we define the `main` method for the Java class. In the `main` method, we create an instance of the `CreateXMLDocument` class and invoke the `createXMLDocument` method.

```
    public static void main(String[] argv) {
CreateXMLDocument createXMLDocument = new CreateXMLDocument();
    createXMLDocument.createXMLDocument();
    }
}
```

Parsing an XML document with the DOM API

In this section we shall parse an XML document (the XML document that was created in the previous section) with a DOM parser. DOM parsing creates an in-memory tree-like structure of an XML document, which may be navigated with the DOM API. We shall iterate over the XML document parsed, and output elements and attribute node values.

The DOM parsing API classes are in the `oracle.xml.parser.v2` package and the DOM parser factory and parser classes are in the `oracle.xml.jaxp` package. First, import these packages into the `DOMParserApp.java` class in JDeveloper:

```
import oracle.xml.jaxp.*;
import oracle.xml.parser.v2.*;
```

Creating the factory

Create a `JXDcoumentBuilderFactory` object with the static method `newInstance()`. The factory object is used to obtain a parser that may be used to create a DOM document tree from an XML document:

```
JXDocumentBuilderFactory factory = (JXDocumentBuilderFactory)
JXDocumentBuilderFactory.newInstance();
```

Set the `ERROR_STREAM` and `SHOW_WARNINGS` attributes on the factory object with the `setAttribute()` method. The `ERROR_STREAM` attribute specifies the error stream, while the `SHOW_WARNINGS` attribute specifies if warnings are to be shown. The value of the `ERROR_STREAM` attribute is an `OutputStream` object or a `PrintWriter` object. The value of the `SHOW_WARNINGS` attribute is a Boolean, which can be set to `Boolean.TRUE` or `Boolean.FALSE`. With the `OutputStream` or `PrintWriter` specified in the `ERROR_STREAM` attribute, parsing errors (if any) get outputted to the specified file. If `ErrorHandler` is also set, `ERROR_STREAM` is not used. The `SHOW_WARNINGS` attribute outputs warnings also:

```
factory.setAttribute(JXDocumentBuilderFactory.ERROR_STREAM,
   new FileOutputStream(new File("c:/output/errorStream.txt")));
factory.setAttribute(JXDocumentBuilderFactory.SHOW_WARNINGS,
   Boolean.TRUE);
```

Creating a DOM document object

Create a `JXDocumentBuilder` object from the factory object by first creating a `DocumentBuilder` object with `newDocumentBuilder()` method and subsequently casting the `DocumentBuilder` object to `JXDocumentBuilder`. `JXDocumentBuilder` is the implementation class in Oracle XDK 11g for the abstract class `DocumentBuilder`:

```
JXDocumentBuilder documentBuilder = (JXDocumentBuilder) factory.
newDocumentBuilder();
```

The JXDocumentBuilder object is used to create a DOM document object from an XML document. A Document object may be obtained using the JXDocumentBuilder object with one of the parse() methods in the JXDocumentBuilder class. The input to the parser may be specified as InputSource, InputStream, File object, or a String URI. Create an InputStream for the example XML document and parse the document with the parse(InputStream) method:

```
InputStream input = new FileInputStream(new File("catalog.xml"));
XMLDocument xmlDocument = (XMLDocument) (documentBuilder.
parse(input));
```

The parse() methods of the JXDocumentBuilder object return a Document object, which may be cast to an XMLDocument object, as the XMLDocument class implements the Document interface.

Outputting the XML document components' values

Output the encoding in the XML document using the getEncoding method, and output the version of the XML document using the getVersion method:

```
System.out.println("Encoding: " + xmlDocument.getEncoding());
System.out.println("Version: " + xmlDocument.getVersion());
```

The XMLDocument class has various getter methods to retrieve elements in a document. Some of these methods are listed in the following table:

Method Name	Description
getDocumentElement()	Returns the root element.
getElementById(String)	Returns element for a specified ID. An element that has an ID attribute may be retrieved using this method. An attribute named "id" is not necessarily an ID attribute. An ID attribute is defined in an XML Schema with the xs:ID type and in a DTD with ID attribute type.
getElementsByTagName (String)	Returns a NodeList of elements for a specified tag name. The elements are returned in the order defined in the DOM tree. All the elements of the specified tag name are returned, not just the top-level elements. If the tag name is specified as "*", all the elements in the document are returned.
getElementsByTagNameN S(String namespaceURI, String localName)	Returns a NodeList of elements for a specified namespace URI and local name.

As an example, retrieve `title` elements in the namespace `http://xdk.com/catalog/journal` using the `getElementsByTagNameNS` method:

```
NodeList namespaceNodeList = xmlDocument.getElementsByTagNameNS("http
://xdk.com/catalog/journal","title");
```

Iterate over the `NodeList` to output element namespace, element namespace prefix, element tag name, and element text. The `getNamespaceURI()` method returns the namespace URI of an element. The `getPrefix()` method returns the prefix of an element in a namespace. The `getTagName()` method returns the element tag name. Element text is obtained by first obtaining the text node within the element node using the `getFirstChild()` method and subsequently the value of the text node:

```
for (int i = 0; i < namespaceNodeList.getLength(); i++) {
XMLElement namespaceElement = (XMLElement) namespaceNodeList.item(i);
                System.out.println("Namespace URI: " +
                    namespaceElement.getNamespaceURI());
                System.out.println("Namespace Prefix: " +
                    namespaceElement.getPrefix());
                System.out.println("Element Name: " +
                    namespaceElement.getTagName());
                System.out.println("Element text:  " +
                  namespaceElement.getFirstChild().getNodeValue());
}
```

Obtain the root element in the XML document with the `getDocumentElement()` method. The `getDocumentElement` method returns an `Element` object that may be cast to an `XMLElement` object if any of the methods defined only in the `XMLElement` class are to be used. The `Element` object is not required to be cast to an `XMLElement` object. We have cast the `Element` object to `XMLElement` as `XMLElement` is Oracle XDK 11g's implementation class for the `Element` interface, and we are discussing Oracle XDK 11g:

```
XMLElement rootElement = (XMLElement)
  (xmlDocument.getDocumentElement());
System.out.println("Root Element is: " + rootElement.getTagName());
```

Next, we shall iterate over all the subnodes of the root element. Obtain a `NodeList` of subnodes of the root element with the `getChildNodes()` method. Create a method `iterateNodeList()` to iterate over the subnodes of an `Element`. Iterate over the `NodeList` and recursively obtain the subelements of the elements in the `NodeList`. The method `hasChildNodes()` tests to see if a node has subnodes. Ignorable whitespace is also considered a node, but we are mainly interested in the subelements in a node. The `NodeList` interface method `getLength()` returns the length of a node list, and method `item(int)` returns the `Node` at a specified index. As class `XMLNode` is Oracle XDK 11g's implementation class for the `Node` interface, cast the `Node` object to `XMLNode`:

```
if (rootElement.hasChildNodes()) {
    NodeList nodeList = rootElement.getChildNodes();
    iterateNodeList(rootElement, nodeList);
}
```

If a node is of type element, the tag name of the element may be retrieved. Node type is obtained with the `getNodeType()` method, which returns a `short` value. The `Node` interface provides static fields for different types of nodes. The different types of nodes in an XML document are listed in the following table:

Node Type	Description
ELEMENT_NODE	Element node.
ATTRIBUTE_NODE	Attribute node.
TEXT_NODE	Text node, for example the text in an element such as `<elementA>Element A Text</elementA>`.
CDATA_SECTION_NODE	CDATA section node. We discussed a CDATA section in an earlier table.
ENTITY_REFERENCE_NODE	Entity reference node. An entity reference refers to the content of a named entity.
ENTITY_NODE	Entity node. An entity is defined in a DOCTYPE declaration or an external DTD, and represents an abbreviation for data that is to be used repeatedly.
PROCESSING_INSTRUCTION_NODE	Processing Instruction node. We discussed a processing instruction in an earlier section.
COMMENT_NODE	Comment node. We discussed a comment node in an earlier section.
DOCUMENT_NODE	Document node. The document node represents the complete DOM document tree.

Node Type	Description
DOCUMENT_TYPE_NODE	Doctype node represents the DOCTYPE declaration.
DOCUMENT_FRAGMENT_NODE	DocumentFragment node. A document fragment is a segment of a document.
NOTATION_NODE	Notation node. A notation is defined in a DOCTYPE declaration or an external DTD. Notations represent the format of unparsed entities (non-XML data that a parser does not parse), format of elements with a notation attribute, and the application to which a processing instruction is sent. An example of a notation is as follows: `<!NOTATION gif PUBLIC "gif viewer">`

For an element node, cast the node to XMLElement and output the element tag name:

```
if (node.getNodeType() == XMLNode.ELEMENT_NODE) {
    XMLElement element = (XMLElement) node;
    System.out.println("Element Tag Name:"+
    element.getTagName))
}
```

The attributes in a element node are retrieved with the getAttributes() method, which returns a NamedNodeMap of attributes. The getLength() method of NamedNodeMap returns the length of an attribute node list. The method item(int) returns an Attr object for the attribute at the specified index. As class XMLAttr implements the Attr interface, cast the Attr object to XMLAttr. Iterate over the NamedNodeMap to output the attribute name and value. The hasAttributes() method tests if an element node has attributes:

```
if (element.hasAttributes()) {
  NamedNodeMap attributes = element.getAttributes();
   for (int i = 0; i < attributes.getLength(); i++) {
  XMLAttr attribute = (XMLAttr)attributes.item(i);
   System.out.println(" Attribute: " + attribute.getName() +
  " with value " +attribute.getValue());
  }
}
```

Running the Java application

The complete `DOMParserApp.java` Java application code listing is listed as follows with notes about the different sections in the Java class:

1. First, we add the `package` and `import` statements.

   ```
   package xmlparser;

   import java.io.*;
   import oracle.xml.jaxp.*;
   import oracle.xml.parser.v2.*;
   import javax.xml.parsers.ParserConfigurationException;
   import org.w3c.dom.*;
   import org.xml.sax.SAXException;
   ```

2. Next, we add Java class `DOMParserApp`.

   ```
   public class DOMParserApp {
   ```

3. Then, we add the `parseXMLDocument` method to parse an XML document.

   ```
   public void parseXMLDocument() {
       try {
   ```

4. Now, we create the `XMLDocument` object by parsing the XML document `catalog.xml`.

   ```
   JXDocumentBuilderFactory factory = (JXDocumentBuilderFactory)
   JXDocumentBuilderFactory.newInstance();
   factory.setAttribute(JXDocumentBuilderFactory.ERROR_STREAM,
   new FileOutputStream(new  File("c:/output/errorStream.txt")));
   factory.setAttribute(JXDocumentBuilderFactory.SHOW_WARNINGS,
                        Boolean.TRUE);
   JXDocumentBuilder documentBuilder = (JXDocumentBuilder)
   factory.newDocumentBuilder();
   InputStream input = new FileInputStream(new File("catalog.xml"));
   XMLDocument xmlDocument =
   (XMLDocument)(documentBuilder.parse(input));
   ```

5. Here, we output the document character encoding, the XML version, and namespace node values from the parsed XML document.

   ```
   System.out.println("Encoding: " + xmlDocument.getEncoding());
   System.out.println("Version: " + xmlDocument.getVersion());
   NodeList namespaceNodeList = xmlDocument.getElementsByTagNameNS
   ("http://xdk.com/catalog/journal", "title");
   for (int i = 0; i < namespaceNodeList.getLength(); i++) {
   ```

```
        XMLElement namespaceElement =
        (XMLElement)namespaceNodeList.item(i);
        System.out.println("Namespace Prefix: " + namespaceElement.
         getNamespaceURI());
         System.out.println("Namespace URI: " + namespaceElement.
         getPrefix());
         System.out.println("Element Name: " + namespaceElement.
         getTagName());
         System.out.println("Element text:   " + namespaceElement.
getFirstChild().getNodeValue());
    }
```

6. Next, we obtain the subnodes of the root element and invoke the
   iterateNodeList method to iterate over the subnodes.

```
XMLElement rootElement =
    (XMLElement)(xmlDocument.getDocumentElement());
System.out.println("Root Element is: " +  rootElement.
getTagName());
if (rootElement.hasChildNodes()) {
NodeList nodeList = rootElement.getChildNodes();
iterateNodeList(rootElement, nodeList);
}
        }
        catch (ParserConfigurationException e) {
            System.err.println(e.getMessage());
        } catch (FileNotFoundException e) {
            System.err.println(e.getMessage());
        } catch (IOException e) {
            System.err.println(e.getMessage());
        } catch (SAXException e) {
            System.err.println(e.getMessage());
        }
    }
```

7. The iterateNodeList method has an Element parameter, which represents
   the element with subnodes. The second parameter is of the type NodeList,
   which is the NodeList of subnodes of the Element represented by the
   first parameter.

```
public void iterateNodeList(Element elem, NodeList nodeList) {
    if (nodeList.getLength() > 1) {
        System.out.println("Element " + elem.getTagName() +
            " has sub-elements\n");
    }
```

8. Iterate over the `NodeList`.

```
for (int i = 0; i < nodeList.getLength(); i++) {
XMLNode node = (XMLNode)nodeList.item(i);
```

9. If a node is of type `Element`, output the `Element` tag name and element text.

```
if (node.getNodeType() == XMLNode.ELEMENT_NODE) {
    XMLElement element = (XMLElement)node;
    System.out.println("Sub-element of " + elem.getNodeName());
System.out.println("Element Tag Name:" + element.getTagName());
System.out.println("Element text:   " + element.getFirstChild().
getNodeValue());
```

10. If an `Element` has attributes, output the attributes.

```
if (element.hasAttributes()) {
    System.out.println("Element has attributes\n");
    NamedNodeMap attributes = element.getAttributes();
    for (int j = 0; j < attributes.getLength(); j++) {
        XMLAttr attribute = (XMLAttr)attributes.item(j);
        System.out.println("Attribute: " +attribute.getName() +
        " with value "+ attribute.getValue());
    }
}
```

11. If an `Element` has subnodes, obtain the `NodeList` of subnodes and iterate over the `NodeList` by invoking the `iterateNodeList` method again.

```
if (element.hasChildNodes()) {
    iterateNodeList(element, element.getChildNodes());
        }
      }
    }
}
```

12. Finally, we add the `main` method. In the `main` method, we create an instance of the `DOMParserApp` class and invoke the `parseXMLDocument` method.

```
public static void main(String[] argv) {
        DOMParserApp domParser = new DOMParserApp();
        domParser.parseXMLDocument();
    }
}
```

13. To run the `DOMParserApp.java` in JDeveloper, right-click on the **DOMParserApp.java** node in **Application Navigator** and select **Run**.

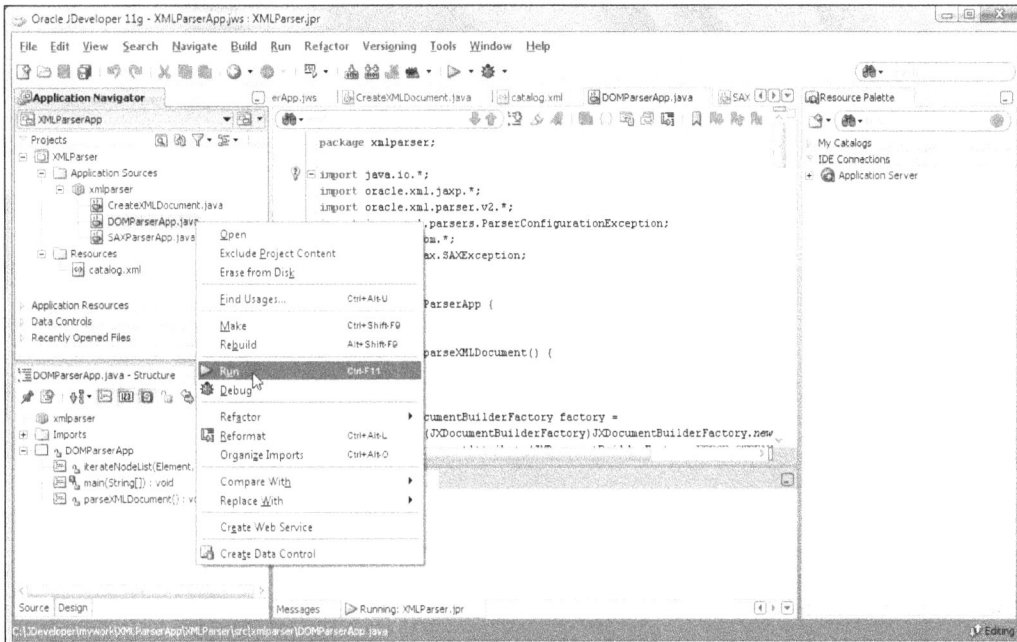

14. The element and attribute values from the XML document get outputted.

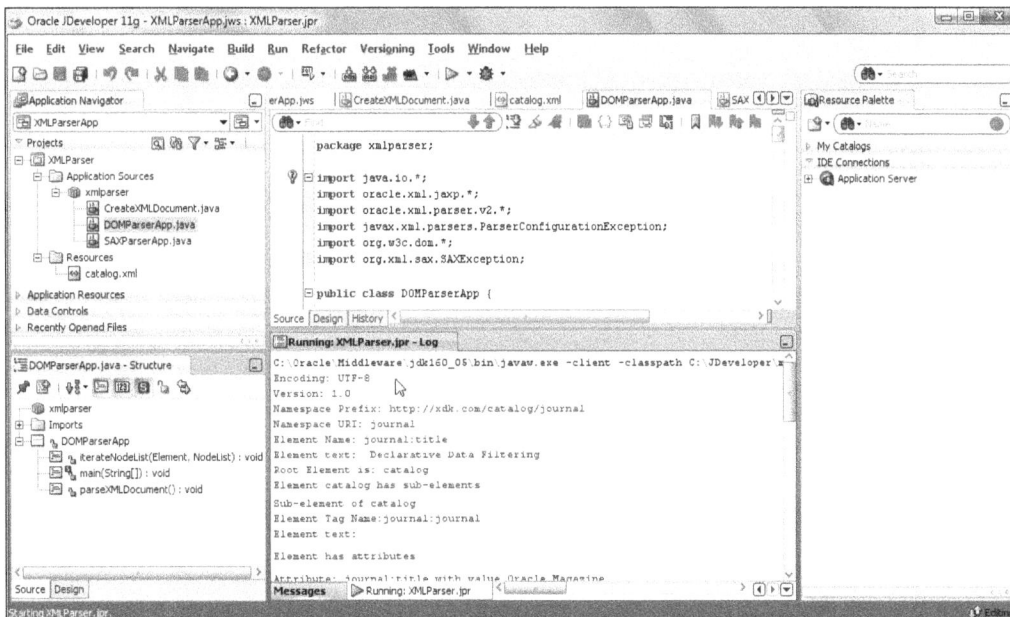

The complete output from the DOM parsing application is as follows:

```
Encoding: UTF-8
Version: 1.0
Namespace Prefix: http://xdk.com/catalog/journal
Namespace URI: journal
Element Name: journal:title
Element text:  Declarative Data Filtering
Root Element is: catalog
Element catalog has sub-elements

Sub-element of catalog
Element Tag Name:journal:journal
Element text:

Element has attributes

Attribute: journal:title with value Oracle Magazine
Attribute: journal:publisher with value Oracle Publishing
Attribute: journal:edition with value March-April 2008
Attribute: xmlns:journal with value http://xdk.com/catalog/journal
Element journal:journal has sub-elements

Sub-element of journal:journal
Element Tag Name:journal:article
Element text:

Element has attributes

Attribute: journal:section with value Oracle Developer
Element journal:article has sub-elements

Sub-element of journal:article
Element Tag Name:journal:title
Element text:  Declarative Data Filtering
Sub-element of journal:article
Element Tag Name:journal:author
Element text:  Steve Muench
Sub-element of catalog
Element Tag Name:journal
Element text:

Element has attributes

Attribute: title with value Oracle Magazine
Attribute: publisher with value Oracle Publishing
Attribute: edition with value September-October 2008
Element journal has sub-elements

Sub-element of journal
```

```
Element Tag Name:article
Element text:

Element has attributes

Attribute: section with value FEATURES
Element article has sub-elements

Sub-element of article
Element Tag Name:title
Element text:  Share 2.0
Sub-element of article
Element Tag Name:author
Element text:  Alan Joch
```

To demonstrate error handling with the ERROR_STREAM attribute, add an error in the example XML document. For example, remove a </journal> tag. Run the DOMParserApp.java application in JDeveloper. An error message gets outputted to the file specified in the ERROR_STREAM attribute:

```
<Line 15, Column 10>: XML-20121: (Fatal Error) End tag
does not match start tag 'journal'.
```

Parsing an XML document with the SAX API

SAX parsing is based on the push model in which events are generated by an SAX parser and a document handler receives notification of the events. The SAX parsing model is faster than DOM parsing, but is limited in its scope to generating parsing events, without any provision for navigating the nodes or retrieving nodes with XPath. In this section, we shall parse the example XML document with a SAX parser and output the events generated by the parser. The SAX parsing application will be developed in JDeveloper in the Java application SAXParserApp.java. First, import the oracle.xml.jaxp package:

```
import oracle.xml.jaxp.*;
```

An SAX parsing application typically extends the DefaultHandler class, which has event-notification methods for the parse events. The DefaultHandler class implements the ErrorHandler interface. A DefaultHandler object may also be used for error handling.

Creating the factory

Create a JXSAXParserFactory object with the static method newInstance().
The newInstance() method returns a SAXParserFactory object that may be
cast to JXSAXParserFactory as the JXSAXParserFactory class extends the
SAXParserFactory class. Why cast, you might ask? We are using Oracle XDK 11g's
implementation classes for various standard interfaces and abstract classes.

```
JXSAXParserFactory factory = (JXSAXParserFactory) JXSAXParserFactory.
newInstance();
```

The factory object is used to obtain a SAX parser that may be used to parse an
XML document.

Parsing the XML document

Create a SAXParser object from the factory object with the newSAXParser() method.
As class JXSAXParser extends the SAXParser class, a SAXParser object may be cast
to JXSAXParser:

```
JXSAXParser saxParser = (JXSAXParser) factory.newSAXParser();
```

Create an InputStream for the XML document to parse, and parse the XML
document with one of the parse() methods in the SAXParser class. The parse
methods take an XML document in the form of InputSource, InputStream, URI,
or File, and an event handler such as the DefaultHandler.

```
InputStream input = new FileInputStream(new File("catalog.xml"));
 saxParser.parse(input, this);
```

The DefaultHandler class provides the parsing event notification methods and
error handling methods. Event notification and error handling methods may be
overridden in the SAX parsing application for application-specific events and error
handling. Some of the event notification methods in the DefaultHandler class are
listed in the following table:

Method Name	Description
startDocument()	Receive notification of the start of the document. The startDocument method is invoked before the XML declaration.
endDocument()	Receive notification of the end of the document. The endDocument method is invoked after the closing tag of the root element.

Method Name	Description
`startElement(java.lang.String uri, java.lang.String localName, java.lang.String qName, Attributes attributes)`	Receive notification of the start of an element. The URI parameter specifies the namespace URI. LocalName specifies the element local name, which is the element name without the prefix. QName specifies the qualified element name; element name with prefix. The attributes parameter specifies the list of attributes in an element.
`endElement(java.lang.String uri, java.lang.String localName, java.lang.String qName)`	Receive notification of the end of an element.
`characters(char[] ch, int start, int length)`	Receive notification of the character data (text).
`ignorableWhitespace(char[] ch, int start, int length)`	Receive notification of the ignorable whitespace in an element.
`notationDecl(String name, String publicId, String systemId)`	Receive notification of a notation.
`processingInstruction(String target, String data)`	Receive notification of a processing instruction.

`unparsedEntityDecl(String name, String publicId, String systemId, String notationName)`	Receive notification of an unparsed entity declaration. Unparsed entity declarations are entities that refer to non-XML data that a parser does not have to parse. For example:
	
	`<!ENTITY banner SYSTEM "http://www.logos.net/logo.jpg" NDATA jpeg>`
	
	`<!NOTATION jpeg PUBLIC "jpeg viewer">`

`skippedEntity(String name)`	Receive notification of a skipped entity. Skipped entity notifications may be received when using a non-validating parser, which is not required to parse an external DTD and thus not required to resolve all entity references. Entity references that are not resolved are skipped entities.
`startPrefixMapping(String prefix, String uri)`	Receive notification of the start of a namespace mapping. An example of a namespace mapping is as follows: `xmls:xsd="http://www.w3.org/2001/XMLSchema"`
`endPrefixMapping(String prefix)`	Receive notification of the end of a namespace mapping.

In the `SAXParserApp.java` application, some of the notification methods are overridden to output the event type, element name, element attributes, and element text. For example, the attributes represented by the `Attributes` object in the `startElement(java.lang.String uri, java.lang.String localName, java.lang.String qName, Attributes atts)` method may be iterated to output the attribute name, namespace URI, and attribute value:

```
for (int i = 0; i < atts.getLength(); i++) {
  System.out.println("Attribute QName:" +atts.getQName(i));
  System.out.println("Attribute Local Name:"+ atts.getLocalName(i));
  System.out.println("Attribute Namespace URI:" + atts.getURI(i));
  System.out.println("Attribute Value:"+atts.getValue(i));
}
```

The error handler methods in `DefaultHandler` may also be overridden. In the `SAXParserApp.java` application, the error handler methods are overridden to output the error message. We shall demonstrate error handling in a SAX parsing application with an example. Error handler methods in the `DefaultHandler` class are listed in the following table:

Method Name	Description
`error(SAXParseException exception)`	Receives notification of a recoverable error
`fatalError(SAXParseException exception)`	Receives notification of a non-recoverable error
`warning(SAXParseException exception)`	Receives notification of a warning

Running the Java application

The `SAXParserApp.java` application is listed as follows with notes about the different sections of the Java class:

1. Add the package and import statements.

```
package xmlparser;
import oracle.xml.jaxp.*;
import org.xml.sax.Attributes;
import org.xml.sax.SAXException;
import org.xml.sax.SAXParseException;
import org.xml.sax.helpers.DefaultHandler;
import java.io.*;
import javax.xml.parsers.ParserConfigurationException;
```

2. Next, we add the Java class `SAXParserApp`.

```
public class SAXParserApp extends DefaultHandler {
```

3. Next, we add a method `parseXMLDocument` to parse the XML document, `catalog.xml`.

```
public void parseXMLDocument() {
    try {
JXSAXParserFactory factory = (JXSAXParserFactory)
JXSAXParserFactory.newInstance();
JXSAXParser saxParser = (JXSAXParser) factory.newSAXParser();
InputStream input = new FileInputStream(new File("catalog.xml"));
        saxParser.parse(input, this);
}catch (ParserConfigurationException e) {
 System.err.println(e.getMessage());
}catch (FileNotFoundException e) {
System.err.println(e.getMessage());
}catch (IOException e) { System.err.println(e.getMessage());
}catch (SAXException e) { System.err.println(e.getMessage());
    }
  }
```

4. The `startDocument` event notification method notifies about the start of an XML document.

```
public void startDocument() throws SAXException {
    System.out.println("SAX Event : Start Document");
}
```

5. The `endDocument` event notification method notifies about the end of an XML document.

```
public void endDocument() throws SAXException {
    System.out.println("SAX Event : End Document");
}
```

6. The `startElement` event notification method notifies about the start of an element.

```
public void startElement(java.lang.String namespaceURI,
java.lang.String localName, java.lang.String qName, Attributes
atts)throws SAXException {
    System.out.println("SAX Event : Start Element");
    System.out.println("Element QName:" + qName);
    System.out.println("Element Local Name:" + localName);
    System.out.println("Element Namespace URI:"+namespaceURI);
    for (int i = 0; i < atts.getLength(); i++) {
      System.out.println("Attribute QName:"+atts.getQName(i));
System.out.println("Attribute Local Name:"+ atts.getLocalName(i));
System.out.println("Attribute Namespace URI:"+ atts.getURI(i));
System.out.println("Attribute Value:"+atts.getValue(i));
      }
    }
```

7. The event notification method `endElement` notifies about the end of an element.

    ```java
    public void endElement(java.lang.String namespaceURI,
        java.lang.String localName, java.lang.String qName)
        throws SAXException {
        System.out.println("SAX Event : End Element");
        System.out.println("Element QName:" + qName);
    }
    ```

8. The event notification method `characters` notifies about character text.

    ```java
    public void characters(char[] ch, int start, int length)
        throws SAXException {
        System.out.println("SAX Event : Text");
        String text = new String(ch, start, length).trim();
        if (text.length() > 0) {
            System.out.println("Text:" + text);
        }
    }
    ```

9. Here, the error handling method `error` handles recoverable errors.

    ```java
    public void error(SAXParseException e) throws SAXException {
        System.err.println("Error:" + e.getMessage());
    }
    ```

10. The error handling method `fatalError` handles non-recoverable errors.

    ```java
    public void fatalError(SAXParseException e) throws SAXException {
        System.err.println("Fatal Error:" + e.getMessage());
    }
    ```

11. The error handling method `warning` handles parser warnings.

    ```java
    public void warning(SAXParseException e) throws SAXException {
        System.out.println("Warning:" + e.getMessage());
    }
    ```

12. Finally, add the `main` method. In the `main` method, create an instance of the `SAXParserApp` class and invoke the `parseXMLDocument` method.

```java
public static void main(String[] argv) {
    SAXParserApp saxParser = new SAXParserApp();
    saxParser.parseXMLDocument();
    }
}
```

13. To run the `SAXParserApp.java` application in JDeveloper, right-click on the **SAXParserApp.java** node in **Application Navigator**, and select **Run**.

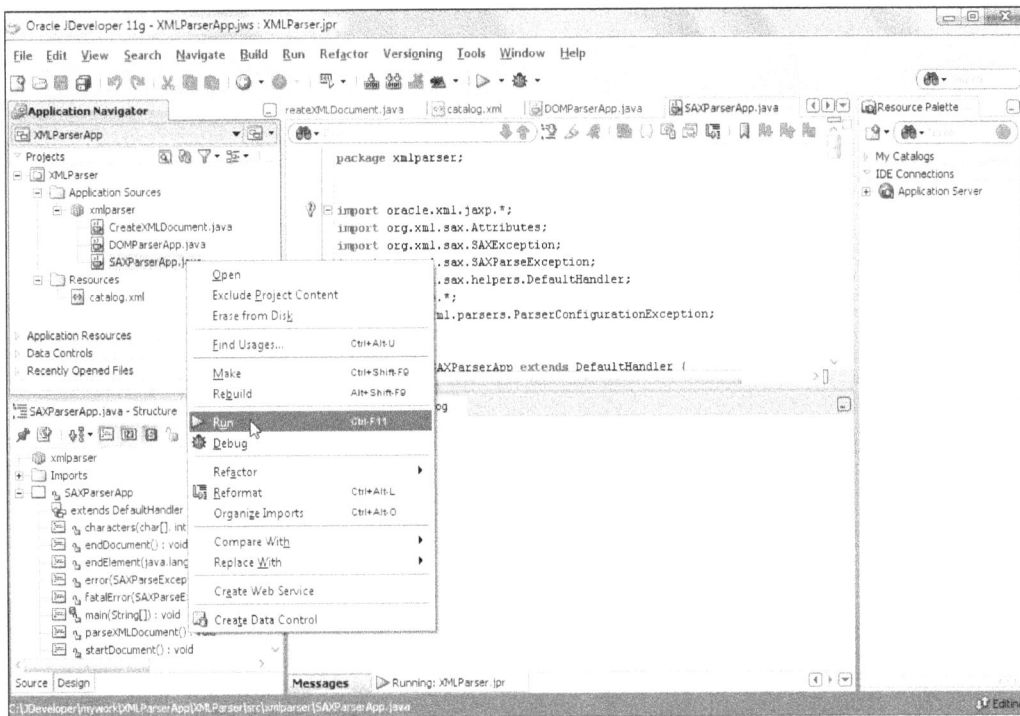

The output from the SAX parsing application lists the SAX events, elements, and attributes in the parsed XML document.

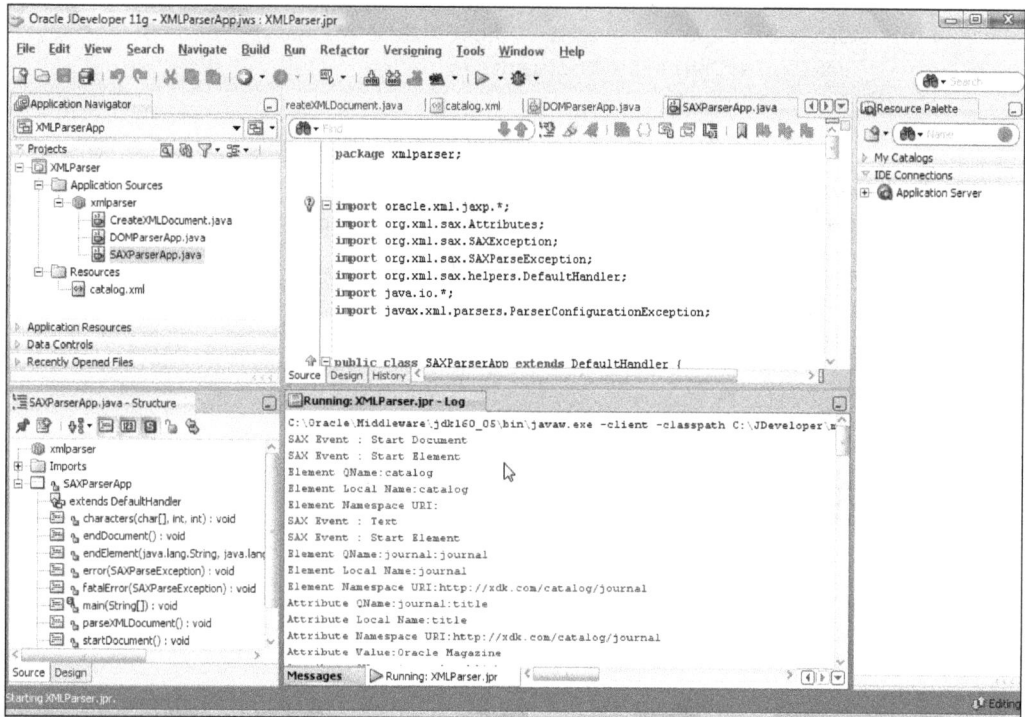

The complete output from the SAX parsing application is listed as follows:

```
SAX Event : Start Document
SAX Event : Start Element
Element QName:catalog
Element Local Name:catalog
Element Namespace URI:
SAX Event : Text
SAX Event : Start Element
Element QName:journal:journal
Element Local Name:journal
Element Namespace URI:http://xdk.com/catalog/journal
Attribute QName:journal:title
Attribute Local Name:title
Attribute Namespace URI:http://xdk.com/catalog/journal
Attribute Value:Oracle Magazine
Attribute QName:journal:publisher
Attribute Local Name:publisher
Attribute Namespace URI:http://xdk.com/catalog/journal
```

```
Attribute Value:Oracle Publishing
Attribute QName:journal:edition
Attribute Local Name:edition
Attribute Namespace URI:http://xdk.com/catalog/journal
Attribute Value:March-April 2008
Attribute QName:xmlns:journal
Attribute Local Name:journal
Attribute Namespace URI:http://www.w3.org/2000/xmlns/
Attribute Value:http://xdk.com/catalog/journal
SAX Event : Text
SAX Event : Start Element
Element QName:journal:article
Element Local Name:article
Element Namespace URI:http://xdk.com/catalog/journal
Attribute QName:journal:section
Attribute Local Name:section
Attribute Namespace URI:http://xdk.com/catalog/journal
Attribute Value:Oracle Developer
SAX Event : Text
SAX Event : Start Element
Element QName:journal:title
Element Local Name:title
Element Namespace URI:http://xdk.com/catalog/journal
SAX Event : Text
Text:Declarative Data Filtering
SAX Event : End Element
Element QName:journal:title
SAX Event : Text
SAX Event : Start Element
Element QName:journal:author
Element Local Name:author
Element Namespace URI:http://xdk.com/catalog/journal
SAX Event : Text
Text:Steve Muench
SAX Event : End Element
Element QName:journal:author
SAX Event : Text
SAX Event : End Element
Element QName:journal:article
SAX Event : Text
SAX Event : End Element
Element QName:journal:journal
SAX Event : Text
SAX Event : Start Element
```

```
Element QName:journal
Element Local Name:journal
Element Namespace URI:
Attribute QName:title
Attribute Local Name:title
Attribute Namespace URI:
Attribute Value:Oracle Magazine
Attribute QName:publisher
Attribute Local Name:publisher
Attribute Namespace URI:
Attribute Value:Oracle Publishing
Attribute QName:edition
Attribute Local Name:edition
Attribute Namespace URI:
Attribute Value:September-October 2008
SAX Event : Text
SAX Event : Start Element
Element QName:article
Element Local Name:article
Element Namespace URI:
Attribute QName:section
Attribute Local Name:section
Attribute Namespace URI:
Attribute Value:FEATURES
SAX Event : Text
SAX Event : Start Element
Element QName:title
Element Local Name:title
Element Namespace URI:
SAX Event : Text
Text:Share 2.0
SAX Event : End Element
Element QName:title
SAX Event : Text
SAX Event : Start Element
Element QName:author
Element Local Name:author
Element Namespace URI:
SAX Event : Text
Text:Alan Joch
SAX Event : End Element
Element QName:author
SAX Event : Text
SAX Event : End Element
```

```
Element QName:article
SAX Event : Text
SAX Event : End Element
Element QName:journal
SAX Event : Text
SAX Event : End Element
Element QName:catalog
SAX Event : End Document
```

To demonstrate error handling, add an error in the example XML document. For example, remove a `</journal>` node, as we did earlier. Run the `SAXParserApp.java` application in JDeveloper. An error message gets outputted:

```
Fatal Error:<Line 15, Column 10>: XML-20121: (Fatal Error) End tag
does not match start tag 'journal'.
```

Summary

In this chapter we demonstrated the DOM and SAX approaches to parsing an XML document. DOM parsing is suitable if document nodes are to be modified and navigated with random access. SAX parsing is useful if you want to go through the XML document once, responding to nodes as you encounter them. If you want to create an encapsulation of the XML document as a DOM tree that you can manipulate later, you need to use DOM parsing.

In this chapter we created an XML document using the JAXP API. In the next chapter, we will create an XML document from an XML Schema. First, we will create an XML Schema in JDeveloper and subsequently we will instantiate an XML document from the XML Schema.

2
Creating an XML Schema

While XML has become the standard medium for exchanging data, it's the XML schema that defines the structure, content, and semantics of the XML documents. Before you create an XML document that conforms to an XML schema, create the XML schema with the procedure explained in this chapter. Why is it better to start off from an XML schema instead of directly creating the XML document without a schema? Consider a shipping company that sends XML documents containing details on a cargo shipment to a client. If the XML documents are not based on an XML schema, the shipping company might send XML documents containing different sets of elements and attributes. The client won't be able to interpret the XML documents if the XML documents contain different sets of elements and attributes. If the XML documents are based on an XML schema, the client would receive similar XML documents and be able to interpret them. An XML schema makes XML documents understandable to the different parties involved.

JDeveloper 11g provides various wizards for processing an XML schema. In the **New Gallery** a new schema file may be created. To construct a schema, select XML schema components from the schema **Component Palette**. A schema may be registered from the **Tools** menu. Subsequently, an XML document may be created from a registered schema.

In this chapter we shall create an XML schema in JDeveloper 11g. We shall register an XML document in JDeveloper and subsequently create an XML document instance from the XML schema. The example XML schema document that we shall create is catalog.xsd and is listed here:

```
<?xml version="1.0" encoding="utf-8"?>
<xsd:schema xmlns:xsd="http://www.w3.org/2001/XMLSchema">
<xsd:element name="catalog" type="catalogType"/>
   <xsd:complexType name="catalogType">
    <xsd:sequence>
     <xsd:element ref="journal" minOccurs="0" maxOccurs="unbounded"/>
```

```
       </xsd:sequence>
     </xsd:complexType>
     <xsd:element name="journal" type="journalType"/>
     <xsd:complexType name="journalType">
      <xsd:sequence>
       <xsd:element ref="article"  minOccurs="0"
       maxOccurs="unbounded"/>
      </xsd:sequence>
      <xsd:attribute name="title" type="xsd:string"/>
      <xsd:attribute  name="publisher"  type="xsd:string"/>
      <xsd:attribute  name="edition"  type="xsd:string"/>
     </xsd:complexType>
    <xsd:element name="article" type="articleType"/>
    <xsd:complexType name="articleType">
     <xsd:sequence>
      <xsd:element name="title" type="xsd:string"/>
       <xsd:element name="author" type="xsd:string"/>
     </xsd:sequence>
     <xsd:attribute  name="section" type="xsd:string"/>
    </xsd:complexType>
  </xsd:schema>
```

The XML document instance that we shall generate from the schema is `catalog.xml`
and is listed as follows:

```
<?xml version="1.0" encoding="utf-8"?>
<catalog>
<journal title="Oracle Magazine" publisher="Oracle
Publishing" edition="September-October 2008">
  <article section="Features">
    <title>Share 2.0</title>
    <author>Alan Joch</author>
   </article>
 </journal>
<journal title="Oracle Magazine" publisher="Oracle
Publishing" edition="March-April 2008">
  <article section="Oracle Developer">
    <title>Declarative Data Filtering</title>
    <author>Steve Muench</author>
   </article>
</journal></catalog>
```

An overview of XML Schema

The structure of an XML document is represented by an XML schema.
An XML schema is also an XML document in the namespace
`http://www.w3.org/2001/XMLSchema`.

Root element

The root element in a schema is `schema`. The schema namespace is specified
in the root element with the declaration `xmlns:xs=http://www.w3.org/2001/`
`XMLSchema`. A prefix other than `xs` may be used, such as `xsd`. A `schema` element
may have attributes `targetNamespace`, `version`, `attributeFormDefault`,
and `elementFormDefault`.

- `targetNamespace` specifies the namespace described in the schema.
  "An XML namespace is a collection of names, identified by a URI reference,
  which are used in XML documents as element types and attribute names."
  (`http://www.w3.org/TR/1999/REC-xml-names-19990114/`)

- `elementFormDefault` and `attributeFormDefault` specify whether
  elements and attributes in the `targetNamespace` are required to be
  qualified by default.

A qualified name consists of a prefix that is mapped to a namespace URI followed
by a single colon, which is followed by the local name. A value of `unqualified`
(default value) indicates that elements and attributes may be specified without a
prefix. The value `qualified` indicates that attributes and elements must be qualified
with a `prefix`. The default values apply only to local elements and attributes. The
top-level elements and attributes need to be `qualified`. The default values may be
overridden by the `form` attribute in an attribute or element. The attribute `version`
specifies the version of XML schema. An example of a schema element is shown in
the following listing:

```
<xsd:schema version="1.0" xmlns:xsd="http://www.w3.org/2001/XMLSchema"
targetNamespace=" http://xdk11g.com/journal" xmlns:journal="http://
xdk11g.com/journal"></xsd:schema>
```

All other schema constructs are specified in the `schema` element.

Element component

An XML document element is represented in a schema with the `element` construct. Some of the attributes an element may have are `name`, `type`, `minOccurs`, and `maxOccurs`.

- `name` specifies the element name. Element and attribute tags can be used to either define a component or to use a component by reference. The attribute `ref` may be used instead of the attribute `name`. The attribute `ref` specifies a reference to a top-level element declaration.

- `type` specifies the element type, which may be one of the schema built-in types, such as `xsd:string` or `xsd:integer`, or a defined `simpleType` or `complexType`. We shall discuss `simpleType` and `complexType` later.

- The cardinality (the number of elements in a set) of an element is specified with the attributes `minOccurs` and `maxOccurs`. The attribute `minOccurs` specifies the minimum occurrences of an element, and the attribute `maxOccurrs` specifies the maximum occurrences of an element. The attributes `minOccurs` and `maxOccurs` may only be specified for local elements, not top-level element declarations. Local elements are elements that are defined within another element definition or within a `complexType` definition. Top-level elements are elements that are defined at the top level directly within the root element schema.

An element may be declared in the `schema` element as a top-level declaration or in `choice`, `sequence`, `all`, or `group` declarations, which are discussed later. An example element declaration is shown in the following listing:

```
<xsd:element name="catalog" type="catalogType"  minOccurs="0"
maxOccurs="unbounded"/>
```

An XML document attribute is represented in an XML schema with the `attribute` construct. Some of the attributes that an attribute construct may have are `name`, `type`, `default`, `fixed`, and `use`.

The attribute `name` specifies attribute name. The attribute `ref` may be used instead of `name` to refer to a top-level attribute declaration or an `attributeGroup` declaration, which we shall discuss later. If `ref` is specified, `name` and `type` attributes must not be specified.

The attribute `type` specifies the type of an attribute. The attribute `default` specifies the default value of an attribute. The attribute `fixed` specifies the fixed value of an attribute. One of `default` or `fixed` may be used. The attribute `use` specifies if the attribute is a required attribute, and may have values `optional`, `required`, or `prohibited`. An attribute may be declared as a top-level declaration in `schema` element or in `attributeGroup`, `complexType`, `restriction`, or `extension` elements. An example attribute declaration is shown in the following listing:

```
<xsd:attribute name="title" type="xsd:string" use="required"/>
```

The schema construct `attributeGroup` specifies a group of attributes. An `attributeGroup` may refer to another `attributeGroup` declaration with the `ref` attribute. An example of an `attributeGroup` declaration is this:

```
<xsd:attributeGroup name="journalAttr">
<xsd:attribute name="title: type="xsd:string"/>
<xsd:attribute name="publisher" type="xsd:string"/>
<xsd:attribute name="edition" type="xsd:string"/>
</xsd:attributeGroup>
```

SimpleType component

The schema construct `simpleType` is used to constrain character data in elements and attributes. The text in an element is actually an XML node, which is a text node. The text node within an element is a text child node of the element. A `simpleType` may be defined with `restriction`, `list`, or `union` constructs. A new data type may be defined with `simpleType`. For example, define a `simpleType` called `stringType` to constrain the `xsd:string` data type to a minimum length of 25 as follows:

```
<xsd:simpleType name="stringType">
<xsd:restriction base="xsd:string">
<xsd:minLenth value="25"/>
</xsd:restriction>
</xsd:simpleType>
```

The following is an example of an attribute that uses a `simpleType` definition where the attribute `title` will have a maximum length of 25:

```
<xsd:attribute name="title">
<xsd:simpleType>
<xsd:restriction base="xsd:string">
<xsd:maxLength value="25"/>
</xsd:restriction>
</xsd:simpleType>
</xsd:attribute>
```

With `simpleType`, an element may be defined as a list of values of a specified data type using the `list` construct. For example, define an element that contains a list of integer values like this:

```
<xsd:simpleType name="listType">
<xsd:list  itemType="xsd:integer"/>
</xsd:simpleType>
```

An element construct of type `listType` may be declared as follows in an XML schema:

```
<xsd:element name="list"  type="listType"/>
```

An example of a `listType` element is shown here:

```
<list>1 5 10 12 15</list>
```

The `union` construct defines a collection of simple types. For example, define a `simpleType` that is the union of the `xsd:string` and `xsd:integer` simple types:

```
<xsd:simpleType name="unionType">
<xsd:union  memberTypes="xsd:integer xsd:string"/>
</xsd:simpleType>
```

`SimpleType unionType` is a combination of `xsd:integer` and `xsd:string`, which implies that an element or attribute of type `unionType` may either be an integer or a string. In the built-in data type hierarchy, string and integer are defined as different data types.

An element, `elementA`, of type `unionType` may be declared as follows:

```
<elementA>Element A</elementA>
```

A `unionType` element may also be declared as follows:

```
<elementA>25</elementA>
```

The XML schema specification provides some built-in simple data types (`http://www.w3.org/TR/xmlschema-2/#built-in-datatypes`).

ComplexType component

The `complexType` construct is used to define the structure of an element. A `complexType` is used for the following:

- Constraining an element definition by providing attribute declarations governing the appearance and content of attributes

- Constraining element children to conform to a specified element-only or mixed-content model, or constraining character data to conform to a specified simple type definition, or constraining element children to be empty
- Deriving a complex type from another simple type or complex type

A `complexType` may be declared at the top level in the schema element or in an element declaration. If a `complexType` is defined at the top level, it is used in an element declaration using the `type` attribute. If an element uses a lot of complex type/simple type definitions, it is better to define the complex types at the top level to keep the element declaration simple. A sequence of elements is defined with the `sequence` construct within a `complexType` construct. An example is:

```
<xsd:complexType name="journalType">
<xsd:sequence>
<xsd:element name="title" type="xsd:string"/>
<xsd:element name="edition" type="xsd:string"/>
</xsd:sequence>
<xsd:attribute name="publisher" type="xsd:string"/>
</xsd:complexType>
```

An example of using a `complexType` in an `element` declaration with the `type` attribute is as follows:

```
<xsd:element name="journal" type="journalType"/>
```

The order of elements in an XML document should be the same as in the `sequence` construct. An example of using the `journal element` declaration in an XML document is as follows:

```
<journal publisher="Oracle Publishing">
<title>Oracle Magazine</title>
<edition>Jan-Feb 2008</edition>
</journal>
```

As the `journal` element is of type `journalType`, it has an attribute `publisher` and a sequence of elements `title` and `edition` with the `title` element preceding the `edition` element. If you need multiple elements, but do not want them to be in a particular order, use the `all` construct. An example of using the `all` construct is as follows:

```
<xsd:complexType name="journalType">
<xsd:all>
<xsd:element name="title" type="xsd:string"/>
<xsd:element name="edition" type="xsd:string"/>
</xsd:all>
</xsd:complexType>
```

A `complexType` may also be defined with a choice of elements with the `choice` construct, which implies that an element of type `journalType` may contain either the `date` subelement or the `edition` subelement, but not both, and it must contain one of the two:

```
<xsd:complexType name="journalType">
<xsd:choice>
<xsd:element name="date" type="xsd:string"/>
<xsd:element name="edition" type="xsd:string"/>
</xsd:choice>
</xsd:complexType>
```

An example XML element `journal` with `choice` content is as follows:

```
<journal>
<date>Jan-Feb 2008</date>
</journal>
```

Similar to setting cardinality on individual elements, cardinality may be set on `sequence`, `all`, and `choice` constructs with `minOccurs` and `maxOccurs`. Cardinality set on a `sequence` construct implies that the `sequence` may be repeated the specified number of times. A `complexType` may be defined to have mixed content, that is, text and elements. A mixed content `complexType` is specified with the attribute `mixed`, which has a Boolean value. The default value of `mixed` is `false`. ComplexType `journalType` may be defined with mixed content as listed:

```
<xsd:complexType name="journalType" mixed="true">
<xsd:sequence>
<xsd:element name="title" type="xsd:string"/>
<xsd:element name="edition" type="xsd:string"/>
</xsd:sequence>
</xsd:complexType>
```

An example XML construct based on the mixed content schema construct is as follows:

```
<journal>
The journal is
<title>Oracle Magazine</title>
The edition is
<edition>Jan-Feb 2008</edition>
</journal>
```

A `complexType` may be defined with `simpleContent` and `complexContent` constructs. `SimpleContent` specifies restrictions and extensions on a text-only complex type, which is a complex type with character data, attributes, and no elements, or on a simple type. In an example of a `simpleContent` with extension, an attribute is added on a text-only `complexType`. For example, define a text only complex type `journalType`:

```
<xsd:complexType name="journalType">
   <xsd:simpleContent>
      <xsd:extension base="xsd:string">
         <xsd:attribute name="publisher" type="xsd:string"/>
      </xsd:extension>
   </xsd:simpleContent>
  </xsd:complexType>
```

Define a complex type that uses a simple content extension to add an attribute to the `journalType` complex type:

```
<xsd:complexType name="journalTypeExtension">
<xsd:simpleContent>
<xsd:extension base="journalType">
<xsd:attribute name="edition" type="xsd:string"/>
</xsd:extension>
</xsd:simpleContent>
</xsd:complexType>
```

An example XML element `journal` based on the `journalTypeExtension` is shown here:

```
<journal publisher="Oracle Publishing" edition="Jan-Feb 2008">Oracle
Magazine</journal>
```

Actually, we used a simple content example in which we used a `simpleContent` for the `journalType` definition. The simple content in the `journalType` definition extends the simple type `xsd:string`. A `simpleContent` may also be declared with a `restriction`. In this example of a `simpleContent` with `restriction`, an element length is restricted to `10`:

```
<xsd:element name="journal">
<xsd:complexType>
<xsd:simpleContent>
<xsd:restriction base="xsd:string">
<xsd:maxLength value="10"/>
</xsd:restriction>
</xsd:simpleContent>
</xsd:complexType>
</xsd:element>
```

An example XML document element `journal` with simple content restriction is shown here:

```
<journal>Oracle Mag</journal>
```

The `complexContent` construct is used to define extensions and restrictions on an element-only (which includes attributes), or mixed content `complexType`. In this example of a `complexContent` with extension, a `complexType`, named `journalType` here, is extended to add another element and attribute in complex type `journalTypeExten` as follows:

```
<xsd:complexType name="journalType">
<xsd:sequence>
<xsd:element name="title"  type="xsd:string"/>
<xsd:element name="publisher" type="xsd:string"/>
</xs:sequence>
</xsd:complexType>

<xsd:complexType name="journalTypeExten">
<xsd:complexContent>
<xsd:extension base="journalType">
<xsd:sequence>
<xsd:element name="edition"  type="xsd:string"/>
</xsd:sequence>
<xsd:attribute name="section" type="xsd:string"/>
</xsd:extension>
</xsd:complexContent>
</xsd:complexType>
```

An example XML document element `journal` of type `journalTypeExten` may be defined as follows:

```
<journal section="XML">
<title>Oracle Magazine</title>
<publisher>Oracle Publishing</publisher>
<edition>Jan-Feb 2006</edition>
</journal>
```

To review what we have discussed in the introduction on XML schema, the following table compares the simple type and complex type structures:

XML Structure	Description
Simple type	Constrains character data in elements and attributes.
Complex type with simple content	Specifies restrictions and extensions on a text-only complex type, which is a complex type with character data attributes and no elements, or on a simple type.

XML Structure	Description
Complex type with complex content	Specifies extensions and restrictions on a content model that includes elements and attributes, or a mixed content complexType. The difference between simple content and complex content is that simple content does not have elements.
Complex type with mixed content	Specifies a content model that includes elements, attributes, and character data. The character data may be specified between elements in addition to within elements.

A more detailed discussion on XML schema structures is in the *XML Schema Structures W3C Recommendation* (http://www.w3.org/TR/xmlschema-1/).

Setting the environment

Create an application and a project in JDeveloper by selecting **File | New**, and subsequently selecting **Categories | General** and **Items | Generic Application** in the **New Gallery** window. In the **Create Generic Application** window specify the **Application Name**, XMLSchema for example, and click on **Next**. In the **Name your Generic project** window specify a **Project Name**, **XMLSchema** for example, and click on **Finish**.

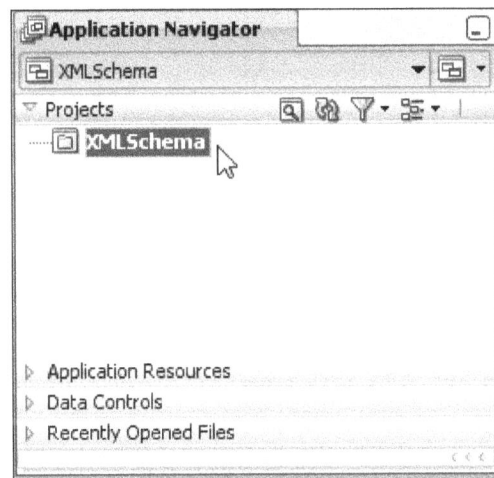

Creating an XML schema

In this section we shall create an XML schema, `catalog.xsd` (as listed in the introduction), in JDeveloper Schema Visual Editor. First, add a schema file to project **XMLSchema**. Select the **XMLSchema** node in **Application Navigator** and select **File | New**. In the **New Gallery** window select **General | XML** in **Categories**, and **XML schema** in **Items**. Click on the **OK** button.

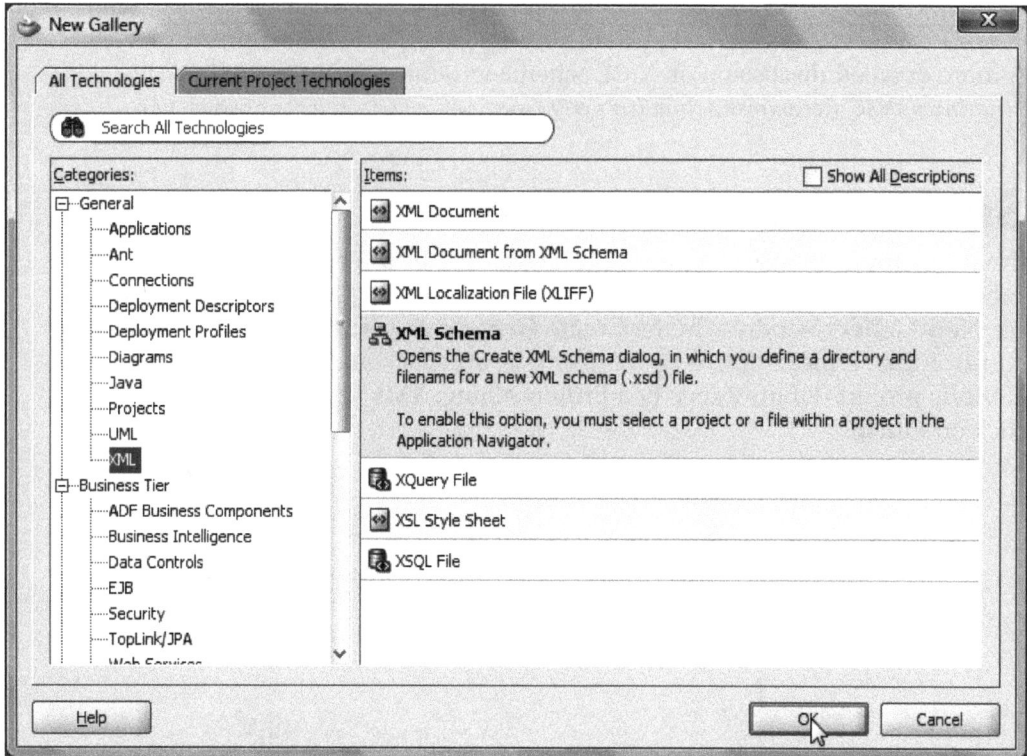

In the **Create XML schema** window specify a **File Name**, `catalog.xsd`, and click on **OK**. An XML schema gets added to project **XMLSchema**. In the **Design** view, the different components of the schema are displayed in the schema visual editor. In the **Source** view, the schema document source is listed. The different schema components available to add to a schema are listed in the **Schema Components Component Palette**.

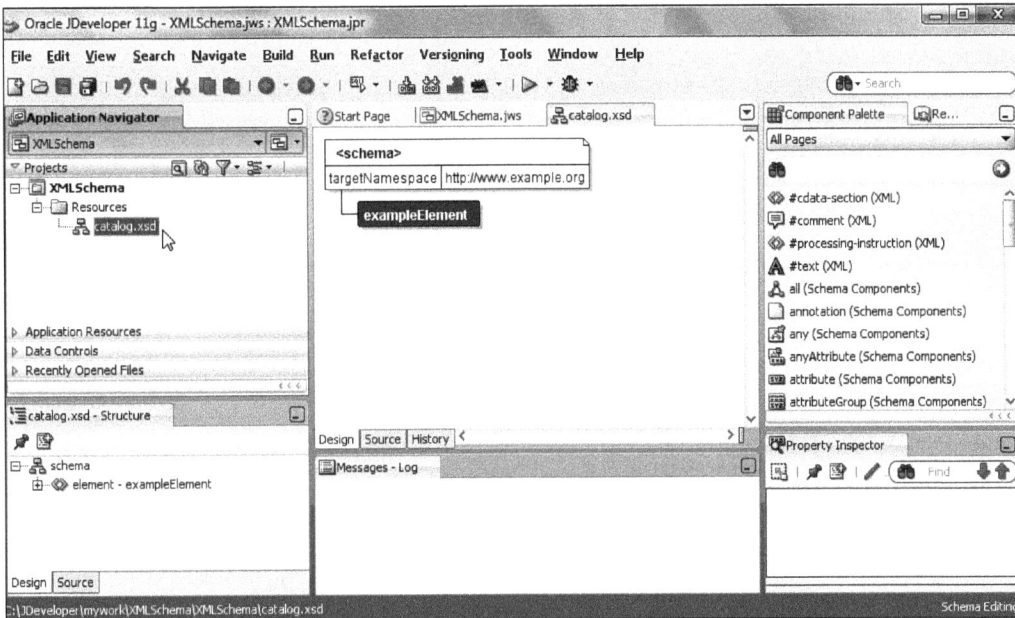

Components may be added to an XML schema either from the **Component Palette** or a component node in the schema. As an example of adding a component from a component node, add root element **catalog**. Right-click on **<schema>** node in **Design** view, and select **Insert inside schema | element**.

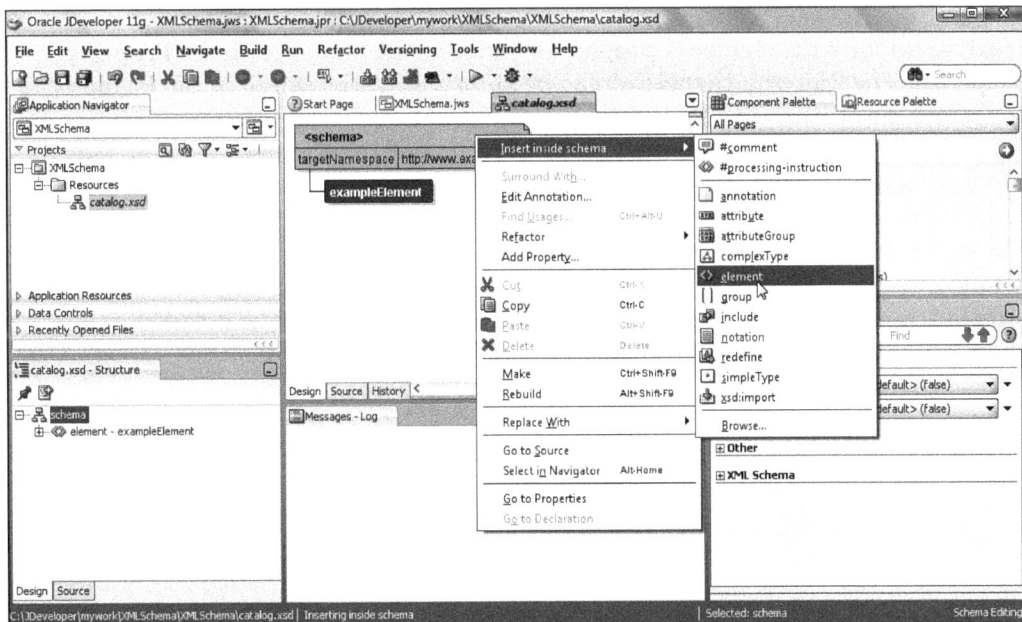

An element, **element1** gets added to the **schema** element.

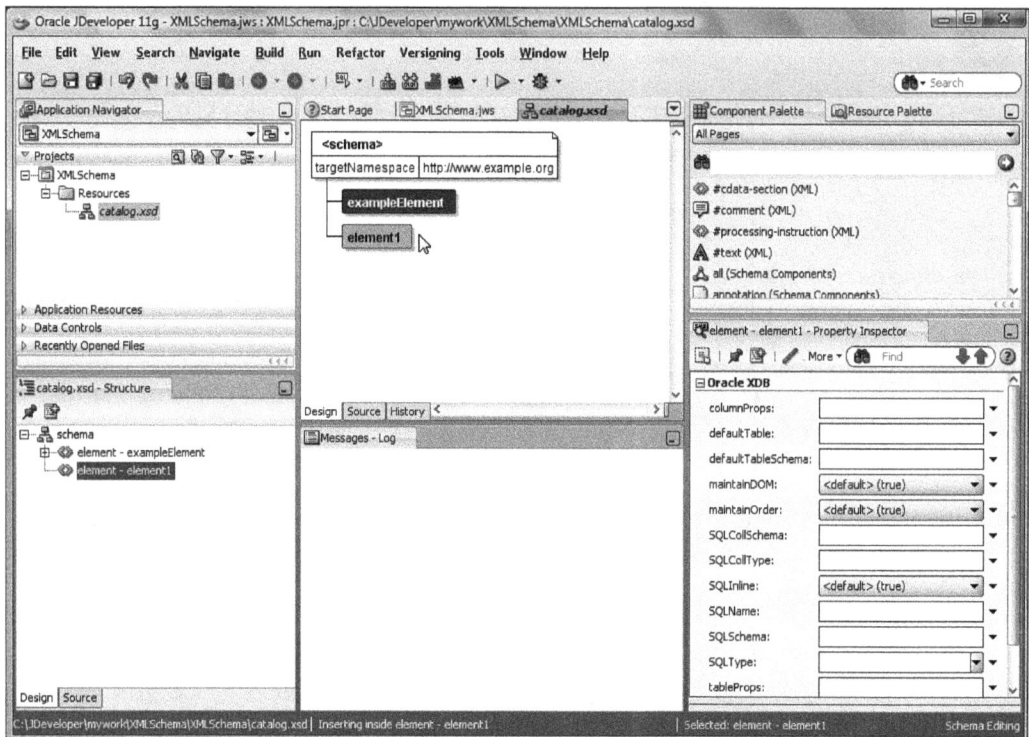

Next, we modify the **element1** properties such as name and type in the **Property Inspector**. The **Property Inspector** may be started either by selecting the **Property Inspector** tab or by right-clicking on the component node and selecting **Go To Properties**. The Property Inspector UI in JDeveloper 11g is on the righthand side of the screen by default, but you have the option to drag the **Property Inspector** window to the bottom where it is easier to read. In the **Property Inspector**, select the **XMLSchema** tree and modify the element name to **catalog**. Specify **type** as **catalogType**. Properties **abstract**, **block**, **default**, **final**, **fixed**, **id**, **nillable**, and **substitutionGroup** may also be set in the **Property Inspector**. The detail of these properties may be referred to in the *W3C XML Schema Structures* (http://www.w3.org/TR/xmlschema-1/#cElement_Declarations).

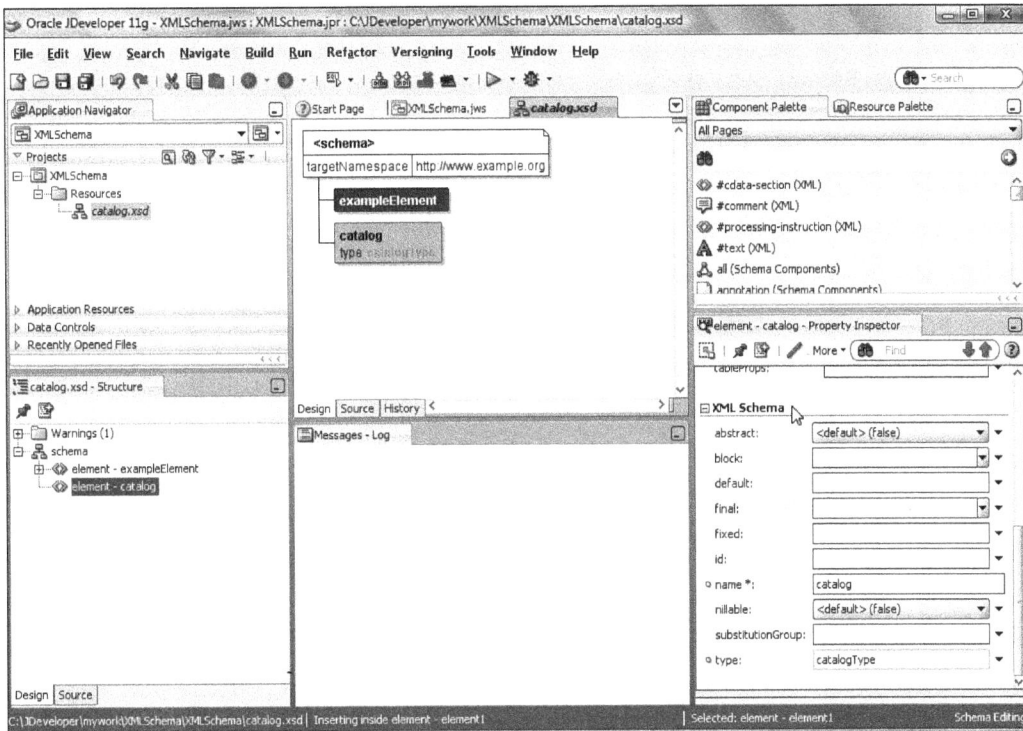

An element may also be added by selecting in **Design** view the node to which the element is to be added and selecting **element** in the **Component Palette**. A component may also be added from the **Component Palette** to a **Design** view component by selecting the component in the **Component Palette** and dragging the component to the **Design** view component and dropping it.

Element properties such as element `name`, element type, and other properties may still be modified in the **Property Inspector**. To delete the **exampleElement** element, right-click on the **exampleElement** node and select **Delete**. Next, we add **complexType catalogType** to the **<schema>** node from the **Component Palette**. Select the schema component in the **Design** view and select **complexType** from the **Component Palette**.

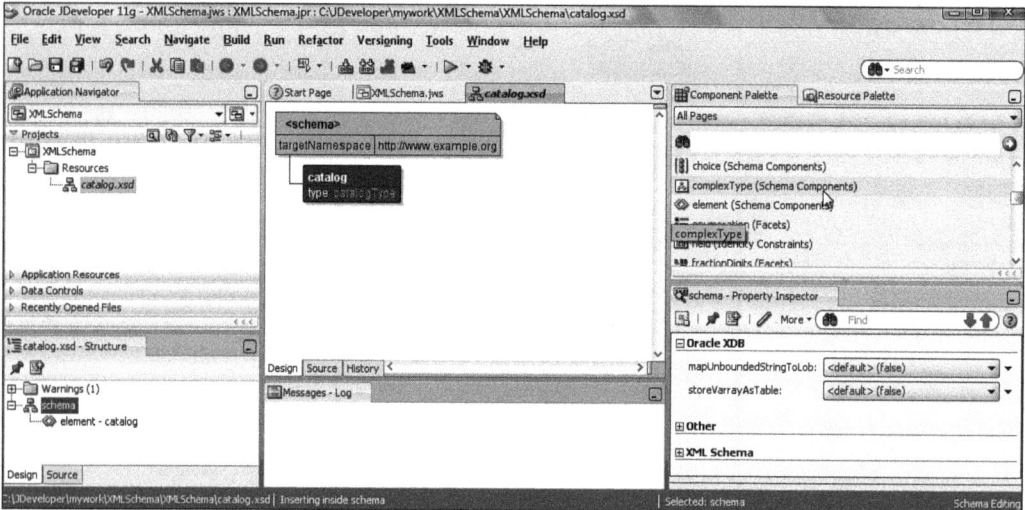

A **complexType** gets added to the **schema** element. Set the **complexType** name and other properties in the **Property Inspector**.

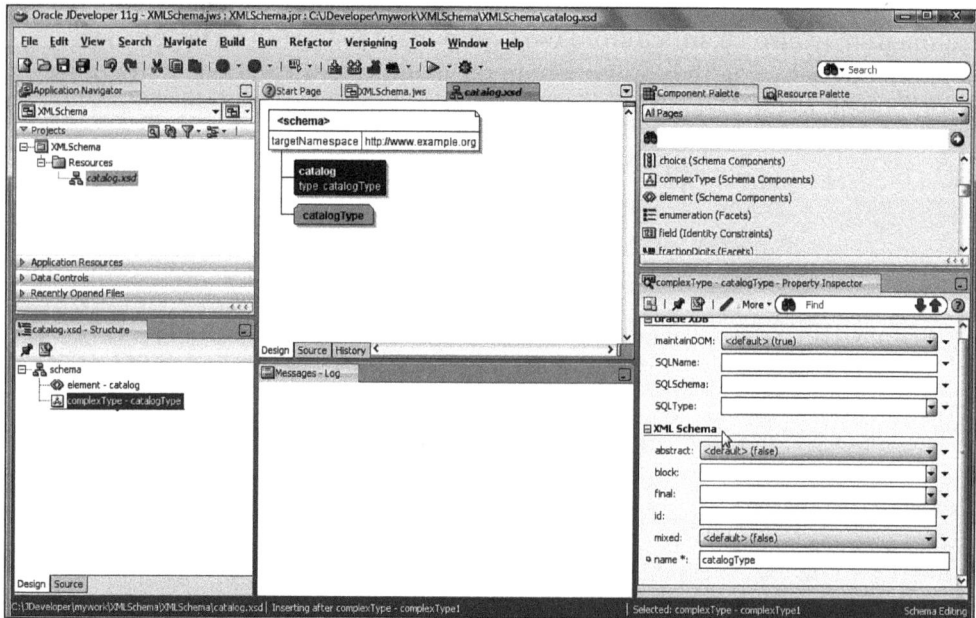

A **complexType** may also be added from the **Design** view by right-clicking on the schema node and selecting **Insert inside schema | complexType**. Next, add a **sequence** element to **complexType-catalogType**. Right-click on the **catalogType** node and select **Insert inside complexType | sequence**.

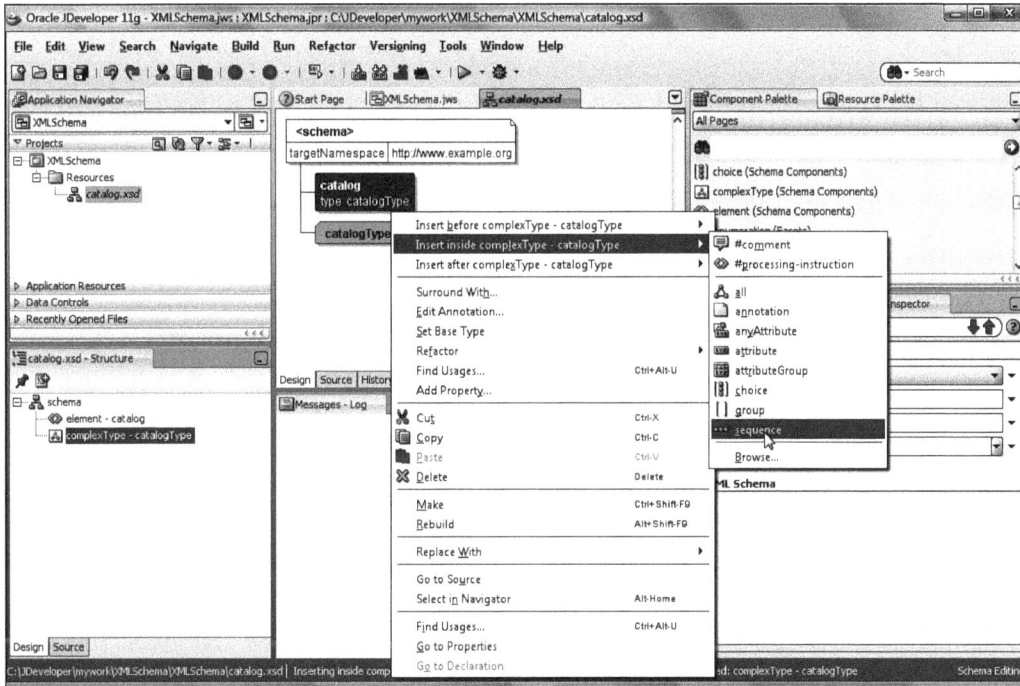

A **sequence** node gets added to the **catalogType** node. The **sequence** node has a default cardinality of **1**. Next, we shall add a **journal** element to the **sequence** node. Right-click on the **sequence** node and select **Insert inside sequence | element**.

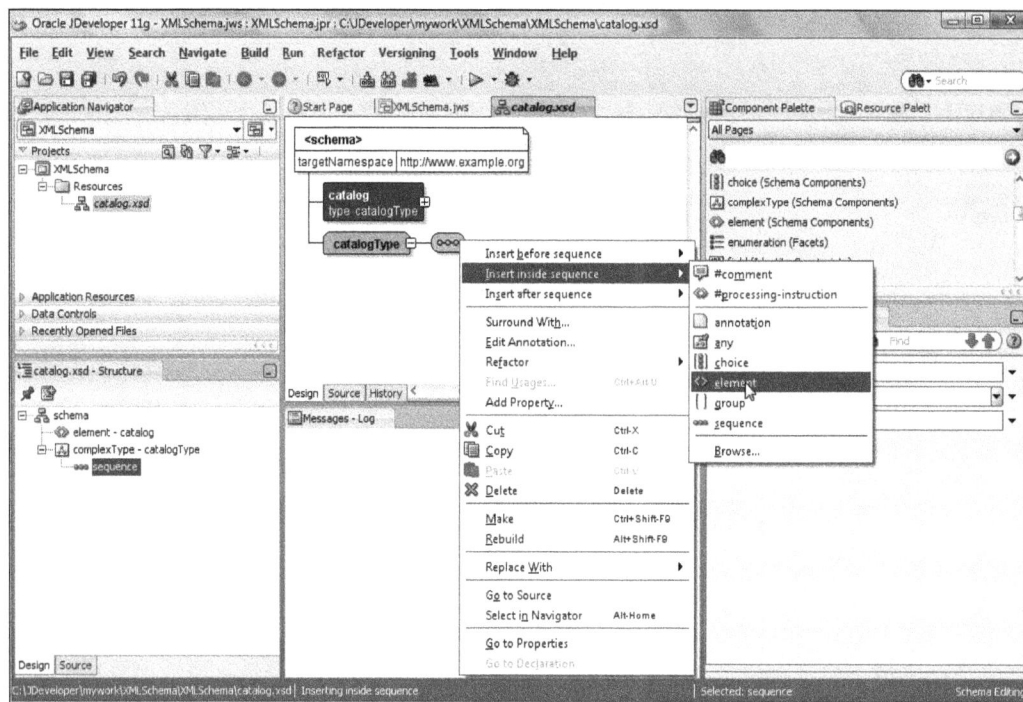

An **element** node gets added to the **sequence** node. In the **Property Inspector** specify element name as **journal** and type as **journalType**. Also, set the attribute **minOccurs** to **0**, and **maxOccurs** to **unbounded**. The type of the element may also be set by right-clicking on the element and selecting **Set Type**.

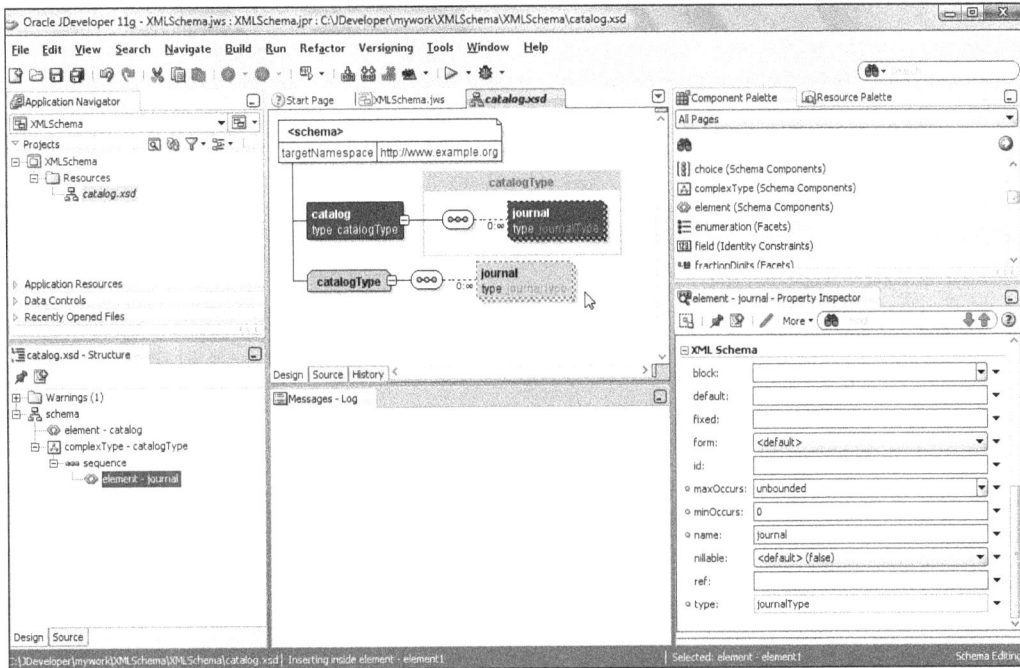

The properties of any of the nodes may be modified by selecting the node in the
Design view and setting the properties in the **Property Inspector**. Next, we add
complexType journalType to the **schema** element. Right-click on the **schema**
element and select **Insert inside schema | complexType**.

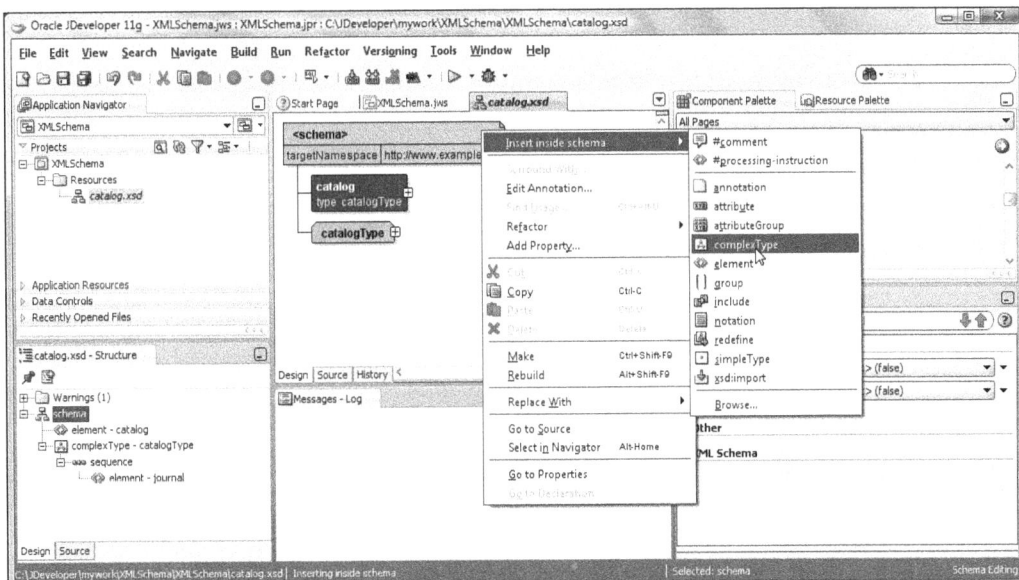

A **complexType** may also be added from the **Component Palette**. A **complexType** node gets added to the **schema** node. Next, we add an element sequence to **journalType** node. Set the **complexType** name to **journalType** in the **Property Inspector**. Right-click on the **complexType** node and select **Insert inside complexType | sequence**. A sequence may also be added by selecting the **journalType** node, and selecting **sequence** in the **Component Palette**.

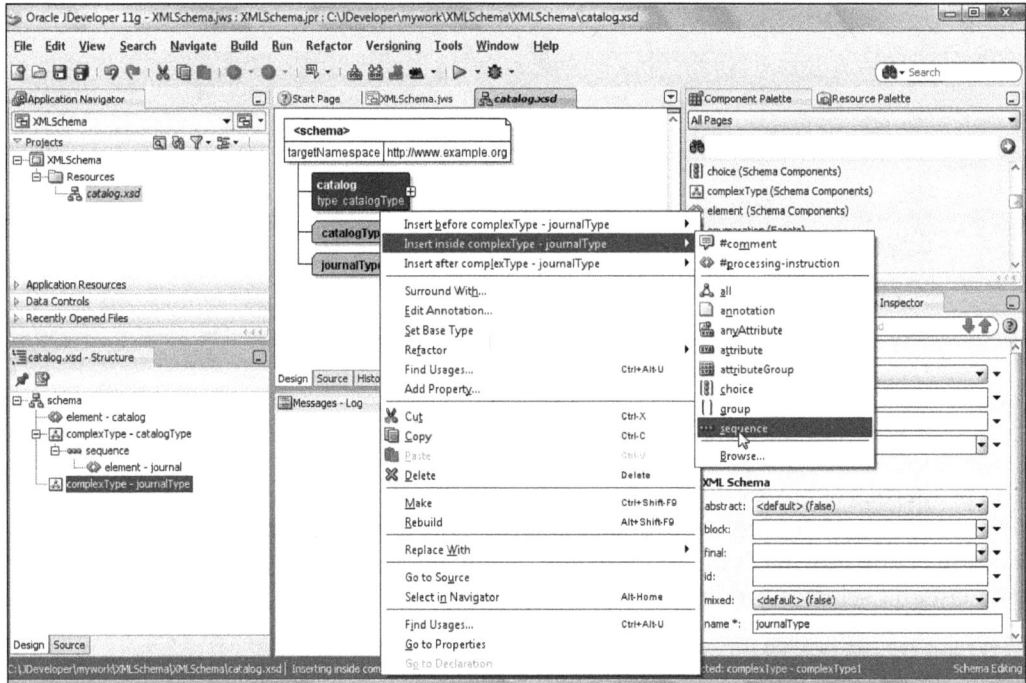

A **sequence** node gets added. Next, we add the **article** element to the **sequence**. Right-click on the **sequence** node and select **Insert inside sequence | element**. An element may also be added to the sequence from the **Component Palette**.

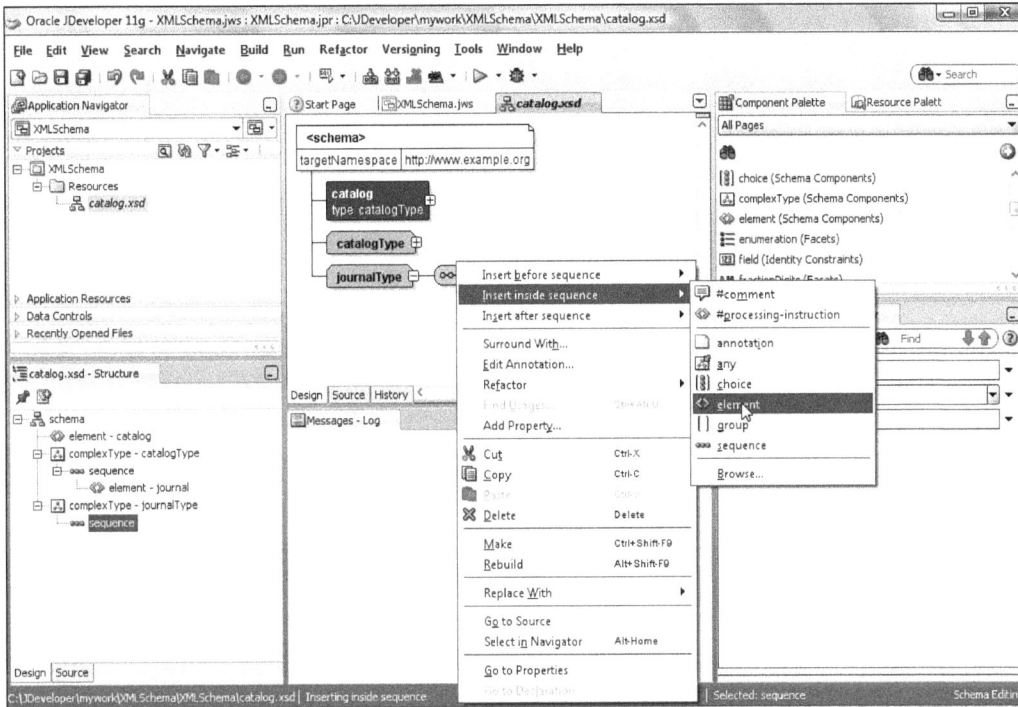

An **element** node gets added to the element sequence. In the **Property Inspector**, set the element **name** to **article**, **minOccurs** to **0** and **maxOccurs** to **unbounded**, and **type** to **articleType**.

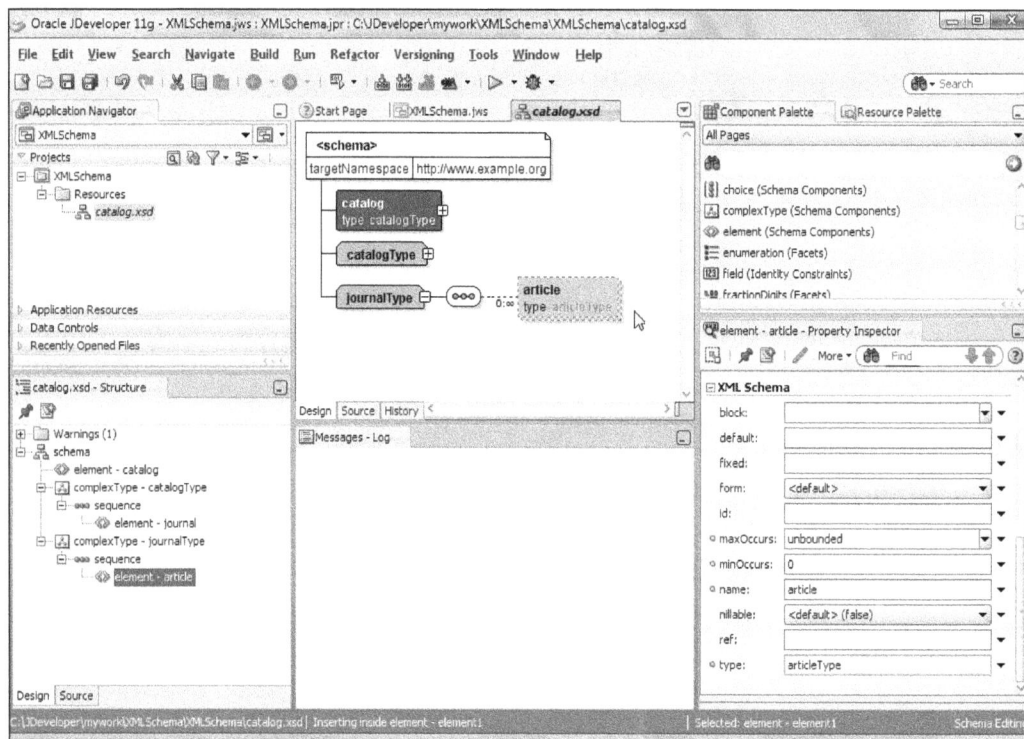

Next, add the attributes **title**, **publisher**, and **edition** to **journalType complexType**. To add an attribute, right-click on the **journalType** node and select **Insert inside complexType-journalType | attribute**. An attribute may also be added by selecting the **journalType** node and selecting **attribute** in the **Component Palette**.

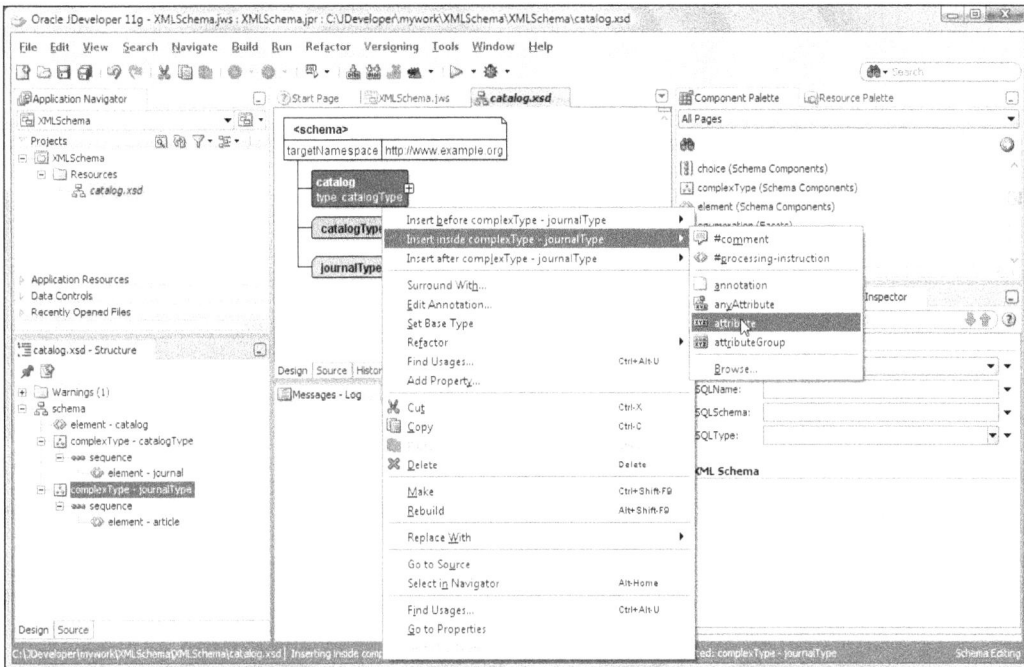

Set the attribute name to **title** and **type** to **xsd:string** in the **Property Inspector**.

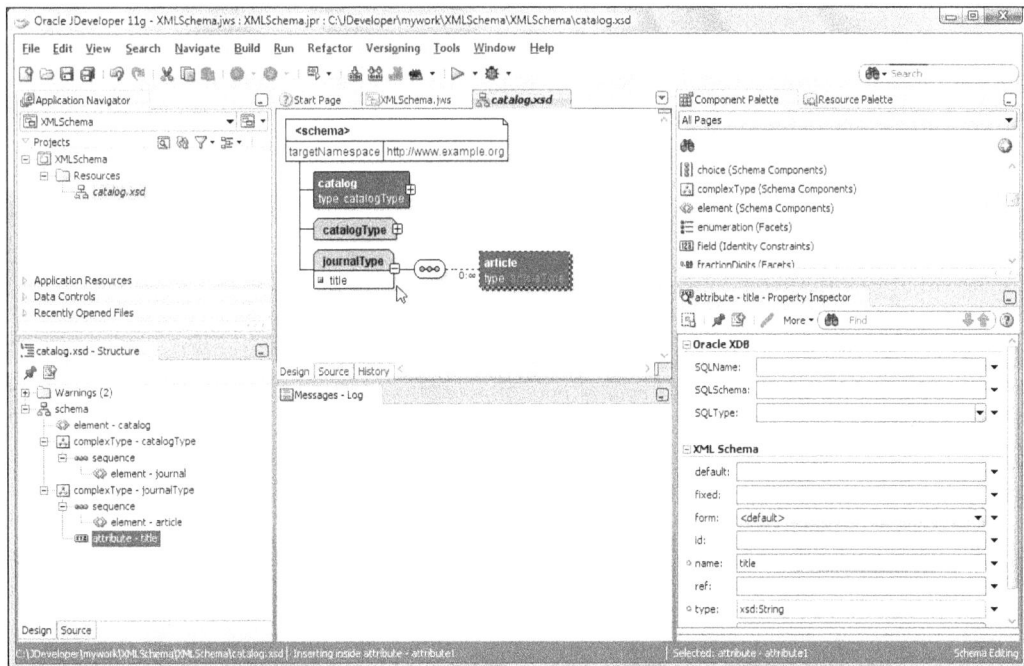

Similarly, add the attributes **publisher** and **edition** to **journalType complexType**.

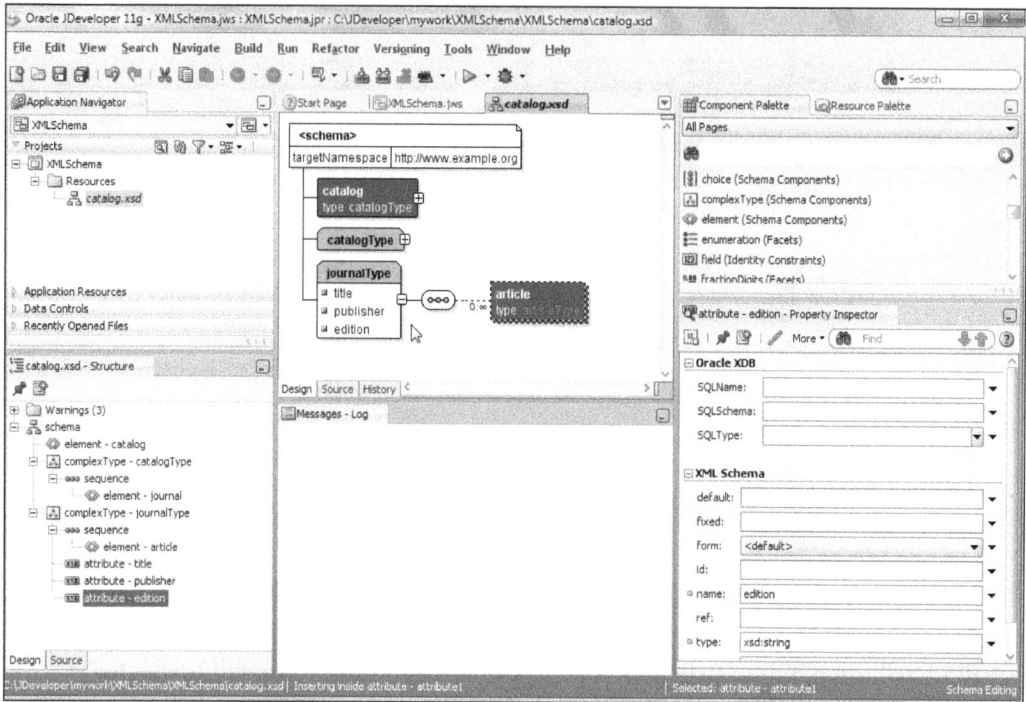

Add **complexType-articleType** to the **schema** node with the procedure with which **catalogType** and **journalType** were added; either from the **Component Palette** or by right-clicking on the **schema** node and selecting **Insert inside schema | complexType**. Set the **complexType** name to **articleType** in the **Property Inspector**. Next, add an element sequence to **articleType** either from the **Component Palette**, or by right-clicking on the **articleType** and selecting **Insert inside complexType | sequence**. Right-click on the **sequence** node and select **Insert inside sequence | element** to add an **element** node to the **sequence** node.

An **element** node may also be added from the **Component Palette**. In the **Property Inspector** set the element **name** to **title**, and **type** to **xsd:string** in the **Property Inspector**. Similarly, add element **author** of type **xsd:string** to the sequence.

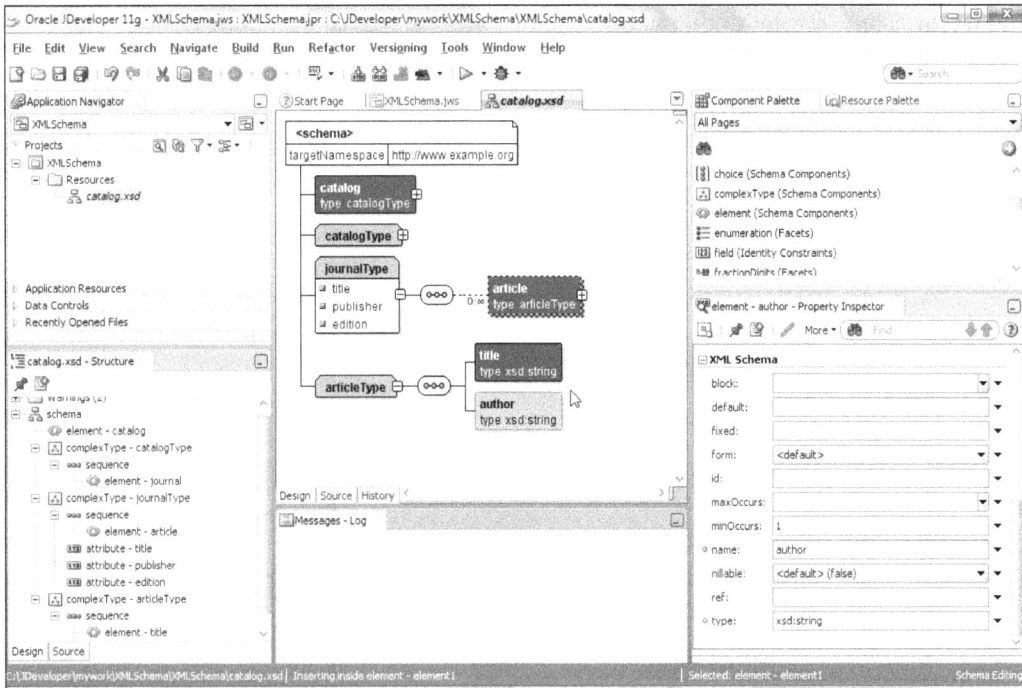

ComplexType-articleType also has an attribute **section**. To add an attribute right-click on the **articleType** node and select **Insert inside complexType | attribute**. The **section** attribute may also be added to **articleType** from the **Component Palette**. Set the attribute **name** to **section** and **type** to **xsd:string** in the **Property Inspector**. The complete schema document, **catalog.xsd**, is shown in **Design** view in the following illustration. Select **File | Save** to save the XML schema.

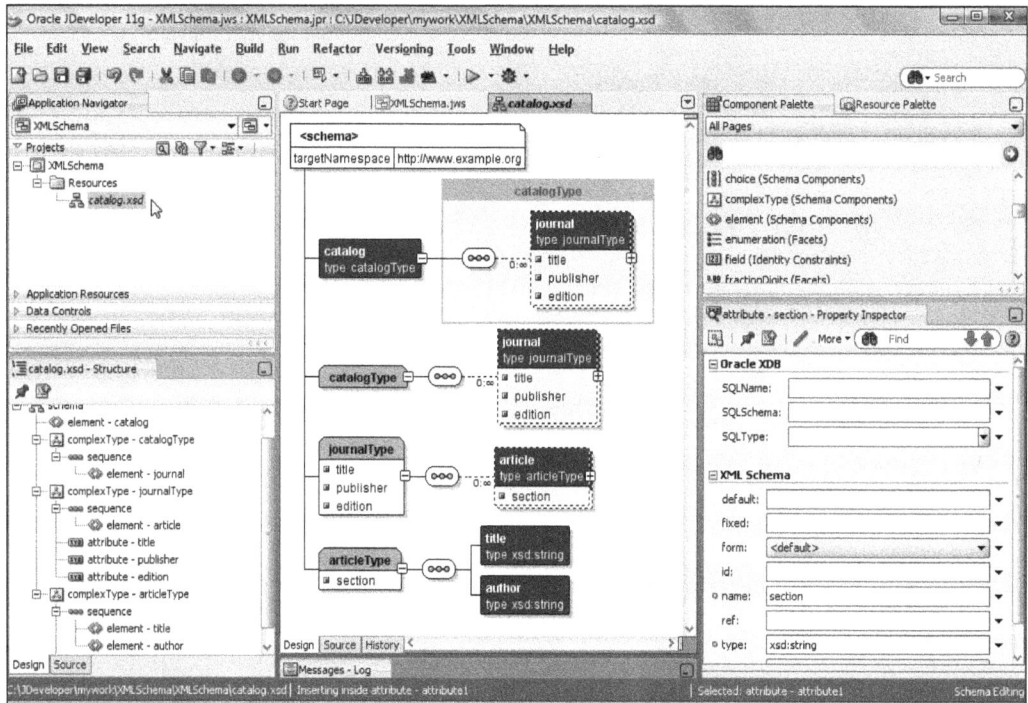

Registering an XML schema

In this section we shall register an XML schema in JDeveloper for XML editing. A registered schema may be used to create an instance of an XML document that conforms to the schema. To register a schema, select **Tools | Preferences**. In the **Preferences** window select **XML schemas**. In the **XML schemas** frame, click the **Add** button to register a schema.

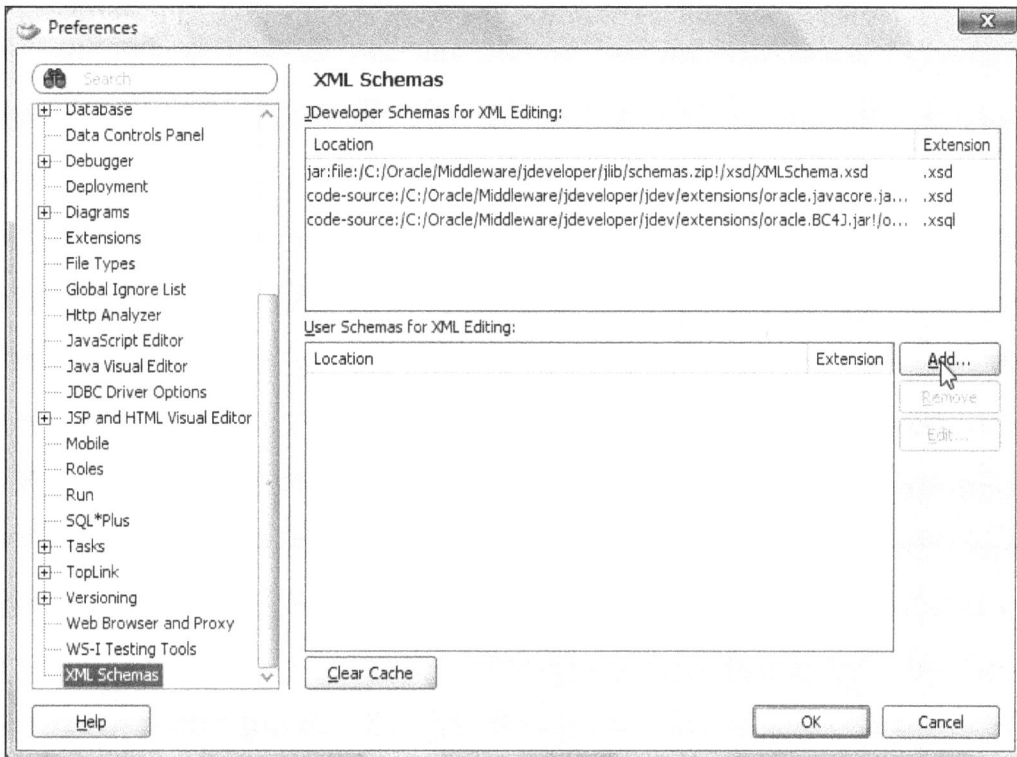

In the **Add Schema** window, click the **Browse** button to select a schema. In the
Open window, select **catalog.xsd** (which was created in the previous section). The
catalog.xsd schema gets added to the **Add Schema** window. **Extension** specifies the
extension of the file type from which the registered schema may be used to create an
XML document instance. We have specified **Extension** as **.xml**, which implies that
the registered schema may be used to create .xml documents. If you were registering
an XML schema to create XSLT files, you would specify **Extension** as .xslt.

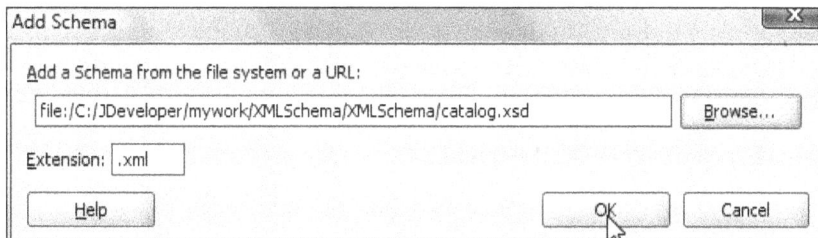

The XML schema **catalog.xsd** gets added to **User Schemas for XML Editing**. Click on the **OK** button to apply the schema registration.

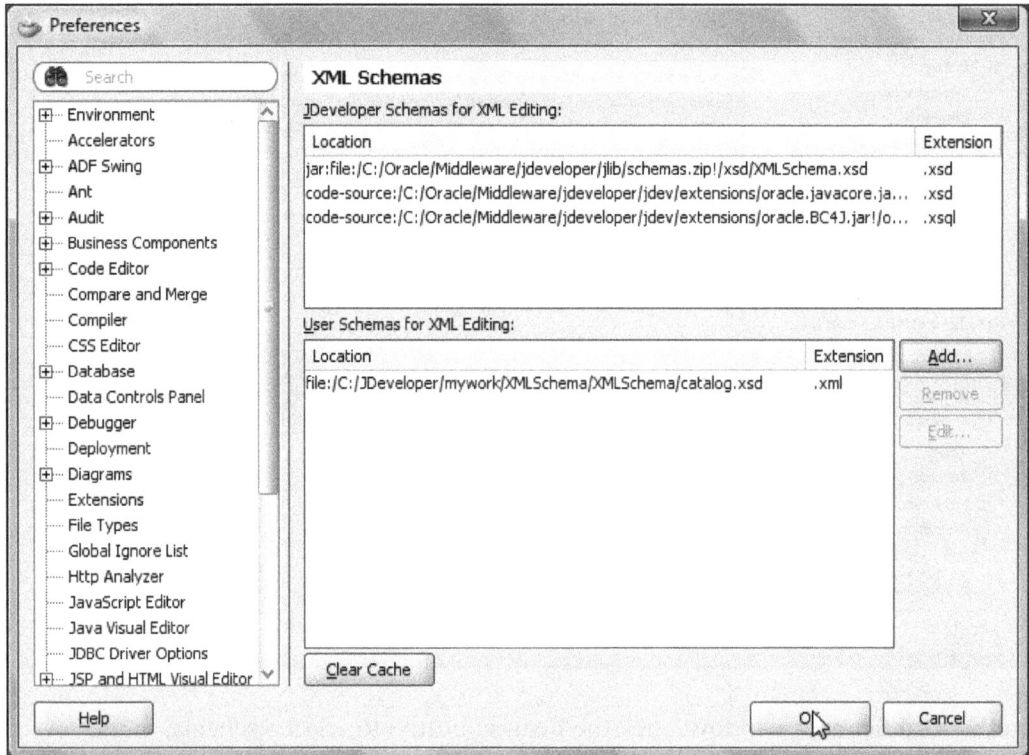

Creating an XML document from the XML schema

In this section we shall create an XML document instance, **catalog.xml** (which was listed in the introduction), from the registered schema **catalog.xsd**. We're using a registered schema, but it is not essential as it's also possible to create an XML document instance using an XML schema in the file system.

However, using a registered XML schema does have an advantage. You may associate it with a specific file extension. For example, to register an XML schema for generating only .xslt files you would associate the .xslt extension with the XML schema.

Select project node **XMLSchema** in **Application Navigator**, and select **File | New**. In the **New Gallery** window select **Categories | General | XML**. Select **XML Document from XML schema** in the **Items** listed. Click on the **OK** button.

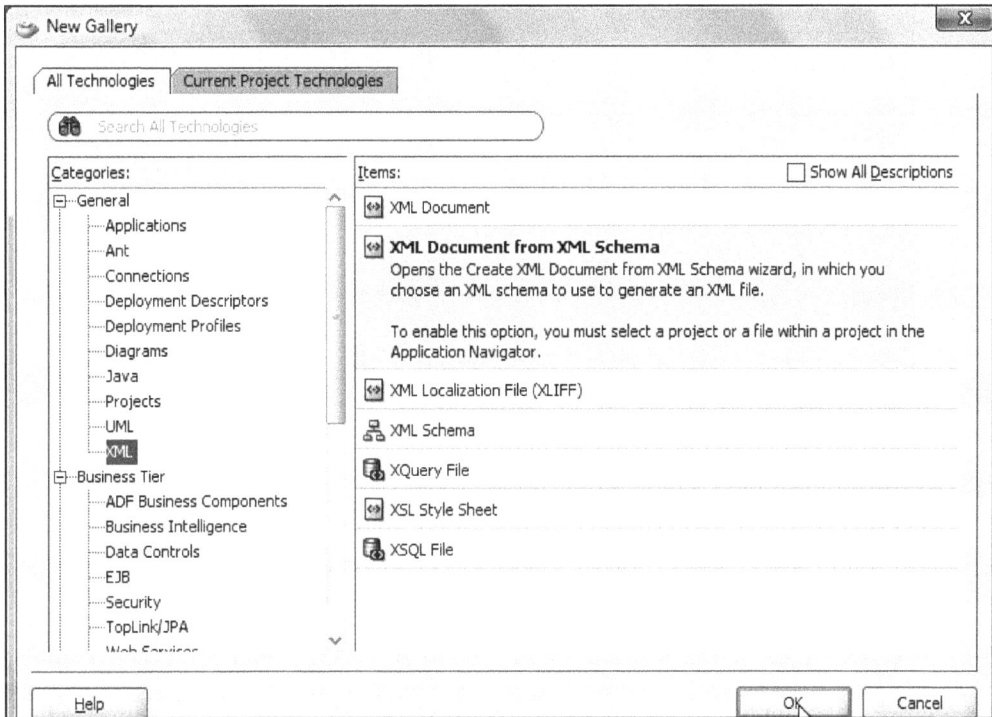

The **Create XML Document from XML schema** wizard gets started. Click on the **Next** button.

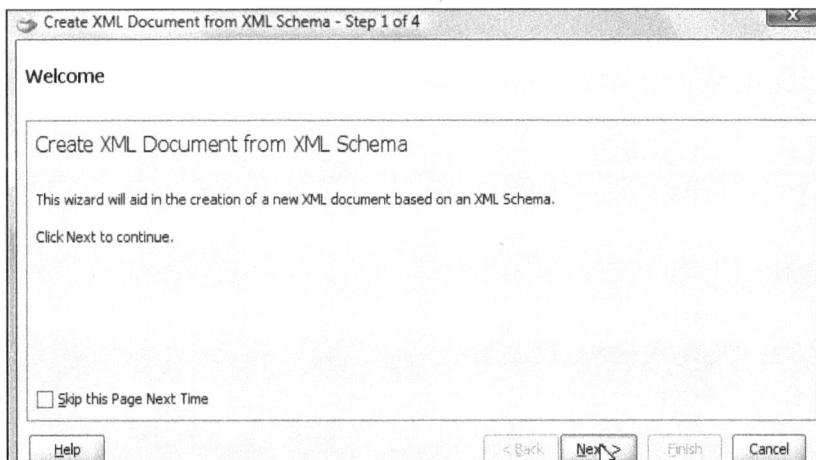

In the **File Location** window specify the **XML File** name as **catalog.xml**. Select **Use Registered Schemas** to create an XML document from a registered schema. Click on the **Next** button.

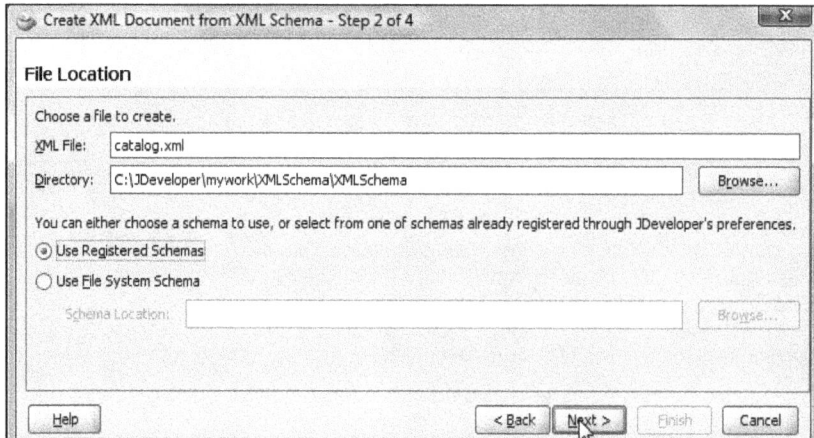

In the **Options** window select **Root Element** as **catalog**. Any of the global elements in a registered XML schema may be selected as the root element. To create an XML document from an XML schema fragment select another global element as the root element. If you want to generate XML document fragments, specify element constructs in an XML schema using the global element declarations and refer to the elements within a complexType using the ref attribute. The other options that may be specified are the **Depth** of the XML document to be generated in terms of element levels, **encoding**, and the option to **Generate Only Required Elements**. Click on the **Next** button.

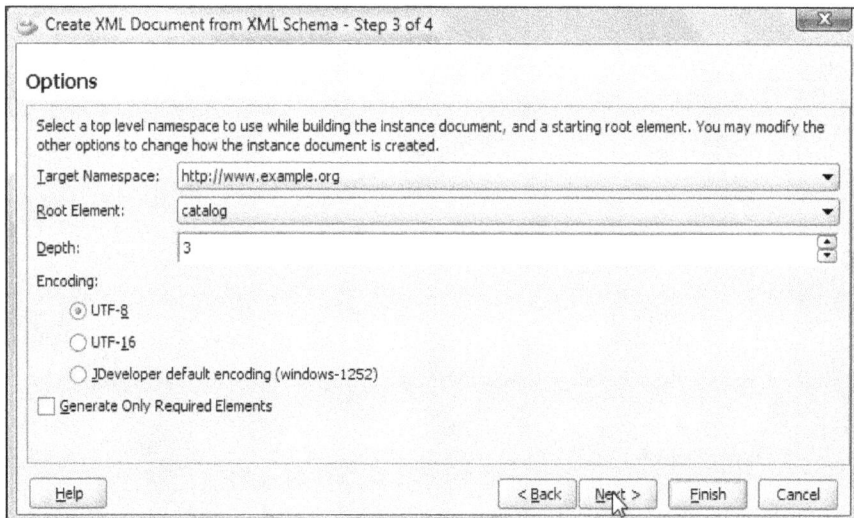

In the **Finish** window, click on the **Finish** button. An XML document, `catalog.xml`, instance gets added to the **Application Navigator**. The XML document has all of the elements defined in the XML schema from which the XML document is instantiated. The default document created has a single instance of elements defined with cardinality greater than 1 in the XML schema. For example, only one instance of the **journal** element is added by default in the XML document instantiated from **catalog. xsd**. Additional **journal** elements may be added as required. If a `choice` is defined in the XML schema, the default XML document generated has the first of the elements specified in the choice.

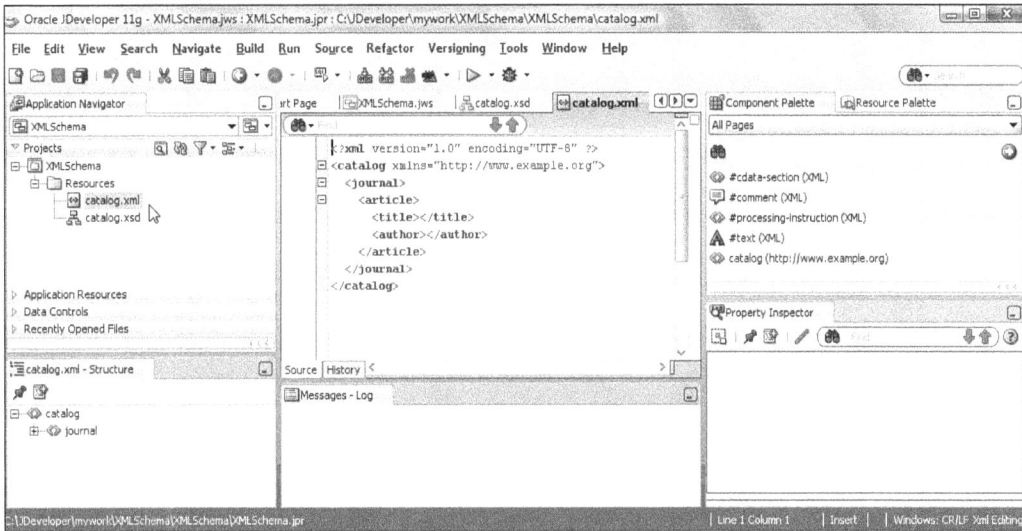

Next, we shall add element and attribute values to the XML schema to construct the XML document **catalog.xml**. Select the **journal** node in the **Structure** view. In the **Property Inspector** specify values for the attributes **title**, **publisher**, and **edition**.

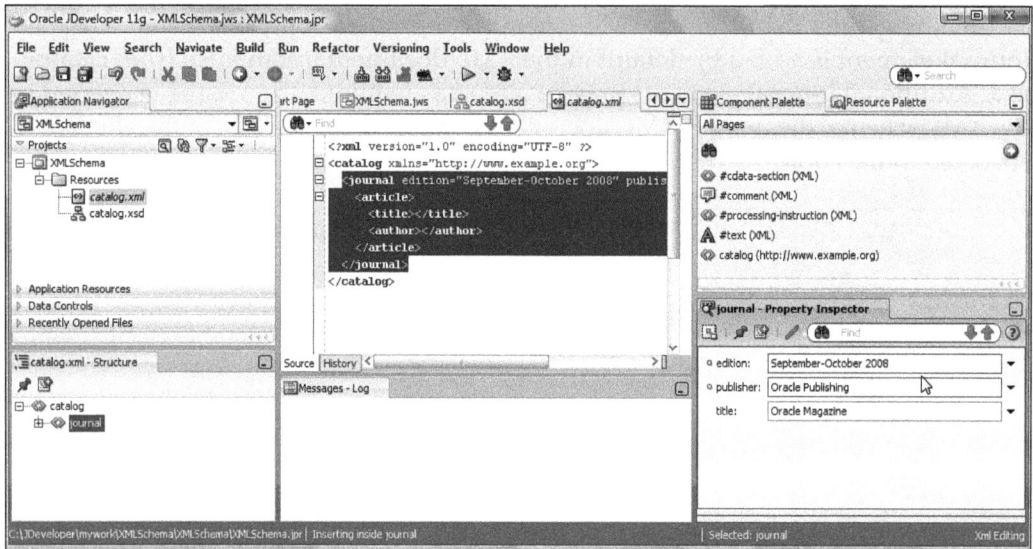

Select the **article** element node in the **Structure** view and specify the value for the **section** attribute and the **title** and **author** elements in the **Property Inspector**.

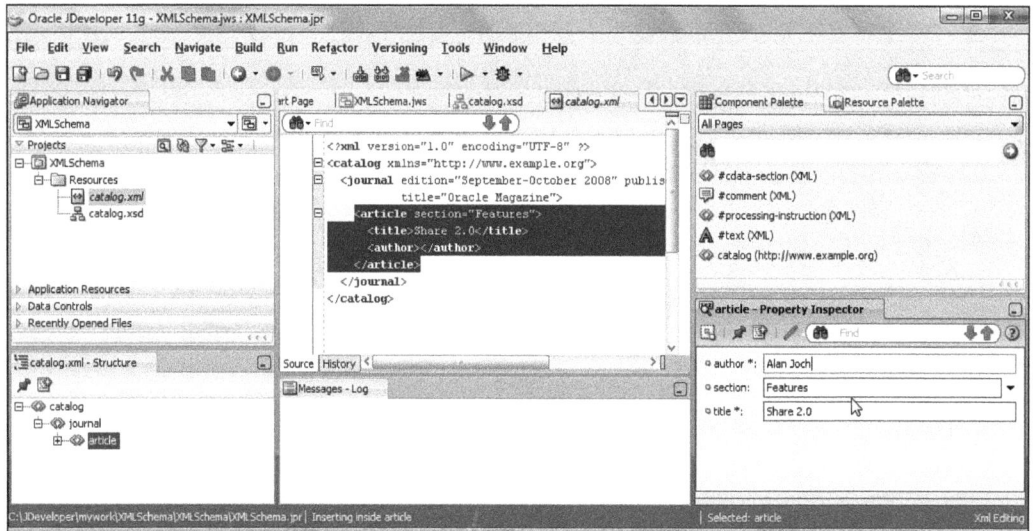

To add another **journal** element, right-click on the **catalog** node in the **Structure** view and select **Insert inside catalog | journal**.

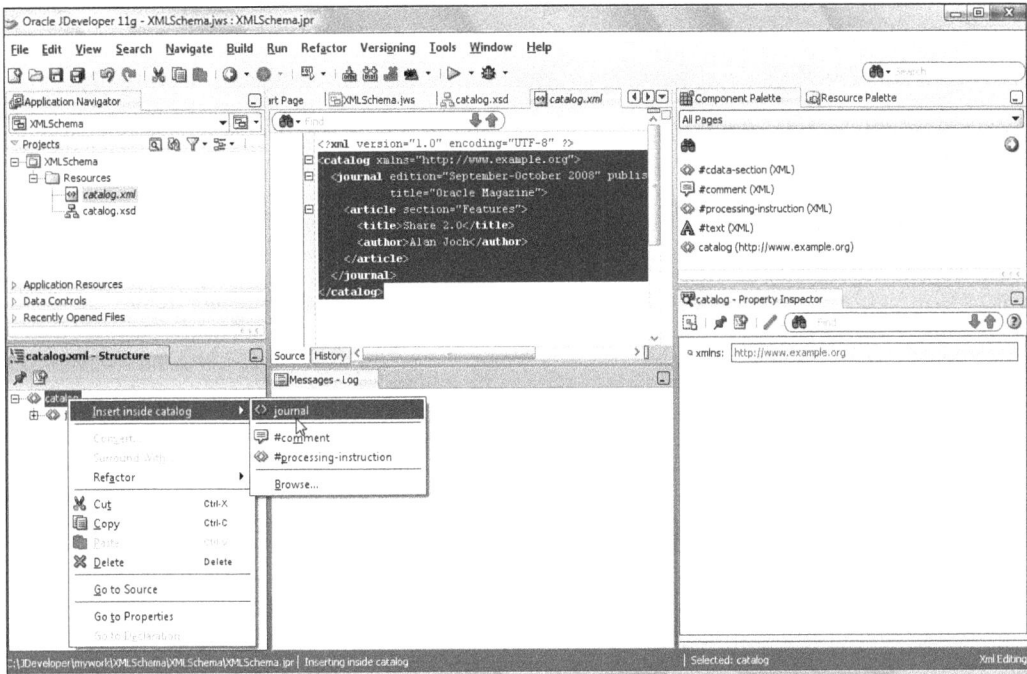

A **** node gets added to the **catalog** element.

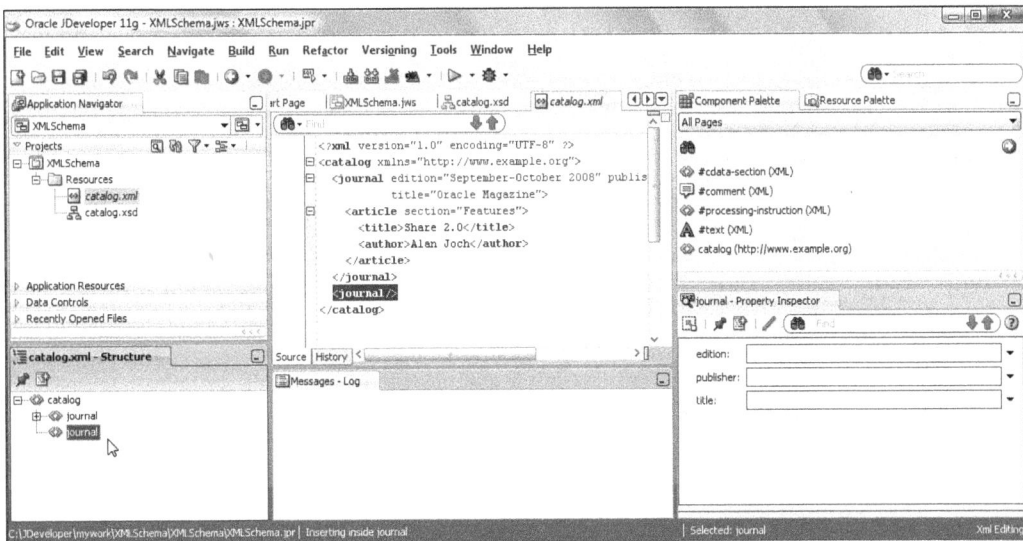

Select the **journal** node in the **Structure** view and add values for **title**, **publisher**, and **edition** attributes in the **Property Inspector**.

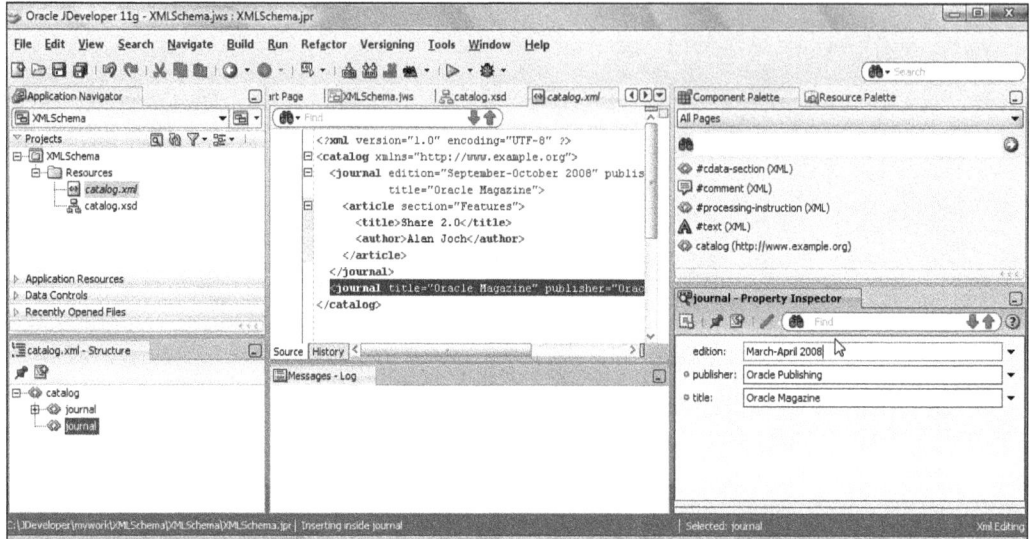

Next, add an **article** element node to the **journal** element. In the **Structure** view, right-click on the **journal** node and select **Insert inside journal | article**.

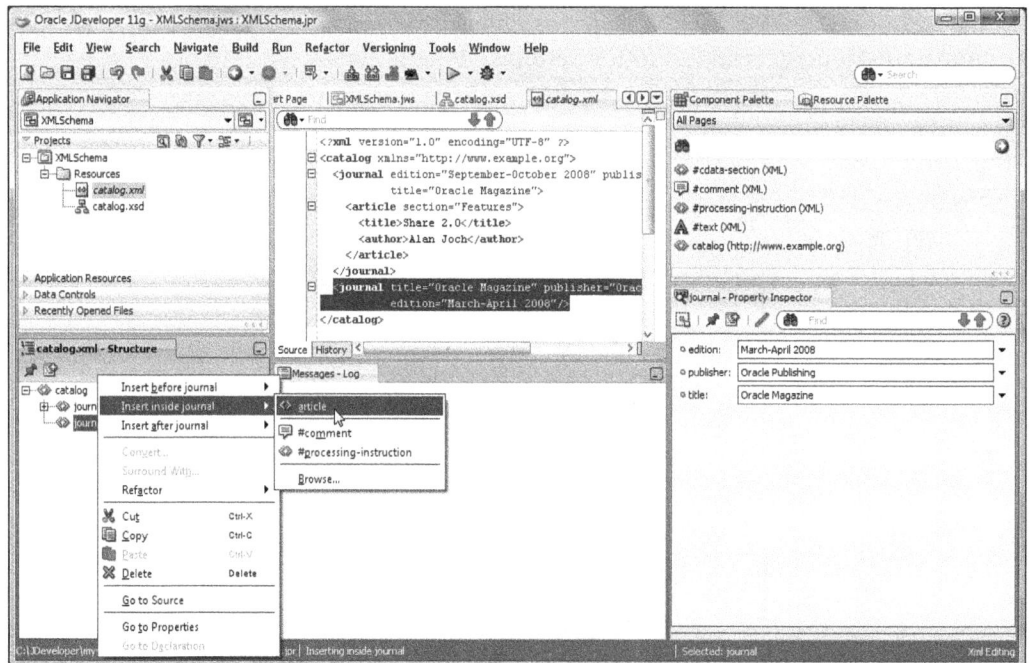

In the **Insert article** window, specify values for **author** and **title** elements. Click on the **OK** button.

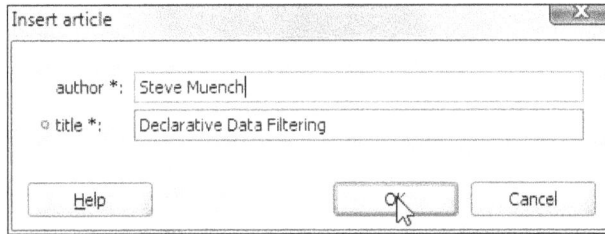

In **Property Inspector** specify a value for the **section** attribute. The **section** attribute was not in the **Insert article** window because it is an optional attribute.

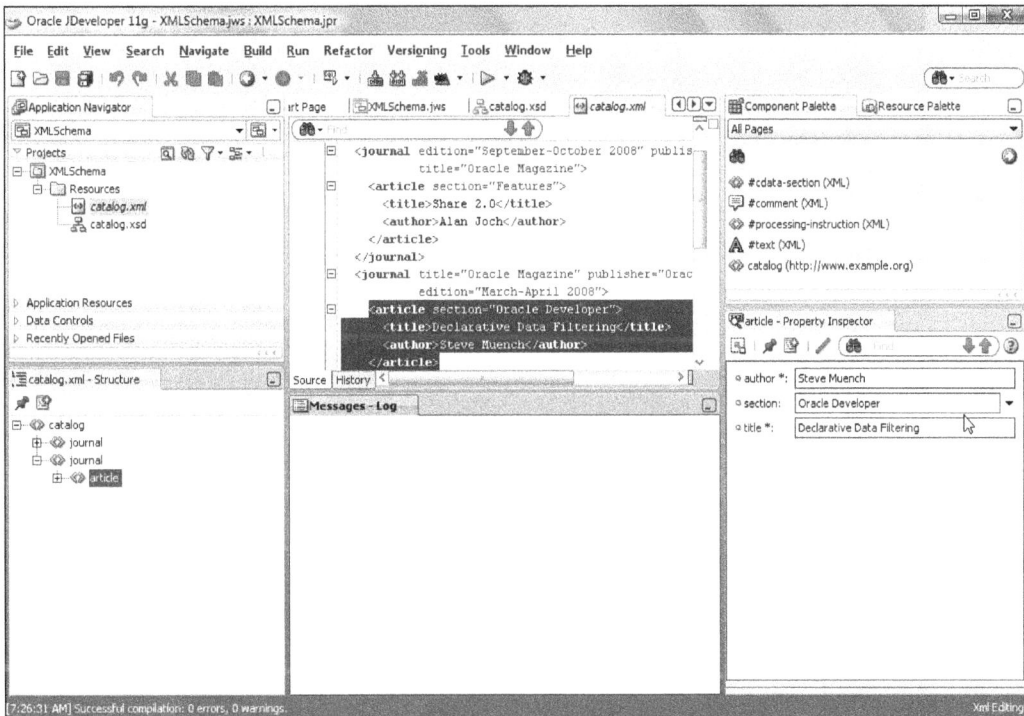

A **journal** element including the attributes and subelements gets added to the **catalog.xml** document.

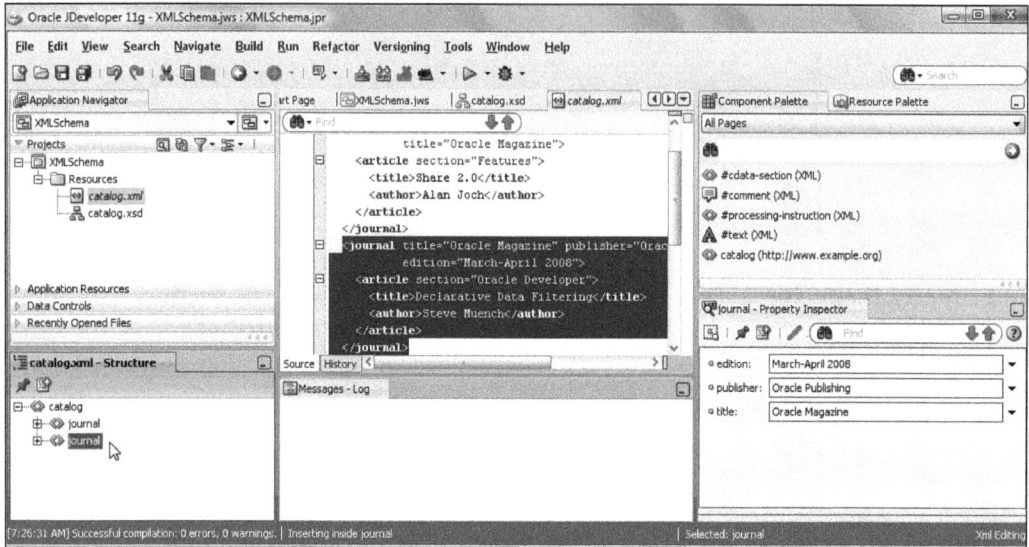

A registered schema also supports editing the XML in the source editor with code help. The complete XML document, **catalog.xml**, instantiated from the XML schema **catalog.xsd** is shown in the following illustration:

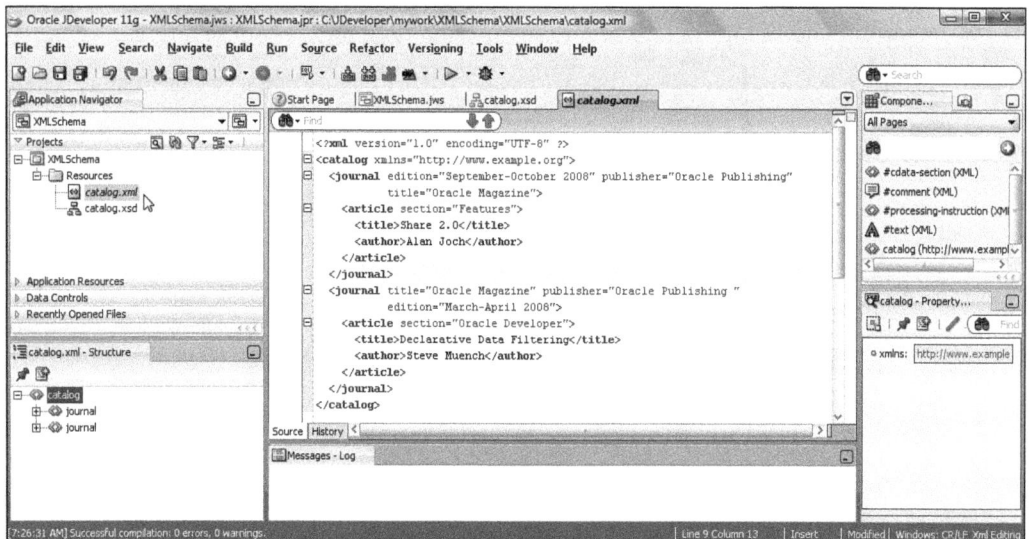

Summary

In this chapter we introduced the commonly used XML schema structures. We created an XML schema in Oracle JDeveloper Schema Visual Editor. We discussed the various methods by which XML schema components may be added to an XML schema. Subsequently, we registered the XML schema in JDeveloper. Registering a schema associates the schema with a specific file extension. We created an XML document that conformed to the XML schema. In the next chapter we shall validate an XML document with an XML schema.

3
XML Schema Validation

As we discussed in the previous chapter, an XML schema document defines the structure, content, and semantics for XML documents. In the previous chapter, we discussed the procedure to create an XML schema in JDeveloper and an XML document instance that conforms to the schema. But if you receive XML documents from another party, the validity of the documents has to be ascertained before the documents may be read and processed. That is what this chapter is about—validating an XML document with an XML schema. An instance document may be processed against a schema to verify whether the XML document conforms to the rules specified in the schema, a process called **schema validation**.

JDeveloper built-in schema validation

Oracle JDeveloper 11g has built-in support for XML schema validation. If an XML document includes a reference to an XML schema, the XML document may be validated with the XML schema using the built-in feature. An XML schema may be specified in an XML document using the `xsi:noNamespaceSchemaLocation` attribute or the `xsi:namespaceSchemaLocation` attribute. Before we discuss when to use which attribute, we need to define the target namespace. A schema is a collection of type definitions and element declarations whose names belong to a particular namespace called a **target namespace**. Thus, a target namespace distinguishes between type definitions and element declarations from different collections. An XML schema doesn't need to have a target namespace. If the XML schema has a target namespace, specify the schema's location in an XML document using the `xsi:namespaceSchemaLocation` attribute. If the XML schema does not have a target namespace, specify the schema location using the `xsi:noNamespaceSchemaLocation` attribute. The `xsi:noNamespaceSchemaLocation` and `xsi:namespaceSchemaLocation` attributes are a hint to the processor about the location of an XML schema document. Taking the example XML schema `catalog.xsd` and the example XML document, `catalog.xml` from the previous chapter, specify the XML schema location in the XML document using the following attribute declaration:

```
xsi:noNamespaceSchemaLocation="catalog.xsd"
```

The XML schema may be in any directory. The example XML document does not include any namespace elements. Therefore, the schema is specified with the `xsi:noNamespaceSchemaLocation` attribute in the root element **catalog**. The XML schema may be specified with a relative URL, or a file, or an HTTP URL. The `xsi:noNamespaceSchemaLocation` attribute we added specifies the relative path to the XML schema document `catalog.xsd`. To validate the XML document with the XML schema, right-click on the XML document and select **Validate XML**.

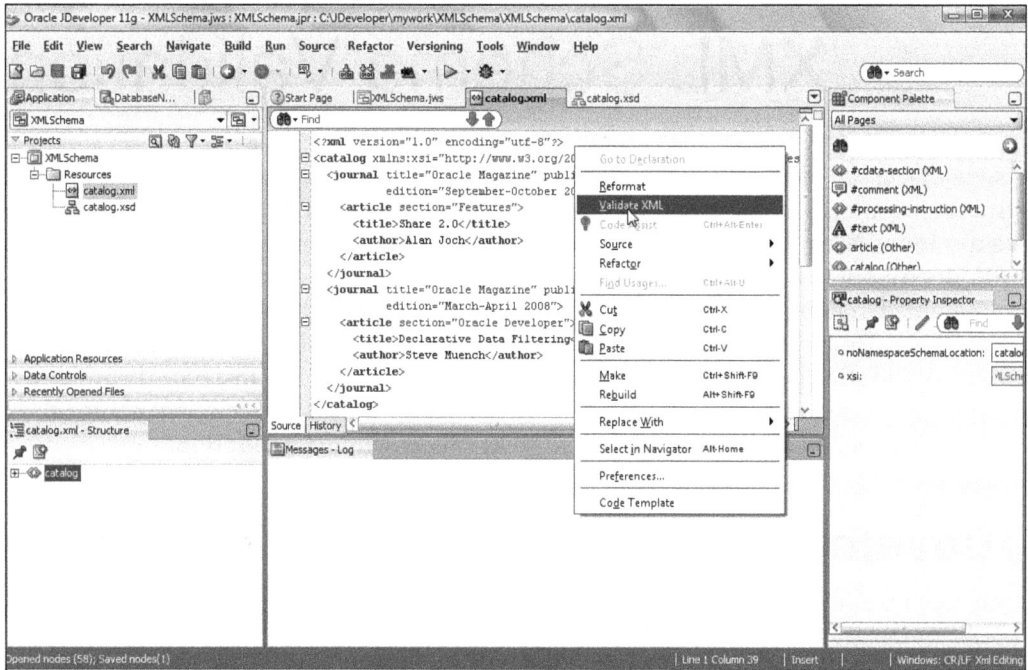

The XML document gets validated with the XML schema and the output indicates that the XML document does not have any validation errors.

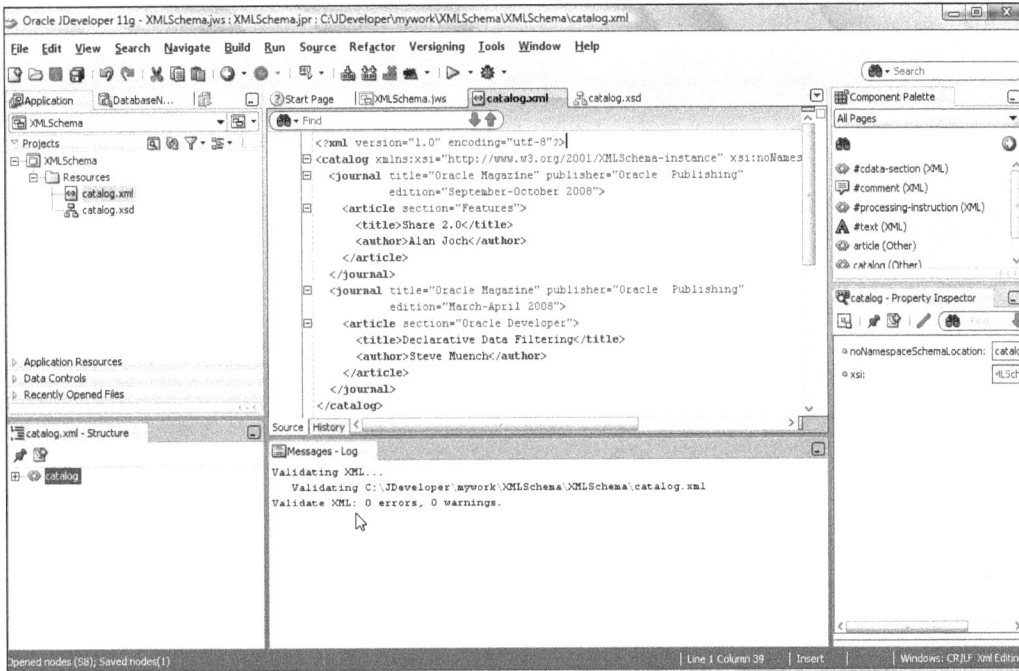

To demonstrate validation errors, add a non-valid element to the XML document. As an example, add the following element to the `catalog` element after the first `journal` element:

<article></article>

To validate the modified XML document, right-click on the XML document and select **Validate XML**. The output indicates validation errors. All the elements after the non-valid element become non-valid. For example, the `journal` element is valid as a subelement of the `catalog` element, but because the second `journal` element is after the non-valid `article` element, the `journal` element also becomes non-valid as indicated in the validation output.

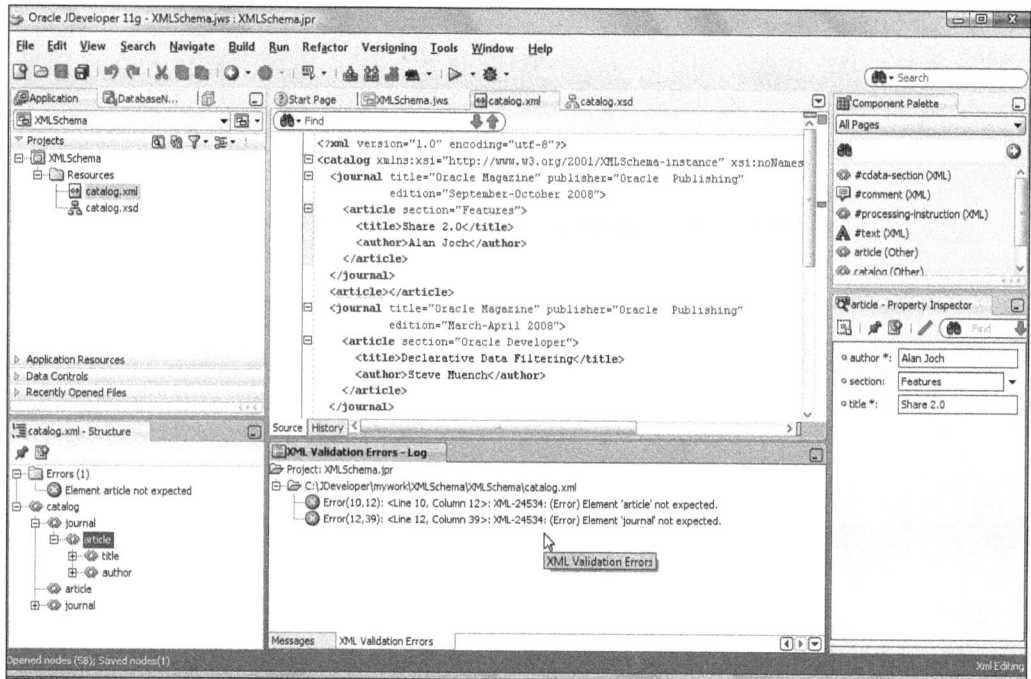

Schema validation in XDK 11g

XDK 11g provides the **Simple API** for **XML** (**SAX**) and the **Document Object Model** (**DOM**) API for parsing an XML document. XDK 11g is included with JDeveloper 11g. XDK 11g parsers DOMParser and SAXParser may be configured for schema validation. In this chapter, we will discuss the procedure to validate an XML document with the SAXParser and the DOMParser. XDK 11g also provides a schema validation-specific API known as XSDValidator to validate an XML document with an XML schema. The choice of validation method depends on the additional functionality required in the validation application. SAXParser is recommended if SAX parsing event notification is required in addition to validation with a schema. DOMParser is recommended if the DOM tree structure of an XML document is required for random access and modification of the XML document. SAX and DOM parsing were discussed in Chapter 1. XSDValidator is suitable for validation if all that is required is schema validation, and SAX parsing event notification or DOM parsing DOM tree for random access and document modification are not required.

Setting the environment

Create an application (**SchemaValidation**, for example) and a project (**SchemaValidation**, for example) in JDeveloper. To create an application and a project select **File | New**. In the **New Gallery** window, select **Categories | General** and **Items | Generic Application**. Click on **OK**. In the **Create Generic Application** window, specify an **Application Name** and click on **Next**. In the **Name your Generic project** window, specify a **Project Name** and click on **Finish**. An application and a project get created. Next, add some XDK 11g JAR files to the project classpath. Select the project node in **Application Navigator**, and select **Tools | Project Properties**. In the **Project Properties** window, select **Libraries and Classpath**. Click on the **Add Library** button to add a library. In the **Add Library** window, select the **Oracle XML Parser v2** library and click on the **OK** button. The **Oracle XML Parser v2** library gets added to the project **Libraries**. Select the **Add JAR/Directory** button to add JAR file xml.jar from the C:\Oracle\Middleware\jdeveloper\ modules\oracle.xdk_11.1.1 directory.

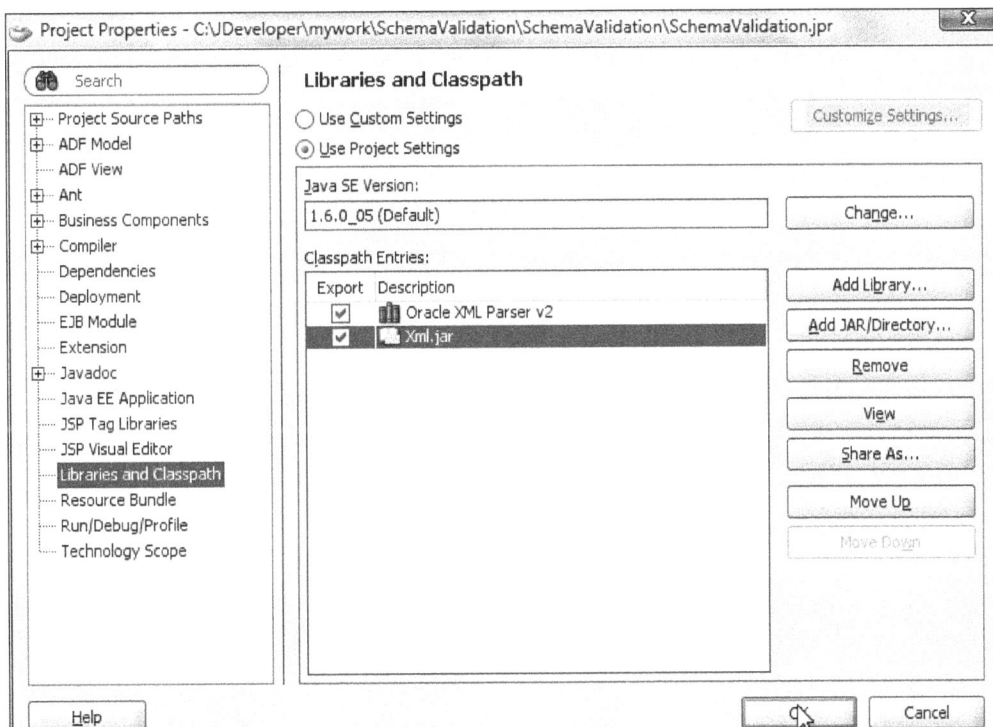

In this chapter, we shall validate an example XML document with an example XML schema using `DOMParser`, `SAXParser`, and `XSDValidator`. We shall also demonstrate error handling in validating an XML document.

First, create an XML document and an XML schema in JDeveloper. To create an XML document, select **File | New**. In the **New Gallery** window select **Categories | General | XML**. In the **Items** listed select **XML Document**, and click on the **OK** button.

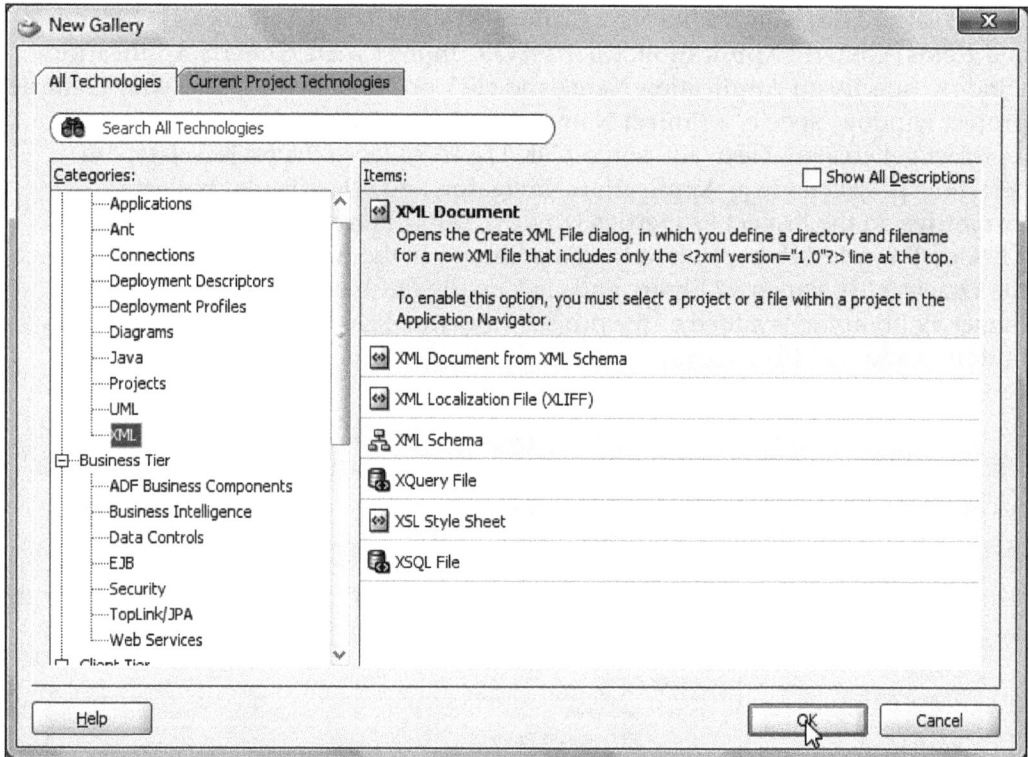

In the **Create XML File** wizard, specify the XML file name, `catalog.xml,` and click on the **OK** button. An XML document gets added to the **SchemaValidation** project in **Application Navigator**. To add an XML schema, select **File | New**, and **General | XML** in the **New Gallery** window. Select **XML schema** in the **Items** listed. Click on the **OK** button.

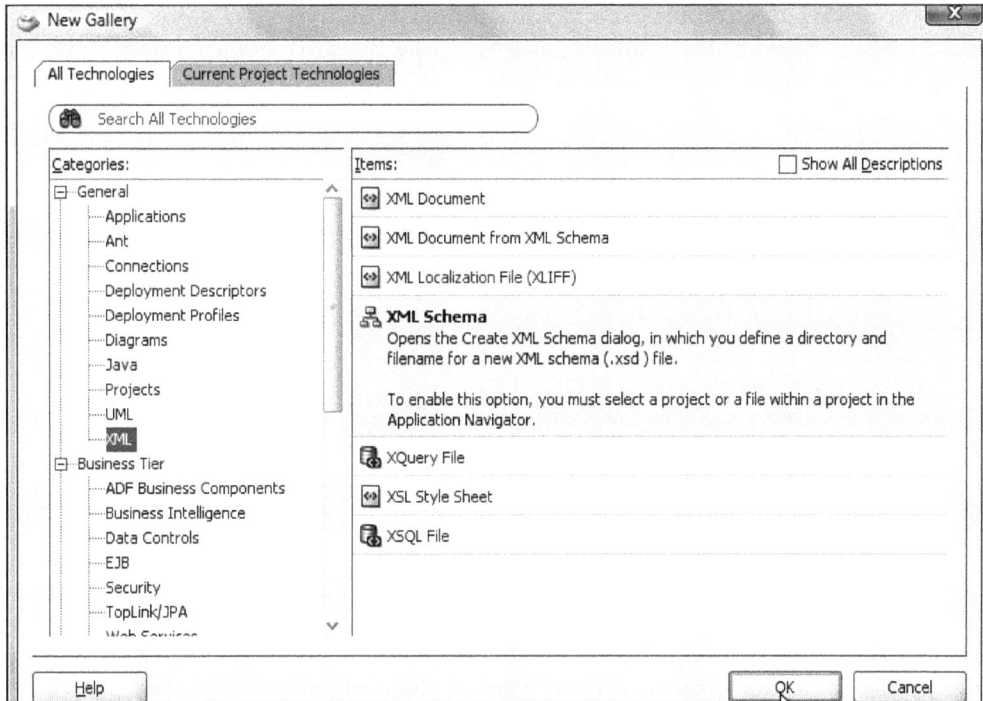

An XML schema document gets added to **SchemaValidation** project.

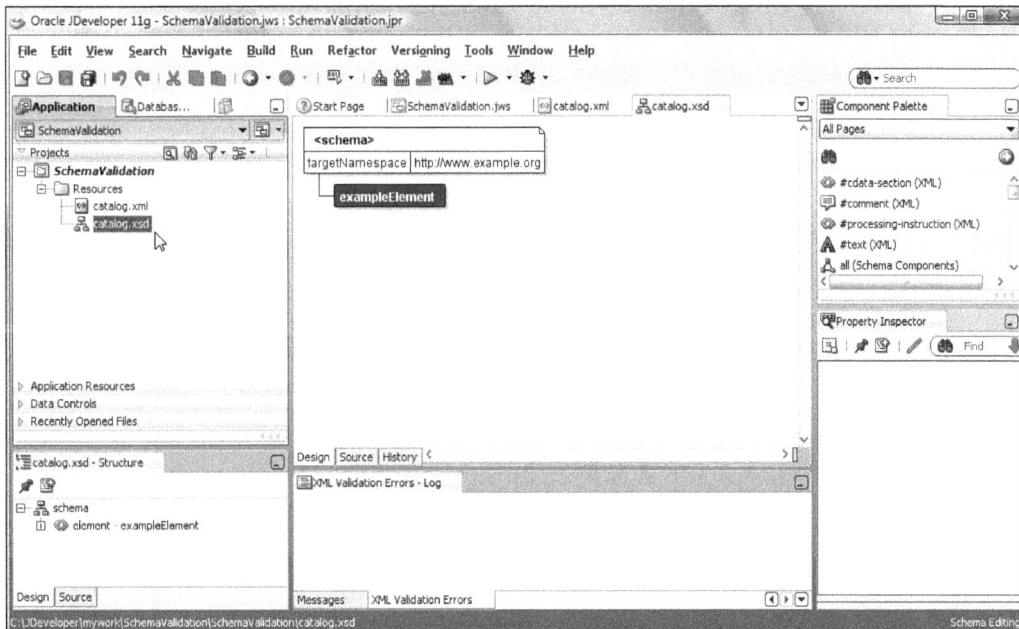

The example XML document, `catalog.xml`, consists of a `journal` catalog. `catalog.xml` is listed in the following listing. Copy the XML document to the `catalog.xml` file in the JDeveloper project.

```
<?xml version="1.0" encoding="utf-8"?>
<catalog title="Oracle Magazine" publisher="Oracle
Publishing">
<journal edition="September-October 2008">
  <article section="Features">
    <title>Share 2.0</title>
    <author>Alan Joch</author>
  </article>
 </journal>
<journal edition="March-April 2008">
  <article section="Oracle Developer">
    <title>Declarative Data Filtering</title>
    <author>Steve Muench</author>
  </article>
</journal></catalog>
```

As explained in the *W3C XML schema Primer*: *"When we want to check that an instance document conforms to one or more schemas (through a process called schema validation), we need to identify which element and attribute declarations and type definitions in the schemas should be used to check which elements and attributes in the instance document."*

The example XML document does not specify the location of the XML schema document to which the XML document must conform to, because we will be setting the XML schema document in the schema validation application. If the XML schema document is specified in the XML document and the schema validation application, the schema document set in the schema validation application is used.

Next, copy the example XML schema document, `catalog.xsd`, listed here to **catalog.xsd** in the JDeveloper project **Schema Validation**:

```
<?xml version="1.0" encoding="utf-8"?>
<xs:schema xmlns:xs="http://www.w3.org/2001/XMLSchema">
  <xs:element name="catalog">
    <xs:complexType>
      <xs:sequence>
        <xs:element ref="journal" minOccurs="0"
        maxOccurs="unbounded"/>
      </xs:sequence>
      <xs:attribute name="title" type="xs:string"/>
      <xs:attribute name="publisher" type="xs:string"/>
    </xs:complexType>
  </xs:element>
  <xs:element name="journal">
    <xs:complexType>
```

```
    <xs:sequence>
      <xs:element ref="article" minOccurs="0"
      maxOccurs="unbounded"/>
    </xs:sequence>
    <xs:attribute name="edition" type="xs:string"/>
  </xs:complexType>
</xs:element>
<xs:element name="article">
  <xs:complexType>
    <xs:sequence>
      <xs:element name="title" type="xs:string"/>
      <xs:element name="author" type="xs:string"/>
    </xs:sequence>
    <xs:attribute name="section" type="xs:string"/>
  </xs:complexType>
</xs:element>
</xs:schema>
```

Each XML schema is required to be in the XML schema namespace
`http://www.w3.org/2001/XMLSchema`. The XML schema namespace is specified
with a namespace declaration in the root element, `schema`, of the XML schema. A
namespace declaration is of the format `xmlns:xs=<namespace URL>`. Though any
prefix may be used, `xs` or `xsd` is commonly used as shown here:

```
<xs:schema xmlns:xs="http://www.w3.org/2001/XMLSchema">
```

Next, we will create Java classes for schema validation. Select **File | New** and
subsequently **Categories | General** and **Items | Java Class** in the **New Gallery**
window to create a Java class for schema validation. Click on the **OK** button. In
the **Create Java Class** window specify a **Class Name**, `XMLSchemaValidator`, and a
package name, `schemavalidation`, and click on the **OK** button. A Java class gets
added to the **SchemaValidation** project. Similarly, add Java classes, `DOMValidator`
and `SAXValidator`. The schema validation applications are shown in the
Application Navigator.

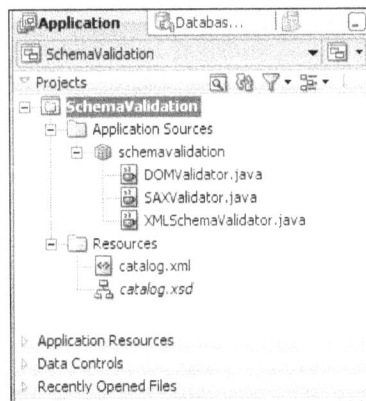

Schema validation with XSDValidator

In this section, we shall create a schema validation application using the schema validator class oracle.xml.schemavalidator.XSDValidator. The application is created in the XMLSchemaValidator class. Import the oracle.xml.parser.schema package and the oracle.xml.schemavalidator.XSDValidator class.

Creating a schema validator

The XSDValidator class is used to validate an XML document that has been built into a DOM tree. First, we need to create an XSDValidator object:

```
XSDValidator xsdValidator = new XSDValidator ();
```

The XML schema with which an XML document is validated is set with the setSchema(XMLSchema) method. An XMLSchema object represents a schema document as a DOM tree. An XSDBuilder object is used to create an XMLSchema object from an XML schema document. Create an XSDBuilder object:

```
XSDBuilder builder = new XSDBuilder();
```

Build an XMLSchema object from an InputSource object using the build(InputSource) method. The XSDBuilder class provides the overloaded build methods discussed in the following table:

Method	Description
build(InputSource source)	Builds an XMLSchema object from an InputSource object. The InputSource class represents a single input source for an XML entity.
build(java.io.InputStream in, java.net.URL baseurl)	Builds an XMLSchema object from an InputStream. The baseurl is used to resolve any relative references to external schemas included with import/include.
build(java.io.Reader r, java.net.URL baseurl)	Builds an XMLSchema object from a Reader. The baseurl is used to resolve any relative references.
build(java.lang.String systemId)	Builds an XMLSchema object from an XML schema document represented with a systemId. A systemId is a URI.
build(java.lang.String ns, java.lang.String systemId)	Builds an XMLSchema object from a XML schema document represented with a String systemId. The ns parameter specifies the schema target namespace and is used to validate the targetNamespace specified in the XML schema document.

Method	Description
`build(java.lang.String ns,java.net.URL systemId)`	Builds an `XMLSchema` object from an XML schema document represented with a `systemId`specified as a URL. The `ns` parameter specifies the schema target namespace to validate `targetNamespace`.
`build(java.net.URL schemaurl)`	Builds an `XMLSchema` object from a XML schema document represented as a URL object.
`build(XMLDocument [] schemaDoc,java.net.URL baseurl)`	Builds an `XMLSchema` object from an array of XML schema documents. The `baseurl` parameter specifies the base URL to be used for any import/include in the schemas.
`build(XMLDocument schemaDoc,java.net.URL baseurl)`	Builds an `XMLSchema` object from an XML schema document specified as `XMLDocument` object and a base URL for any import/include in the schema.

Create an `InputSource` object from schema document and invoke the `build(InputSource)` method of `XSDBuilder` object. We have used `InputSource` for the input because most SAX parser implementations convert the input to `InputSource`, and most parsers are SAX based. It is better to specify the input directly as `InputSource` rather than have the SAX or JAXP implementation convert the input to `InputSource`. Set the `XMLSchema` object returned by the `build` method on the `XSDValidator` object created earlier. The procedure to create an `XMLSchema` object from a schema document, and set the schema on an `XSDValidator` object is as follows:

```
InputStream inputStream=new FileInputStream(new File("catalog.xsd"));
InputSource inputSource=new InputSource(inputStream);
XMLSchema schema =  builder.build(inputSource);
xsdValidator.setSchema(schema);
```

Setting the error handler

When validating an XML document errors might get generated. For error handling, create and register an `ErrorHandler` object with the `XSDValidator` object. The `ErrorHandler` interface is the basic error handler for SAX parsing. The SAX standard for reporting errors is the most commonly used error handling model because most XML processing including DOM parsing is based on SAX parsing. The `DefaultHandler` class implements the `ErrorHandler` interface. Create a class `CustomErrorHandler` that extends the `DefaultHandler` class. In the error handling class `CustomErrorHandler`, override the error handling methods of class `DefaultHandler`. Add variable `hasValidationError` of type `boolean` and `saxParseException` of type `SAXParseException`. An error handling method gets invoked if a validation error is generated. In the error handling methods set instance variable `hasValidationError` to `true`, and `saxParseException` to the `SAXParseException` parameter value. The custom error handling class is shown in the following listing:

```
private class CustomErrorHandler extends DefaultHandler
    {
        protected boolean  hasValidationError = false;
        protected SAXParseException saxParseException=null;

        public void error(SAXParseException exception)
        {
            hasValidationError = true;
            saxParseException=exception;
        }
        public void fatalError(SAXParseException exception)
        {
            hasValidationError = true;
            saxParseException=exception;
        }
        public void warning(SAXParseException exception)
        {
        }
    }
```

Create a `CustomErrorHandler` object for error handling. The class that holds an error message including the line number is `oracle.xml.parser.v2.XMLError`. Create an object of type `XMLError` and register the `CustomErrorHandler` with the `XMLError` object with the `setErrorHandler(ErrorHandler)` method. Set the `XMLError` object on the `XSDValidator` object created earlier with the `setError(XMLError)` method. The procedure to create and set an `ErrorHandler` object on an `XSDValidator` object is shown in the following listing:

```
CustomErrorHandler errorHandler=new CustomErrorHandler();
XMLError xmlError=new XMLError();
xmlError.setErrorHandler(errorHandler);
xsdValidator.setError(xmlError);
```

Validating the XML document

The XSDValidator class provides an overloaded validate method to validate an XML document with an XML schema. The XML document input to the validate method may be in the form of an XMLDocument object, an InputStream object, or a URL object. We shall validate with the validate(InputStream) method. Create an InputStream object from the XML document catalog.xml, and validate it with the XML schema document using the validate(InputStream) method of class XSDValidator, as shown in the following listing:

```
InputStream inputStream=new FileInputStream(new File("catalog.xml"));
xsdValidator.validate(inputStream);
```

Running the Java application

To run the XMLSchemaValidator.java application, right-click on **XMLSchemaValidator.java** in **Application Navigator** and select **Run**. As catalog.xml does not have any validation errors, the output **XML Document validates with XML schema** gets generated.

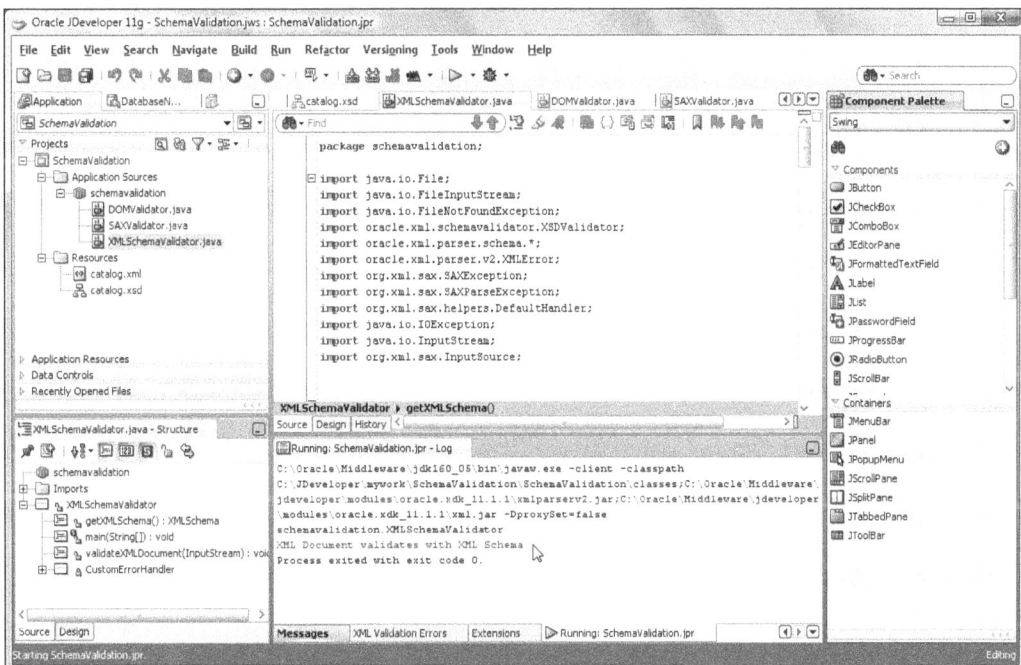

To demonstrate error handling, add an error in the XML document. As an example, add a `title` element in a `journal` element:

```
<journal>
<title>Oracle Magazine   </title>
</journal>
```

Run the `XMLSchemaValidator` application again. A validation error gets generated:

XML Document has Validation Error:XML-24534: (Error) Element 'title' not expected.

`XMLSchemaValidator.java` is listed here with explanations about the different sections of the Java application.

1. First, we declare the `import` statements for the different classes that we need.

```java
import java.io.File;
import java.io.FileInputStream;
import java.io.FileNotFoundException;
import oracle.xml.schemavalidator.XSDValidator;
import oracle.xml.parser.schema.*;
import oracle.xml.parser.v2.XMLError;
import org.xml.sax.SAXException;
import org.xml.sax.SAXParseException;
import org.xml.sax.helpers.DefaultHandler;

import java.io.IOException;
import java.io.InputStream;
import org.xml.sax.InputSource;
```

2. Next, we add the Java class declaration `XMLSchemaValidator`.

```java
public class XMLSchemaValidator{
```

3. Next, we define the method `validateXMLDocument` to validate an XML document.

```java
public void validateXMLDocument(InputStream input)
    {
      try {
```

4. We create an `XSDValidator` object and set the XML schema on the `XSDValidator`.

```java
XSDValidator xsdValidator=new XSDValidator();
XMLSchema schema =getXMLSchema();
xsdValidator.setSchema(schema);
```

5. We create an error handler and set the error handler on the XSDValidator. We validate the XML document and output the validation errors (if any).

```
CustomErrorHandler errorHandler=new CustomErrorHandler();
XMLError xmlError=new XMLError();
xmlError.setErrorHandler(errorHandler);
xsdValidator.setError(xmlError);
   xsdValidator.validate(input);


if(errorHandler.hasValidationError==true)
System.err.println("XML Document has  Validation
Error:"+errorHandler.saxParseException.getMessage());

else

System.out.println("XML Document validates with XML schema");

  }catch(IOException e)
  {
    System.err.println("IOException "+e.getMessage());
  }catch (SAXException e) {
    System.err.println("SAXException "+e.getMessage());
     }catch (XSDException e) {
    System.err.println("XSDException "+e.getMessage());
  }
  }
```

6. We define the custom error handler inner class CustomErrorHandler, which extends the DefaultHandler class.

```
private class CustomErrorHandler extends DefaultHandler
  {
      protected boolean  hasValidationError = false;
      protected SAXParseException saxParseException=null;

      public void error(SAXParseException exception)
      {
          hasValidationError = true;
          saxParseException=exception;
      }
      public void fatalError(SAXParseException exception)
      {
          hasValidationError = true;
          saxParseException=exception;
      }
      public void warning(SAXParseException exception)
      {
      }
  }
```

7. We define the `getXMLSchema` method to create an `XMLSchema` object from an XML schema document.

```
public XMLSchema getXMLSchema() {

    try {
        XSDBuilder builder = new XSDBuilder();
        InputStream inputStream =
            new FileInputStream(new File("catalog.xsd"));
        InputSource inputSource = new InputSource(inputStream);
        XMLSchema schema = builder.build(inputSource);
        return schema;
    } catch (XSDException e) {
        System.err.println("XSDException " + e.getMessage());
    }catch (FileNotFoundException e) {
        System.err.println("FileNotFoundException " +
        e.getMessage());
    }
    return null;
}
```

8. Finally, we add the `main` method in which we create an instance of the `XMLSchemaValidator` class and invoke the `validateXMLDocument` method.

```
public static void main(String[] argv) {
    try {
            InputStream inputStream =
            new FileInputStream(new File("catalog.xml"));
            XMLSchemaValidator validator = new
            XMLSchemaValidator();
            validator.validateXMLDocument(inputStream);
    } catch (FileNotFoundException e) {
            System.err.println("FileNotFoundException " +
            e.getMessage());

    }

}
}
```

Schema validation with a SAX parser

In this section we shall validate the example XML document `catalog.xml` with XML schema document `catalog.xsd`, with the `SAXParser` class. Import the `oracle.xml.parser.schema` and `oracle.xml.parser.v2` packages.

Creating a SAX parser

Create a `SAXParser` object and set the validation mode of the `SAXParser` object to `SCHEMA_VALIDATION`, as shown in the following listing:

```
SAXParser saxParser=new SAXParser();
saxParser.setValidationMode(XMLParser.SCHEMA_VALIDATION);
```

The different validation modes that may be set on a `SAXParser` are discussed in the following table; but we only need the SCHEMA-based validation modes:

Validation Mode	Description
NONVALIDATING	The parser does not validate the XML document.
PARTIAL_VALIDATION	The parser validates the complete or a partial XML document with a DTD or an XML schema if specified.
DTD_VALIDATION	The parser validates the XML document with a DTD if any.
SCHEMA_VALIDATION	The parser validates the XML document with an XML schema if any specified.
SCHEMA_LAX_VALIDATION	Validates the complete or partial XML document with an XML schema if the parser is able to locate a schema. The parser does not raise an error if a schema is not found.
SCHEMA_STRICT_VALIDATION	Validates the complete XML document with an XML schema if the parser is able to find a schema. If the parser is not able find a schema or if the XML document does not conform to the schema, an error is raised.

Next, create an `XMLSchema` object from the schema document with which an XML document is to be validated. An `XMLSchema` object represents the DOM structure of an XML schema document and is created with an `XSDBuilder` class object. Create an `XSDBuilder` object and invoke the `build(InputSource)` method of the `XSDBuilder` object to obtain an `XMLSchema` object. The `InputSource` object is created with an `InputStream` object created from the example XML schema document, `catalog.xsd`. As discussed before, we have used an `InputSource` object because most SAX implementations are `InputSource` based. The procedure to obtain an `XMLSchema` object is shown in the following listing:

```
XSDBuilder builder = new XSDBuilder();
InputStream inputStream=new FileInputStream(new File("catalog.xsd"));
InputSource inputSource=new InputSource(inputStream);
XMLSchema schema =  builder.build(inputSource);
```

Set the XMLSchema object on the SAXParser object with
setXMLSchema(XMLSchema) method:

```
saxParser.setXMLSchema(schema);
```

Setting the error handler

As in the previous section, define an error handling class, CustomErrorHandler that
extends DefaultHandler class. Create an object of type CustomErrorHandler, and
register the ErrorHandler object with the SAXParser as shown here:

```
CustomErrorHandler errorHandler = new CustomErrorHandler();
saxParser.setErrorHandler(errorHandler);
```

Validating the XML document

The SAXParser class extends the XMLParser class, which provides the overloaded
parse methods discussed in the following table to parse an XML document:

Method	Description
parse(InputSource in)	Parses an XML document from an org.xml. sax.InputSouce object. The InputSource-based parse method is the preferred method because SAX parsers convert the input to InputSource no matter what the input type is.
parse(java.io.InputStream in)	Parses an XML document from an InputStream.
parse(java.io.Reader r)	Parses an XML document from a Reader.
parse(java.lang.String in)	Parses an XML document from a String URL for the XML document.
parse(java.net.URL url)	Parses an XML document from the specified URL object for the XML document.

Create an InputSource object from the XML document to be validated, and parse
the XML document with the parse(InputSource) object:

```
InputStream inputStream=new FileInputStream(new
File("catalog.xml"));
InputSource inputSource=new InputSource(inputStream);
saxParser.parse(inputSource);
```

Running the Java application

The validation application `SAXValidator.java` is listed in the following listing with additional explanations:

1. First we declare the `import` statements for the classes that we need.

```
import java.io.File;
import java.io.FileInputStream;
import java.io.FileNotFoundException;
import oracle.xml.parser.schema.*;
import oracle.xml.parser.v2.*;
import java.io.IOException;
import java.io.InputStream;
import org.xml.sax.SAXException;
import org.xml.sax.SAXParseException;
import org.xml.sax.helpers.DefaultHandler;
import org.xml.sax.InputSource;
```

2. We define the Java class `SAXValidator` for SAX validation.

```
public class SAXValidator {
```

3. In the Java class we define a method `validateXMLDocument`.

```
public void validateXMLDocument(InputSource input) {
    try {
```

4. In the method we create a `SAXParser` and set the XML schema on the `SAXParser`.

```
SAXParser saxParser = new SAXParser();
saxParser.setValidationMode(XMLParser.SCHEMA_VALIDATION);
XMLSchema schema=getXMLSchema();
saxParser.setXMLSchema(schema);
```

5. To handle errors we create a custom error handler. We set the error handler on the `SAXParser` object and parse the XML document to be validated and also output validation errors if any.

```
CustomErrorHandler errorHandler = new CustomErrorHandler();
saxParser.setErrorHandler(errorHandler);
saxParser.parse(input);
   if (errorHandler.hasValidationError == true) {
      System.err.println("XML Document has
Validation Error:" + errorHandler.saxParseException.getMessage());
   } else {
      System.out.println("XML Document validates
with XML schema");
```

```
        }
    } catch (IOException e) {
    System.err.println("IOException " + e.getMessage());
    } catch (SAXException e) {
        System.err.println("SAXException " + e.getMessage());
    }
}
```

6. We add the Java method getXMLSchema to create an XMLSchema object.

```
public XMLSchema getXMLSchema() {
    try {
        XSDBuilder builder = new XSDBuilder();
        InputStream inputStream =
            new FileInputStream(new File("catalog.xsd"));
        InputSource inputSource = new
InputSource(inputStream);
        XMLSchema schema = builder.build(inputSource);
        return schema;
    } catch (XSDException e) {
        System.err.println("XSDException " + e.getMessage());
    } catch (FileNotFoundException e) {
        System.err.println("FileNotFoundException " +
e.getMessage());
    }
    return null;
}
```

7. We define the main method in which we create an instance of the SAXValidator class and invoke the validateXMLDocument method.

```
public static void main(String[] argv) {
    try {
        InputStream inputStream =
        new FileInputStream(new File("catalog.xml"));
        InputSource inputSource=new InputSource(inputStream);
        SAXValidator validator = new SAXValidator();
        validator.validateXMLDocument(inputSource);
    } catch (FileNotFoundException e) {
        System.err.println("FileNotFoundException " +
e.getMessage());
    }
}
```

8. Finally, we define the custom error handler class as an inner class CustomErrorHandler to handle validation errors.

```
        private class CustomErrorHandler extends DefaultHandler {
            protected boolean hasValidationError = false;
            protected SAXParseException saxParseException = null;
```

```
    public void error(SAXParseException exception)
        {
        hasValidationError = true;
        saxParseException = exception;
    }
    public void fatalError(SAXParseException exception)
        {
        hasValidationError = true;
        saxParseException = exception;
    }
    public void warning(SAXParseException exception)
        {
        }
    }
}
```

Copy the SAXValidator.java application to SAXValidator.java in the
SchemaValidation project. To demonstrate error handling, add a title
element to the journal element.

To run the SAXValidator.java application, right-click on **SAXValidator.java**
in **Application Navigator**, and select **Run**. A validation error gets outputted.
The validation error indicates that the **title** element is not expected.

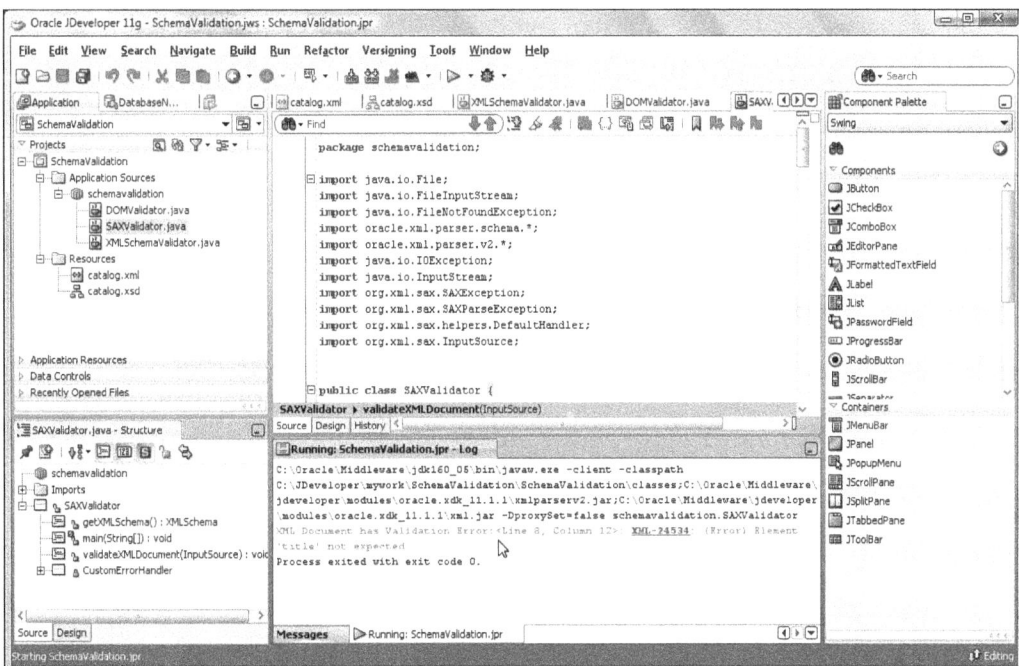

Schema validation with a DOM parser

In this section, we shall validate the example XML document, `catalog.xml`, against `catalog.xsd` with the `DOMParser` class. The procedure to validate with a `DOMParser` is the same as with a `SAXParser`, except that the parser class is different. First, import the `oracle.xml.parser.schema` and the `oracle.xml.parser.v2` packages.

Creating a DOM parser

Create a `DOMParser` object and set validation mode to `SCHEMA_VALIDATION`, as shown in the following listing:

```
DOMParser domParser=new DOMParser();
domParser.setValidationMode(XMLParser.SCHEMA_VALIDATION);
```

Create an `XMLSchema` object, which represents the DOM structure of an XML schema document, from the example schema document. To create an `XMLSchema` object, first create an `XSDBuilder` object. Next, create an `InputStream` object from `catalog.xsd` and subsequently create an `InputSource` object from the `InputStream` object. Create an `XMLSchema` object with the `build(InputSource)` method of the `XSDBuilder` class. The procedure to obtain an `XMLSchema` object is shown in the following listing:

```
XSDBuilder builder = new XSDBuilder();
InputStream inputStream=new FileInputStream(new File("catalog.xsd"));
InputSource inputSource=new InputSource(inputStream);
XMLSchema schema =  builder.build(inputSource);
```

Set the `XMLSchema` object on the `DOMParser` object with the `setXMLSchema(XMLSchema)` method:

```
domParser.setXMLSchema(schema);
```

Setting the error handler

As in the `SAXParser` section, define an error handling class, `CustomErrorHandler`. Create a `CustomErrorHandler` object, and register the `ErrorHandler` object with the `DOMParser` using the `setErrorHandler` method.

```
CustomErrorHandler errorHandler = new CustomErrorHandler();
 domParser.setErrorHandler(errorHandler);
```

We have used a SAX-based error handler for a DOM parser because most DOM parsers use a SAX parser internally.

Parsing the XML document

The DOMParser class extends the XMLParser class that provides the overloaded parse methods discussed in the previous section to parse an XML document. The preferred parse method is parse(InputSource) because the DOM parser uses an SAX parser internally and SAX parsers use an InputSource object for parsing. If another input type is specified, the input is converted to an InputSource by the SAX parser. Create an InputStream object from the example XML document, catalog.xml, and create an InputSource object from the InputStream object. Subsequently, parse the XML document using the parse(InputSource) method:

```
InputStream inputStream=new FileInputStream(new
File("catalog.xml"));
InputSource inputSource=new InputSource(inputStream);
domParser.parse(inputSource);
```

Running the Java application

The validation application DOMValidator.java is listed in the following listing with explanations:

1. First, we declare the import statements for the classes that we need.

   ```
   import java.io.File;
   import java.io.FileInputStream;
   import java.io.FileNotFoundException;
   import oracle.xml.parser.schema.*;
   import oracle.xml.parser.v2.*;
   import java.io.IOException;
   import java.io.InputStream;
   import org.xml.sax.SAXException;
   import org.xml.sax.SAXParseException;
   import org.xml.sax.helpers.DefaultHandler;
   import org.xml.sax.InputSource;
   ```

2. We define the Java class DOMValidator.

   ```
   public class DOMValidator {
   ```

3. In the Java class we add a method validateXMLDocument.

   ```
   public void validateXMLDocument(InputSource input) {
           try {
   ```

4. We create a `DOMParser` object and set the XML schema on the `DOMParser`.

```
DOMParser domParser = new DOMParser();
domParser.setValidationMode(XMLParser.SCHEMA_VALIDATION);
XMLSchema schema=getXMLSchema();
domParser.setXMLSchema(schema);
```

5. We create a `CustomErrorHandler` object and set the error handler on the `DOMParser`. We parse the XML document and output the validation errors, if any.

```
CustomErrorHandler errorHandler = new CustomErrorHandler();
domParser.setErrorHandler(errorHandler);
domParser.parse(input);

  if (errorHandler.hasValidationError == true) {
     System.err.println("XML Document has
Validation Error:" + errorHandler.saxParseException.getMessage());
  } else {
     System.out.println("XML Document validates
with XML schema");
     }
} catch (IOException e) {
System.err.println("IOException " + e.getMessage());
} catch (SAXException e) {
     System.err.println("SAXException " + e.getMessage());
  }
}
```

6. We define the `getXMLSchema` method to create an `XMLSchema` object.

```
public XMLSchema getXMLSchema() {

   try {
      XSDBuilder builder = new XSDBuilder();
      InputStream inputStream =
         new FileInputStream(new File("catalog.xsd"));
      InputSource inputSource = new InputSource(inputStream);
      XMLSchema schema = builder.build(inputSource);
      return schema;
   } catch (XSDException e) {
        System.err.println("XSDException " + e.getMessage());
   } catch (FileNotFoundException e) {
        System.err.println("FileNotFoundException " +
        e.getMessage());
   }
   return null;
}
```

7. We add the `main` method in which we create an instance of the `DOMValidator` class and invoke the `validateXMLDocument` method.

```
public static void main(String[] argv) {
  try {
            InputStream inputStream =
                  new FileInputStream(new File("catalog.xml"));
            InputSource inputSource=new InputSource(inputStream);
        DOMValidator validator = new DOMValidator();
        validator.validateXMLDocument(inputSource);
    } catch (FileNotFoundException e) {
        System.err.println("FileNotFoundException " +
        e.getMessage());
    }
}
```

8. Finally, we define the `CustomErrorHandler` inner class.

```
    private class CustomErrorHandler extends DefaultHandler {
        protected boolean hasValidationError = false;
        protected SAXParseException saxParseException = null;
        public void error(SAXParseException exception)
            {
            hasValidationError = true;
            saxParseException = exception;
        }
        public void fatalError(SAXParseException exception)
            {
            hasValidationError = true;
            saxParseException = exception;
        }
        public void warning(SAXParseException exception)
            {
        }
    }
}
```

To demonstrate error handling, add a `title` element to the `journal` element. A `title` element is not valid in a `journal` element.

Copy the `DOMValidator.java` application to the `DOMValidator.java` application in **SchemaValidation** project. To run the `DOMValidator.java` application, right-click on **DOMValidator.java** in **Application Navigator**, and select **Run**. A validation error gets outputted, indicating that the `title` element is not valid. If the `title` element in the `journal` element is removed and the `DOMValidator.java` application is re-run, a validation message gets outputted to indicate that the XML document is valid.

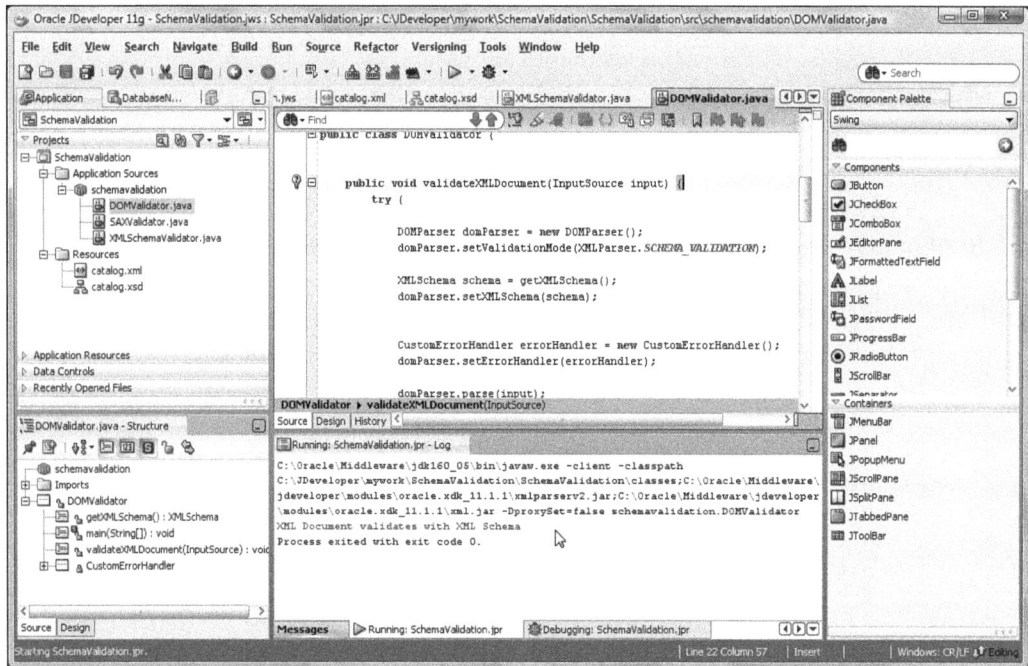

Summary

An XML schema defines the structure of an XML document. In this chapter we discussed validating an XML document with an XML schema. JDeveloper 11g provides built-in support for validating an XML document with an XML schema. JDeveloper also includes the XDK 11g through which an XML document may be validated with an XML schema in a Java application. We discussed the `XSDValidator`, `SAXPaser`, and `DOMParser` classes to validate an XML document.

In the next chapter we shall discuss the built-in XPath support in JDeveloper and also the XPath support in XDK 11g.

4
XPath

As mentioned in the earlier chapters, XML documents can be used for the transfer of data. The data in an XML document may be retrieved either with the **JAXP** (**Java API** for **XML Processing**) DOM and SAX APIs, or with the JAXP XPath API. Addressing an XML document with XPath has the advantage that a single node may be selected directly without iterating over a node set. With SAX and DOM APIs, node lists have to be iterated over to access a particular node. Another advantage of navigating an XML document with XPath is that an attribute node may be selected directly. With DOM and SAX APIs, an element node has to be selected before an element attribute can be selected. In this chapter we shall discuss XPath support in JDeveloper.

What is XPath?

XPath is a language for addressing an XML document's elements and attributes. As an example, say you receive an XML document that contains the details of a shipment and you want to retrieve the element/attribute values from the XML document. You don't just want to list the values of all the nodes, but also want to output the values of specific elements or attributes. In such a case, you would use XPath to retrieve the values of those elements and attributes. XPath constructs a hierarchical structure of an XML document, a tree of nodes, which is the XPath data model. The XPath data model consists of seven node types. The different types of nodes in the XPath data model are discussed in the following table:

Node Type	Description
Root Node	The root node is the root of the DOM tree. The document element (the root element) is a child of the root node. The root node also has the processing instructions and comments as child nodes.
Element Node	This represents an element in an XML document. The character data, elements, processing instructions, and comments within an element are the child nodes of the element node.

Node Type	Description
Attribute Node	This represents an attribute other than the xmlns-prefixed attribute, which declares a namespace.
Text Node	The character data within an element is a text node. A text node has at least one character of data. A whitespace is also considered as a character of data. By default, the ignorable whitespace after the end of an element and before the start of the following element is also a text node. The ignorable whitespace can be excluded from the DOM tree built by parsing an XML document. This can be done by setting the whitespace-preserving mode to false with the setPreserveWhitespace (boolean flag) method.
Comment Node	This represents a comment in an XML document, except the comments within the DOCTYPE declaration.
Processing Instruction Node	This represents a processing instruction in an XML document except the processing instruction within the DOCTYPE declaration. The XML declaration is not considered as a processing instruction node.
Namespace Node	This represents a namespace mapping, which consists of a xmlns:-prefixed attribute such as xmlns:xsd="http://www.w3.org/2001/XMLSchema". A namespace node consists of a namespace prefix (xsd in the example) and a namespace URI (http://www.w3.org/2001/XMLSchema in the example).

Specific nodes including element, attribute, and text nodes may be accessed with XPath. XPath supports nodes in a namespace. Nodes in XPath are selected with an XPath expression. An expression is evaluated to yield an object of one of the following four types: node set, Boolean, number, or string.

For an introduction on XPath refer to the *W3C Recommendation for XPath* (http://www.w3.org/TR/xpath). As a brief review, expression evaluation in XPath is performed with respect to a **context node**. The most commonly used type of expression in XPath is a **location path**. XPath defines two types of location paths: **relative location paths** and **absolute location paths**. A relative location path is defined with respect to a context node and consists of a sequence of one or more location steps separated by "/". A **location step** consists of an **axis**, a **node test**, and **predicates**.

An example of a location step is:

```
child::journal[position()=2]
```

In the example, the child axis contains the child nodes of the context node. Node test is the journal node set, and predicate is the second node in the journal node set. An absolute location path is defined with respect to the root node, and starts with "/". The difference between a relative location path and an absolute location path is that a relative location path starts with a location step, and an absolute location path starts with "/".

XPath support in Oracle XDK 11g

As we discussed in Chapter 1, Oracle XML Developer's Kit 11g, which is included in JDeveloper, provides the DOMParser class to parse an XML document and construct a DOM structure of the XML document. An XMLDocument object represents the DOM structure of an XML document. An XMLDocument object may be retrieved from a DOMParser object after an XML document has been parsed. The XMLDocument class provides select methods to select nodes in an XML document with an XPath expression.

In this chapter we shall parse an example XML document with the DOMParser class, obtain an XMLDocument object for the XML document, and select nodes from the document with the XMLDocument class select methods. The different select methods in the XMLDocument class are discussed in the following table:

Method Name	Description
selectSingleNode(String XPathExpression)	Selects a single node that matches an XPath expression. If more than one node matches the specified expression, the first node is selected. Use this method if you want to select the first node that matches an XPath expression.
selectNodes(String XPathExpression)	Selects a node list of nodes that match a specified XPath expression. Use this method if you want to select a collection of similar nodes.
selectSingleNode(String XPathExpression, NSResolver resolver)	Selects a single namespace node that matches a specified XPath expression. Use this method if the XML document has nodes in namespaces and you want to select the first node that is in a namespace and matches an XPath expression.
selectNodes(String XPathExpression, NSResolver resolver)	Selects a node list of nodes that match a specified XPath expression. Use this method if you want to select a collection of similar nodes that are in a namespace.

The example XML document that is parsed in this chapter has a namespace declaration `xmlns:journal="http://www.xdk11g.com/xpath"` for elements in the namespace with the prefix `journal`. For an introduction on namespaces in XML refer to the *W3C Recommendation on Namespaces in XML 1.0* (`http://www.w3.org/ TR/REC-xml-names/`). `catalog.xml`, the example XML document, is shown in the following listing:

```
<?xml version="1.0" encoding="UTF-8"?>
<catalog xmlns:journal="http://www.xdk11g.com/xpath"
    title="Oracle Magazine" publisher="Oracle Publishing">
 <journal:journal  journal:date="November-December 2008">
  <journal:article journal:section="ORACLE DEVELOPER">
    <title>Instant ODP.NET Deployment</title>
    <author>Mark A. Williams</author>
   </journal:article>
   <journal:article journal:section="COMMENT">
    <title>Application Server Convergence</title>
    <author>David Baum</author>
   </journal:article>
  </journal:journal>
 <journal  date="March-April 2008">
  <article section="TECHNOLOGY">
    <title>Oracle Database 11g Redux</title>
    <author>Tom Kyte</author>
   </article>
  <article section="ORACLE DEVELOPER">
    <title>Declarative Data Filtering</title>
    <author>Steve Muench</author>
   </article>
  </journal>
</catalog>
```

Setting the environment

Create an application (called `XPath`, for example) and a project (called `XPath`) in JDeveloper as explained in the earlier chapters. The XPath API will be demonstrated in a Java application. Therefore, create a Java class in the `XPath` project with **File | New**. In the **New Gallery** window select **Categories | General** and **Items | Java Class**. In the **Create Java Class** window, specify the class name (**XPathParser**, for example), the package name (**xpath** in the example application), and click on the
OK button.

To develop an application with XPath, add the required libraries to the project classpath. Select the project node in **Application Navigator** and select **Tools | Project Properties**. In the **Project Properties** window, select the **Libraries and Classpath** node. To add a library, select the **Add Library** button. Select the **Oracle XML Parser v2** library. Click on the **OK** button in the **Project Properties** window. We also need to add an XML document that is to be parsed and navigated with XPath. To add an XML document, select **File | New**. In the **New Gallery** window, select **Categories | General | XML** and **Items | XML Document**. Click on the **OK** button. In the **Create XML File** window specify the file name `catalog.xml` in the **File Name** field, and click on the **OK** button. Copy the `catalog.xml` listing to the **catalog.xml** file in the **Application Navigator**. The directory structure of the XPath project is shown in the following illustration:

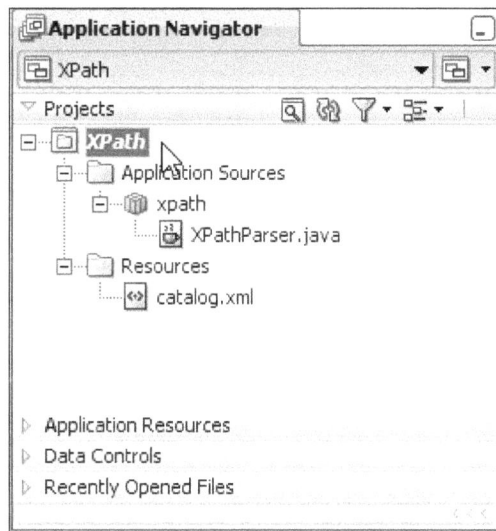

XPath search

In this section, we shall select nodes from the example XML document, `catalog.xml`, with the **XPath Search** tool of JDeveloper 11g. The **XPath Search** tool consists of an **Expression** field for specifying an XPath expression. Specify an XPath expression and click on **OK** to select nodes matching the XPath expression. The **XPath Search** tool has the provision to search for nodes in a specific namespace. An XML namespace is a collection of element and attribute names that are identified by a URI reference. Namespaces are specified in an XML document using namespace declarations. A namespace declaration is an `xmlns`-prefixed attribute in an element that consists of a namespace prefix in the attribute name with the namespace URI as the attribute value.

If you want to select nodes in a specific namespace or nodes from different namespaces, first add the namespace **Prefix** and **URI** to the **XPath Search** tool using the **Add** button. Subsequently, include namespace prefixes in the XPath expression. The **XPath Search** tool is shown here:

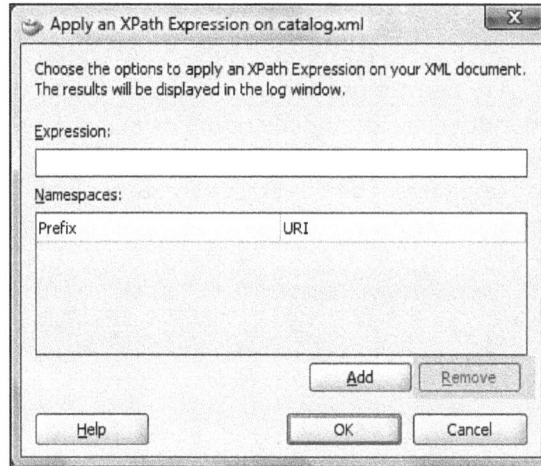

To navigate catalog.xml with XPath, select **catalog.xml** in the **Application Navigator** and select **Search | XPath Search**.

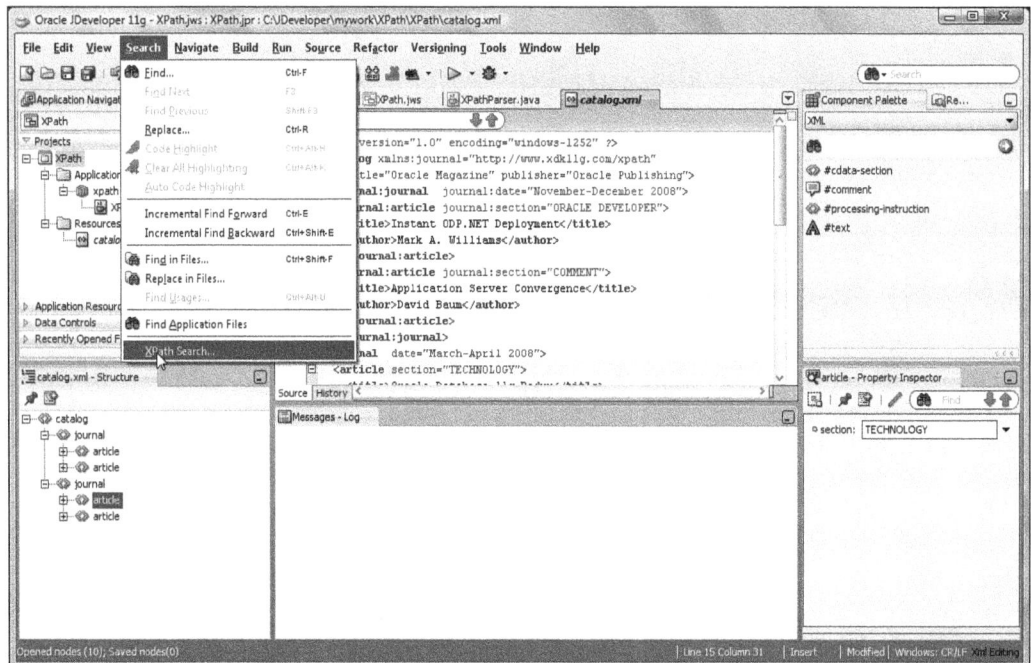

In the following subsections, we shall select example nodes using absolute location paths and relative location paths. Use a relative location path if the XML document is large and a specific node is required. Also, use a relative path if the node from which subnodes are to be selected and the relative location path are known. Use an absolute location path if the XML document is small, or if the relative location path is not known. The objective is to use minimum XPath navigation. Use the minimum number nodes to navigate in order to select the required node.

Selecting nodes with absolute location paths

Next, we shall demonstrate with various examples of selecting nodes using XPath. As an example, select all the title elements in catalog.xml. Specify the XPath expression for selecting the title elements in the **Expression** field of the **Apply an XPath Expression on catalog.xml** window. The XPath expression to select all title elements is **/catalog/journal/article/title**. Click on the **OK** button to select the title elements.

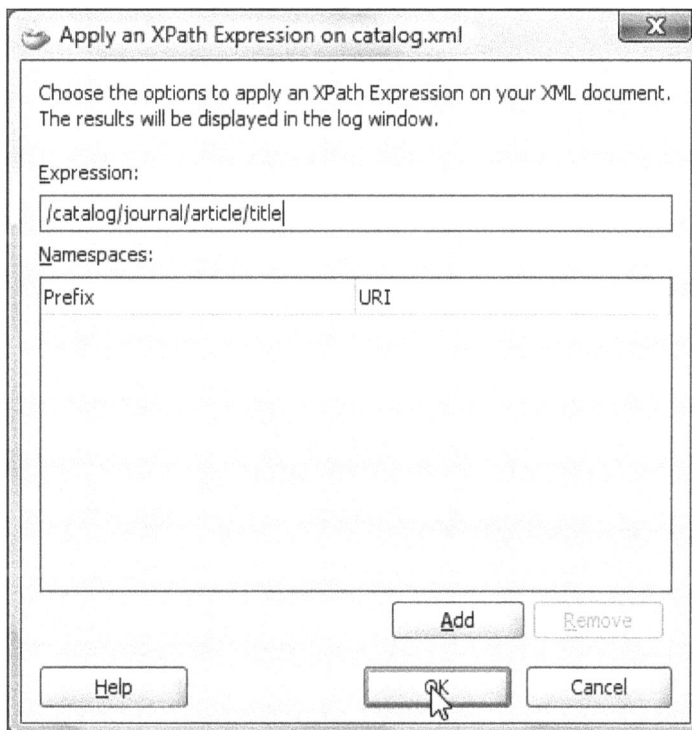

The `title` elements get selected. `Title` elements from the `journal:article` elements in the `journal` namespace do not get selected because a namespace has not been applied to the XPath expression.

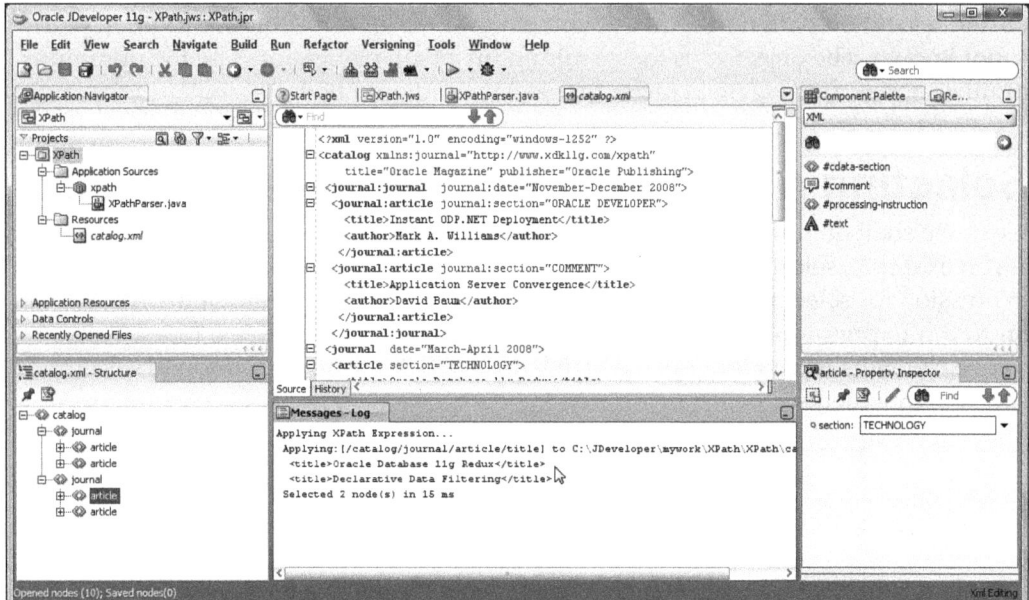

As another example, select the `title` element in the first `article` element using the XPath expression **/catalog/journal/article[1]/title**. We are not using namespaces yet. The XPath expression is specified in the **Expression** field.

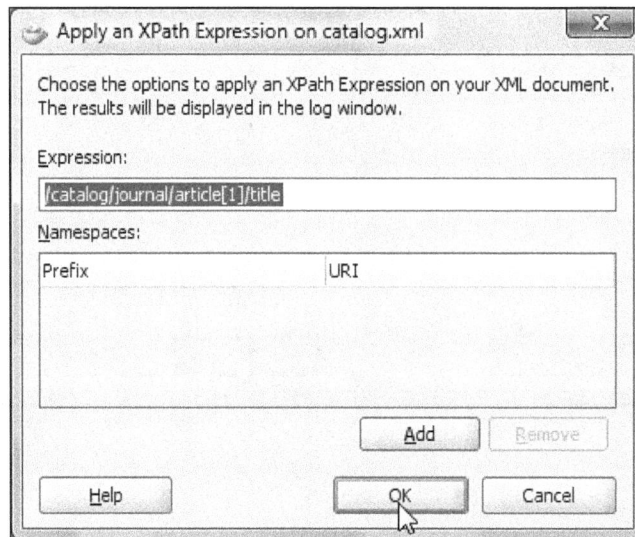

The `title` of the first `article` element gets selected as shown in the
JDeveloper output:

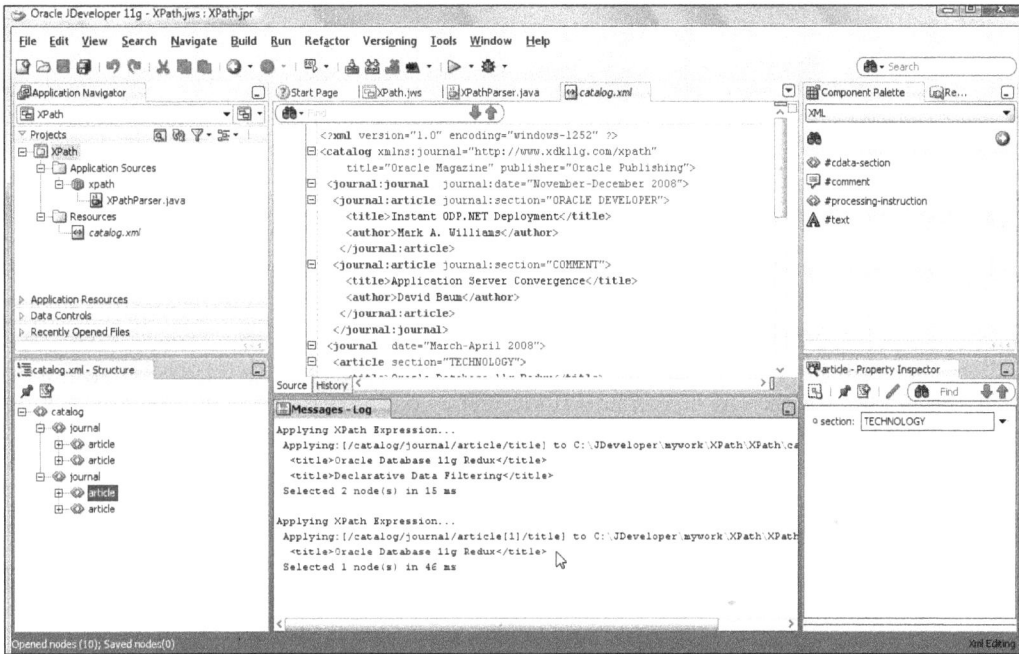

Attribute nodes may also be selected with XPath. Attributes are selected by using the
"@" prefix. As an example, select the `section` attribute in the first `article` element
in the `journal` element. The XPath expression for selecting the `section` attribute is
/catalog/journal/article[1]/@section and is specified in the **Expression** field. Click on
the **OK** button to select the `section` attribute.

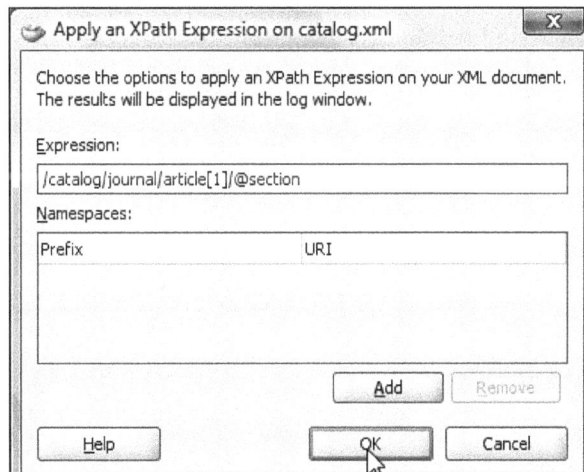

The attribute `section` gets outputted in JDeveloper.

```
Applying XPath Expression...
 Applying:[/catalog/journal/article[1]/@section ] to C:\JDeveloper\mywork\XPath\X
   section="TECHNOLOGY"
 Selected 1 node(s) in 0 ms
```

Selecting nodes with relative location paths

In the previous examples, an absolute location is used to select nodes. Next, we shall demonstrate selecting an element with a relative location path. As an example, select the `title` of the first `article` element in the `journal` element. The relative location path for selecting the `title` element is **child::catalog/journal/article[position()=1]/ title**. Specifying the axis as `child` and node test as `catalog` selects all the child nodes of the `catalog` node and is equivalent to an absolute location path that starts with `/catalog`. If the child nodes of the `journal` node were required to be selected, specify the node test as `journal`. Specify the XPath expression in the **Expression** field and click on the **OK** button.

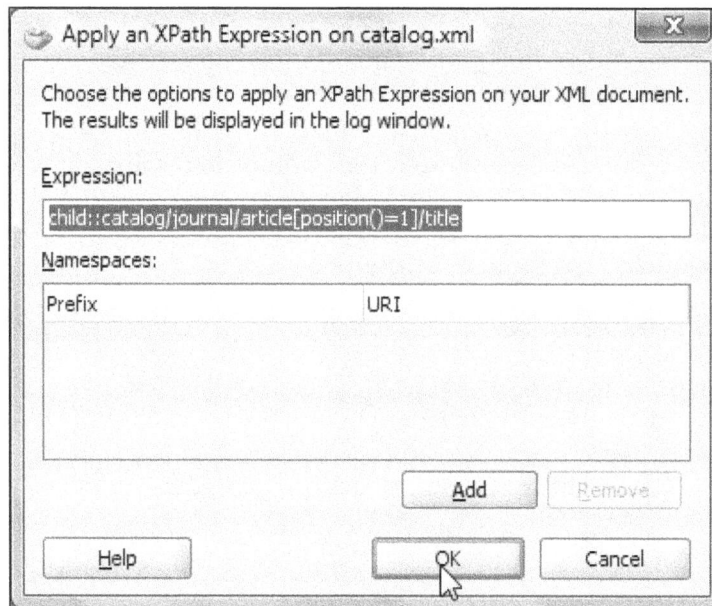

The `title` of the first `article` element in the `journal` element gets selected as shown here:

```
Applying XPath Expression...
 Applying:[child::catalog/journal/article[position()=1]/title] to C:\JDeveloper\n
  <title>Oracle Database 11g Redux</title>
 Selected 1 node(s) in 0 ms
```

Selecting namespace nodes

XPath Search also has the provision to select elements and attributes in a namespace. To illustrate, select all the `title` elements in the `journal` element (that is, in the `journal` namespace) using the XPath expression **/catalog/journal:journal/journal:article/title**. First, add the namespaces of the elements and attributes to be selected in the **Namespaces** text area. `Prefix` and `URI` of namespaces are added with the **Add** button. Specify the prefix in the **Prefix** column, and the URI in the **URI** column. Multiple namespace mappings may be added. XPath expressions that select namespace nodes are similar to no-namespace expressions, except that the namespace prefixes are included in the expressions. Elements in the default namespace, which does not have a namespace prefix, are also considered to be in a namespace. Click on the **OK** button to select the nodes with XPath.

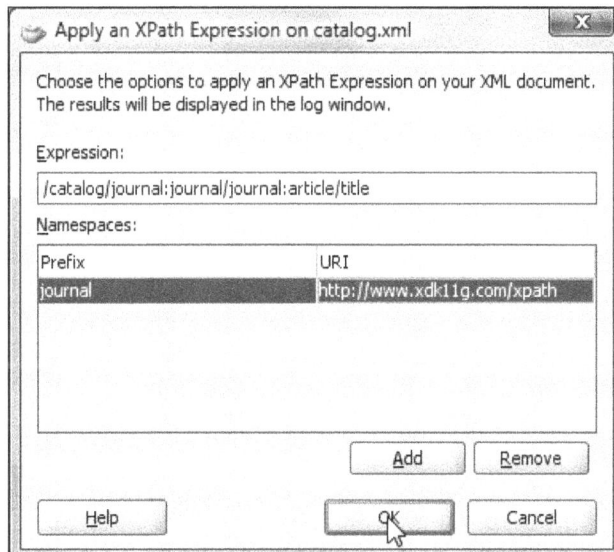

The `title` elements in the `journal` element (in the `journal` namespace) get selected and outputted in JDeveloper.

```
Applying XPath Expression...
 Applying:[/catalog/journal:journal/journal:article/title] to
C:\JDeveloper\mywork\XPath\XPath\catalog.xml
 with [http://www.xdk11g.com/xpath] as [journal]
  <title>Instant ODP.NET Deployment</title>
  <title>Application Server Convergence</title>
 Selected 2 node(s) in 0 ms
```

Attributes in a namespace may also be selected with **XPath Search**. As an example, select the `section` attributes in the `journal` namespace. Specify the XPath expression to select the `section` attributes in the **Expression** field and click on the **OK** button.

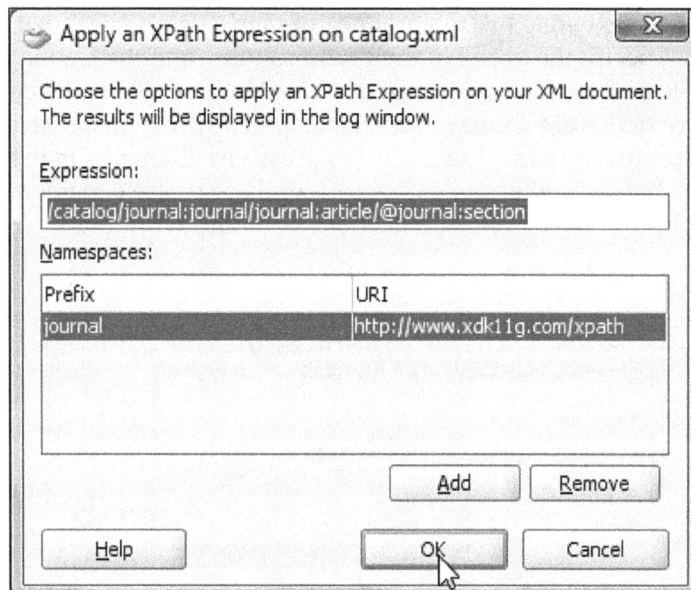

`Section` attributes in the `journal` namespace get selected.

```
Applying XPath Expression...
 Applying:[/catalog/journal:journal/journal:article/@journal:section] to C:\JDeve
 with [http://www.xdk11g.com/xpath] as [journal]
   journal:section="ORACLE DEVELOPER"
   journal:section="COMMENT"
 Selected 2 node(s) in 0 ms
```

Selecting nodes with XPath API

In the previous section, XML document nodes were selected automatically with the **XPath Search** tool in JDeveloper. In this section, we shall select nodes with the XPath API in the **XPathParser** class. JDeveloper XPath searches with the XPath Search tool are for the convenience of the developer as they find nodes faster than when looking through the XML file. The XPath searches, using the XPath API, actually let your application find nodes via XPath.

The XMLDocument class has select methods to select nodes with an XPath expression. A single node may be selected or a NodeList of nodes may be selected. Nodes declared in a namespace may also be selected. First, we need to import the oracle.xml.parser.v2 package that has the XMLDocument class and the parser class DOMParser, from which an XMLDocument may be obtained.

```
import oracle.xml.parser.v2.*;
```

Creating the DOM parser

Next, we need to parse an XML document and create a DOM structure for the XML document before being able to select nodes with XPath. Therefore, create a DOMParser using:

```
DOMParser domParser=new DOMParser();
```

The DOMParser class, which extends the XMLParser class, has overloaded the parse methods to parse an XML document from different input sources. An XML document may be parsed from InputSource, InputStream, Reader, String, or URL. In the example application XPathParser.java, we shall parse an example document from a FileReader.

Create a FileReader object from a File object and parse it with the parse(Reader) method as shown in the following listing:

```
domParser.parse(new FileReader(xmlDocument));
```

Variable xmlDocument is the File representation of the XML document catalog.xml. The class that provides XPath functionality is XMLDocument. Obtain an XMLDocument object from the DOMParser object with the getDocument() method.

```
XMLDocument document=domParser.getDocument();
```

Method selectSingleNode(String)

The XMLDocument class method selectSingleNode(String) selects a single node specified by an XPath expression. If more than one nodes match the XPath expression, the first node that matches the XPath expression gets selected. As an example, select the title of the first article node with section attribute value ORACLE DEVELOPER. The title element is selected with the selectSingleNode(String) method as shown here:

```
XMLNode titleNode=(XMLNode)document.selectSingleNode("/catalog/
journal/article[@section='ORACLE DEVELOPER']/title");
```

The title element value may be selected by first selecting the text node in the title element node using the getFirstChild() method and subsequently selecting the text node value using the getNodeValue() method, as shown in the following listing:

```
String title=titleNode.getFirstChild().getNodeValue();
```

As another example of the selectSingleNode(String) method, select the author of the article with the title Oracle Database 11g Redux, as shown here:

```
XMLNode authorNode=(XMLNode)document.selectSingleNode("/catalog/
journal/article[title= Oracle Database 11g Redux']/author");
```

The author element text value is outputted by first selecting the text node within the author element node using the getFirstChild() method and subsequently selecting the text node value using the getNodeValue() method, as shown here:

```
String author=authorNode.getFirstChild().getNodeValue();
```

The XMLDocument class selectSingleNode(String) may also be used to select an attribute node. As an example, select the section attribute of the second article in the journal of date March-April 2008:

```
XMLNode sectionNode=(XMLNode)document.selectSingleNode("/catalog/
journal[@date=March-April 2008]/article[2]/@section");
```

The section node value may be selected with the getNodeValue() method:

```
String section=sectionNode.getNodeValue();
```

Method selectNodes(String)

The XMLDocument class method selectNodes(String XPathExpression) selects all the nodes specified by an XPath expression. As an example, select all the title elements for the journal of date March-April 2008, as shown in the following listing:

```
NodeList nodeList=document.selectNodes("/catalog/journal[@date='March-
April 2008']/article/title");
```

The method selectNodes(String) returns a NodeList that may be iterated over to output title elements:

```
for(int i=0; i<nodeList.getLength(); i++){
        titleNode=(XMLElement)nodeList.item(i);
        title=titleNode.getFirstChild().getNodeValue();
        System.out.println(title);
}
```

The method selectNodes(String) may also be used to select attribute nodes. For example, select all the section attributes for the articles in the journal of date March-April 2008:

```
NodeList
nodeList=document.selectNodes("/catalog/journal[@date='March- April
2008]/article/@section");
```

The NodeList of section nodes may be iterated over to output section node values as shown in the following listing:

```
for(int i=0; i<nodeList.getLength(); i++){
        XMLNode     sectionNode=(XMLNode)nodeList.item(i);
        String   section=sectionNode.getNodeValue();
        System.out.println(section+" ");
}
```

Method selectSingleNode(String,NSResolver)

The XMLDocument class method selectSingleNode(String XSLPattern, NSResolver resolver) selects a single node specified by an XPath expression. NSResolver is used to resolve any namespace prefixes that may occur in the XPath expression.

To select nodes in a namespace, create a class (for example, `CustomNSResolver`) that implements the `NSResolver` interface. In the implementation class, implement the `NSResolver` method `resolveNamespacePrefix(String prefix)` as shown in the following listing:

```
class CustomNSResolver implements NSResolver{
    public java.lang.String resolveNamespacePrefix(java.lang.String
    prefix){

        if(prefix.equals("journal")){
        return new String("http://www.xdk11g.com/xpath");
        }
}
}
```

The `resolveNamespacePrefix` method accepts a prefix and returns a URI. Create an `NSResolver` object. Set the namespace prefix to resolve using the `resolveNamespacePrefix` method:

```
CustomNSResolver  resolver=new CustomNSResolver();
resolver.resolveNamespacePrefix("journal");
```

In the example XML document, `catalog.xml`, one of the `journal` elements is in the `journal` namespace. As an example, select the `section` attribute in the `journal` namespace in the first `article` element (in `journal` namespace) in the `journal` element (in `journal` namespace). The `section` attribute value will be outputted with the `getNodeValue()` method, as shown in the following listing:

```
XMLNode sectionNode= (XMLNode)document.selectSingleNode("/catalog/
journal:journal/journal:article/@journal:section", resolver);
section=sectionNode.getNodeValue();
```

As a contrast between the `selectSingleNode` method that takes an `NSResolver` and the `selectSingleNode` method that doesn't, the method that doesn't take an `NSResolver` does not select nodes in a namespace. On the other hand, the one that does selects nodes in a namespace. If the method that does not take an `NSResolver` is invoked with an XPath expression containing namespace nodes, the following error is generated:

```
XSLException Namespace prefix 'journal' used but not declared.
```

Method selectNodes(String,NSResolver)

The XMLDocument class method selectNodes(String XPathExpression, NSResolver resolver) selects all the namespace nodes resolved by an NSResolver that are specified in an XPath expression. NSResolver is used to resolve any prefixes that may occur in the XPath expression. For example, select all the title elements in journal (in journal namespace) of date (in journal namespace) November-December 2008, as shown in the following listing:

```
NodeList nodeList=document.selectNodes("/catalog/journal:journal[@
journal:date='November-December 2008']/journal:article/title",
resolver );
```

The namespace prefix journal in the XPath expression is resolved with an NSResolver object. The NodeList returned by the selectNodes(String, NSResolver) method may be iterated over to output the title elements.

```
for(int i=0; i<nodeList.getLength(); i++){
            titleNode=(XMLElement)nodeList.item(i);
            title=titleNode.getFirstChild().getNodeValue();
            System.out.println(title);
}
```

Running the Java application

The Java program XPathParser.java is used to select nodes from the XML document catalog.xml. The Java application is listed with additional explanations about the application as follows:

1. First, we import the required packages from XDK 11g.

   ```
   import oracle.xml.parser.v2.*;
   import java.io.*;
   import org.xml.sax.SAXException;
   import org.w3c.dom.*;
   ```

2. Next, we add the XPathParser Java class declaration.

   ```
   public class XPathParser{
   ```

3. We define the parseDocument method to parse an XML document with the DOMParser.

   ```
   public void parseDocument(File xmlDocument){

     try{
   ```

4. Next, we create a `DOMParser` object and parse the XML document.

```
DOMParser domParser=new DOMParser();
domParser.parse(new FileReader(xmlDocument));
XMLDocument document=domParser.getDocument();
```

5. We specify the `NSResolver` object to resolve namespaces.

```
CustomResolver resolver=new CustomResolver();
resolver.resolveNamespacePrefix("journal");
```

6. Next, we select nodes using the `selectSingleNode(String)` method.

```
XMLNodetitleNode=(XMLNode)document.selectSingleNode
("/catalog/journal/article[@section=' ORACLE DEVELOPER']/title");

String title=titleNode.getFirstChild().getNodeValue();

System.out.println("Title of first Article in ORACLE DEVELOPER
Section (with nodes not in any namespace) is "+ title);

XMLNode authorNode=(XMLNode)document.selectSingleNode("/catalog/
journal/article[title= Oracle Database 11g Redux']/author");

String author=authorNode.getFirstChild().getNodeValue();

    System.out.println("Author of Title Oracle Database 11g Redux
    is "+ author);

    XMLNode sectionNode=(XMLNode)document.selectSingleNode
    ("/catalog/journal[@date=March-April 2008']/article[2]
     /@section");

String section=sectionNode.getNodeValue();

System.out.println("Section of 2nd Article in Journal of date
March-April 2008 is   "+ section);
```

7. We select nodes using the `selectNodes(String)` method.

```
NodeList nodeList = document.selectNodes("/catalog/journal[@date=
'March-April 2008']/article/title");

System.out.println("Article Titles published in journal of March-
April 2008 are: ");

            for(int i=0; i<nodeList.getLength(); i++){

                titleNode=(XMLElement)nodeList.item(i);
                title=titleNode.getFirstChild().getNodeValue();
                System.out.println(title);
            }

nodeList=document.selectNodes("/catalog/journal[@date='March-April
2008']/article/@section");
```

```
System.out.println("Articles in journal of March-April 2008 were
published in Sections: ");
            for(int i=0; i<nodeList.getLength(); i++){
                sectionNode=(XMLNode)nodeList.item(i);
                 section=sectionNode.getNodeValue();
                 System.out.println(section+" ");
            }
```

8. Next, we select nodes using the `selectSingleNode(String,NSResolver)` method.

```
sectionNode=(XMLNode)document.selectSingleNode("/catalog/journal:
journal/journal:article/@journal:section", resolver);

section=sectionNode.getNodeValue();
System.out.println("Section of first article in first journal
(nodes being in journal namespace) is "+section+" ");

System.out.println("Titles for articles in journal of date
November-December 2008 (journal, article, and date nodes being in
journal namespace) are   ");
```

9. We also select nodes using the `selectNodes(String,NSResolver)` method.

```
nodeList=document.selectNodes("/catalog/journal:journal[@journal:
date= 'November-December 2008']/journal:article/title",
resolver );
            for(int i=0; i<nodeList.getLength(); i++){
                titleNode=(XMLElement)nodeList.item(i);
                title=titleNode.getFirstChild().getNodeValue();
                System.out.println(title);
             }
        }catch(IOException e){
System.err.println("IOException"+e.getMessage());
        }
        catch(XMLDOMException e){
System.err.println("XMLDOMException"+e.getMessage());
        }
catch(XMLParseException e)
{System.err.println("XMLParseException"+e.getMessage());
        }
        catch(XSLException e){
            System.err.println("XSLException"+e.getMessage());
        }
        catch(SAXException e){
            System.err.println("SAXException"+e.getMessage());
        }
    }
```

10. We add the Java class that extends the NSResolver class.

```
class CustomResolver implements NSResolver{
public java.lang.String
resolveNamespacePrefix(java.lang.String prefix){
if(prefix.equals("journal")){
        return new "http://www.xdk11g.com/xpath";
        }else
        return null;
    }

}
```

11. Finally, we define the main method in which we create an instance of the XPathParser class and invoke the parseDocument method.

```
        public static void main(String[] argv){
                XPathParser  parser=new XPathParser();
                    parser.parseDocument(new File("catalog.xml"));
        }
    }
```

To run the XPathParser.java application in JDeveloper, right-click on the **XPathParser.java** node in the **Application Navigator**, and select **Run**. The output from the XPathParser.java application is shown in the following illustration:

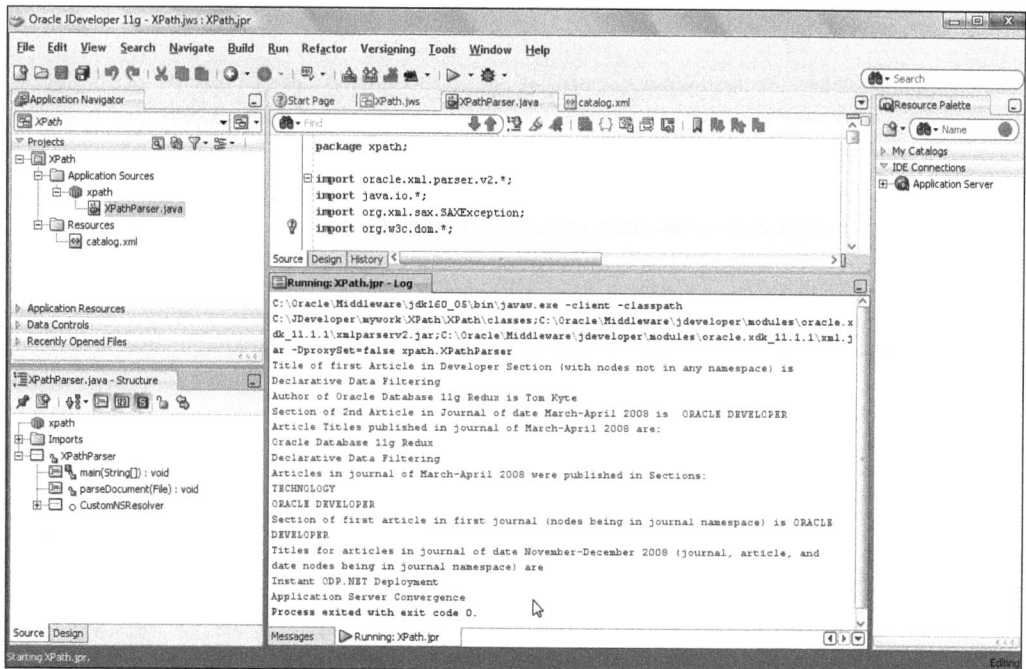

Summary

In this chapter you learned about XPath support in JDeveloper 11g. JDeveloper provides an **XPath Search** GUI tool to select nodes from an XML document using XPath. We selected nodes using absolute location paths and relative location paths, and also selected namespace nodes. We discussed the XDK's XMLDocument class select methods to select elements and attributes in an XML document with XPath. The select methods may be used to select single nodes or collections of nodes. The select methods may also be used to select nodes in a namespace.

In the next chapter, you will learn about **XSLT**(**Extensible Stylesheet Language Transformation**) support in JDeveloper.

5

Transforming XML with XSLT

XSLT (Extensible Stylesheet Language Transformations) is a language for transforming XML documents into other documents. JDeveloper 11g supports the development of XSLT applications using the built-in Oracle XML Parser v2 library. The Java API for transforming XML documents using XSLT is the **TrAX (Transformation API for XML)**, and the TrAX API is included in the XDK's `javax.xml.transform` package. Using an XSLT stylesheet, an XML document may be transformed to another XML document or an HTML document, or another implementation-supported format such as XHTML.

XSLT uses XPath to select nodes in a source DOM tree and construct a result tree. XSLT 1.0 also provides for implementation-specific extension functions that may be used in a stylesheet. The Oracle XSLT processor supports XSLT extension functions to access Java class functions (methods) from an XSLT stylesheet. The XSLT extension functions add the functionality to access Java classes and methods in an XSLT stylesheet.

JDeveloper 11g provides a **New Gallery** wizard to add an XSL stylesheet to a project. XSLT is a component of **XSL (Extensible Stylesheet Language—** `http://www.w3.org/Style/XSL/`), which also includes XPath (discussed in Chapter 4) and XSL-FO; XSL-FO specifies the formatting of an XML document and will be discussed in Chapter 11. JDeveloper 11g also provides a **Component Palette** for adding XSLT components to an XSLT stylesheet.

What we will cover in this chapter

In this chapter, we will develop a TrAX application to convert an XML document to an HTML document using an XSLT stylesheet. An XSLT stylesheet may need to call Java classes and class methods for functionality not available in standard XSLT functions. Java class methods can be invoked in an XSLT stylesheet using the XSLT extension functions. The Java methods accessed in an XSLT stylesheet may be static methods or non-static methods. In this chapter, we will discuss procedures that configure XSLT extension functions in an XSLT stylesheet. To demonstrate the application of the XSLT extension functions, we shall parse and modify an example XML document.

Setting the environment for XSLT transformation

We need to create an application and a project in JDeveloper 11g to develop a TrAX application. To create an application select **File | New**. In the **New Gallery** window select **Categories | General** and **Items | Generic Application**. Click on **OK**. In the **Create Generic Application** window specify the application name (Trax for example) and click on **Next**. In the **Name your Generic project** window specify a project name (Trax for example) and click on **Finish**. An application and a project get created.

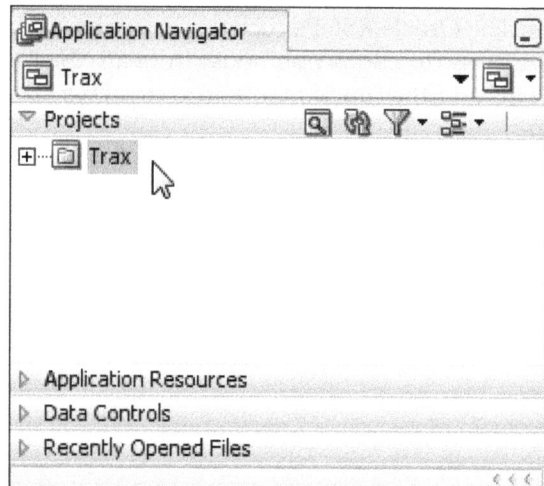

To the project, add an XML document by selecting **File | New** and subsequently selecting **Categories | General | XML** and **Items | XML Document** in the **New Gallery** window. Click on the **OK** button.

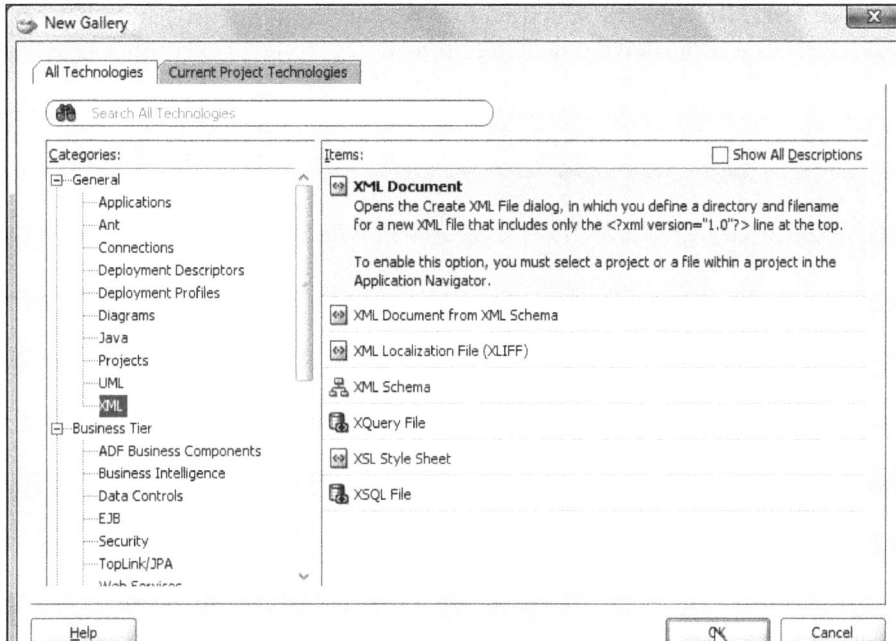

In the **Create XML File** window specify a **File Name** (catalog.xml for example) and click on **OK**. Add an XSLT stylesheet by selecting **File | New**. In the **New Gallery** window select **Categories | General | XML** and **Items | XSL Style Sheet**. Click on **OK**.

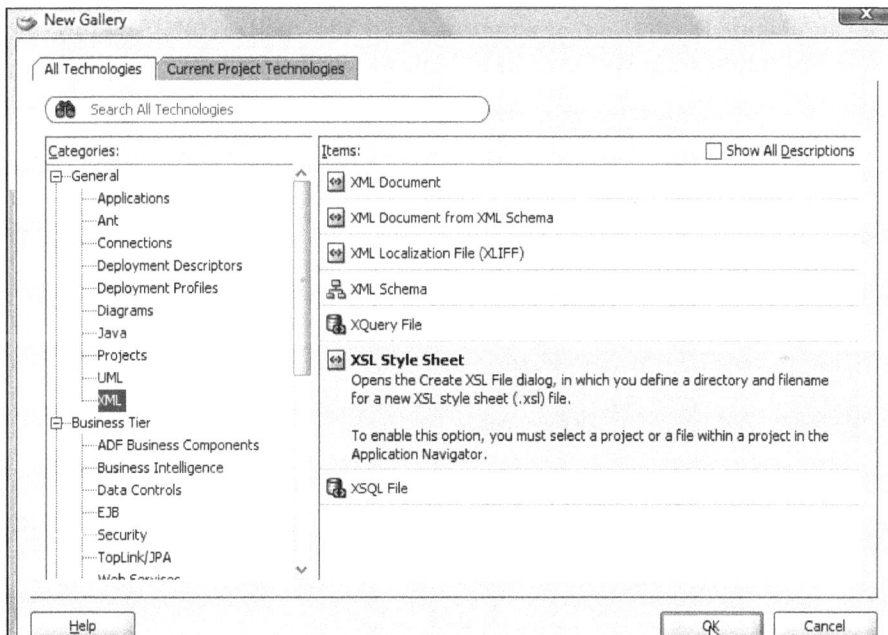

In the **Create XSL File** window specify a **File Name**, `catalog.xsl`, and click on **OK**. An XSL stylesheet gets added to the **Trax** project. XSL stylesheet components may be added to a stylesheet from the **XSL Component Palette**.

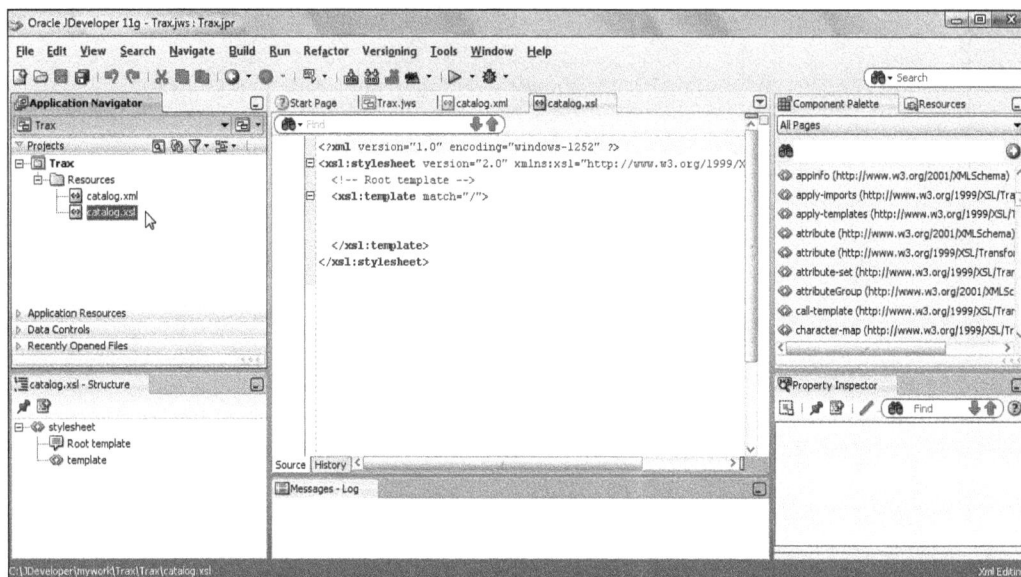

We also need to add a Java class by selecting **File | New**. In the **New Gallery** window select **Categories | General** and **Items | Java Class**. In the **Create Java Class** window specify a class **Name** (`XSLTransform` for example) and click on **OK**. The directory structure of the application is shown in the following illustration:

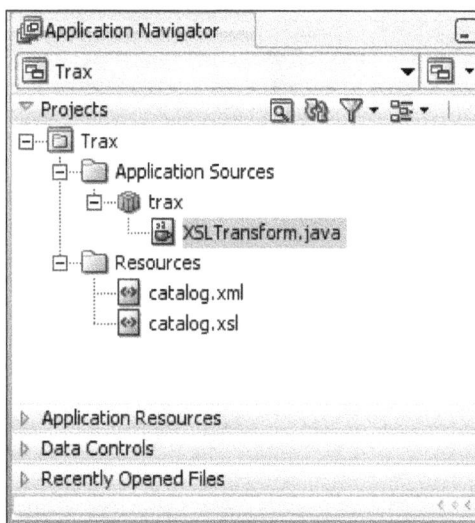

We also need to add the **Oracle XML Parser v2** library to the project. Add the library by selecting **Tools | Project Properties**. In the **Project Properties** window, select the **Libraries and Classpath** node and add the **Oracle XML Parser v2** library with the **Add Library** button.

Transforming an XML document

In this section, we will develop a Java application for the TrAX to convert an example XML document, `catalog.xml`, to an HTML document. The procedure to transform an XML document is as follows:

1. Parse the XML Document.
2. Create a TransformerFactory object.
3. Set an error listener on the TransformerFactory object.
4. Create a Transformer object.
5. Set an error listener on the Transformer object.
6. Set output properties.
7. Transform an XML document.

The example XML document `catalog.xml` that we shall transform is listed as follows:

```
<?xml version="1.0" encoding="windows-1252" ?>
<catalog>
  <journal title="Oracle Magazine" publisher="Oracle Publishing"
  edition="March-April 2008">
    <article section="ORACLE DEVELOPER">
      <title>Declarative Data Filtering</title>
      <author>Steve Muench</author>
    </article>
  </journal>
  <journal title="Oracle Magazine" publisher="Oracle Publishing"
  edition="November-December 2008">
    <article section="COMMENT">
      <title>Application Server Convergence</title>
      <author>David Baum</author>
    </article>
  </journal>
</catalog>
```

Copy the `catalog.xml` listing to the `catalog.xml` document in the `Trax` JDeveloper project. The example stylesheet, `catalog.xsl`, is used to transform the example XML document and is listed as follows:

```
<?xml version="1.0" encoding="windows-1252" ?><xsl:stylesheet
version="1.0" xmlns:xsl="http://www.w3.org/1999/XSL/Transform">
<xsl:output encoding="ISO-8859-1"  method="text/html" />
<xsl:template match="/catalog">
<html>
  <head>
    <title>Oracle Catalog</title>
  </head>
  <body>
    <table border="1" cellspacing="0">
        <tr>
         <th>Journal</th>
         <th>Publisher</th>
         <th>Edition</th>
         <th>Section</th>
         <th>Title</th>
         <th>Author</th>
        </tr>
      <xsl:for-each select="journal">
        <tr>
         <td><xsl:value-of select="@title"/></td>
         <td><xsl:value-of select="@publisher"/></td>
         <td><xsl:value-of select="@edition"/></td>
          <td><xsl:value-of select="article/@section"/></td>
         <td><xsl:value-of select="article/title"/></td>
         <td><xsl:value-of select="article/author"/></td>
        </tr>
      </xsl:for-each>

    </table>
  </body>
</html>
</xsl:template>
</xsl:stylesheet>
```

The XSLT stylesheet has an `xsl:template` tag to match the root element `catalog`. The `xsl:for-each` tag is used to iterate over the `journal` tags. The `xsl-value` tag is used to output element/attribute values. Copy the `catalog.xsl` listing to the `catalog.xsl` file in the JDeveloper project: `Trax`. In the `XSLTransform.java` application, import the JAXP classes required for parsing and transforming an XML document.

Parsing the XML document

As explained in Chapter 1, create a `DocumentBuilderFacory` object using the static method `newInstance()`. `DocumentBuilderFactory` is a factory class for obtaining a parser.

```
DocumentBuilderFactory factory = DocumentBuilderFactory.newInstance();
```

Obtain a `DocumentBuilder` object from the factory object using the `newDocumentBuilder()` method.

```
DocumentBuilder builder = factory.newDocumentBuilder();
```

Parse the example XML document using the `DocumentBuilder` object and obtain a `Document` object. The `DocumentBuilder` class provides overloaded `parse()` methods to parse an XML document from a `File`, `InputSource`, or `InputStream` object or a `String` URI.

```
File xmlFile = new File("catalog.xml");
Document document = builder.parse(xmlFile);
```

Creating the TransformerFactory

The `TransformerFactory` class is an abstract factory class to create `Transformer` objects. Oracle XDK provides an implementation class `oracle.xml.jaxp.JXSAXTransformerFactory` that is a subclass of the `TransformerFactory` class. For creating a `Transformer` and subsequently transforming an XML document, first we need to create a `JXSAXTransformerFactory` object. Create a `JXSAXTransformerFactory` object using the `newInstance()` static method of the `JXSAXTransformerFactory` class.

```
JXSAXTransformerFactory tFactory = (JXSAXTransformerFactory)
                        (JXSAXTransformerFactory.newInstance());
```

The `newInstance()` method uses the following ordered lookup procedure to determine the `TransformerFactory` implementation class used:

1. Use the `javax.xml.transform.TransformerFactory` system property.
2. Use the properties file `lib/jaxp.properties` in the JRE directory, which specifies the implementation class for the `javax.xml.transform.TransformerFactory` system property.
3. Use the Services API to obtain a implementation class classname from the file `META-INF/services/javax.xml.transform.TransformerFactory` in JARs available to the runtime.
4. Platform default `TransformerFactory` instance.

The **TrAX** (**Transformation API** for **XML**) defines objects and methods for processing input and generating output in different formats including DOM documents, SAX event streams, and character streams. Different XSLT processors support different features. The features are defined as un-resolvable URL strings that are also available as named constants. The features that are supported by an implementation may be obtained using the getFeature method of the XSLT engine factory class. The getFeature method can be invoked using a URL or named constant as the method argument and a Boolean value indicating if the feature is supported gets returned. The following table lists the different features as URLs and named constants and specifies which features are supported by the Oracle XSLT engine factory class oracle.xml.jaxp.JXSAXTransformerFactory.In the table DOMSource, SAXSource and StreamSource are classes that are holders of the transformation source tree and DOMResult, SAXResult, and StreamResult are classes that are holders of the transformation result tree.

Feature URL	Feature Named Constant	Description	Supported by Oracle XSLT Engine
http://javax.xml. transform.dom. DOMResult/feature	javax.xml.transform. dom.DOMResult.FEATURE	The implementation supports transformation output as a DOMResult object.	Yes
http://javax.xml. transform.dom. DOMSource/feature	javax.xml.transform. dom.DOMSource.FEATURE	The implementation supports processing of XML input as a DOMSource object.	Yes
http://javax.xml. transform.sax. SAXResult/feature	javax.xml.transform. sax.SAXResult.FEATURE	The implementation supports transformation output as a SAXResult object.	Yes
http://javax.xml. transform.sax. SAXSource/feature	javax.xml.transform. sax.SAXSource.FEATURE	The implementation supports processing of XML input as a SAXSource object.	Yes
http://javax.xml. transform.sax. SAXTransformerFactory /feature	javax.xml. transform.sax. SAXTransformerFactory	The implementation provides a SAXTransformerFactory class as a subclass of TransformerFactory.	Yes
http://javax.xml. transform.sax. SAXTransformerFactory /feature/xmlfilter	javax.xml. transform.sax. SAXTransformerFactory. FEATURE_XMLFILTER	The implementation supports the XMLFilter interface for using the output of one transformation as input to another transformation.	Yes

Feature URL	Feature Named Constant	Description	Supported by Oracle XSLT Engine
`http://javax.xml.` `transform.stream.` `StreamResult/feature`	`javax.xml.transform.` `stream.StreamResult.` `FEATURE`	The implementation supports generating transformation output as a StreamResult object.	No
`http://javax.xml.` `transform.stream.` `StreamSource/feature`	`javax.xml.transform.` `stream.StreamSource.` `FEATURE`	The implementation supports processing of XML input as a StreamSource object.	No

Next, we set the error event listener for the `TransformerFactory` using the `setErrorListener` method. The error event listener processes the errors generated in the processing of transformation instructions, not the transformation itself. First, we need to create an error listener class that implements the `ErrorListener` interface. In the `ErrorListener` class, `CustomErrorListener`, provide an implementation for the methods `error`, `fatalError`, and `warning`. The `error` method receives notification of recoverable errors. The `fatalError` method receives notification of non-recoverable errors and the `warning` method receives notification of warnings.

```
private class CustomErrorListener implements ErrorListener
    {
        public void error(TransformerException exception)
        {
            System.err.println("TransformerException: " + exception);
        }
        public void fatalError(TransformerException exception)
        {
            System.err.println("TransformerException: " + exception);
        }
        public void warning(TransformerException exception)
        {
            System.err.println("TransformerException: " + exception);
        }
    }
```

Create an instance of the `CustomErrorListener` class and set the error listener object on the transformation factory class.

```
CustomErrorListener errorListener = new CustomErrorListener();
    tFactory.setErrorListener(errorListener);
```

Creating the Transformer

Next, we create a `Transformer` object from the `TransformerFactory` object. The `Transformer` class is an abstract class that is used to transform a source tree into a result tree. Oracle XDK provides an implementation class `oracle.xml.jaxp.JXTransformer` that extends the `Transformer` class and provides additional methods. The `JXSAXTransformerFactory` class provides two methods that are discussed in the following table to create a `Transfomer` object:

Method	Description
`newTransformer()`	The `Transformer` object created performs a copy of the source to the result.
`newTransformer (Source source)`	The `Transformer` object created performs a transformation of the `source` to the result using an XSLT stylesheet specified as a Source object. `DOMSource`, `SAXSource`, and `StreamSource` classes implement the `Source` interface.

As we shall be using an XSLT stylesheet, create a `Transformer` object using the `newTransformer(Source)` method and cast the `Transformer` object to `JXTransformer`. The `Source` parameter may be specified as a `SAXSource`, `DOMSource`, or `StreamSource` object that represents a stylesheet.

```
StreamSource stylesource = new StreamSource(stylesheet);
JXTransformer transformer = (JXTransformer)tFactory.newTransformer
                                (stylesource);
```

Next, we shall create another `CustomErrorListener` object and set an error listener on the `Transformer` object using the `setErrorListener` method. The error listener set on the `Transformer` object processes the errors generated in the actual transformation of the XML document.

```
CustomErrorListener errorListener2 = new CustomErrorListener ();
transformer.setErrorListener(errorListener2);
```

The `Transformer` class provides the `setOutputProperty` method to optionally specify output properties. As an example, set output properties for indentation and encoding.

```
transformer.setOutputProperty(OutputKeys.INDENT, "yes");
transformer.setOutputProperty(OutputKeys.ENCODING, "UTF-8");
```

The various output properties that may be specified for an XSLT processor are discussed in the following table:

Output Property	Description
OutputKeys.CDATA_SECTION_ELEMENTS	Specifies the whitespace-delimited names of elements whose text node children should be outputted using CDATA sections.
OutputKeys.DOCTYPE_PUBLIC	Specifies the public identifier to be used in the DOCTYPE declaration of the XML document output. A public identifier is a globally unique, abstract name.
OutputKeys.DOCTYPE_SYSTEM	Specifies the system identifier to be used in the DOCTYPE declaration of the XML document output. A system identifier is a URI reference for a resource file such as an XML Schema or DTD document. For further explanation on public and system identifiers refer to http://www.docbook.org/tdg/en/html/ch02.html#s-pid-sid-catalogs.
OutputKeys.ENCODING	Specifies the encoding for the result XML document.
OutputKeys.INDENT	Specifies if the result tree output XML document should be indented. Value may be "yes" or "no". A default value is used for indenting.
OutputKeys.MEDIA_TYPE	Specifies the media type (MIME content type) of the transformation result. For example, for HTML you would use "text/html" and for PDF output you would use "application/pdf". The default value is "text/xml". For other MIME types refer to http://www.iana.org/assignments/media-types/.
OutputKeys.METHOD	Specifies the method used for outputting the result. Standard values are "xml", "html", and "text", but other values such as "xhtml" that are supported by the implementation may also be specified. The default is "xml".
OutputKeys.OMIT_XML_DECLARATION	Specifies if the XML declaration is to be omitted from the output XML document. Value may be "yes" or "no". An XML document is not required to have an XML declaration; however, the W3C Recommendation for XML 1.0 specifies that "*XML documents SHOULD begin with an XML declaration which specifies the version of XML being used*". The default value is "no".
OutputKeys.STANDALONE	Specifies if the transformer is to output a standalone document declaration. A standalone document was defined in Chapter 1. The default value is "no".
OutputKeys.VERSION	Specifies the version of the output format. Only used for "xml" and "html" output methods. Default value for "xml" output method is "1.0". Default value for "html" output method is "4.0".

Transform the example XML document using the `transform(Source, Result)` method. The `Source` parameter represents a source tree to be transformed and a `DOMSource`, `SAXSource`, or `StreamSource` object may be specified for that parameter. The `Result` parameter specifies a result tree and a `SAXResult`, `DOMResult`, or a `StreamResult` object may be specified for the parameter.

```
DOMSource source = new DOMSource(document);
StreamResult result = new StreamResult(new File("catalog.html"));
transformer.transform(source, result);
```

Running the application

The `XSLTransform.java` application with additional explanations is listed as follows:

1. First, we specify the package declaration and the import statements.

```
package trax;

import javax.xml.parsers.DocumentBuilder;
import javax.xml.parsers.DocumentBuilderFactory;
import javax.xml.parsers.ParserConfigurationException;

import org.xml.sax.SAXException;

import org.w3c.dom.Document;

import javax.xml.transform.TransformerException;

import oracle.xml.jaxp.JXSAXTransformerFactory;
import oracle.xml.jaxp.JXTransformer;

import javax.xml.transform.TransformerConfigurationException;
import javax.xml.transform.dom.DOMSource;
import javax.xml.transform.stream.StreamSource;
import javax.xml.transform.stream.StreamResult;

import java.io.*;

import javax.xml.transform.ErrorListener;
import javax.xml.transform.OutputKeys;
```

2. Add a Java class declaration `XSLTransform`.

```
public class XSLTransform {
```

3. Define the `main` method in which an instance of the `XSLTTransform` class is created and the `transformXML` method, which is used for the transformation, is invoked.

```
public static void main(String[] argv) {
  File stylesheet = new File("catalog.xsl");
  File xmlFile = new File("catalog.xml");

  XSLTransform xsltTransform = new XSLTransform();
  xsltTransform.transformXML(xmlFile, stylesheet);
}
```

4. Define the `transformXML` method, which takes an XML file and an XSL file and transforms the XML file using the XSL file.

```
public void transformXML(File xmlFile, File xslFile) {

        try {
```

5. Parse the XML document.

```
DocumentBuilderFactory factory =
DocumentBuilderFactory.newInstance();
DocumentBuilder builder = factory.newDocumentBuilder();
Document document = builder.parse(xmlFile);
```

6. Create a `TransformerFactory` object and set the error listener on the factory object.

```
JXSAXTransformerFactory tFactory =
(JXSAXTransformerFactory)(JXSAXTransformerFactory.newInstance());
CustomErrorListener errorListener = new CustomErrorListener();
tFactory.setErrorListener(errorListener);
```

7. Create a `Transformer` object and set an error listener on the `Transformer` object. Also set the output properties.

```
StreamSource stylesource = new StreamSource(xslFile);
JXTransformer transformer = (JXTransformer)tFactory.newTransformer
                            (stylesource);
CustomErrorListener errorListener2 = new CustomErrorListener();
transformer.setErrorListener(errorListener2);
transformer.setOutputProperty(OutputKeys.INDENT, "yes");
 transformer.setOutputProperty(OutputKeys.ENCODING, "UTF-8");
```

8. Transform the XML document using an XSLT stylesheet.

```
DOMSource source = new DOMSource(document);
StreamResult result = new StreamResult(new File("catalog.html"));
transformer.transform(source, result);
        } catch (TransformerConfigurationException e) {
System.err.println("TransformerConfigurationException   " +
                                e.getMessage());
        } catch (TransformerException e) {
System.err.println("TransformerException   " + e.getMessage());
        } catch (SAXException e) {
System.err.println("SAXException  " + e.getMessage());
        } catch (ParserConfigurationException e) {
System.err.println("ParserConfigurationException   " +
                                e.getMessage());
        } catch (IOException e) {
System.err.println("IOException   " + e.getMessage());
        }

    }
```

9. Define the error listener class that implements the `ErrorListener` interface.

```
private class CustomErrorListener implements ErrorListener

{
    public void error(TransformerException exception)

    {
     System.err.println("TransformerException: " + exception);
    }
    public void fatalError(TransformerException exception)

    {
     System.err.println("TransformerException: " + exception);
    }

    public void warning(TransformerException exception)

    {
     System.err.println("TransformerException: " + exception);
    }
  }
}
```

10. Copy the `XSLTransformer.java` listing to the `XSLTransformer.java` class in the **Trax** project. To run the `XSLTTransform.java` application, right-click on `XSLTTransform.java` in the **Application Navigator** and select **Run**.

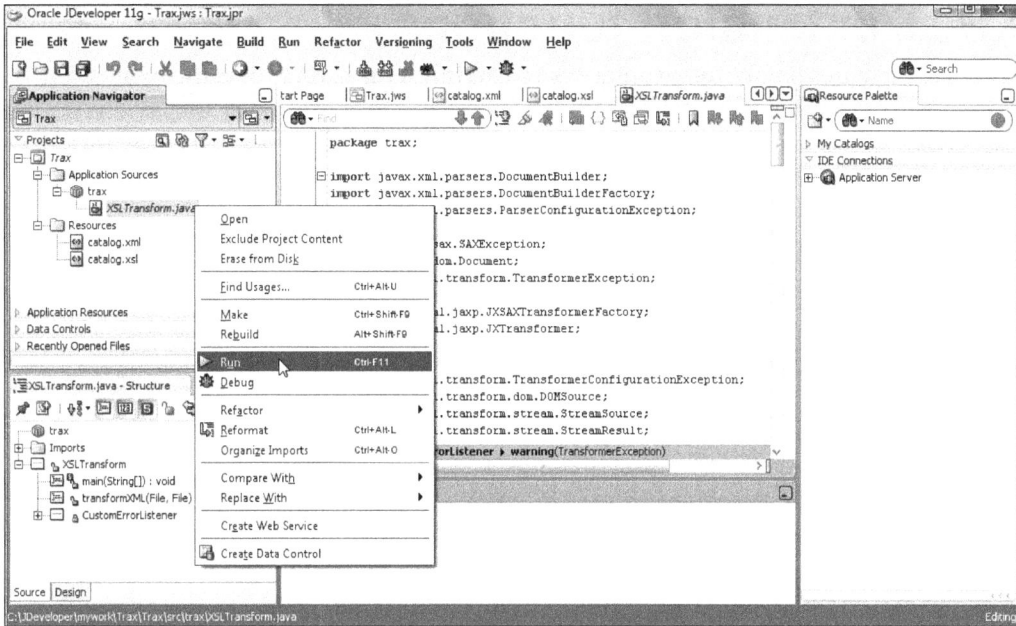

The XML document `catalog.xml` gets transformed to `catalog.html` with the stylesheet `catalog.xsl`. Select **View | Refresh** to add the `catalog.html` document to the **Trax** project in the **Application Navigator**.

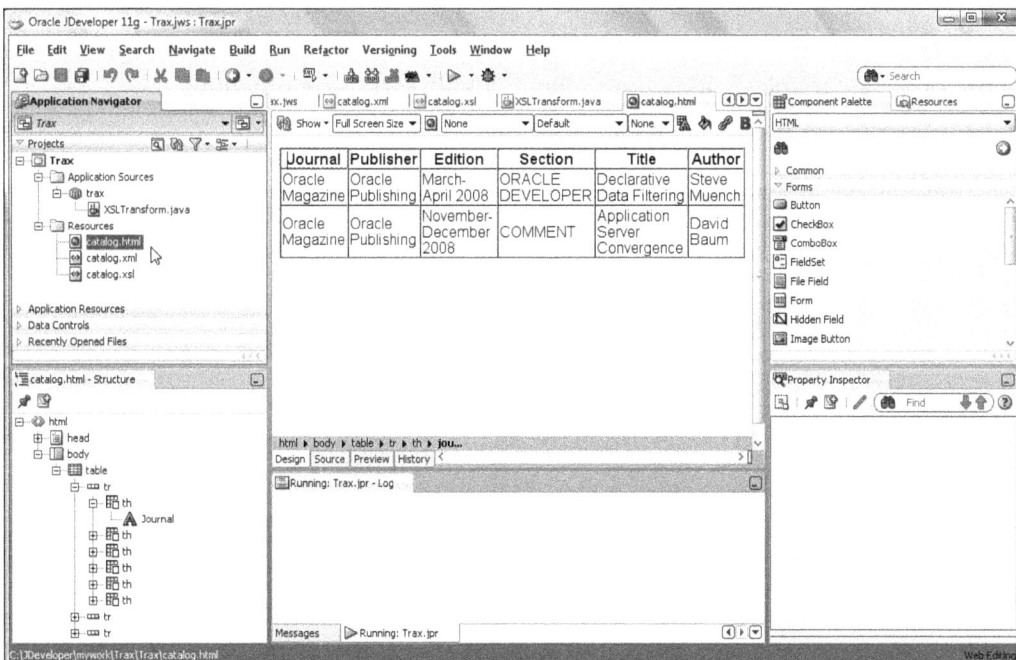

XSLT extension functions

XSLT 1.0 provides a way for developers to call implementation-specific extension functions from within a stylesheet. With the Oracle XSLT processor for Java, you use XSLT extension functions to access Java class functions (methods) from an XSLT stylesheet, letting you use Java to augment native XSLT transformations. Typically you'd use XSLT extension functions to:

- Perform a conversion. For example you might need to convert Fahrenheit to Celsius, or perform math functions that are not included in XSLT's library functions.

- Create XSLT variables from result values. It's sometimes convenient to get the results of a process into an XSLT variable. Using extension functions is a convenient way to achieve that.

This section explains how to configure XSLT extension functions, as implemented in XDK 11g, for use in an XSLT stylesheet. We will be parsing and modifying an XML document using extension functions, as an example. It's important to note that this example makes no modifications that you can't do in a standard XSLT stylesheet. Instead, it focuses on demonstrating all the features of XSLT extension functions, which are:

- Use of static methods
- Use of non-static methods
- Use of custom classes
- Use of variables with values obtained with extension functions
- Using constructor extension functions

The example XML, document `catalog.xml`, parsed and modified with the XSLT extension functions is listed as follows:

```
<?xml version="1.0" encoding="windows-1252" ?><catalog  title="Oracle
Magazine" publisher="Oracle Publishing">
   <journal date="November-December 2008">
      <article section="COMMENT">
        <title>Application Server Convergence</title>
        <author>David Baum</author>
      </article>
   </journal>
</catalog>
```

After modifying the input document with the XSLT extension features, it is slightly different, shown as follows. Specifically, the `<journal>` and `<article>` element attributes have changed, as have the `<title>` and `<author>` element values.

```
<?xml version="1.0" encoding="windows-1252" ?><catalog  title="Oracle
Magazine" publisher="Oracle Publishing">
   <journal date="March-April 2008">
      <article section="TECHNOLOGY">
         <title>Oracle Database 11g Redux</title>
         <author>Tom Kyte</author>
      </article>
   </journal>
</catalog>
```

Setting the environment for XSLT extension functions

As in the previous section create an application (called XSLTExtensions) and a project (called XSLTExtensions) in JDeveloper. Add a Java class XSLTransform for the XSLT transformation. Also add a Java class NodeConversionUtil that will be invoked in the XSL stylesheet that uses the XSLT extension functions. Create an XML document (catalog.xml) that is to be processed using the XSLT extension functions. Copy the catalog.xml listed in the beginning of this section to catalog.xml in the JDeveloper project. Also, create an XSL stylesheet (parser.xsl) that will contain the XSLT extension functions. The directory structure of the XSLT extension functions application is shown in the following illustration:

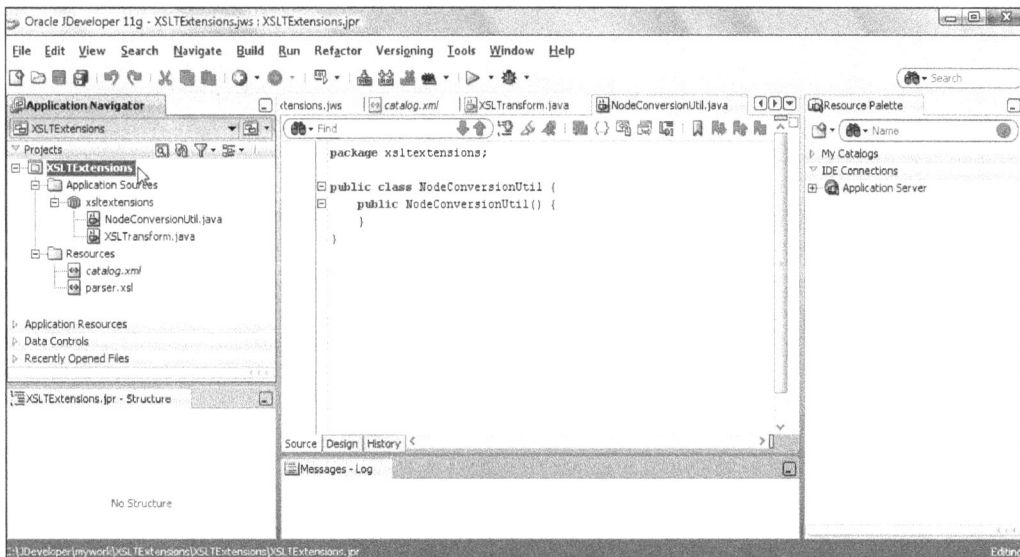

We also need to add the Oracle XML Parser v2 library to the XSLT extension functions application. Select **Tools | Project Properties** to add a library. In the **Project Properties** window select **Libraries and Classpath** and add the **Oracle XML Parser v2** library with the **Add Library** button. Click on **OK** in the **Project Properties** window.

Creating the stylesheet containing the extension functions

Next, we shall create the `parser.xsl` XSL stylesheet that will use the XSLT extension functions. To configure XSLT extension functions in an XSLT stylesheet you must declare the namespace of the extension functions in the XSLT stylesheet. This example uses Java class methods from the following classes:

- `oracle.xml.parser.v2.DOMParser`
- `oracle.xml.parser.v2.XMLDocument`
- `oracle.xml.parser.v2.XMLPrintDriver`
- `org.w3c.dom.Element`
- `org.w3c.dom.Node`
- `org.w3c.dom.NodeList`
- `xsltextensions.NodeConversionUtil`

Add the namespace declarations for these Java classes to the `xsl:stylesheet` element of the XSLT stylesheet. Each namespace represents a Java class. The syntax for declaring a Java extension function namespace is as follows:

```
xmlns:<classprefix>=
    "http://www.oracle.com/XSL/Transform/java/<classname>"
```

Looking at the syntax of the above example, `<classprefix>` is a name you choose that you'll later use in the stylesheet to invoke methods on the matching Java class, and `<classname>` is the Java class on which you want to call the methods. For example, here are two of the namespace declarations for the classes listed earlier.

```
xmlns:parser="http://www.oracle.com/XSL/Transform/java/oracle.xml.
parser.v2.DOMParser"
xmlns:document="http://www.oracle.com/XSL/Transform/java/oracle.xml.
parser.v2.XMLDocument"
```

XSLT extension functions do not have any provision for casting Java objects; however, because many `select` calls used to retrieve XML DOM objects return `Node` objects—even though you actually want to use an `Element` object—you often need to make type casts, such as from `Node` to `Element`. To convert one class to another you need a custom Java class. The example XSLT, `parser.xsl`, uses the custom Java utility class `NodeConversionUtil` to cast `org.w3c.dom.Node` types to `org.w3c.dom. Element` types. Here's the `NodeConversionUtil` class.

```
import org.w3c.dom.*;
public class NodeConversionUtil{
    public static Element nodeToElement(Node node){
        Element element=null;
         if(node instanceof Element)
           element=(Element)node;
        return element;
    }
}
```

Copy the `NodeConversionUtil` utility class listing to the `NodeConversionUtil. java` application in the **XSLTExtensions** JDeveloper project.

Instantiating Java classes

The XSLT extension functions are invoked in the `select` attribute of XSL stylesheet tags such as `xsl:variable` and `xsl:value-of`. In general, the syntax to create a class object in XSLT using XSLT Extension functions is as follows:

```
<xsl:variable name="<classobject>"
    select="<classprefix>:new('param1', 'param2', 'param3')"/>
```

Tag `xsl:variable` is an XSL stylesheet element. Variable `<classobject>` is the name of the XSLT variable you will use to refer to the class object in the XSLT stylesheet, and `<classprefix>` is the namespace prefix for the Java class that you declared in the `xsl:stylesheet` element of the XSLT. The `param1`, `param2`, and `param3` items in the remainder of the syntax represent any constructor parameters that might be needed to create a class instance. An example that creates a `DOMParser` object using XSLT extension functions is as follows:

```
<xsl:variable name="parser" select="parser:new()"/>
```

In a similar fashion, you create a `java.io.File` instance and a `java.io.FileReader` instance.

```
<xsl:variable name="xmlDocument"
    select="file:new('catalog.xml')"/>
<xsl:variable name="file-reader"
    select="fileReader:new($xmlDocument)"/>
```

Parsing the XML

Now you can parse the example XML document with the `DOMParser` class's `parse(java.io.Reader)` method. The `parse` method is a non-static method of the `DOMParser` class. The syntax for invoking a Java class non-static method in an XSLT stylesheet with extension functions is as follows:

```
select="<classprefix>:<classmethod>(<classobject>,<methodparam1>,
<methodparam2>)"
```

In a non-static method invocation, the first parameter is the instance on which the method is invoked and the remaining parameters are passed to the method in the specified order. Because we are invoking a method of the `DOMParser` class we shall use the `parser` prefix, which we defined in the namespace declaration for the `DOMParser` class. Because the return type of the `parse` method is `void` we shall use the `xsl:value-of` XSLT stylesheet tag, which does not have a `name` attribute to store the result of the method invocation. Because we are invoking a non-static method, the first parameter is the variable name representing a `DOMParser` object.

```
<xsl:value-of select="parser:parse($parser, $file-reader)"/>
```

By now you should have become familiar with the extension functions notation for invoking a non-static method:

- `<classprefix>` is the namespace prefix specified in the namespace declaration corresponding to the Java class in the `xsl:stylesheet` element
- `<classmethod>` is the Java class method you want to call
- `<classobject>` is the XSLT variable name representing the class instance on which you want to call the non-static method
- `<methodparam1>`, `<methodparm2>` are the method parameters

Storing Java results in XSLT—non-static method

You can place values returned from non-static methods into XSLT variables. For example, to obtain the parsed `XMLDocument` object using the non-static method `getDocument` of the `DOMParser` class and save it into a variable named `parsedDocument`, you could specify the following:

```
<xsl:variable name="parsedDocument" select="parser:
getDocument($parser)"/>
```

You can use that to query the document further. To get the root node of the parsed XML document using the `getDocumentElement` method of the `XMLDocument` class and store the result in a variable, specify the following:

```
<xsl:variable name="catalogElement"   select="document:getDocumentElem
ent($parsedDocument)"/>
```

You can obtain node lists as well as individual nodes. To modify the first `journal` node, first retrieve the list of `journal` nodes from the parsed XML document using the `getElementsByTagName` method of the `Element` object.

```
<xsl:variable name="journalNodeList"
   select="element:getElementsByTagName(
   $catalogElement,'journal')"/>
```

Then select the first node from the list using the `item` method of the `NodeList` object.

```
<xsl:variable name="journalNode"
   select="nodelist:item($journalNodeList, 0)"/>
```

Storing Java results in XSLT—static method

Because XSLT can't cast objects you have to convert the `journal` node, which is of type `org.w3c.dom.Node`, to an `org.w3c.dom.Element` using the Java `NodeConversionUtil` utility class's `nodeToElement(Node node)` method. You assign the result to an XSLT variable.

```
<xsl:variable name="journalElement"
select="nodeConvUtil:nodeToElement($journalNode)"/>
```

Note that the call was slightly different, because `nodeToElement()` is a static method. The syntax for a static method in an XSLT stylesheet is as follows:

```
select="<classprefix>:<classmethod>(<methodparam1>, <methodparam2>)"
```

Variable `<classprefix>` is the namespace prefix in the namespace declaration corresponding to the Java class, `<classmethod>` is the static method you're calling, and `<methodparam1>`, `<methodparam2>`, and so on are the static method parameters. The difference from a non-static method call is that the first parameter is not the class instance variable.

Modifying attributes

To modify an element's attributes, you first remove the attribute, and then add a new attribute and value to the element. So, for example, to change the `date` attribute in the `journal` element, first remove it using the `removeAttribute` method of the `Element` object.

```
<xsl:value-of select="element:removeAttribute(
   $journalElement, 'date')"/>
```

Then create a new attribute and add it to the `journal` element using the `setAttribute` method of the `Element` object.

```
<xsl:value-of select="element:setAttribute($journalElement,
    'date', 'March-April 2008')"/>
```

The sample XSLT stylesheet uses a similar process to modify the `article` element's `section` attribute.

Modifying element text

To modify the text in the `title` element, first retrieve the text node within the title node. Obtain a `NodeList` of title nodes using the `getElementsByTagName` method. Obtain the first item in the `NodeList` using the `item` method. Obtain the text node using the `getFirstChild` method.

```
<xsl:variable name="titleNodeList"
    select="element:getElementsByTagName(
    $articleElement, 'title')"/>
<xsl:variable name="titleNode"
    select="nodelist:item($titleNodeList, 0)"/>
<xsl:variable name="titleTextNode"
    select="node:getFirstChild($titleNode)"/>
```

Then you can modify the `text` node's value directly using the `setNodeValue` method.

```
<xsl:value-of select="node:setNodeValue(
    $titleTextNode, 'Oracle Database 11g Redux')"/>
```

Modifying the author node is similar.

Stylesheet with extension functions

The example XSLT stylesheet, `parser.xsl`, used to modify the example XML document is listed as follows:

```
<xsl:stylesheet version="1.0" xmlns:xsl="http://www.w3.org/1999/XSL/
Transform"

xmlns:parser="http://www.oracle.com/XSL/Transform/java/oracle.xml.
parser.v2.DOMParser"
xmlns:document="http://www.oracle.com/XSL/Transform/java/oracle.xml.
parser.v2.XMLDocument"
xmlns:element="http://www.oracle.com/XSL/Transform/java/org.w3c.dom.
Element"
```

```
xmlns:node="http://www.oracle.com/XSL/Transform/java/org.w3c.dom.Node"
xmlns:nodelist="http://www.oracle.com/XSL/Transform/java/org.w3c.dom.
NodeList"
xmlns:nodeConvUtil="http://www.oracle.com/XSL/Transform/java/trax.
NodeConversionUtil"
xmlns:file="http://www.oracle.com/XSL/Transform/java/java.io.File"
xmlns:fileReader="http://www.oracle.com/XSL/Transform/java/java.
io.FileReader"
xmlns:outputStream="http://www.oracle.com/XSL/Transform/java/java.
io.FileOutputStream"
xmlns:printDriver="http://www.oracle.com/XSL/Transform/java/oracle.
xml.parser.v2.XMLPrintDriver">
 <xsl:output  method="text" />

 <xsl:template match="/">
    <xsl:variable name="parser" select="parser:new()"/>
    <xsl:variable name="xmlDocument" select="file:new('catalog.xml')"/>
    <xsl:variable name="file-reader" select="fileReader:
new($xmlDocument)"/>
    <xsl:value-of select="parser:parse($parser, $file-reader)"/>
    <xsl:variable name="parsedDocument" select="parser:
getDocument($parser)"/>
    <xsl:variable name="catalogElement" select="document:getDocumentEle
ment($parsedDocument)"/>

    <xsl:variable name="journalNodeList" select="element:getElementsByT
agName($catalogElement, 'journal')"/>
    <xsl:variable name="journalNode" select="nodelist:
item($journalNodeList, 0)"/>
    <xsl:variable name="journalElement"  select="nodeConvUtil:nodeToEle
ment($journalNode)"/>
    <xsl:value-of select="element:removeAttribute($journalElement,
'date')"/>
    <xsl:value-of select="element:setAttribute($journalElement, 'date',
'March-April 2008')"/>

    <xsl:variable name="articleNodeList" select="element:getElementsByT
agName($journalElement, 'article')"/>
    <xsl:variable name="articleNode" select="nodelist:
item($articleNodeList, 0)"/>
    <xsl:variable name="articleElement" select="nodeConvUtil:nodeToElem
ent($articleNode)"/>
    <xsl:value-of select="element:removeAttribute($articleElement,
'section')"/>
    <xsl:value-of select="element:setAttribute($articleElement,
'section', 'TECHNOLOGY')"/>
```

```
    <xsl:variable name="titleNodeList" select="element:getElementsByTag
Name($articleElement, 'title')"/>
    <xsl:variable name="titleNode" select="nodelist:
item($titleNodeList, 0)"/>
    <xsl:variable name="titleTextNode" select="node:getFirstChild($tit
leNode)"/>
    <xsl:value-of select="node:setNodeValue($titleTextNode, 'Oracle
Database 11g Redux')"/>

    <xsl:variable name="authorNodeList" select="element:getElementsByTa
gName($articleElement, 'author')"/>
    <xsl:variable name="authorNode" select="nodelist:
item($authorNodeList, 0)"/>
    <xsl:variable name="authorTextNode" select="node:getFirstChild($au
thorNode)"/>
    <xsl:value-of select="node:setNodeValue($authorTextNode, 'Tom
Kyte')"/>

    <xsl:variable name="outputFile" select="file:new('catalog-modified.
xml')"/>
    <xsl:variable name="fileOutputStream" select="outputStream:
new($outputFile)"/>
    <xsl:variable name="xmlPrintDriver" select="printDriver:new($fileOu
tputStream)"/>
    <xsl:value-of select="printDriver:setEncoding($xmlPrintDriver,
'utf-8')"/>
    <xsl:value-of select="printDriver:printDocument($xmlPrintDriver,
$parsedDocument)"/>
    <xsl:value-of select="printDriver:close($xmlPrintDriver)"/>

 </xsl:template>

</xsl:stylesheet>
```

Next, we shall run the XSLT stylesheet containing the XSLT extension function in JDeveloper. Copy the `parser.xsl` listing to the `parser.xsl` in the JDeveloper extension functions project.

Processing the extension functions

We shall use the same `XSLTransform.java` application that we used in the previous section to transform an XML document to an HTML document. Copy the `XSLTransform` class from the previous section to the `XSLTransform` class in the `XSLTExtensions` project in the **Application Navigator**. Modify the `XSLTTransform.java` application to specify `parser.xsl` as the input XML file and `parser.xsl` as the stylesheet. Another XML file may be specified as the input XML file, because the transformation does not require an input XML file to be named. Normally, the input XML file is the file the stylesheet will process; however, because this sample stylesheet doesn't use a source XML document, the input file is irrelevant. Still, it's required, and it has to be a valid file, therefore use the stylesheet file again. In this case, the transformation will transform identically, regardless of which file you use for the input file.

```
File stylesheet = new File("parser.xsl");
File xmlFile = new File("parser.xsl");
```

Also modify the `StreamResult` object, which specifies the output from the transformation. Specify the output file as `catalog-modified.xml`.

```
StreamResult result = new StreamResult(new File(
"catalog-modified.xml"));
```

To run **XSLTransform.java**, right-click on the application node and select **Run**. The example XML document gets modified using the XSLT extension functions. Select **View | Refresh** to add the `catalog-modified.xml` to the `XSLTExtensions` project in the **Application Navigator**. The outputted XML document is shown in the following illustration:

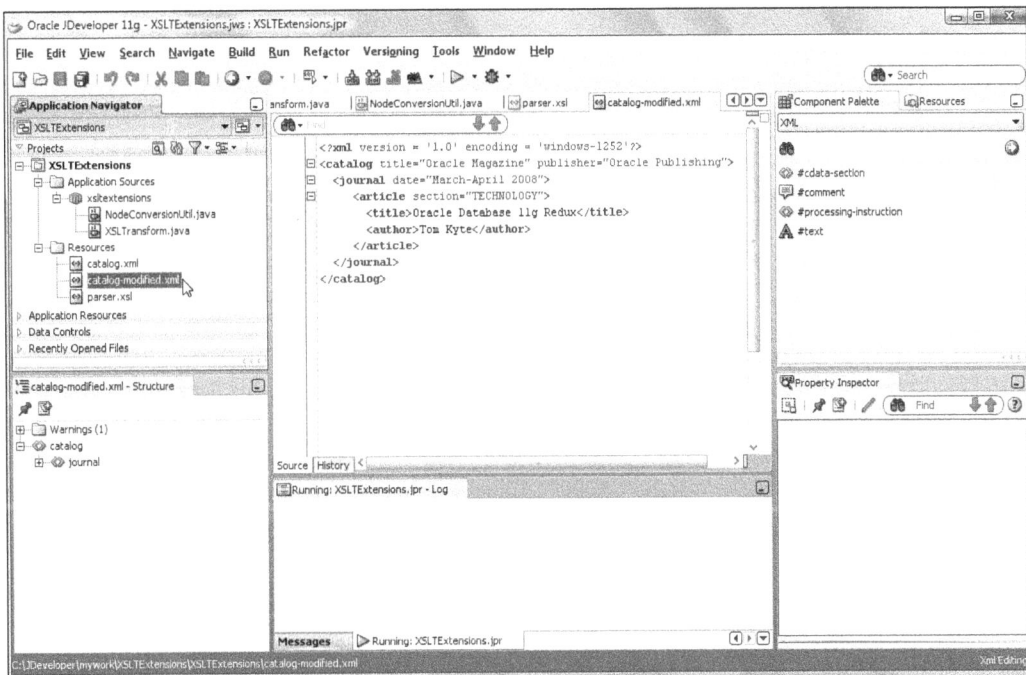

In this section, you learned how to add additional functionality to an XSLT stylesheet by loading an XML file and altering its contents using Java class methods from within the XSLT stylesheet itself, using the XSLT extension functions to call the Java class methods from the XSLT stylesheet.

We discussed two implementations of XSLT in the Packt Publishing book *JDBC 4.0 and Oracle JDeveloper for J2EE Development*. In the JDBC 4.0 book we discussed XSQL in which an XSLT stylesheet was used to transform XML output generated with XSQL to HTML. We also discussed the XML SQL Utility (included in XDK). In it we used an XSLT stylesheet to transform an XML document with attributes to another XML document without attributes for storage in an Oracle database. We also used an XSLT stylesheet to transform an XML document without attributes, generated from the database using the XML SQL Utility, to an XML document with attributes. The XSQL and XML SQL Utility chapters from the JDBC 4.0 book are not required for this chapter. But, if you want to learn about other implementations of XSLT in XDK and JDeveloper, refer to the XSQL and XML SQL Utility chapters in the *JDBC 4.0 and Oracle JDeveloper for J2EE Development* book.

Summary

In this chapter, XSLT support in JDeveloper 11g was discussed. An example XML document was transformed into an HTML document using the TrAX API. The application of XSLT extension functions was demonstrated by parsing and modifying an XML document. The XSLT extension functions add the provision to invoke Java class methods in an XSLT stylesheet. To wrap up, you can use XSLT extension functions to extend the library of functions that XSLT provides. You can store the return values of XSLT extension functions in XSLT variables to use them in your stylesheets. Although—for demonstration purposes—this sample doesn't reflect the rule, you should normally use XSLT extension functions only if the XSLT doesn't provide the required functionality.

In the next chapter you will learn about processing XML with the JSTL XML tag library in JDeveloper.

6
JSTL XML Tag Library

Tag libraries are used to include custom actions in a JSP page. The **JavaServer Pages Standard Tag Library (JSTL)** tag library provides XML tags for processing an XML document. JSTL 1.2 requires a JSP container that supports (at least) Servlet specification 2.5 and JSP specification 2.1. JSTL 1.2 XML support is included in JDeveloper 11g. JSTL 1.2 XML tags may be selected from a **Component Palette** and added to a JSP page to include XML processing in a JSP page. In this chapter we shall develop a web application in JDeveloper 11g to parse an XML document, and transform the XML document with an XSLT stylesheet using the JSTL XML tag library in a JSP page. The JSTL XML 1.2 tag library may also be used in a JSF page as the JSTL 1.2 version aligns the JSP and JSF specifications with support for the Unified Expression Language.

Overview of the JSTL XML tag library

In this section we shall discuss the XML tags in the JSTL XML tag library. We will use some of the tags in a subsequent section in a JSTL XML example application. The JSTL XML tag library provides various tags for parsing an XML document, selecting nodes in an XML document with XPath, iterating over document nodes, and transforming an XML document. The JSTL XML tag library URI is `http://java.sun.com/jsp/jstl/xml`. The syntax for including the JSTL XML tag library in a JSP page is the following `taglib` directive:

```
<%@ taglib prefix="x" uri="http://java.sun.com/jsp/jstl/xml" %>
```

The different tags in the JSTL XML tag library are discussed in the table that follows. All of the attributes are of type `java.lang.String`, except the `begin`, `end`, and `step` attributes in the `forEach` tag, which are of type `int`, and attributes are not required unless specified to be required.

Tag Name	Description	Attributes
parse	Parses an XML document and saves the resulting object in the specified var attribute variable. The XML document may be specified with the doc attribute or in the body of the tag.	`var` — Scoped variable for parsed XML document. The type of the scoped variable is implementation based. `varDom` — Scoped variable for parsed XML document of type `org.w3c.dom.Document`. `scope` — Scope for var. The scope value may be one of page, request, session and application, the standard scopes defined in the JSP specification (`https://cds.sun.com/is-bin/INTERSHOP.enfinity/WFS/CDS-CDS_JCP-Site/en_US/-/USD/ViewFilteredProducts-SimpleBundleDownload`). `scopeDom` — Scope of varDom. `doc` — Source XML document to be parsed. The XML document is specified as a URL. In the example JSTL XML application in a later section we create a variable for the source XML document specified as a relative URL.
transform	Transforms an XML document with a XSLT stylesheet. The XML document may be specified using the doc attribute or in the tag body.	`var` — Exported scoped variable for transformed XML document. The type of the variable is `org.w3c.dom.Document`. By default (if var is not specified) the result of the transformation is output to the page. `scope` — Scope for variable. `result` — Result object that is a holder of the transformation result tree . The type of result is `javax.xml.transform.Result`. `doc` — Source XML document to be transformed specified as a URL. `xslt` — Transformation stylesheet as a String, Reader, or Source object. Reader or Source objects may be specified with expressions that evaluate to a Reader or a Source object. The URL for the stylesheet may also be specified in xslt. `docSystemId` — The system identifier (URI) for parsing the XML document to be transformed. Only one of doc or `docSystemId` may be specified. `xsltSystemId` — The system identifier (URI) for the stylesheet. Only one of xslt or `xsltSystemId` may be specified.

Tag Name	Description	Attributes
param	Specifies parameter for the transform tag. Must be nested within the transform tag. Param value may be set using the value attribute or in the body of the tag.	name (required)-Name of parameter. value – Value of parameter. For a further explanation of XSLT parameters refer to the *W3C Recommendation for XSLT* (http://www.w3.org/TR/xslt).
set	Evaluates an XPath expression and stores result in a variable.	var (required) – Exported scoped variable to store the result of the XPath expression evaluation. var is of the type the XPath expression evaluates to. select – XPath expression to be evaluated in the context of the parsed XML document. scope-Scope of var.
out	Outputs the value of an XPath expression.	select (required) – XPath expression to be evaluated in the context of the parsed document. escapeXml – Specifies if characters <, >, ', " in the result tree should be converted to their corresponding character encoding codes. Default is true.
if	Conditional tag that evaluates the content in the body of the tag if an XPath expression evaluates to true.	select (required) – XPath expression that evaluates to a Boolean. var – Exported scoped variable for the result of evaluating the XPath expression. Variable type is Boolean. scope – Scope of var.
forEach	XML iteration tag	var – Exported scoped variable for current item of iteration. Its type is based on the result of the XPath expression in the select attribute. select(required)-XPath expression to be evaluated. begin – Index with which to begin iteration. The first item index is 0. If begin is omitted the iteration starts from index 0. end – Index with which to end iteration. If end is omitted the iteration ends at the last item in the collection. step – Iteration increment. The default value of step is 1.

Tag Name	Description	Attributes
choose	Conditional tag for conditional operations. The choose tag contains 1 or more 'when' subtags and 1 'otherwise' subtag. The tag content of the first 'when' subtag, whose XPath expression, specified in the 'select' attribute of the 'when' tag, evaluates to true, is evaluated. The tag content in the 'otherwise' tag is evaluated if the XPath expression in the 'select' attribute of none of the 'when' tags evaluates to true.	
when	Subtag of `<choose/>`. Conditional tag that processes the content in the body of the tag if its test condition evaluates to true. Only the tag content of the first 'when' tag whose test expression evaluates to true is included.	select (required) — XPath expression, which evaluates to a Boolean.
otherwise	Subtag of `<choose/>` that follows `<when/>` tags and processes the tag content only if test expressions in none of the `<when/>` tags evaluate to true.	

Setting the environment

In this section we shall discuss the preliminary setup required for the JSTL XML tag library. In JDeveloper create an application for the JSTL XML tag library. Select **File | New**. In the **New Gallery** window select **General** in the **Categories** list and **Generic Application** in the **Items** list. Click on **OK**. In the **Create Generic Application** window specify an **Application Name**, JSTLXML for example, and click on **Finish**. An application and a project node get added to the **Application Navigator**. We need to delete the default project because we shall be adding a **Web Project** to the application. Select the project node in the **Application Navigator** and select **Edit | Delete**. Select **File | New** to add a **Web project** to the JSTLXML application. In **Categories** select **General | Projects** and then select **Web Project** in the **Items** listed. Click on the **OK** button.

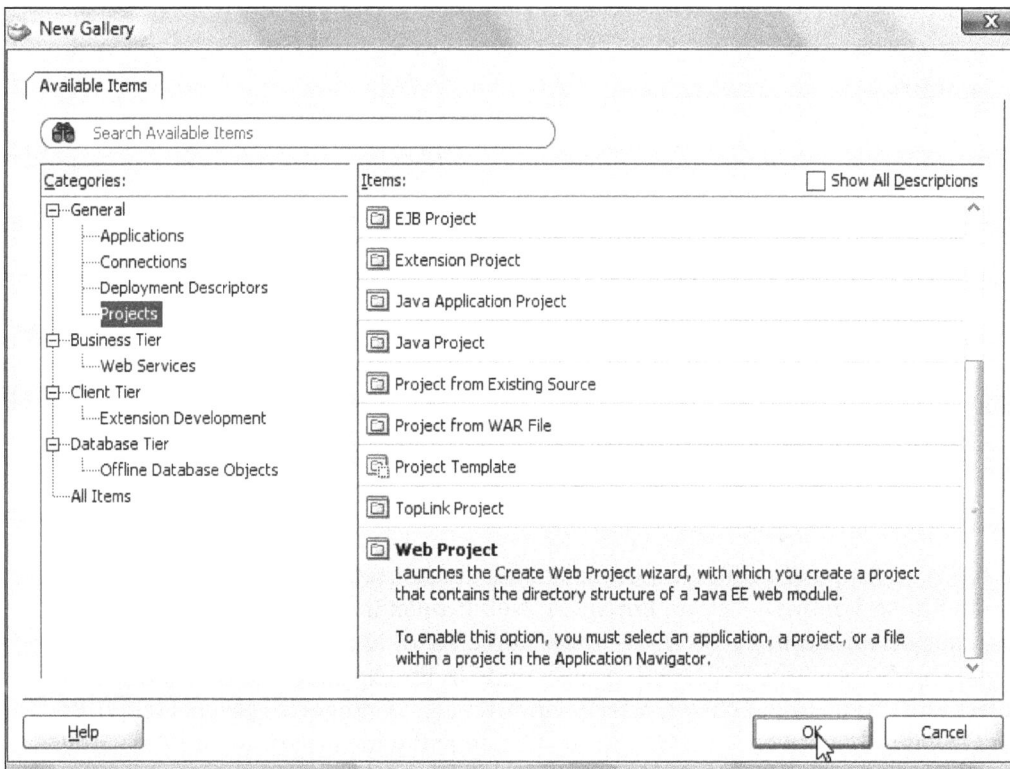

In the **Create Web Project** window, click on **Next**. In the **Location** window specify a **Project Name**, JSTLXML for example, and click on **Next**. In the **Web Application** window, select **Web Application Version** as **Java EE 1.5** and click on **Next**. In the **Page Flow Technology** window select **None** and click on **Next**. In the **Tag Libraries** window, select the **JSTL XML 1.2** and **JSTL Core 1.2** tag libraries and click on **Next**.

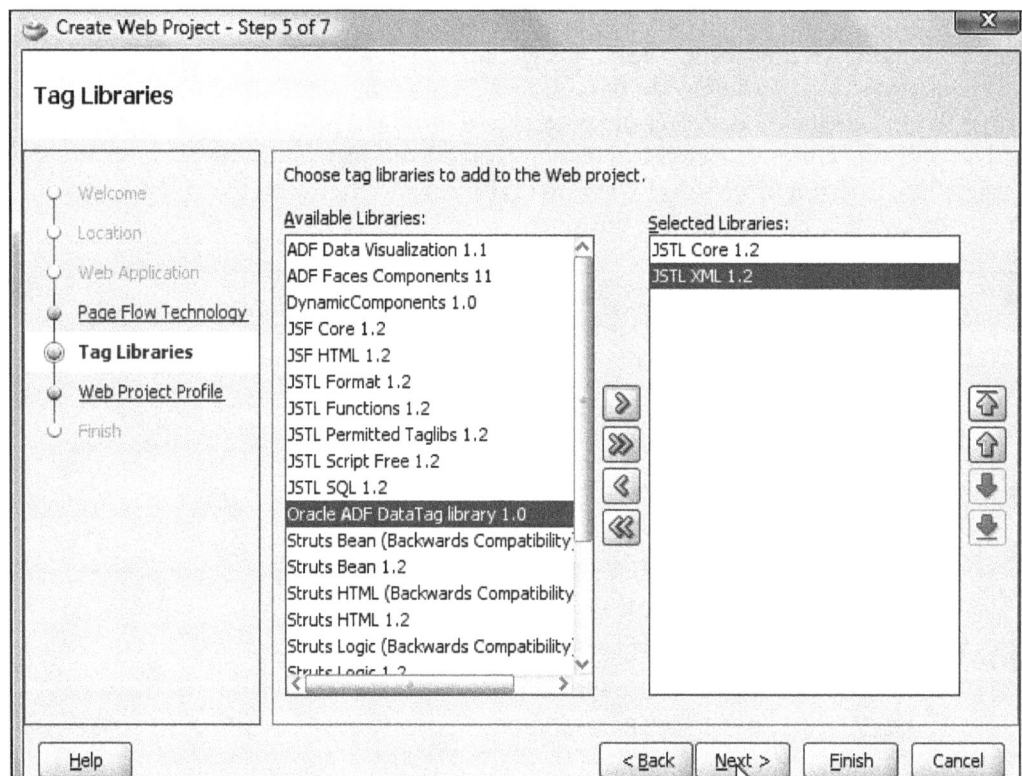

In the **Web Project Profile** window select the default settings and click on **Next**. In the **Finish** window click on **Finish**. A **Web Project** including a WEB-INF/web. xml file gets added to the JSTLXML application. Next, we add a JSP page to the web project. Select the **JSTLXML** project node in the **Application Navigator** and select **File | New**. In the **New Gallery** window select **Categories | Web Tier | JSP** and **Items | JSP**, and click on **OK**. In the **Create JSP** window specify a **File Name**, parseXML.jsp, and click on **OK**. A JSP gets added to the project. Similarly, add a JSP transformXML.jsp. Create an XML document, catalog.xml, which is to be parsed with the JSTL XML tag library, with **File | New**. In the **New Gallery** window select **Categories | General | XML** and **Items | XML Document**, and click on **OK**. In the **Create XML File** window specify a **File Name**, catalog.xml, and click on **OK**. An XML document gets added in the **Resources** folder. Copy the following catalog.xml listing to the catalog.xml file in the JSTLXML project.

```
<?xml version="1.0" encoding="windows-1252" ?><catalog title="Oracle
Magazine" publisher="Oracle
Publishing" edition="March-April 2008">
<journal section="Oracle Developer">
  <article>
    <title>Declarative Data Filtering</title>
    <author>Steve Muench</author>
  </article>
 </journal>

<journal section="Technology">
  <article>
    <title>Oracle Database 11g Redux</title>
    <author>Tom Kyte</author>
  </article>
</journal>
</catalog>
```

Save catalog.xml to the public_html directory of the **JSTLXML** project with
File | Save As. Similarly create an XSL stylesheet, catalog.xsl, which is used for
transforming the XML document catalog.xml, with **File | New**. In the **New Gallery**
window select **Categories | General | XML** and **Items | XSL Style Sheet**, and click on
OK. In the **Create XSL File** window specify a **File Name**, catalog.xsl, and click on
OK. An XSL stylesheet gets added to the **Resources** folder. Save the stylesheet to the
public_html directory with **File | Save As**. The directory structure of the **JSTLXML**
application is shown as follows:

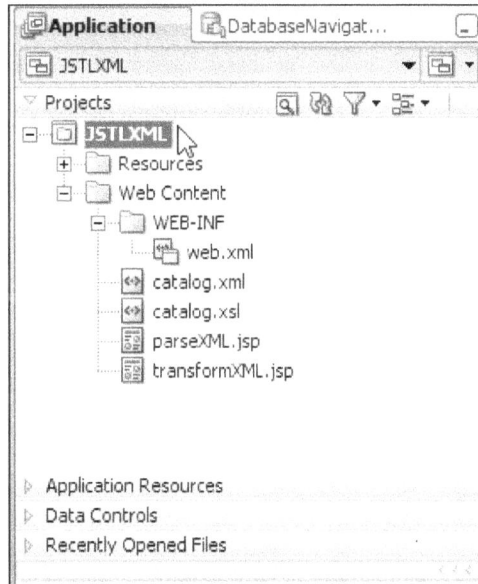

In JDeveloper's **Application Navigator** select the project node and select **Tools | Project Properties**. In the **Project Properties** window select **Libraries and Classpath**. The **JSTL 1.2** and **JSTL 1.2 Tags** libraries are in the **Classpath Entries** as we selected the JSTL XML 1.2 and JSTL Core 1.2 tag libraries when creating the web project. We also need to add an `Xalan-J` JAR file for some required classes from the Xalan-J. Download `xalan-j_2_7_1-bin.zip` from `http://www.apache.org/dyn/closer.cgi/xml/xalan-j` and extract the ZIP file to a directory. Add JAR file **xalan.jar** from the Xalan-J distribution to the project libraries with the **Add JAR/Directory** button. Click on **OK** in the **Project Properties** window. The project libraries are shown as follows:

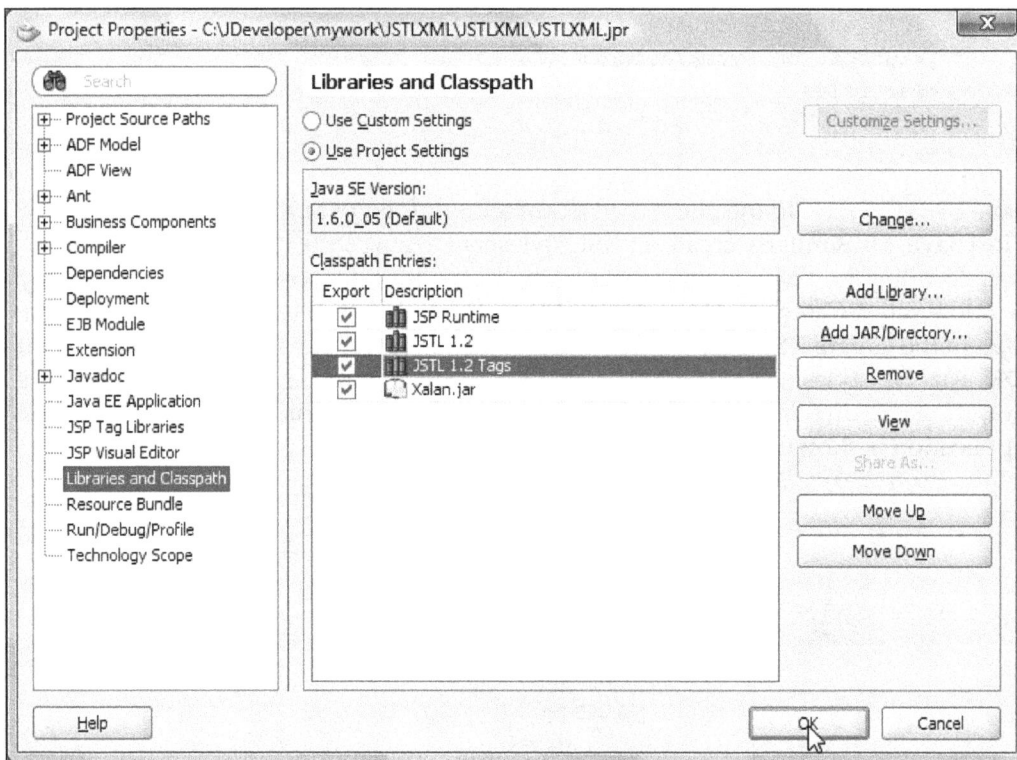

Parsing with the JSTL XML tag library

In this section, we shall parse an XML document using the JSTL 1.2 XML tag library. The example XML document, `catalog.xml`, was added to the JSTLXML project in the previous section.

The parsing application is developed in the `parseXML.jsp` JSP. Open `parseXML.jsp`. Next, import the XML document with the JSTL Core tag `c:import`. Select the **Design** view of **parseXML.jsp** and select **Import** in the **JSTL | Core Component Palette** in the **Design** view.

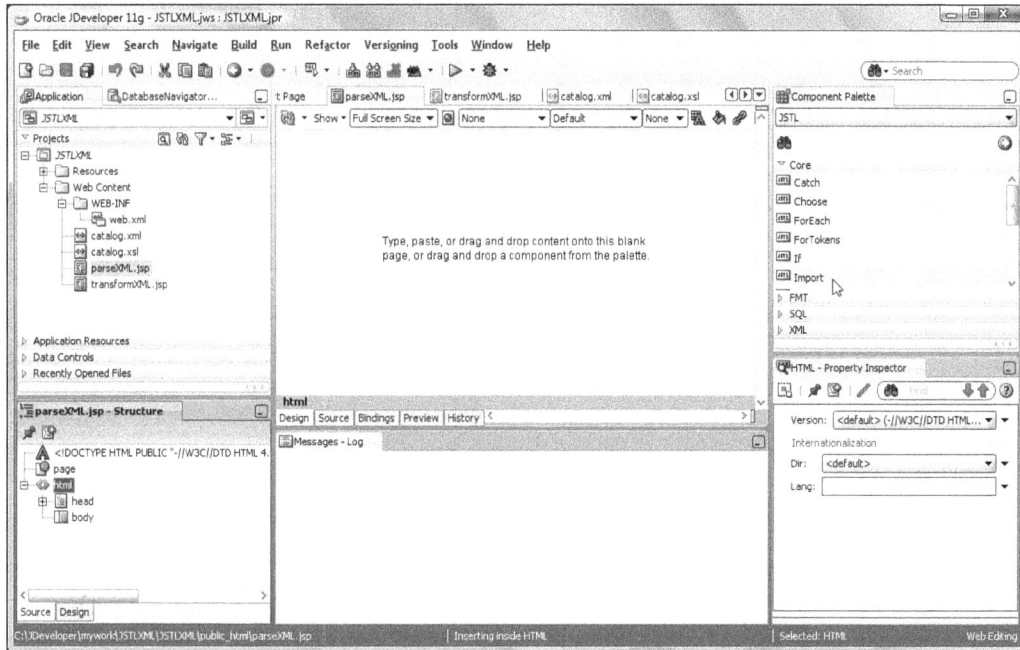

In the **Insert Import** window specify the **Url** for the XML document as **catalog.xml** and click on **OK**.

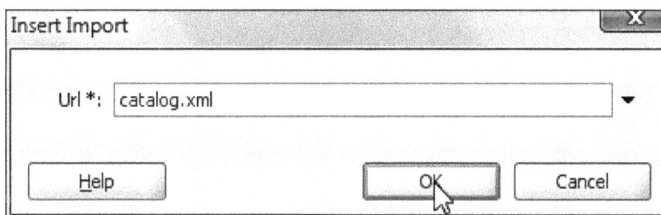

The **Import** tag gets added to the **Design** view. A corresponding `c:import` tag gets added to the **Source** view. Specify a variable name for the XML document imported using the **var** attribute of the **Import** tag in the **Property Inspector**.

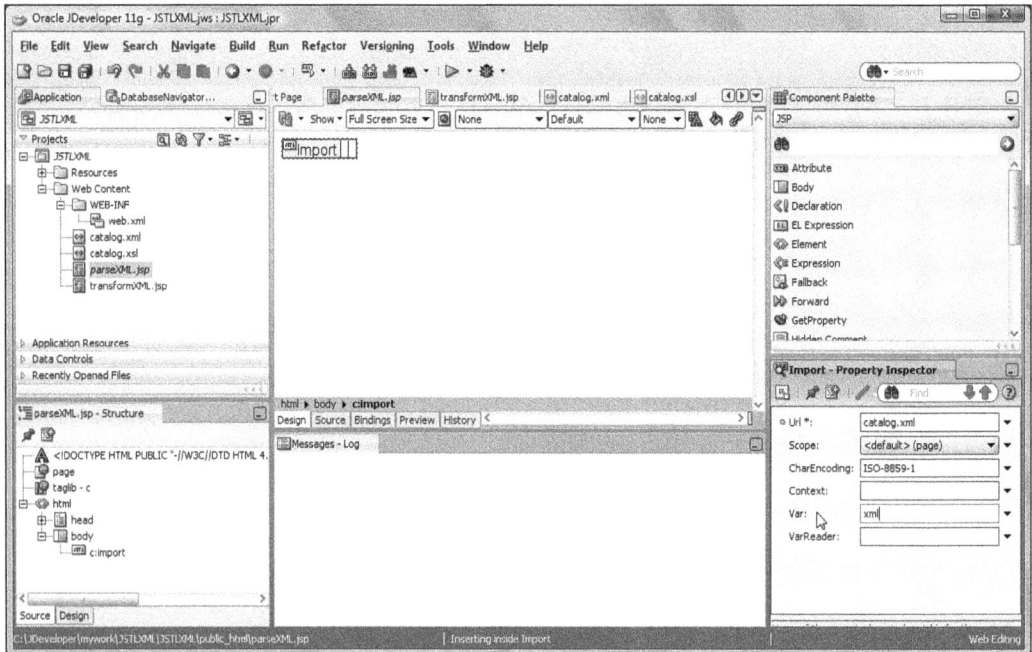

The following `c:import` tag gets added to `parseXML.jsp`:

```
<c:import var="xml" url="catalog.xml"/>
```

The following `taglib` directive for the JSTL Core tag library also gets added to the `parseXML.jsp`:

```
<%@ taglib uri="http://java.sun.com/jsp/jstl/core"
prefix="c"%>
```

Parse the XML document with the JSTL XML `parse` tag. Add the `parse` tag to `parseXML.jsp` after the `c:import` tag from the **JSTL | XML Component Palette** or from the **Design** view menu. To add the `parse` tag from the **Design** view menu right-click in the **Import** tag and select **Insert after Import | JSTL 1.2 XML | Parse**.

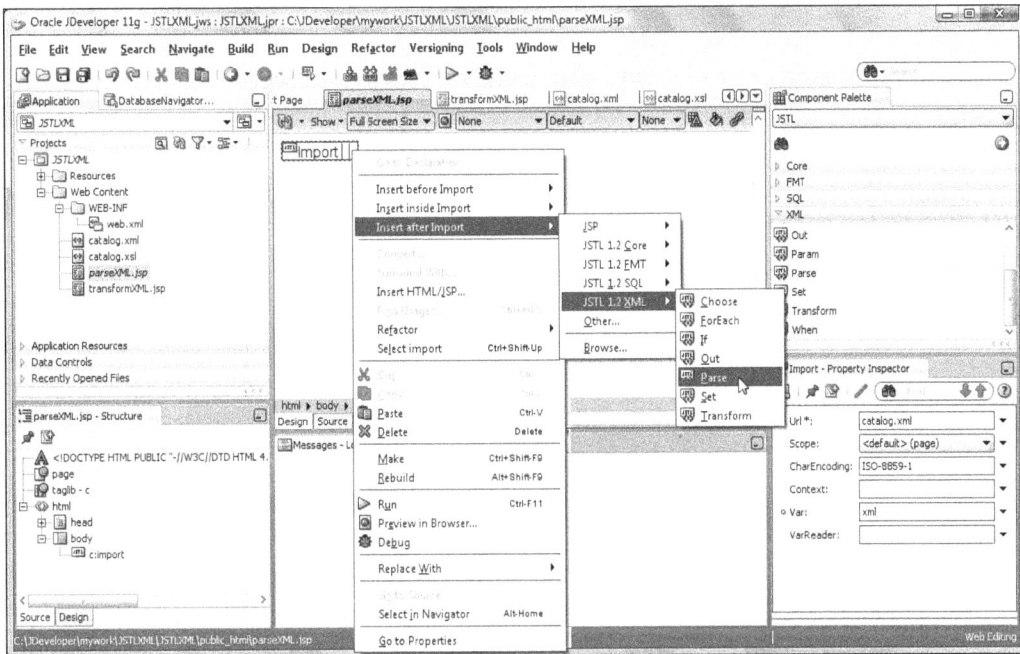

A **Parse** tag gets added after the **Import** tag. The following `taglib` directive for the JSTL XML tag library gets added to the `parseXML.jsp`:

```
<%@ taglib uri="http://java.sun.com/jsp/jstl/xml"
prefix="x"%>
```

In the **Property Inspector** specify the value for the var attribute as xmlDocument. The Property Inspector may be shifted below the JSP. The value for the doc attribute may be specified using an **Expression Builder**. Select the **Expression Builder** from the **Doc** attribute drop-down menu.

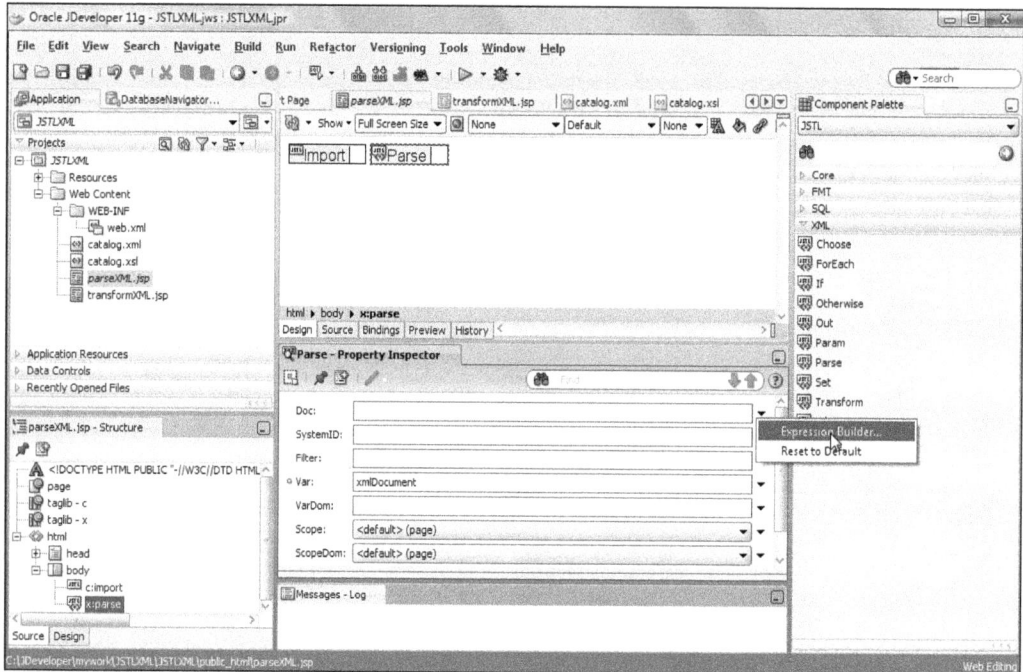

In the **Expression Builder** select the **xml** variable that was created using the c:import tag. Click on **OK**.

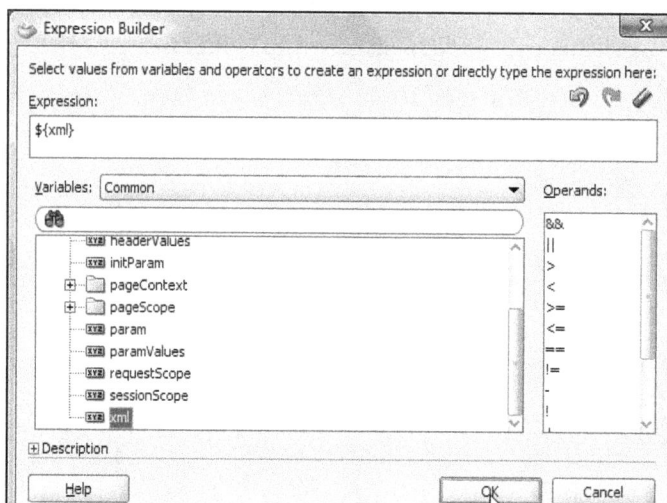

The value for the **Doc** attribute gets specified as **${xml}**.

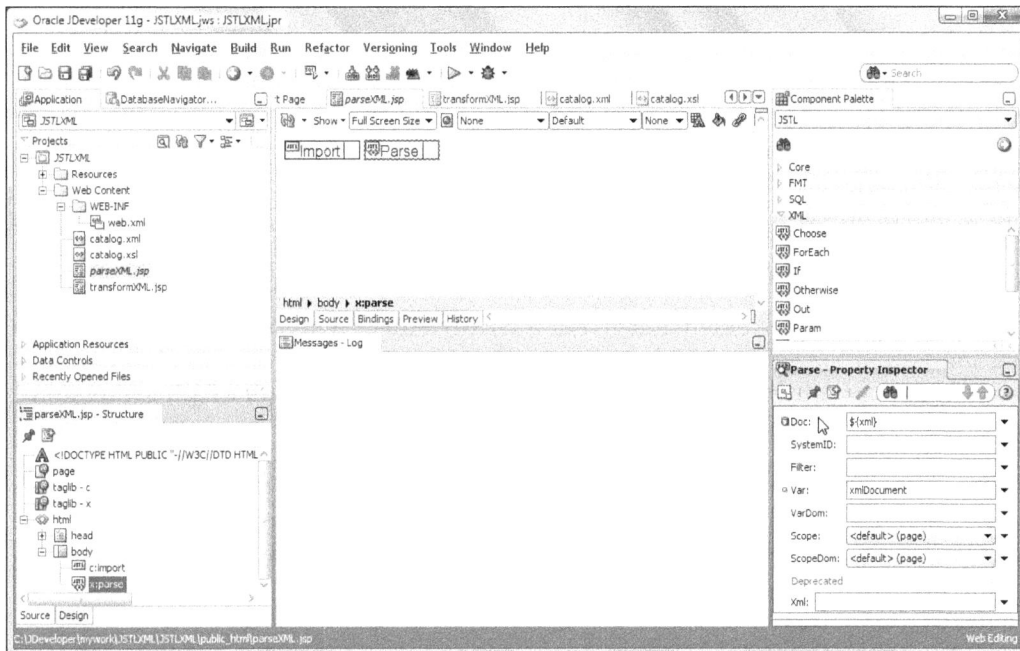

The x:parse tag, which is used to parse an XML document is listed as follows:

```
<x:parse var="xmlDocument" doc="${xml}"/>
```

Alternatively, an XML document may be parsed by specifying the XML document as tag content of the parse tag.

```
<x:parse var="xmlDocument">
<catalog title="Oracle Magazine" publisher="Oracle
Publishing" edition="March-April 2008">
<journal section="Oracle Developer">
  <article>
    <title>Declarative Data Filtering</title>
    <author>Steve Muench</author>
  </article>
 </journal>

<journal section="Technology">
  <article>
    <title>Oracle Database 11g Redux</title>
    <author>Tom Kyte</author>
  </article>
</journal>
</catalog>
```

If an XML document is specified in the doc attribute and also in the body of the parse tag, the XML document in the doc attribute is used.

Similarly add the other JSTL tags from the **Component Palette** (We won't be showing the JSTL Component Palette for each of the tag additions.) Set a variable corresponding to the root element, catalog, with the JSTL XML tag set. The select attribute of the set tag, just like the select attribute of other tags, takes an XPath expression as its input. Expression language is not supported in attribute select. The XPath expression $xmlDocument/catalog selects the root element catalog.

```
<x:set var="catalog" select="$xmlDocument/catalog"/>
```

Iterate over the journal elements in the XML document with the JSTL XML forEach tag and output the values of the attributes and element text with the JSTL XML out tag. The select attributes of the forEach tag and out tag take an XPath expression as input.

In the following code listing, the XPath expression $catalog/journal selects a journal node. The XPath expression @title selects the title attribute of a journal element. The XPath expression article/@section selects the section attribute of the article element. The XPath expression article/title selects the title element text.

```
<x:forEach select="$catalog/journal">
<b>Catalog Title: <x:out select="../@title"/></b><br/>
Catalog Publisher: <x:out select="../@publisher"/> <br/>
Catalog Edition: <x:out select="../@edition"/><br/>
Journal Section: <x:out select="@section"/><br/>
Article Title: <x:out select="article/title"/><br/>
Article Author: <x:out select="article/author"/><br/><br/>
</x:forEach>
```

The JSTL XML if tag may be used to test a Boolean condition. For example, in the following code listing the select attribute XPath expression tests if the edition attribute of the catalog element is March-April 2008.

```
<x:if select="$catalog/@edition='March-April 2008'">
Edition: March-April 2008
</x:if>
```

The JSTL XML choose tag, with the when and otherwise subtags, is used for conditional outputs. The choose tag specifies the context of a conditional selection. If the Boolean expression in a when tag evaluates to true the when tag is run, otherwise the otherwise tag is run. More than one when tag instances may be specified followed by one otherwise tag. If any of the when tags' test conditions evaluates to true the content in the body of the tag is processed. Only one when tag, the first when tag with test condition evaluating to true, is included. If none of the when tags' test conditions evaluates to true the otherwise tag is processed. In the following example, if the section attribute in the second journal element is Technology, output is Title: Oracle Database 11g Redux, otherwise the output is Title: Declarative Data Filtering.

```
<x:choose>
<x:when select="$catalog/journal[2]/@section='Technology'">
Title: Oracle Database 11g Redux
</x:when>

<x:otherwise>
Title: Declarative Data Filtering
</x:otherwise>
</x:choose>
```

JSP parseXML.jsp is listed below. If the parseXML.jsp you created by selecting JSTL components from the **Component Palette** does not match the listing, copy the listing to parseXML.jsp in JDeveloper project JSTLXML.

```
<!DOCTYPE HTML PUBLIC "-//W3C//DTD HTML 4.01 Transitional//EN"
"http://www.w3.org/TR/html4/loose.dtd">
<%@ page contentType="text/html;charset=windows-1252"%>
<%@ taglib uri="http://java.sun.com/jsp/jstl/core" prefix="c"%>
<%@ taglib uri="http://java.sun.com/jsp/jstl/xml" prefix="x"%>
<html>
  <head>
    <meta http-equiv="Content-Type" content=
    "text/html;charset=windows-1252"/>
    <title>parseXML</title>
  </head>
  <body>
    <c:import var="xml" url="catalog.xml"/>
    <x:parse var="xmlDocument" doc="${xml}"/>
    <x:set var="catalog" select="$xmlDocument/catalog"/>
    <x:forEach select="$catalog/journal">
      <b>Catalog Title:
        <x:out select="../@title"/></b>
      <br/>
      Catalog Publisher:
      <x:out select="../@publisher"/>
      <br/>
      Catalog Edition:
      <x:out select="../@edition"/>
      <br/>
      Journal Section:
      <x:out select="@section"/>
      <br/>
      Article Title:
```

```
      <x:out select="article/title"/>
      <br/>
      Article Author:
      <x:out select="article/author"/>
      <br/>
      <br/>
    </x:forEach>
    <x:if select="$catalog/@edition='March-April 2008'">Edition:
    March-April 2008</x:if>
    <br/>
    <x:choose>
      <x:when select=
      "$catalog/journal[2]/@section='Technology'">Title: Oracle
      Database 11g Redux</x:when>
      <x:otherwise>Title: Declarative Data Filtering</x:otherwise>
    </x:choose>
  </body>
</html>
```

To run `parseXML.jsp` in JDeveloper, right-click on the **parseXML.jsp** node and select **Run**. The `parseXML.jsp` runs in the integrated WebLogic Server and the output gets displayed in the browser. The output from `parseXML.jsp` is shown as follows:

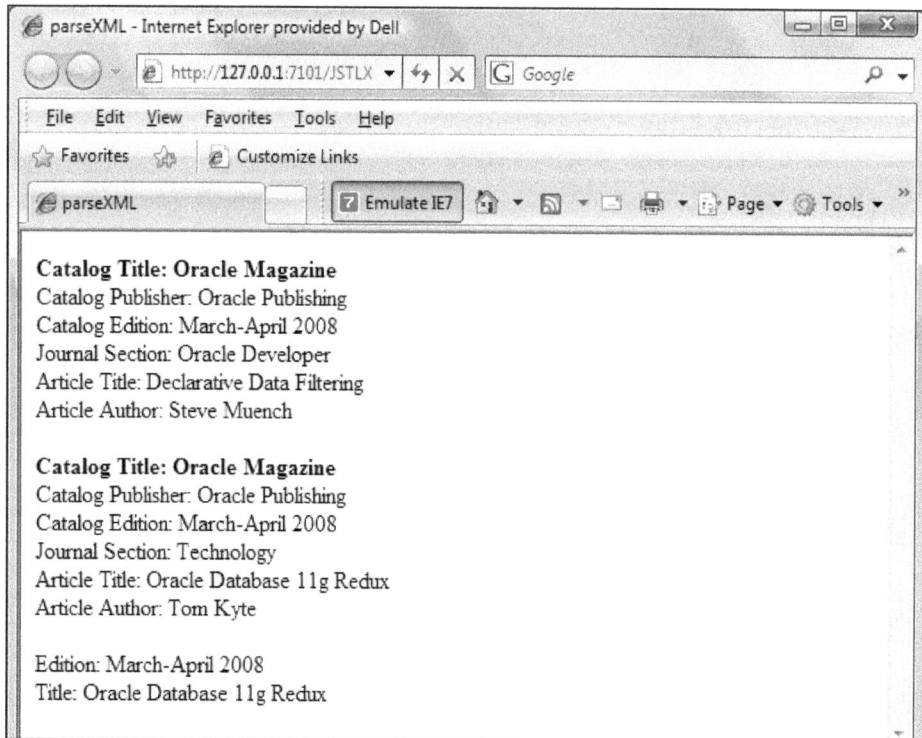

Transforming with the JSTL XML tag library

Next, we shall transform the XML document `catalog.xml` with an XSL stylesheet. We shall use stylesheet `catalog.xsl`, which we created in the *Setting the environment* section to convert the XML document to an HTML document. Stylesheet `catalog.xsl` is listed as follows:

```
<?xml version="1.0" encoding="windows-1252" ?><xsl:stylesheet
version="2.0" xmlns:xsl="http://www.w3.org/1999/XSL/Transform"><xsl:
output encoding="ISO-8859-1"  method="html" />
<xsl:template match="/catalog">
<html>
  <head>
    <title>Journal Catalog</title>
  </head>
  <body>
    <table border="1" cellspacing="0">
        <b><tr>
          <th>Journal</th>
          <th>Publisher</th>
          <th>Edition</th>
          <th>Section</th>
          <th>Title</th>
          <th>Author</th>
        </tr></b>
      <xsl:for-each select="journal">
        <tr>
        <td><xsl:value-of select="../@title"/></td>
        <td><xsl:value-of select="../@publisher"/></td>
        <td><xsl:value-of select="../@edition"/></td>
          <td><xsl:value-of select="@section"/></td>
        <td><xsl:value-of select="article/title"/></td>
        <td><xsl:value-of select="article/author"/></td>
        </tr>
      </xsl:for-each>
    </table>
  </body>
</html>
</xsl:template>
</xsl:stylesheet>
```

Copy the `catalog.xsl` listing to the `catalog.xsl` file in the **Application Navigator**. Open the `transformXML.jsp` and select the **Design** view. Import the XML document, `catalog.xml`, and stylesheet, `catalog.xsl`, with the JSTL Core tag **Import** from the **JSTL | Core Component Palette** as explained in the previous section for `catalog.xml`. Specify the value for the `var` attribute in the **Property Inspector** as explained in the previous section.

```
<c:import var="xml" url="catalog.xml"/>
<c:import var="xslt" url="catalog.xsl"/>
```

Transform the XML document with the stylesheet with the `transform` tag. Position the cursor after the **Import** tags and select the **Transform** tag from the **Component Palette**.

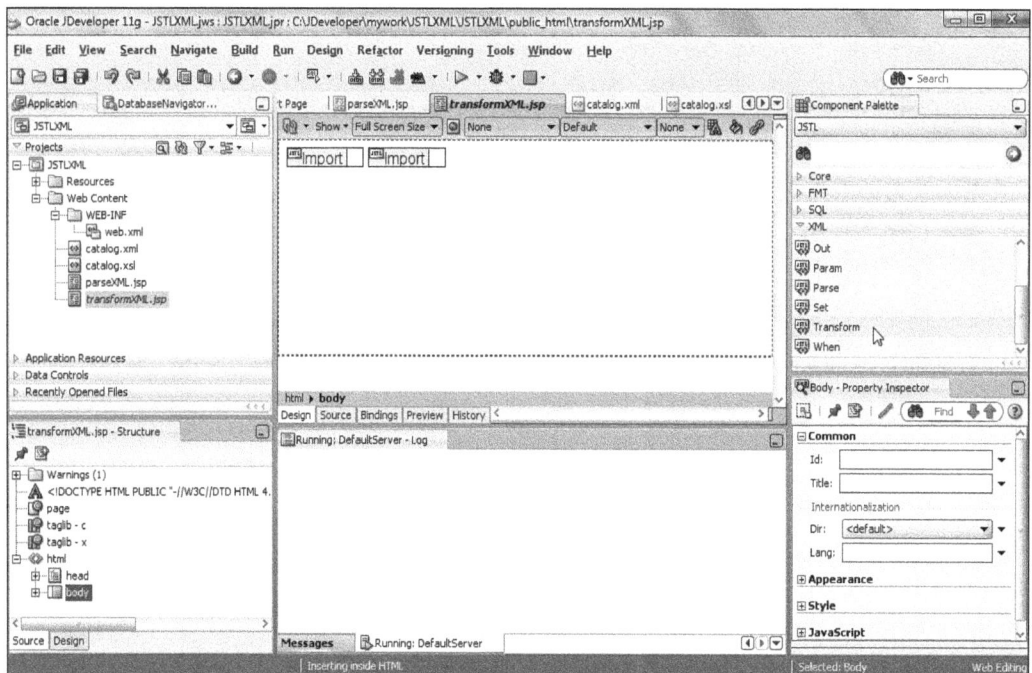

The `doc` attribute of the `transform` tag specifies the XML document to be transformed. Attribute `xslt` specifies the XSL stylesheet. In the **Property Inspector** specify the **Doc** attribute value using the **Expression Builder** as explained in the previous section. Similarly, specify the **Xslt** attribute value using the **Expression Builder**.

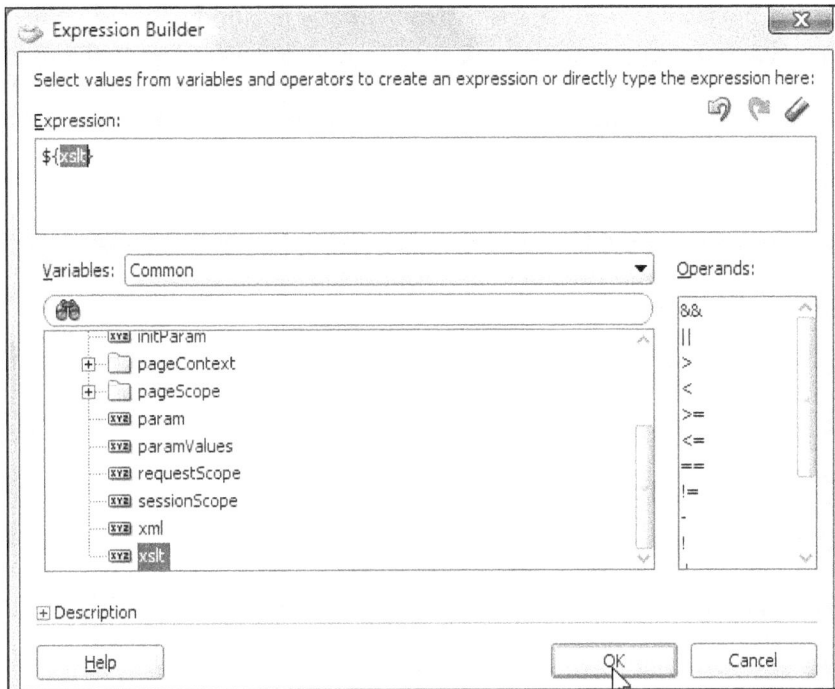

The **Transform** tag with the **Doc** and **Xslt** attributes set is shown as follows:

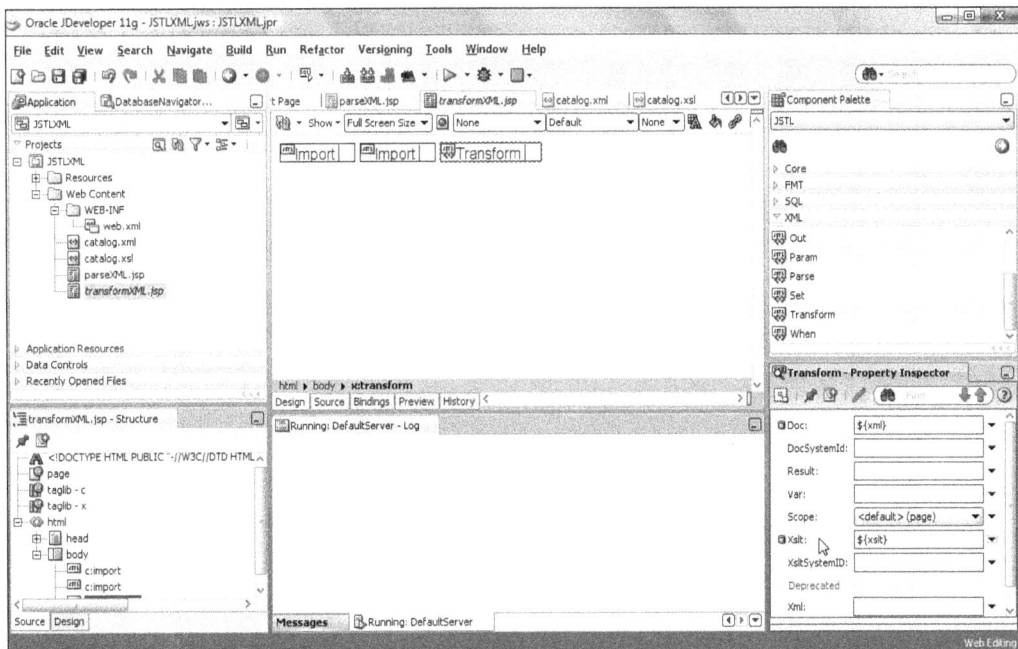

The x:transform tag in transformXML.jsp with the doc and xslt attributes is shown as follows:

```
<x:transform doc="${xml}"  xslt="${xslt}"/>
```

JSP transformXML.jsp is listed as follows:

```
<!DOCTYPE HTML PUBLIC "-//W3C//DTD HTML 4.01 Transitional//EN"
"http://www.w3.org/TR/html4/loose.dtd">
<%@ page contentType="text/html;charset=windows-1252"%>
<%@ taglib uri="http://java.sun.com/jsp/jstl/core" prefix="c"%>
<%@ taglib uri="http://java.sun.com/jsp/jstl/xml" prefix="x"%>
<html>
  <head>
    <meta http-equiv="Content-Type" content="text/html; charset=
    windows-1252"/>
    <title>transformXML</title>
  </head>
  <body>
    <c:import var="xml" url="catalog.xml"/>
    <c:import var="xslt"    url="catalog.xsl"/>
    <x:transform doc="${xml}"   xslt="${xslt}"/>
  </body>
</html>
```

If the transformXML.jsp you generated by selecting components from the JSTL **Component Palette** is different than the listing, copy the transformXML.jsp listing to the **transformXML.jsp** file in the **JSTLXML** project in **Application Navigator**. To run the transformation application, right-click on **transformXML.jsp** and select **Run**. The transformXML.jsp JSP runs in the integrated WebLogic Server and the XML document gets converted to an HTML document, shown as follows:

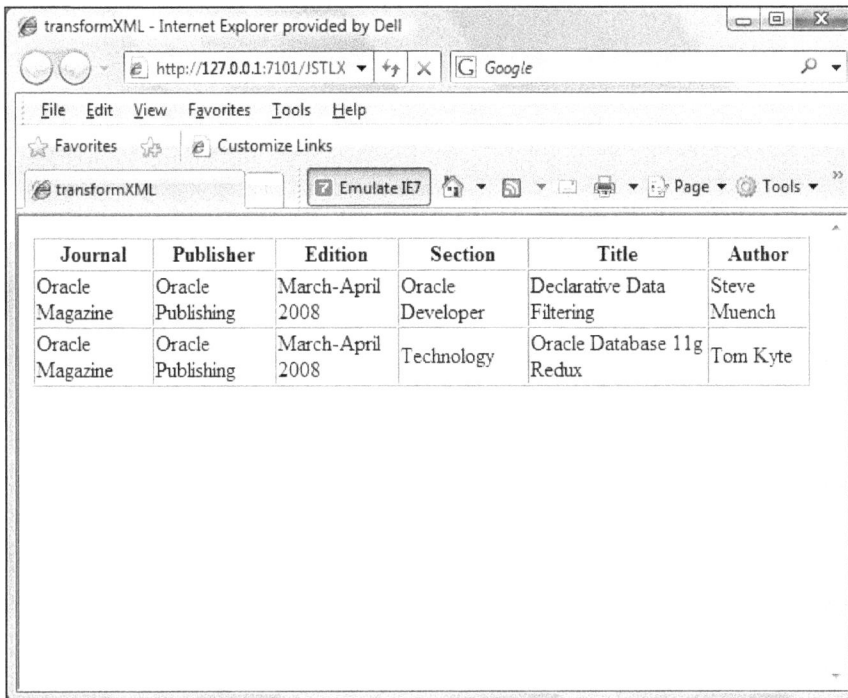

Journal	Publisher	Edition	Section	Title	Author
Oracle Magazine	Oracle Publishing	March-April 2008	Oracle Developer	Declarative Data Filtering	Steve Muench
Oracle Magazine	Oracle Publishing	March-April 2008	Technology	Oracle Database 11g Redux	Tom Kyte

Summary

In this chapter we discussed the JSTL XML tag library, support for which is built into JDeveloper 11g. We parsed an XML document using the JSTL XML tag library tags. Subsequently, we transformed the XML document into an HTML document using the JSTL XML tags for transformation. Use the JSTL XML tag library if XML processing is required in a web application. In the next chapter we will discuss the DOM 3.0 Load and Save API to load and save an XML document.

7
Loading and Saving XML with DOM 3.0 LS

The **Document Object Model (DOM)** Level 3 provides a new specification called the **DOM Level 3 Load** and **Save (LS)** specification for loading, saving, and filtering an XML document. For an introduction on the Document Object Model refer to http://www.w3.org/DOM/, and for an introduction on the various specifications included in the DOM refer to http://www.w3.org/DOM/Activity.

In this chapter we will explain the procedure for loading and saving an XML document with the DOM 3.0 Load and Save (LS) API. We will also discuss the filtering of an XML document. The Oracle XML Parser v2 library in JDeveloper 11g includes an implementation of the DOM Level 3 Load and Save specification. The DOM Level 3 LS specification is influenced by the **JAXP (Java APIs for XML Processing**; refer to https://jaxp.dev.java.net/) and **SAX** APIs (**Simple API for XML**; refer to http://www.saxproject.org/), which were discussed in Chapter 1.

The DOM Level 3 Load and Save API has the following advantages over the JAXP and SAX APIs:

- Event handling in loading: While SAX is an event-based API, the DOM API does not support event handling while loading a document, other than error event handling. The DOM Level 3 Load API supports event handling while loading. The loading process supports LSLoadEvent and LSProgressEvent event types. The LSProgressEvent notifies an application about progress as a document is parsed. LSLoadEvent notifies an application that the loading is complete. Event handling may be implemented by registering an event listener.

- Parsing with context: DOM 3.0 LS has the provision to replace a node in an XML document with an XML fragment from another resource.

- Saving selected nodes: With DOM 3.0 LS, a node in an XML document may be stored instead of the complete document. With the DOM API a `DocumentFragment` must be created from the section of the XML document to be saved.

- String output: A DOM document or a node may be outputted to a String, which can be required by certain web services.

- Filtering: An XML document may be filtered as it is parsed. A DOM document may be filtered as the document is saved to an XML document.

The DOM 3 Load and Save API may be used in applications that require the loading and saving of XML documents as in an XML Editor. The `LSLoadEvent` and `LSProgressEvent` may be used to display the loading status of an XML document in an XML Editor. Parsing with context may be used to build an XML document in an XML Editor with XML fragments from different resources. The DOM 3 Load and Save API may also be used to serialize an XML document to a String in web services.

Background

The **Document Object Model (DOM)** Level 1, Level 2, and Level 3 Core specifications of the **World Wide Web Consortium (W3C)** standard for XML define a platform- and language- neutral interface for programs and scripts to access and update the content and structure of an XML document. But, the DOM Core specifications don't define an interface for XML document loading and saving. This missing API is defined in the DOM Level 3 Load and Save specification. The DOM Level 3 Load and Save specification provides a standard mechanism for loading and saving (serializing) an XML document.

In the DOM Level 3 Load and Save specification (`http://www.w3.org/TR/DOM-Level-3-LS/`): "*This specification defines the Document Object Model Load and Save Level 3, a platform – and language – neutral interface that allows programs and scripts to dynamically load the content of an XML document into a DOM document and serialize a DOM document into an XML document.*"

The **Java APIs** for **XML Parsing (JAXP)** also provide a standard procedure to create a parser and load an XML document, but this is specific to the Java language. The DOM 3 Load and Save API may be implemented in any language including Java; we shall be discussing the Java implementation in this chapter. In addition to facilitating the loading and saving of an XML document, DOM 3 Load and Save provides event handling and filtering of XML documents, as the document is parsed or serialized. Previous to the DOM Level 3 Load and Save specification, XML document loading varied with the parser used to load and parse an XML document, a disadvantage to the portability of XML document parsing applications. With the

DOM Level 3 specification, the loading and saving mechanism is standardized. Loading an XML document implies parsing an XML document into a DOM object. Saving an XML document implies saving a DOM object to an XML document. Platform and language neutral implies that the specifications may be implemented on any platform and language (including scripting languages).

The API

The DOM 3.0 LS API is implemented in the `org.w3c.dom.ls` package. The `DOMImplementationLS` interface contains factory methods for creating Load and Save objects, which are `LSInput`, `LSOutput`, `LSParser`, and `LSSerialize`. The `LSParser` interface is used to parse input data and construct a DOM document structure. The input data may be in the form of a character stream, byte stream, string, public ID or system ID. The `LSInput` interface represents an input data source. The `LSParser` uses the `LSInput` object to parse input data from various types of input sources. `LSParser` scans input sources specified in the `LSInput` object in the following order and uses the first input source that is not null and not an empty string:

1. `LSInput.characterStream`

2. `LSInput.byteStream`

3. `LSInput.stringData`

4. `LSInput.systemId`

5. `LSInput.publicId`

The various input sources that may be specified are character stream, byte stream, string data, system identifier, and public identifier. The `LSParserFilter` interface is an interface to filter nodes as an XML document is parsed. The `LSResourceResolver` interface is used to resolve external resources such as entities. The `LSLoadEvent` interface indicates that an XML document has completed loading. The `LSProgressEvent` interface indicates the progress of document loading. Finally, the `LSSerializer` interface is used to save a DOM document or a document node as an XML document. The `LSSerializerFilter` interface is used to filter nodes as an XML document is saved.

Setting the environment

In this chapter we shall load, save, and filter an XML document using the DOM 3 Load and Save API. The example XML document, `catalog.xml`, is listed as follows:

```xml
<?xml version="1.0" encoding="windows-1252" ?><!--A Oracle Magazine
Catalog-->
<catalog publisher="Oracle Publishing" title="Oracle Magazine">
    <journal date="March-April 2008">
        <article section="Oracle Developer">
            <title>Declarative Data Filtering</title>
            <author>Steve Muench</author>
        </article>
    </journal>

    <journal date="May-June 2008">
        <article section="ORACLE DEVELOPER">
            <title>On the PGA and Indexing Collections</title>
            <author>Steven Feuerstein</author>
        </article>
    </journal>
</catalog>
```

We need to create a JDeveloper application (DOM3LS) and a project (DOM3LS) by selecting **File | New** and subsequently selecting **Categories | General** and **Items | Generic Application** in the **New Gallery** window. Add the Java classes `DOM3Builder.java`, `DOM3Writer.java`, and `DOM3Filter.java` to the JDeveloper project. Create a Java class by selecting **File | New** and subsequently selecting **Categories | General** and **Items | Java Class** in the **New Gallery** window. Create an XML document, `catalog.xml`, by selecting **File | New**, and **Categories | General | XML** and **Items | XML Document** in the **New Gallery** window. Copy the `catalog.xml` listing to the `catalog.xml` file in the **DOM3LS** project. The directory structure of the DOM 3 Load and Save application is shown in the following illustration:

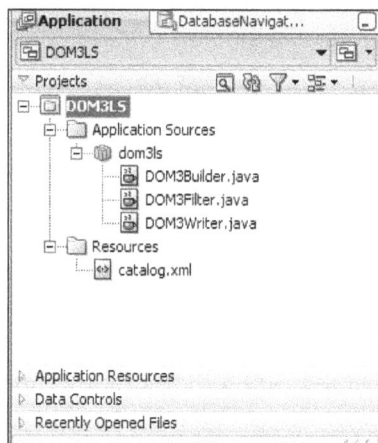

Add the **Oracle XML Parser v2** library to the project by selecting **Tools | Project Properties** and subsequently selecting **Libraries and Classpath** in the **Project Properties** window. Select **Add Library** to add the library.

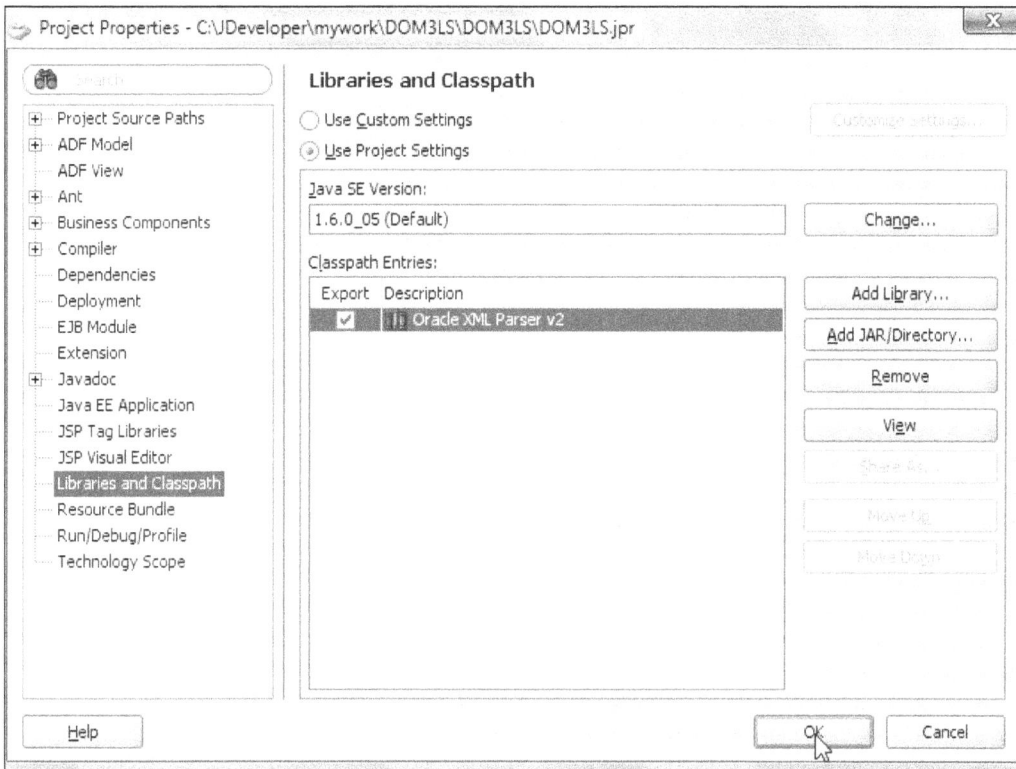

Loading an XML document

In this section, we shall load the example XML document `catalog.xml` using the DOM 3 Load and Save API. The `LSParser` interface in the `org.w3c.dom.ls` package is used to load an XML document, parse an XML document, and obtain a `Document` object. The document loaded by `LSParser` may also be validated with an XML Schema. The following code is the standard way to retrieve a DOM implementation, which can then be used to parse an XML document. Most of the code is simply used to initialize registries and properties so as to extract the final parser. First, we need to import the DOM 3.0 LS package.

```
import org. w3c.dom.ls.*;
```

Creating the LSParser

The `DOMImplementationLS` interface is used to create Load and Save objects, including the `LSParser` object. Create a `DOMImplementationLS` object by creating an instance of the `XMLDOMImplementation` class, which implements the `DOMImplementationLS` interface.

```
DOMImplementationLS domImpl = new XMLDOMImplementation();
```

The `DOMImplementationLS` interface provides methods to create Load and Save objects. Create an `LSParser` object using the `createLSParser(short mode,java.lang.String schemaType)` method.

```
LSParser parser = domImpl.createLSParser(DOMImplementationLS.MODE_
SYNCHRONOUS, null);
```

The `LSParser` mode may be set to `MODE_SYNCHRONOUS` or `MODE_ASYNCHRONOUS`. If the `LSParser` is set to `MODE_SYNCHRONOUS`, the `parse` and `parseURI` methods of the `LSParser` object return an object of type `org.w3c.dom.Document`. If the `LSParser` is set to `MODE_ASYNCHRONOUS`, the methods return `null`, as the document object may not yet be completely loaded when the `parse` or `parseURI` method returns.

Adding event handling

The `DOM3Builder.java` class implements the `EventListener` interface for event handling. To add event handling, register an event listener with the `LSParser` object. Firstly, create an `XMLLSParser` object from the `LSParser` by casting to `XMLLSParser`. The `XMLLSParser` class implements the `LSParser` interface and the `EventTarget` interface. Register an event listener with the `XMLLSParser` object using the `addEventListener(String eventType, EventListener listener, boolean useCapture)` method. `LSParser` supports the `ls-load` event type—the event that is generated after an XML document has been parsed by the `XMLLSParser` object.

```
XMLLSParser lsParser=(XMLLSParser)parser;
lsParser.addEventListener(
"ls-load", new DOM3Builder(), true);
```

Parsing the XML document

Store the XML document in a directory, for example `DOM3.0`, with **File | Save As**. We need to store `catalog.xml` in a directory because the `parseURI` method does not take relative URLs. Parse the XML document using the `parse(LSInput)` or `parseURI(String)` method.

```
Document document=lsParser.parseURI("file://c:/DOM3.0/catalog.xml");
```

The `DOM3Builder.java` class implements the `handleEvent(Event event)` method. An `LSLoadEvent` event is generated when loading of an XML document is complete. In the `handleEvent(Event event)` method, the XML document that generated the `LSLoadEvent` event may be retrieved using the `getNewDocument()` method of `LSLoadEvent`.

Next, we shall use the `parseWithContext(LSInput input, Node contextArg, short action)` method to replace a node in the XML document loaded with a node from another XML document. We have obtained the replacement XML fragment from another document, but the replacement XML fragment may be specified as any of the input sources supported by `LSInput`. As an example, let's replace the `journal` node for `May-June 2008` in `catalog.xml` with the `journal` node in the `replace-node.xml` document listed in the following listing, for which let's add an XML document, `replace-node.xml`, to the `DOM3LS` project.

```
<?xml version="1.0" encoding="windows-1252" ?>
<journal date="March-April 2008">
  <article section="Oracle Developer">
    <title>On BULK COLLECT</title>
    <author>Steven Feuerstein</author>
  </article>
</journal>
```

Copy the `replace-node.xml` listing to the `replace-node.xml` file in the `DOM3LS` project. Store `replace-node.xml` to the `DOM3.0` directory with **File | Save As**.

First, we shall select the `journal` node for the date `May-June 2008` in the XML document, `catalog.xml`, to be replaced with an XPath expression using the `selectSingleNode` method.

```
Node node=((XMLDocument)(document)).selectSingleNode("/catalog/
journal[@date='May-June 2008']");
```

Create an `LSInput` object for the XML document that contains the replacement node using the `createLSInput` method. Create a `URL` object for the `replace-node.xml` document and set the `URL` object converted to `String` on the `LSInput` object.

```
LSInput lsInput=impl.createLSInput();
URL url=new URL("file://c:/DOM3.0/replace-node.xml");
lsInput.setSystemId(url.toString ());
```

Replace the selected `journal` node in `catalog.xml` with the `journal` node in the `replace-node.xml` document using the `parseWithContext` method.

```
lsParser.parseWithContext(lsInput, node , LSParser.ACTION_REPLACE);
```

The LSParser interface supports various actions that are discussed in the following table:

LSParser Action	Description
ACTION_APPEND_AS_CHILDREN	Appends result of parse operation as children of context node, which is required to be an Element or DocumentFragment.
ACTION_REPLACE_CHILDREN	Replaces context node children with the result of the parse operation. Both element and attributes are replaced.
ACTION_INSERT_BEFORE	Inserts result of parse operation before context node.
ACTION_INSERT_AFTER	Inserts result of parse operation after context node.
ACTION_REPLACE	Replaces context node with result of parse operation.

Output the modified XML document with a XMLPrintDriver object. Create an XMLPrintDriver object using a FileOutputStream object. Set the output encoding using the setEncoding method. Output the modified XML document using the printDocument(XMLDocument) method. Close the XMLPrintDriver object after outputting the document using the close method.

```
XMLPrintDriver output=new XMLPrintDriver(new FileOutputStream(new
    File("catalog-modified.xml")));
output.setEncoding("utf-8");
output.printDocument((XMLDocument)document);
output.close();
```

DOM3Builder.java, the Java application that we used to load and replace the XML document, is listed as follows with explanations:

1. Add the package and import statements.

```
package dom3ls;
import org. w3c.dom.ls.*;
import org.w3c.dom.*;
import org.w3c.dom.events.Event;
import org.w3c.dom.events.EventListener;
import oracle.xml.parser.v2.*;
import java.net.URL;
import java.io.*;
```

2. Add the Java class DOM3Builder that implements the EventListener interface.

```
public class DOM3Builder implements EventListener{
```

3. Define a method `loadDocument` to load an XML document with the DOM 3.0 LS API.

```
public void loadDocument(){
    try{
```

4. Create an `LSParser` and set the event listener.

```
DOMImplementationLS domImpl = new
XMLDOMImplementation();
LSParser parser = domImpl.createLSParser
(DOMImplementationLS.MODE_SYNCHRONOUS, null);
XMLLSParser lsParser=(XMLLSParser)parser;
lsParser.addEventListener("ls-load", new
DOM3Builder(), true);
```

5. Parse the XML document and replace a node in the XML document.

```
Document document=lsParser.parseURI
("file://C:/DOM3.0/catalog.xml");
Node node=((XMLDocument)(document)).selectSingleNode
("/catalog/journal[@date='May-June 2008']");
LSInput lsInput=domImpl.createLSInput();
URL url=new URL("file://C:/DOM3.0/
replace-node.xml");
lsInput.setSystemId(url.toString());
lsParser.parseWithContext(lsInput, node ,
LSParser.ACTION_REPLACE);
System.out.println("XML Document Node has been replaced");
```

6. Output the XML document.

```
XMLPrintDriver output=new XMLPrintDriver(new
FileOutputStream(new
            File("catalog-modified.xml")));
            output.setEncoding("utf-8");
            output.printDocument((XMLDocument)document);
            output.close();
}
catch(IOException e){
  System.err.println("IOException "+e.getMessage());
  }
catch(DOMException e){
  System.err.println("DOMException "+e.getMessage());
  }
catch(XSLException e){
  System.err.println("XSLException "+e.getMessage());
  }
}
```

7. Implement the event handling method `handleEvent` from the `EventListener` interface.

```
public void handleEvent( Event event)
  {
  if(event instanceof LSLoadEvent){
  LSLoadEvent loadEvent=(LSLoadEvent)event;
  Document document=loadEvent.getNewDocument();
   System.out.println("XML Document with root element "+document.
getDocumentElement().getTagName()+ " has been loaded.");
  }
  }
```

8. Add the `main` method in which to create an instance of the class `DOM3Builder` and invoke the `loadDocument` method.

```
public static void main(String[] args){
DOM3Builder builder=new DOM3Builder();
builder.loadDocument();
  }
  }
```

9. Copy the listing to the `DOM3Builder.java` application in the **Application Navigator**. To run the `DOM3Builder.java` application, right-click on the **DOM3Builder.java** node in the **Application Navigator** and select **Run**.

The output from the `DOM3Builder.java` application indicates that the example XML document has been loaded and a node has been replaced.

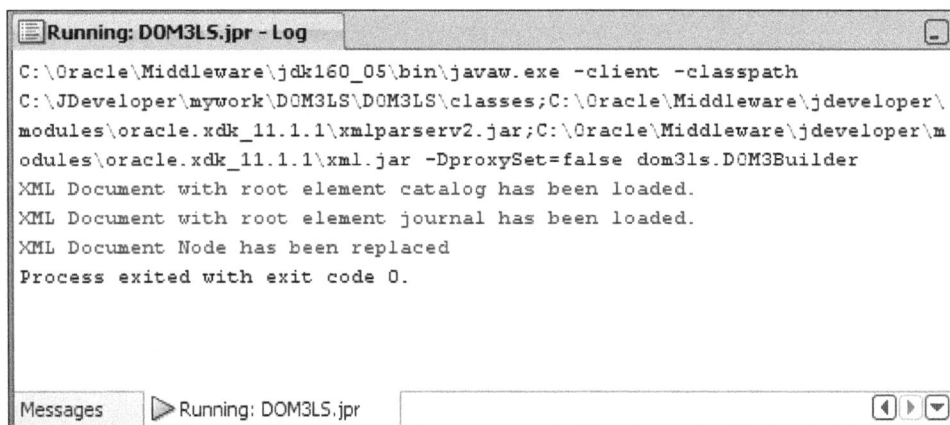

```
Running: DOM3LS.jpr - Log

C:\Oracle\Middleware\jdk160_05\bin\javaw.exe -client -classpath
C:\JDeveloper\mywork\DOM3LS\DOM3LS\classes;C:\Oracle\Middleware\jdeveloper\
modules\oracle.xdk_11.1.1\xmlparserv2.jar;C:\Oracle\Middleware\jdeveloper\m
odules\oracle.xdk_11.1.1\xml.jar -DproxySet=false dom3ls.DOM3Builder
XML Document with root element catalog has been loaded.
XML Document with root element journal has been loaded.
XML Document Node has been replaced
Process exited with exit code 0.

Messages     Running: DOM3LS.jpr
```

Select **View | Refresh** to add the `catalog-modified.xml` file to the **Application Navigator**. The `catalog-modified.xml` document shows that a `journal` node has been replaced with a node from another document.

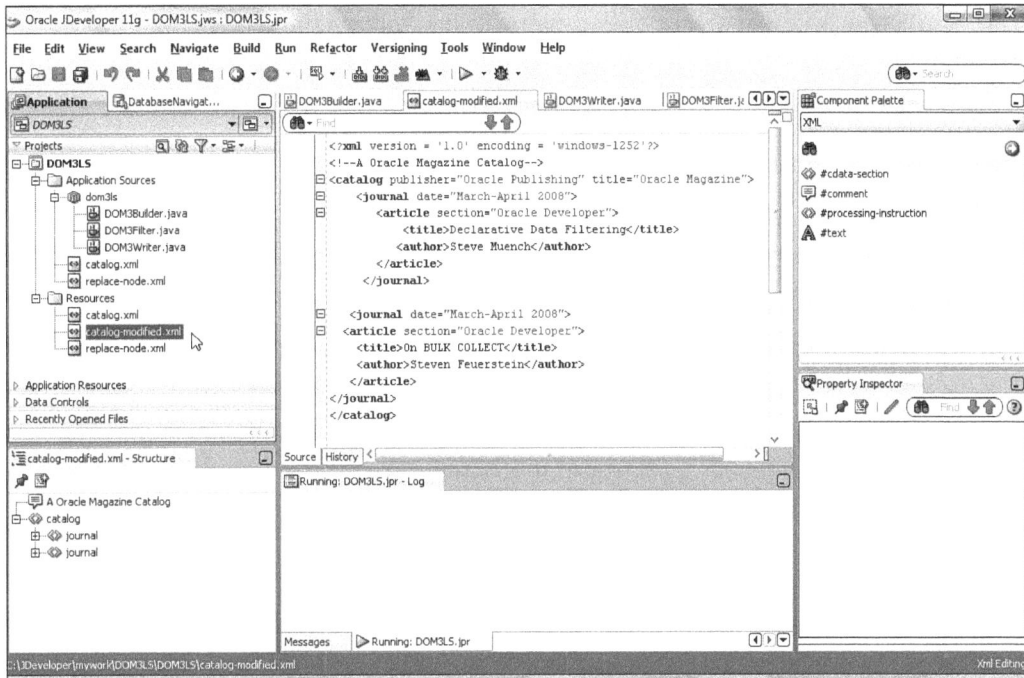

Saving an XML document

In this section, we will save a `DOMDocument` object to an XML document using the DOM 3.0 Load and Save API. We shall use the `LSerializer` interface to save the XML document.

Creating a document object

First, create an `XMLDOMImplementation` class object. The `XMLDOMImplementation` class implements the `DOMImplementationLS` interface and has methods to create Load and Save objects.

```
XMLDOMImplementation impl = new XMLDOMImplementation();
```

Create an `org.w3c.dom.Document` object from the `XMLDOMImplementation` object using the `createDocument(java.lang.String namespaceURI, java.lang.String qualifiedName, DocumentType doctype)` method. Rather logically, the parameter `namespaceURI` specifies the namespace URI of the document element. The parameter `qualifiedName` specifies the qualified name of the document element, and the parameter `doctype` specifies the `DOCTYPE` of the XML document.

```
Document document = impl.createDocument(null, null, null);
```

Create and add elements and attributes to the XML document.

```
Element catalog = document.createElement("catalog");
    catalog.setAttribute("title", "Oracle Magazine");
    document.appendChild(catalog);
    Element journal = document.createElement("journal");
    journal.setAttribute("date", "Sept-Oct 2008");
    journal.setAttribute("section", "Oracle Developer");
    catalog.appendChild(journal);
```

Creating an LSSerializer

Create a `DOMImplementationLS` object, and create an `LSSerializer` object from the `DOMImplementationLS` object using the `createLSSerializer()` method. The `LSSerializer` object is used to save a `Node` object.

```
LSSerializer domWriter = impl.createLSSerializer();
```

The `LSSerializer` interface has methods `write(Node nodeArg, LSOutput destination)`, `writeToString(Node nodeArg)`, and `writeToURI(Node nodeArg, String uri)` to output a document to a string, a URI or, an `LSOutput` object, which represents an output destination for data.

Outputting the document object

First we need to create an `LSOutput` object using the `createLSOutput()` method of the `DOMImplementationLS` interface. An `LSOutput` object encapsulates the output destination in a single object. Multiple output destinations may be specified in an `LSOutput` object. The `LSSerializer` object will use the `LSOutput` object to determine the serialization destination. `LSSerializer` scans output destinations specified in the `LSOutput` in the following order and uses the first output destination that is not null and not an empty string.

1. `LSOutput.characterStream`
2. `LSOutput.byteStream`
3. `LSOutput.systemId`

Create a byte output stream and set the output stream on the LSOutput object. Set encoding for the output. Output the document using the write(Node, LSOutput) method.

```
LSOutput output= impl.createLSOutput();
OutputStream outputStream=new FileOutputStream(new File("output.
xml"));
output.setByteStream(outputStream);
output.setEncoding("UTF-8");
domWriter.write(document, output);
```

The write() method has the provision to save a selected node instead of the complete document. As an example, save only the journal node in the document. Create an output stream for the journal node and output the node using the write(Node, LSOutput) method.

```
Node journalNode=catalog;OutputStream outputStream=new
FileOutputStream(new File("nodeOutput.xml"));
output.setByteStream(outputStream);
domWriter.write(journal,output);
```

The journal node is outputted to the output file nodeOutput.xml as shown in the following listing.

```
<journal date="Sept-Oct 2008" section="Oracle Developer"/>
```

The document or a node in the document may also be outputted to a String object using the writeToString(Node) method.

```
String nodeString=domWriter.writeToString(journal);
System.out.println(nodeString);
```

DOM3Writer.java, the Java application that we used to save a document to an OutputStream, is listed as follows with explanations:

1. Add the package and import statements.

    ```
    package dom3ls;
    import org.w3c.dom.ls.*;
    import oracle.xml.parser.v2.*;
    import org.w3c.dom.*;
    import java.io.*;
    ```

2. Define the Java class DOM3Writer.

    ```
    public class DOM3Writer {
    ```

3. Define the Java method `saveDocument` to save a `Document` object using the DOM 3.0 LS API.

```
public void saveDocument(){
try{
```

4. Create a `Document` object.

```
XMLDOMImplementation impl =
new XMLDOMImplementation();
Document document = impl.createDocument(
     null, null, null);
     Element catalog = document.createElement("catalog");
     catalog.setAttribute("title", "Oracle Magazine");
     document.appendChild(catalog);
     Element journal = document.createElement("journal");
     journal.setAttribute("date", "Sept-Oct 2008");
     journal.setAttribute("section", "Oracle Developer");

     catalog.appendChild(journal);
```

5. Create an `LSSerializer` object, and output the `Document` object and a `Node` object.

```
     LSSerializer domWriter = impl.createLSSerializer();
     LSOutput output= impl.createLSOutput();
     OutputStream outputStream=new FileOutputStream(new
     File("output.xml"));
     output.setByteStream(outputStream);
     output.setEncoding("UTF-8");
     domWriter.write(document, output);
     Node journalNode=catalog;
     outputStream=new FileOutputStream(new
     File("nodeOutput.xml"));
     output.setByteStream(outputStream);
     domWriter.write(journalNode,output);
     String nodeString=domWriter.writeToString(journalNode);
     System.out.println(nodeString);
}
catch(IOException e){ System.err.println("IOException "+e.
getMessage()); }
catch(DOMException e){System.err.println("DOMException "+e.
getMessage());}
}
```

6. Add the `main` method in which to create an instance of the `DOM3Writer` object and invoke the `saveDocument` method.

```
public static void main(String[] argv){
DOM3Writer writer=new DOM3Writer();
writer.saveDocument();
}
}
```

7. Copy the listing to the `DOM3Writer.java` application in the **Application Navigator**. To run the `DOM3Writer.java` application, right-click on the **DOM3Writer.java** node and select **Run**.

The output from the application shows that the `Document` object is outputted to XML document `output.xml`, and the `journal` node is outputted to a `String` object.

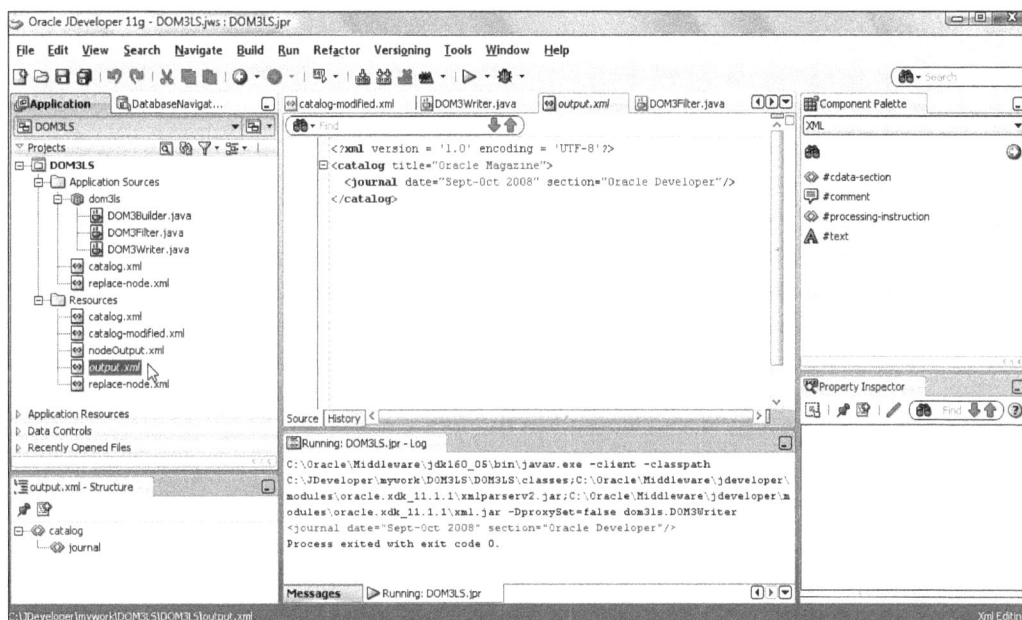

Filtering an XML document

An XML developer may be interested in filtering an XML document as the document is loaded, or as the document is stored. Filtering is used if you only need to load or save a section of an XML document. In this section we shall filter nodes with the DOM 3 Load and Save API. We shall load an XML document by selecting nodes from the input, and save an XML document by selecting nodes from the DOM object to be saved. The DOM 3.0 LS API provides interfaces to filter input from an XML document and filter output to an XML document. The `LSParserFilter` interface is used to filter input and the `LSSerializerFilter` interface is used to filter output.

Filtering the input

First, we need to define a class that implements the `LSParserFilter` interface.
In the class that implements the `LSParserFilter` interface, implement methods
`acceptNode(Node)`, `getWhatToShow()`, and `startElement(Element)`. The input
filter class is listed as follows:

```
private class InputFilter implements LSParserFilter{
    public   short acceptNode(Node node){
           return NodeFilter.FILTER_ACCEPT;
     }

    public   int getWhatToShow(){
        return NodeFilter.SHOW_ALL;
    }
    public   short startElement(Element element){
        System.out.println("Element Parsed "+ element.getTagName());
        return NodeFilter.FILTER_ACCEPT;
    }
}
```

The `getWhatToShow()` method returns a value to indicate which of the nodes are
shown to the filter. For example, if the value returned is `NodeFilter.SHOW_ELEMENT`,
only the element nodes are shown to the filter. The nodes that are not shown to the
filter are automatically included in the DOM object built from an XML document.
Nodes marked by the `getWhatToShow()` method will be passed to the `acceptNode()`
method for acceptance/rejection or skipping. The different values that may be
returned by an input filter are discussed in the following table:

Return Value (short)	Description
SHOW_ALL	Show all Nodes.
SHOW_CDATA_SECTION	Show CDATASection nodes.
SHOW_COMMENT	Show comment nodes.
SHOW_ELEMENT	Show element nodes.
SHOW_ENTITY_REFERENCE	Show entity reference nodes.
SHOW_PROCESSING_INSTRUCTION	Show processing instruction nodes.
SHOW_TEXT	Show text nodes.

Return values `SHOW_DOCUMENT`, `SHOW_DOCUMENT_TYPE`, `SHOW_NOTATION`,
`SHOW_ENTITY`, and `SHOW_DOCUMENT_FRAGMENT` are not valid for an `LSParserFilter`
and do not show the corresponding nodes to an `LSParserFilter` filter. These return
values should not be specified.

The acceptNode(Node) method is invoked after a node has been parsed completely. This method returns a short value to indicate if the node is to be accepted, rejected, or skipped by the filter, or if the parsing of the document is to be interrupted. For example, if the return value is NodeFilter.FILTER_REJECT the node is filtered out. A node may be modified in this method. Attribute nodes are not inputted to the acceptNode(Node) method. The different short values that may be returned by the acceptNode(Node) method are discussed in the following table:

Return Value (short)	Description
FILTER_ACCEPT	Accept the node including the child nodes.
FILTER_REJECT	Reject the node including the child nodes.
FILTER_SKIP	Skip node, but consider child nodes. When a Element node is skipped the attributes in the Element are also skipped.
FILTER_INTERRUPT	Accept the node and interrupt the processing of the XML document. If the processing is interrupted the resulting DOM tree may not be well formed. The node is accepted.

If a node is accepted with FILTER_ACCEPT, then the node is included in the Document object returned by the parser. If a node is skipped with FILTER_SKIP, only the specified node is skipped; the children of the node are parsed and included in the DOM document. If a node is rejected with FILTER_REJECT, the node and its children are rejected. Note that the acceptNode() method receives a fully parsed node (including its descendants), which you can then accept/reject as just described. If you like, you can modify this node, by adding children, for example.

The startElement(Element) method is called at the start of each element after the start tag has been parsed, but the child nodes have not yet been parsed. Only Element nodes, including element attributes, are inputted to the startElement(Element) method. An element's child nodes are not inputted to the startElement(Element) method. An element's attributes may be modified in the startElement(Element) method. The return value of the startElement(Element) method is a short that indicates if an element is to be accepted, rejected, skipped, or parsing interrupted. The return values of the startElement(Element) method are the same as those for the acceptNode() method, which are discussed in the table above, except that the values apply to an Element instead of a Node. If the return value is FILTER_INTERRUPT the Element is rejected.

The differences between the `acceptNode()` method and the `startElement()` method are:

- Only the `Element` nodes are inputted to the `startElement()` method, as compared to the `acceptNode()` method in which all the nodes except the `Document, DocumentType, Notation, Entity, DocumentFragment,` and `Attribute` nodes may be inputted. The `Attribute` nodes may be inputted to the `acceptNode()` method of the `LSSerializerFilter` interface.

- The `Element` node inputted to `startElement()` will include all the Element's attributes but none of the child nodes that include non-Element nodes. The nodes inputted to the `acceptNode()` method of the `LSParserFilter` include all the child nodes but none of the attribute nodes. The nodes inputted to the `acceptNode()` method of the `LSSerializerFilter` include all the child nodes, and may include the attribute nodes.

In the example input filter class, `InputFilter`, the `getWhatToShow()` method shows all the nodes that may be shown to the input filter. The `acceptNode(Node)` method accepts all the nodes that are shown to the filter. The `startElement(Element)` method prints out the element nodes that are parsed and accepts all the element nodes.

To filter the example XML document, create an `LSParser` object and set an `InputFilter` object on it using the `setFilter()` method.

```
DOMImplementationLS impl = new XMLDOMImplementation();
LSParser parser = impl.createLSParser(
DOMImplementationLS.MODE_SYNCHRONOUS,null);
InputFilter inputFilter=new InputFilter();
parser.setFilter(inputFilter);
```

Load the XML document `catalog.xml` using the `parseURI()` method of the `LSParser` object.

```
Document document=parser.parseURI(
"file://c:/ DOM3.0/catalog.xml");
```

Filtering the output

The document loaded consists of all the elements and attribute nodes in the XML document input. To filter the output, define a class that implements the `LSSerializerFilter` interface. In the class, implement the methods `getWhatToShow()` and `acceptNode(Node)`.

```
private class OutputFilter implements LSSerializerFilter{
        public  short acceptNode(Node node){
        if(node.getNodeType()==Node.ELEMENT_NODE){
```

```
Element element=(Element)node;
if(element.getTagName().equals("journal"))
if(element.getAttribute("date").equals("May-June 2008"))
    return NodeFilter.FILTER_REJECT;}
    return NodeFilter.FILTER_ACCEPT; }
 public  int getWhatToShow(){
    return NodeFilter.SHOW_ALL;
 }
}
```

The getWhatToShow() method returns a short value to indicate which nodes to show to the output filter. In addition, to the return values listed in the second table in this chapter, attribute nodes may be shown to the output filter with the return value of SHOW_ATTRIBUTE. The acceptNode() method accepts, rejects, skips nodes or interrupts saving. Return values of the acceptNode(Node) method are discussed in the third table in this chapter. In the example, the output filter class, OutputFilter, shows all nodes that may be shown to an output filter and accepts all nodes except the journal Element node with date attribute value May-June 2008. To filter the output, create an LSSerializer object and set an output filter on the LSSerializer object using the setFilter() method.

```
LSSerializer domWriter = impl.createLSSerializer();
    OutputFilter outputFilter = new OutputFilter();
    domWriter.setFilter(outputFilter);
```

Create an LSOuput object to output the filtered document. Save the DOM object using the write(Node, LSOutput) method of the LSSerializer interface.

```
LSOutput lsOutput=impl.createLSOutput();
OutputStream outputStream=new FileOutputStream(new File("filter-
output.xml"));
lsOutput.setByteStream(outputStream);
domWriter.write( document, lsOutput);
```

DOM3Filter.java, the Java application used to filter input and output is shown in the following listing with explanations:

1. First specify the package and the import statements.

    ```
    package dom3ls;
    import org.w3c.dom.*;
    import org.w3c.dom.ls.*;
    import oracle.xml.parser.v2.*;
    import org.w3c.dom.traversal.*;
    import java.io.*;
    ```

2. Define the Java class DOM3Filter.

    ```
    public class DOM3Filter {
    ```

3. Define the Java method `filter`.

```
public void filter(){
try{
```

4. Filter the input.

```
DOMImplementationLS impl =
new XMLDOMImplementation();
        LSParser parser = impl.createLSParser(
        DOMImplementationLS.MODE_SYNCHRONOUS,null);
        InputFilter inputFilter=new InputFilter();
        parser.setFilter(inputFilter);
        Document document=parser.parseURI
        ("file://c:/DOM3.0/catalog.xml");
```

5. Filter the output.

```
        LSSerializer domWriter = impl.createLSSerializer();
        OutputFilter outputFilter = new OutputFilter();
        domWriter.setFilter(outputFilter);
        LSOutput lsOutput=impl.createLSOutput();
        OutputStream outputStream=new FileOutputStream(new
        File("filter-output.xml"));
        lsOutput.setByteStream(outputStream);
        domWriter.write( document, lsOutput);

    }
    catch (IOException e) {
      System.err.println("IOException "+e.getMessage());
    }
    catch (DOMException e) {
      System.err.println("DOMException "+e.getMessage());
    }

}
```

6. Define the `main` method in which to create an instance of the `DOM3Filter` class and invoke the `filter` method.

```
public static void main(String[] args) {

  DOM3Filter dom3Filter=new DOM3Filter();
  dom3Filter.filter();
  }
```

7. Define the input filter class `InputFilter`, which implements the `LSParserFilter` interface.

```
private class InputFilter implements LSParserFilter{
    public  short acceptNode(Node node){
            return NodeFilter.FILTER_ACCEPT;
     }
    public  int getWhatToShow(){
        return NodeFilter.SHOW_ALL;
    }

    public  short startElement(Element element){
        System.out.println("Element Parsed "
        + element.getTagName());
        return NodeFilter.FILTER_ACCEPT;
    }
}
```

8. Define the output filter class `OutputFilter`, which implements the `LSSerializer` interface.

```
private class OutputFilter implements LSSerializerFilter{
        public  short acceptNode(Node node){
        if(node.getNodeType()==Node.ELEMENT_NODE){
         Element element=(Element)node;
         if(element.getTagName().equals("journal"))
           if(element.getAttribute("date").equals("May-June 2008"))
             return NodeFilter.FILTER_REJECT;
        }
            return NodeFilter.FILTER_ACCEPT;
        }
          public  int getWhatToShow(){
             return NodeFilter.SHOW_ALL;
        }
    }
}
```

9. Copy the listing to the `DOM3Filter.java` application in the **Application Navigator**. To run the `DOM3Filter.java` application, right-click on the application in **Application Navigator** and select **Run**.

The output from the application lists the `Element` nodes that are parsed. A `journal` node gets filtered out in the output document `filter-output.xml`.

Select **View | Refresh** to add `filter-output.xml` to the **Application Navigator**.

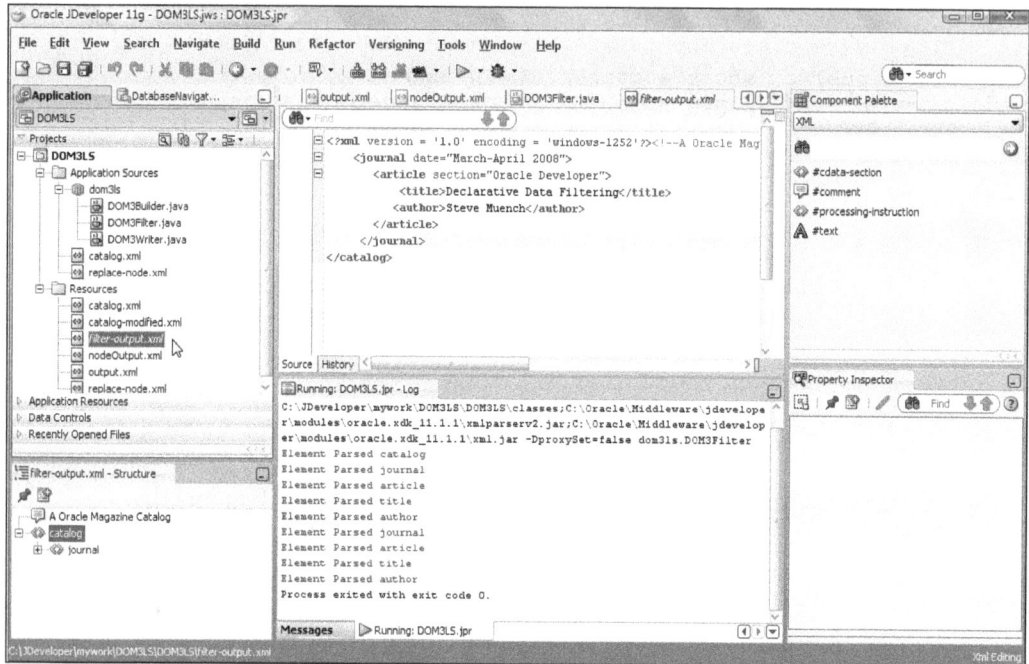

Prior to the DOM Level 3 Load and Save specification, an XML document could not be filtered as the document was parsed or outputted. In the DOM Core API, nodes are removed with the `remove` methods of the `Node` interface after the XML document has been parsed and a DOM tree built.

Summary

The DOM 3 Load and Save specification provides standard mechanisms for loading, saving, and filtering XML documents. In this chapter you have learned how to load an XML document, save an XML document or a node to a file or a String, and filter nodes from an XML document. While the DOM 3 Load and Save API is not as simple as the JAXP APIs, the Load and Save API does have some advantages. If any of the advantages of the DOM 3 Load and Save API are required, use the DOM 3 API. Otherwise use the JAXP API. An example of using DOM 3 Load and Save is in an XML Editor (such as JDeveloper's built-in XML Editor) in which an XML document is loaded into the Editor and saved from the Editor. But, it is up to JDeveloper designers to add the DOM 3 Load and Save feature to the XML Editor. A developer won't be able to use DOM 3 Load and Save with JDeveloper's XML Editor directly. In the next chapter we will validate an XML document with an XML schema using the DOM Level 3 Validation API.

8

Validating an XML Document with DOM 3 Validation

The DOM 3.0 Validation specification provides a means of dynamically updating the content and structure of XML documents while ensuring schema validity for XML documents. The advantage of DOM 3.0 Validation over validation with a validating parser such as the DOMParser is the support for **dynamic validation**. The DOM 3.0 Validation specification implementation retrieves the metadata definitions from the XML schema and provides methods to query the validity of DOM operations — for example the addition and removal of attributes and elements — so that you can validate potential document modifications before actually making them. You would use the parser schema validation, which we discussed in Chapter 3, if the XML document is completely constructed and only the schema validation of the XML document is required. And you would use the DOM 3 Validation if you are constructing or modifying an XML document and you want to validate the different DOM modifications, such as adding elements and attributes, before you actually make the document modifications.

This chapter discusses how to use the DOM 3.0 Validation implementation classes in XDK 11g, which is included in JDeveloper 11g. This chapter uses an example XML document called catalog.xml, and shows how to validate it with an example XML schema document called catalog.xsd as the document is constructed. XDK 11g is the only XML API that implements the DOM Level 3 Validation specification (http://www.w3.org/TR/2003/PR-DOM-Level-3-Val-20031215/); however, some of the DOM 3 Validation features are not implemented by the Oracle XDK 11g API. A test was run by W3C to determine which of the DOM 3 Validation methods are supported by the XDK 11g implementation. You can refer to the results of the DOM3 Validation test (http://www.w3.org/2003/11/26-DOM3-Val-Oracle-Result. html) when developing a DOM 3 Validation application.

Setting the environment

First, we need to create an application and a project in JDeveloper 11g.
Select **File | New** to create an application. In the **New Gallery** window select
Categories | General and **Items | Generic Application**. Click on the **OK** button.
In the **Create Generic Application** window specify an **Application Name**
(DOM3Validation for example) and click on **Next**. In the **Name your Generic Project**
window specify a **Project Name** (DOM3Validation) and click on **OK**. An application
and a project get added to the **Application Navigator**.

To validate an XML document with the DOM 3.0 Validation API we need to
add the libraries/JAR files required for the DOM 3 Validation application. Select
Tools | Project Properties. In the **Project Properties** window select **Libraries and
Classpath**. Click on **Add Library** to add the **Oracle XML Parser v2** library. Click
on the **OK** button.

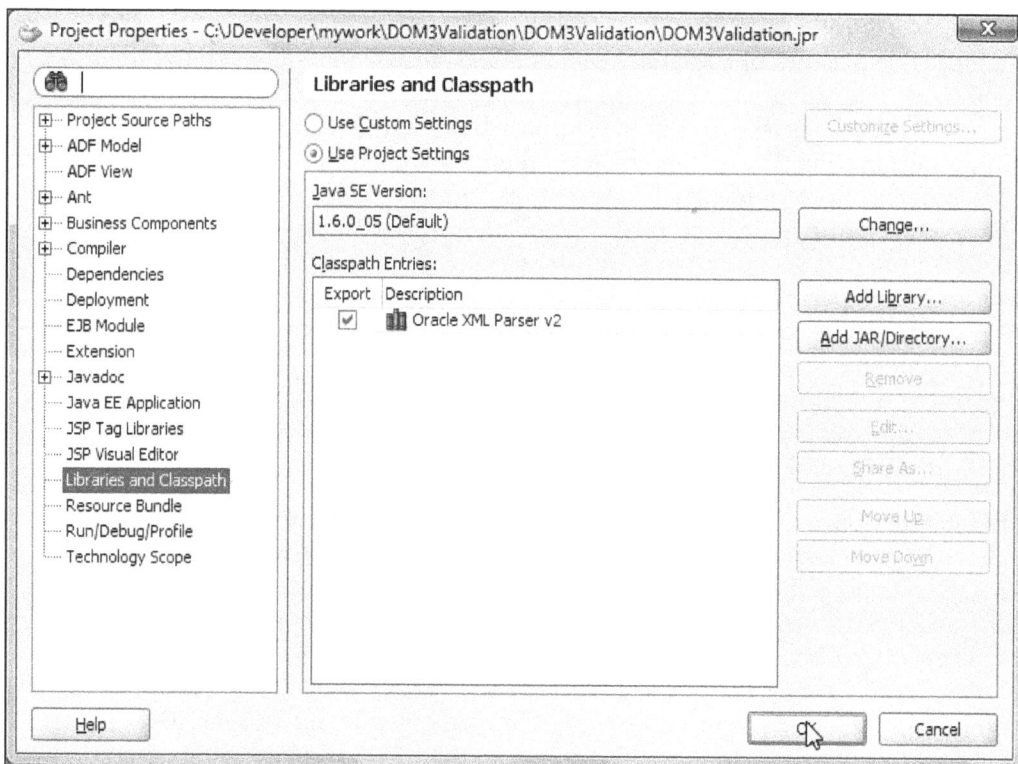

We shall be constructing an XML document and validating the document with an XML schema, `catalog.xsd`, which is listed as follows:

```
<?xml version="1.0" encoding="windows-1252" ?>
<xs:schema xmlns:xs="http://www.w3.org/2001/XMLSchema">
 <xs:element name="catalog">
  <xs:complexType>
   <xs:sequence>
    <xs:element ref="journal" minOccurs="0" maxOccurs="unbounded"/>
   </xs:sequence>
   <xs:attribute name="title" type="xs:string" use="optional"/>
   <xs:attribute name="publisher" type="xs:string" use="required"/>
  </xs:complexType>
 </xs:element>
 <xs:element name="journal">
  <xs:complexType>
   <xs:sequence>
    <xs:element ref="article" minOccurs="0" maxOccurs="unbounded"/>
   </xs:sequence>
   <xs:attribute name="date" type="xs:string"/>
  </xs:complexType>
 </xs:element>
 <xs:element name="article">
  <xs:complexType>
   <xs:sequence>
    <xs:element name="title" type="xs:string"/>
    <xs:element name="author" type="xs:string"/>
   </xs:sequence>
   <xs:attribute name="section">
    <xs:simpleType>
     <xs:restriction base="xs:string">
      <xs:enumeration value="Features"/>
      <xs:enumeration value="SQL"/>
      <xs:enumeration value="PL/SQL"/>
      <xs:enumeration value="JSP"/>
      <xs:enumeration value="XML"/>
     </xs:restriction>
    </xs:simpleType>
   </xs:attribute>
  </xs:complexType>
 </xs:element>
</xs:schema>
```

Create a directory `C:/DOM3Validation` and save the XML schema `catalog.xsd` to the `DOM3Validation` directory.

We need to add a Java class, DOM3Validation.java, by selecting **Categories | General** and **Items | Java Class** in the **New Gallery** window. The directory structure of the DOM3Validation application is shown in the following illustration:

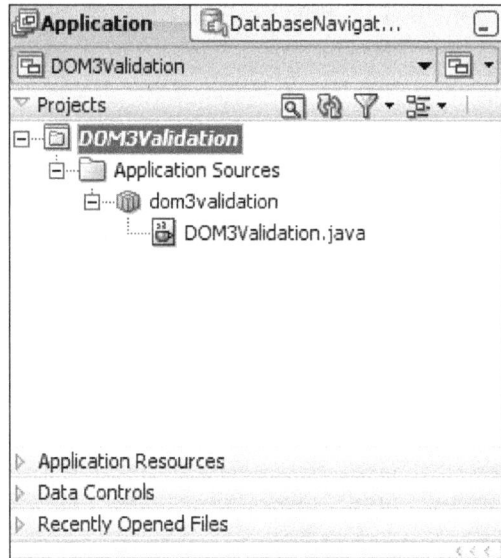

Constructing and validating an XML document

In this section we will construct an example XML document and dynamically validate the XML document with the example XML schema, catalog.xsd, using the DOM 3 Validation API in XDK 11g that is included in JDeveloper 11g. We will be constructing the following XML document, catalog.xml:

```xml
<?xml version = '1.0' encoding = 'windows-1252'?>
<catalog title="Oracle Magazine" publisher="Oracle Publishing">
 <journal date="March-April 2008">
  <article section="ORACLE DEVELOPER">
   <title>Declarative Data Filtering</title>
   <author>Steve Muench</author>
  </article>
 </journal>
 <journal date="May-June 2008">
  <article section="ORACLE DEVELOPER">
   <title>On the PGA and Indexing Collections</title>
   <author>Steven Feuerstein</author>
  </article>
 </journal></catalog>
```

The initial XML document that we will be modifying to construct the required XML document is listed as follows; copy the document to a file `catalog.xml` and save the file in the `C:/DOM3Validation` directory.

```
<?xml version="1.0" encoding="windows-1252" ?>
<catalog title="Oracle Magazine" publisher="Oracle Publishing">
 <journal>
  <article>
   </article>
  </journal>
</catalog>
```

We will be developing the validation application in the `DOM3Validation` Java class. The root interface in the DOM Level 3 Validation API is `NodeEditVAL`, which is similar to the DOM Level 3 Core `Node` interface, with methods for guided document editing. Guided document editing implies that the validity of a modification is ascertained before the modification is performed. The `NodeEditVAL` interface provides the methods discussed in the following table:

Method	Description
`canAppendChild(Node newChild)`	Determines if it is valid to append a child node.
`canInsertBefore(Node newChild, Node refChild)`	Determines if it is valid to insert a node before a specified node.
`canRemoveChild(Node oldChild)`	Determines if it is valid to remove a node.
`canReplaceChild(Node newChild, Node oldChild)`	Determines if it is valid to replace a node.
`getDefaultValue()`	Gets the default value specified in an element or an attribute, or returns null if the default value is not specified.
`getEnumeratedValues()`	Returns a list of distinct values of an element or an attribute, or null if not specified.
`nodeValidity(short wFValidityCheckLevel)`	Determines if a node is valid relative to the specified validity level.

The different validity levels that may be specified in the `nodeValidity` method are represented with static `short` fields and are discussed in the following table:

Validity Level	Description
VAL_INCOMPLETE	Validates if a node's immediate children (level 1) are those expected by the content model. The node's trailing required children (level 2 and latter) could be missing. For example, if an XML document has an element `catalog` that has level 1 sub-element `journal`, which further has sub-elements. Validation of the `catalog` node would only test if the sub-element of `catalog` is `journal`, but won't test the sub-elements of the `journal` element.
VAL_NS_WF	Validates if a node conforms to namespace requirements.
VAL_SCHEMA	Validates if a node's entire subtree is as expected by the content model.
VAL_WF	Validates if a node is well formed.

In XDK 11g, the DOM 3.0 Validation specification is implemented with the `DocumentEditVAL`, `ElementEditVAL`, and `CharacterDataEditVAL` interfaces, which extend the `NodeEditVAL` interface. As the names indicate, you use the three interfaces to dynamically validate a document—that is, the entire document, an element, or character data, respectively. The `oracle.xml.parser.v2.XMLDocument` class implements the `DocumentEditVAL` and `ElementEditVAL` interfaces. The `XMLText` class implements the `CharacterDataEditVAL` interface.

To validate a document, you use the `DocumentEditVAL` interface. The `DocumentEditVAL` interface extends the `NodeEditVAL` interface and provides additional methods, discussed in the following table, for guided document editing.

Method	Description
`getContinuousValidityChecking()`	Returns a Boolean value that specifies if the validity of a document is continuously enforced.
`getDefinedElements(java.lang.String namespaceURI)`	Returns names of globally defined elements in the specified namespace.
`setContinuousValidityChecking(boolean continuousValidityChecking)`	Sets an attribute that specifies if the validity of a document is continuously enforced. The default value is false.
`validateDocument()`	Validates a document against the schema (DTD or XML schema) specified on the document.

Next, we shall construct an XML document and dynamically validate the XML document. In the DOM3Validation Java class, first, import the DOM 3.0 Validation specification classes.

```
import org.w3c.dom.validation.*;
```

Parsing XML document and setting XML schema

Next, create an LSParser and parse the XML document catalog.xml as explained in Chapter 7 on the DOM 3 Load and Save specification.

```
XMLDOMImplementation impl = new XMLDOMImplementation();
LSParser parser = impl.createLSParser(DOMImplementationLS.MODE_
SYNCHRONOUS, "http://www.w3.org/2001/XMLSchema");
XMLDocument document = (XMLDocument)(parser.parseURI
                      ("file://C:/ DOM3Validation/catalog.xml"));
```

Set the XML schema for validating the XML document using an XMLSchema object, which you can obtain from an XSDBuilder object using the build(URL schema) method. The URL parameter specifies the URL for the XML schema. Create a URL object from XML schema catalog.xsd.

```
XSDBuilder builder = new XSDBuilder();
URL url = new URL( "file://c:/DOM3Validation/catalog.xsd");
XMLSchema schemadoc = (XMLSchema)builder.build(url);
```

Set the schema document you want to use to validate the XMLDocument using the setSchema method.

```
document.setSchema(schemadoc);
```

Global elements

You may obtain the global element declarations in an XML schema to determine which element is the root element. A global element is a top level element in an XML schema declared with the xs:element construct. Global elements in an XML document are obtained using the getDefinedElements(String namespaceURI) method. As we are not using a namespace, invoke the getDefinedElement method with a null argument.

```
NameList elementList = document.getDefinedElements(null);
```

Using the sample XML schema, the elementList consists of the following elements:

```
Element at index 0 is catalog
Element at index 1 is journal
Element at index 2 is article
```

The elements title and author in the XML schema do not get listed, because they aren't global elements. The element at index value 0 is the root element. The root element in an XML document based on catalog.xsd is catalog. The catalog. xml document already has the root element and the top-level elements journal and article in the document. The top-level elements are required in an XML document to construct the document using DOM 3 Validation testing. The ElementEditVAL interface extends the NodeEditVAL interface and provides additional methods for dynamically validating an element node. The additional methods of the ElementEditVAL interface are discussed in the following table; a more detailed description and examples of some of these methods are provided later in this chapter.

Method	Description
canRemoveAttribute(java.lang. String attrname)	Determines whether removing the attribute of the specified name would be valid.
canRemoveAttributeNode(Node attrNode)	Determines whether removing the specified attribute node would be valid.
canRemoveAttributeNS(java.lang. String namespaceURI, java.lang. String localName)	Determines whether removing the attribute of the specified local name and namespace would be valid.
canSetAttribute(java.lang. String attrname, java.lang. String attrval)	Determines whether setting the attribute of the specified name and value would be valid.
canSetAttributeNode(Attr attrNode)	Determines whether setting the specified attribute node would be valid.
canSetAttributeNS(java.lang. String namespaceURI, java.lang. String qualifiedName, java. lang.String value)	Determines whether setting the attribute of the specified namespace, qualified name, and value would be valid.
getAllowedAttributes()	Returns a NameList of attributes that are allowed in an element.
getAllowedChildren()	Returns a NameList of allowed children of an element.
getAllowedFirstChildElements()	Returns a NameList of allowed first child elements for an element node.
getAllowedNextSiblings()	Returns a NameList of allowed next siblings for an element.

Method	Description
getAllowedParents()	Returns a NameList of allowed parents for an element.
getAllowedPreviousSiblings()	Returns a NameList of allowed previous siblings for an element.
getContentType()	Returns the content type of an element. The different types of content types are discussed in a subsequent table.
getRequiredAttributes()	Returns a NameList of required attributes of an element.
isElementDefined(java.lang. String name)	Determines if the element of the specified name is defined in the schema. Applies only to global declarations.
isElementDefinedNS(java.lang. String namespaceURI, java.lang. String name)	Determines if the element of the specified name is defined in the specified namespace. Applies to global and local definitions.

The `CharacterDataEditVAL` interface, which extends the `NodeEditVAL` interface, is used to determine the validity of operations on character data. The interface provides additional methods, for guided document editing, which are discussed in the following table:

Method	Description
canAppendData(java.lang.String arg)	Determines if it is valid to append the specified character data.
canDeleteData(int offset, int count)	Determines if it is valid to delete the specified number of characters at the secified offset.
canInsertData(int offset, java.lang.String arg)	Determines if it is valid to insert the specified character data at the specified offset.
canReplaceData(int offset, int count, java.lang.String arg)	Determines if it is valid to replace the specified number of characters at the specified offset with the specified character data.
canSetData(java.lang.String arg)	Determines if it is valid to set the specified data.
isWhitespaceOnly()	Determines if data is only whitespace.

The catalog element

To start constructing the example XML document, retrieve the root element, catalog, using the `getDocumentElement()` method.

```
XMLElement catalogElement =
(XMLElement)(document.getDocumentElement());
```

The `getRequiredAttributes()` method returns a list of required attributes for an element, letting you know in advance which attributes you'll need to add to an element for a valid document. In an XML schema, you specify a required attribute using the `use="required"` syntax. For example, to get the required attributes in the `catalog` element.

```
NameList attrRequired = catalogElement.getRequiredAttributes();
```

After running the preceding line of code, for the sample documents, the `attrRequired NameList` would contain `publisher`, because that's the only `catalog` element attribute specified with `use="required"` in the sample schema.

To retrieve all attributes allowed in an element, invoke the `getAllowedAttributes` method. For example, retrieve the allowed attributes in the `catalog` element as follows:

```
NameList attr = catalogElement.getAllowedAttributes();
```

The output for the allowed attributes for the `catalog` element is as follows:

```
title
publisher
```

Before setting an attribute on an element, invoke the `canSetAttribute` method to test the validity of adding an attribute. For example, the following test returns `VAL_FALSE`, because `section` is not an attribute of the `catalog` element in `catalog.xsd`.

```
short attrSet = catalogElement.canSetAttribute("section", "SQL");
```

Methods that return the validity of an operation return a `short` value that may be represented as a `NodeEditVAL` constant, as discussed in the following table:

short Value	Description
VAL_FALSE	Indicates that the operation is not valid.
VAL_UNKNOWN	Indicates that the validity of the operation is not known. If the XML schema is not able to ascertain the validity of a document modification VAL_UNKNOWN is returned. For example, the canAppendChild validity test for adding a XMLText node to the title element in the example XML document discussed in this chapter returns VAL_UNKNOWN.
VAL_TRUE	Indicates that the operation is valid.

Before removing an attribute, invoke the `canRemoveAttribute` method, which takes an attribute name as the argument, to test the validity of removing an attribute. For example, the test to remove the `title` attribute from `catalog` element returns `VAL_TRUE` because `title` is not a required attribute of the `catalog` element.

```
short attrRemove = catalogElement.canRemoveAttribute("title");
```

As an example, try removing the `publisher` attribute from the `catalog` element. The `publisher` attribute is a required attribute of element `catalog`, so the return value is `VALID_FALSE`.

```
attrRemove = catalogElement.canRemoveAttribute("publisher");
```

The `canRemoveChild()` method tests the validity of removing an element. As an example, if you test to see if you can remove the `journal` element, you'll get a `VALID_TRUE` return value.

```
XMLElement journalNode = (XMLElement)(document.selectSingleNode
                      ("catalog/journal"));
short elementRemove = catalogElement.canRemoveChild(journalNode);
```

Adding journal attributes

Next, we add the attributes to the `journal` node. Obtain the required attributes using the `getRequiredAttributes` method and the allowed attributes using the `getAllowedAttributes` method. The `journal` node does not have any required attributes, and has `date` as the only allowed attribute. Test the validity of adding a `date` attribute to the `journal` element using the `canSetAttribute` method and if it returns `VAL_TRUE`, set the `date` attribute using the `setAttribute` method, which takes two arguments of attribute name and attribute value.

```
short setAttr =
 journalNode.canSetAttribute("date", "March-April 2008");
 if (setAttr == NodeEditVAL.VAL_TRUE)
  journalNode.setAttribute("date", "March-April 2008");
```

Adding article attributes

Similarly, obtain the required and allowed attributes of the `article` element. The `article` element has only one allowed attribute, `section`. Test the validity of setting the `section` attribute using the `canSetAttribute` method and set the `section` attribute using the `setAttribute` method.

```
XMLElement articleNode = (XMLElement)(document.selectSingleNode
                      ("catalog/journal/article"));
setAttr =articleNode.canSetAttribute("section", "ORACLE DEVELOPER");
if (setAttr == NodeEditVAL.VAL_TRUE)
articleNode.setAttribute("section", "ORACLE DEVELOPER");
```

The XML schema `catalog.xsd` only allows an enumeration of values for the `section` attribute. If a value not listed in the enumeration is set on the `section` attribute, the validity test for setting the attribute value returns `VAL_FALSE`. For example, test the validity of setting the `section` attribute value to `XSLT` using the `canSetAttribute` method. The method returns `VAL_FALSE`, because `XSLT` is not a value listed in the `simpleType` enumeration for the `section` attribute in `catalog.xsd`.

```
setAttr = articleNode.canSetAttribute("section", "XSLT");
```

Adding article subelements

The `getContentType()` method returns the content type an element is allowed to have. For example, obtain the valid content type for an `article` element:

```
short contentType=articleNode.getContentType();
```

The method returns a `short` representing the content type; details will be presented later in this section in a table. If the value of the `short` variable returned by the `getContentType()` method is `VAL_ANY_CONTENTTYPE`, the element content could be element, processing instruction, unexpanded entity reference, character, and comment information items. For the `article` element, `getContentType()` returns `VAL_ELEMENTS_CONTENTTYPE`—in other words, the `article` element can contain a sequence of elements.

The return value of the `getContentType` method is a `short` that represents the valid content type as discussed in the following table:

Short Value	Valid Element Content Type
VAL_ELEMENTS_CONTENTTYPE	A sequence of elements optionally separated by whitespace.
VAL_ANY_CONTENTTYPE	Any content type is permitted.
VAL_EMPTY_CONTENTTYPE	Empty; no content is allowed.
VAL_MIXED_CONTENTTYPE	A sequence of ordered elements interspersed with optional character data.
VAL_SIMPLE_CONTENTTYPE	Character data.

The `getAllowedChildren()` method returns a list of elements allowed in an element, providing another way to determine whether adding an element would be a valid action. As an example, output the elements that can be added to the `article` element with `System.out`.

```
elementList = articleNode.getAllowedChildren();

System.out.println("Elements which may be specified in an article
element are: ");
```

```
   for (int i = 0; i < elementList.getLength(); i++)
   System.out.println(elementList.getName(i) + " ");
```

The output from the `getAllowedChildren()` method is as follows:

```
Elements which may be specified in an article element are:
title
author
```

The allowed child elements are outputted in the order specified in the XML schema. Next, we append the `title` and `author` elements to the `article` element. You can test the validity of appending an element using the `canAppendChild()` method. As an example, suppose you want to append a `title` element to the `article` element in the sample document. You first get a XMLElement object for the `article` element using XPath, create the `title` element, and then use the `canAppendChild()` method to check whether appending it to the `article` element would be a valid operation, shown as follows:

```
XMLElement articleNode = (XMLElement)(document.selectSingleNode
                          ("catalog/journal/article"));
XMLElement titleElement = (XMLElement)document.createElement("title");
short editVal = articleNode.canAppendChild(titleElement);
```

Output the result of the validity test with `System.out`. As the `title` element is defined in the `article` element, the output is:

```
Element Addition is VALID_TRUE
```

Add the `title` element to the `article` element using the `appendChild` method.

```
if (editVal == NodeEditVAL.VAL_TRUE) {
   System.out.println("Element addition VALID_TRUE");
articleNode.appendChild(titleElement);
}
```

Similar to the `title` element, test the validity of adding an `author` element using the `canAppendChild` method and if the method returns `VAL_TRUE`, add the `author` element using the `appendChild` method.

```
XMLElement authorElement =
(XMLElement)document.createElement("author");
editVal = articleNode.canAppendChild(authorElement);

if (editVal == NodeEditVAL.VAL_TRUE) {
    articleNode.appendChild(authorElement);
   }
```

We also need to add a text node each to the `title` and `author` elements. Create an XMLText object, which represents a text node, and add the text node with the `appendChild` method.

```
XMLText title =(XMLText)document.createTextNode("Declarative Data
Filtering");
   titleElement.appendChild(title);
   XMLText author = (XMLText)document.createTextNode("Steve Muench");
   authorElement.appendChild(author);
```

We have fully constructed the top-level elements that were in the `catalog.xml` document that we started with. The `nodeValidity()` method tests the validity of a node with respect to a validity level. The different validity levels were discussed in an earlier table. As an example, we are testing the validity of the `journal` node that we have constructed. The `nodeValidity` method returns `VAL_TRUE`.

```
short nodeValid = journalNode.nodeValidity(ElementEditVAL.VAL_SCHEMA);
```

Adding a journal element

Next, we shall add another `journal` element to the `catalog` element. Because the second `journal` element is not already defined in the `catalog.xml` element that we started with, we need to create a `journal` element and add the `journal` element to the `catalog` element. We need to create the complete subtree of the `journal` element. We won't be able to test the validity of adding all the nodes in the subtree of the `journal` node, because a shell of the subtree is not defined in the initial `catalog.xml` for a second `journal` element. We will only be able to test the validity of adding the `journal` node to the `catalog` element.

The `isElementDefined()` method may be used to test if an element is defined in another element. For example, test whether a `title` element is defined in the `catalog` element.

```
short elementDefined = catalogElement.isElementDefined("title");
```

Because the `title` element defined in the `catalog.xsd` schema is not in the `catalog` element the return value is `VALID_FALSE`. If you tested the validity of adding a `title` element to the `catalog` element you would get a `VAL_FALSE`.

```
short editVal = catalogElement.canAppendChild(titleElement);
```

Obtain a `NameList` of elements that may be defined in the `catalog` element using the `getAllowedChildren` method.

```
NameList elementList = catalogElement.getAllowedChildren();
```

Only the `journal` element is outputted as an allowed sub-element of the `catalog`
element. Construct a complete `journal` node using the DOM Core API, which was
discussed in Chapter 1.

```
XMLElement journalElement = (XMLElement)document.createElement
                            ("journal");
journalElement.setAttribute("date", "May-June 2008");
XMLElement articleElement = (XMLElement)document.createElement
                            ("article");
journalElement.appendChild(articleElement);
articleElement.setAttribute("section", "ORACLE DEVELOPER");
titleElement=(XMLElement)document.createElement("title");
articleElement.appendChild(titleElement);
authorElement=(XMLElement)document.createElement("author");
articleElement.appendChild(authorElement);

title = (XMLText)document.createTextNode("On the PGA and Indexing
Collections");
titleElement.appendChild(title);
author = (XMLText)document.createTextNode("Steven Feuerstein");
authorElement.appendChild(author);
```

Test the validity of adding a `journal` element to the `catalog` element using
the `canAppendChild` method and add the `journal` element using the
`appendChild` method.

```
short editVal = catalogElement.canAppendChild(journalElement);
if (editVal == NodeEditVAL.VAL_TRUE) {
  catalogElement.appendChild(journalElement);
            }
```

Validating a document

Validate the XML document `catalog.xml` with the XML schema `catalog.xsd` using
the `validateDocument` method.

```
short valid=document.validateDocument();
```

There are three possible return values. If the XML document is valid, the value of the
`valid` variable will be `VALID_TRUE`; otherwise, it will be `VALID_FALSE`. If the validity
of the XML document is not known, it will be `VAL_UNKNOWN`.

For the example XML document and XML schema document, the `System.out`
output is as follows:

```
Document is VALID_TRUE
```

Running the DOM 3 Validation application

The example validation program, `DOM3Validation.java` is shown in the following listing with explanations:

1. First, we specify the `package` statement and import the required packages.

   ```
   package dom3validation;

   import org.w3c.dom.validation.*;
   import org.w3c.dom.ls.*;
   import oracle.xml.parser.schema.*;
   import oracle.xml.parser.v2.*;
   import org.w3c.dom.*;
   import java.io.*;
   import java.net.*;
   ```

2. Next, define the Java class `DOM3Validation`.

   ```
   public class DOM3Validation {
   ```

3. Add the Java method `validate`.

   ```
       public void validate() {

           try {
   ```

4. Create an `LSParser` object. Parse the XML document `catalog.xml`. Set the XML schema.

   ```
   XMLDOMImplementation impl = new XMLDOMImplementation();
   LSParser parser = impl.createLSParser(DOMImplementationLS.MODE_
   SYNCHRONOUS, "http://www.w3.org/2001/XMLSchema");

   XMLDocument document = (XMLDocument)(parser.parseURI("file://C:/
   DOM3Validation/catalog.xml"));
   XSDBuilder builder = new XSDBuilder();
   URL url = new URL("file://C:/DOM3Validation/catalog.xsd");
   XMLSchema schemadoc = builder.build(url);
   document.setSchema(schemadoc);
   ```

5. Obtain the defined global elements in the XML schema. Retrieve the root element.

   ```
   NameList elementList =document.getDefinedElements(null);
       for (int i = 0; i < elementList.getLength(); i++)
          System.out.println("Element at index " + i + " is " +
          elementList.getName(i));

   XMLElement catalogElement =
       (XMLElement)(document.getDocumentElement());
   ```

6. Obtain the list of required attributes for the `catalog` element.

```
NameList attrRequired = catalogElement.getRequiredAttributes();
System.out.println("The required attributes of the catalog element
are: ");
    for (int i = 0; i < attrRequired.getLength(); i++)
System.out.println(attrRequired.getName(i) + " ");
```

7. Obtain a list of allowed attributes for the `catalog` element.

```
NameList attr = catalogElement.getAllowedAttributes();
System.out.println("The allowed attributes of the catalog element
are: ");
for (int i = 0; i < attr.getLength(); i++)
System.out.println(attr.getName(i) + " ");
```

8. Test the validity of setting an attribute.

```
short attrSet = catalogElement.canSetAttribute
("section", "SQL");
if (attrSet == NodeEditVAL.VAL_TRUE)
   System.out.println("Attribute Addition is VALID_TRUE");
if (attrSet == NodeEditVAL.VAL_FALSE)
   System.out.println("Attribute Addition is VALID_FALSE");
if (attrSet == NodeEditVAL.VAL_UNKNOWN)
   System.out.println("Attribute Addition is VALID_UNKNOWN");
```

9. Test the validity of removing attributes.

```
short attrRemove = catalogElement.canRemoveAttribute("title");
    if (attrRemove == NodeEditVAL.VAL_TRUE)
      System.out.println("Attribute Removal is VALID_TRUE");
    if (attrRemove == NodeEditVAL.VAL_FALSE)
      System.out.println("Attribute Removal is VALID_FALSE");
    if (attrRemove == NodeEditVAL.VAL_UNKNOWN)
       System.out.println("Attribute Removal is VALID_UNKNOWN");

attrRemove =catalogElement.canRemoveAttribute("publisher");

    if (attrRemove == NodeEditVAL.VAL_TRUE)
      System.out.println("Attribute Removal is VALID_TRUE");
    if (attrRemove == NodeEditVAL.VAL_FALSE)
      System.out.println("Attribute Removal is VALID_FALSE");
    if (attrRemove == NodeEditVAL.VAL_UNKNOWN)
      System.out.println("Attribute Removal is VALID_UNKNOWN");
```

10. Select the `journal` node using XPath. Test the validity of removing the `journal` element.

```
XMLElement journalNode = (XMLElement)(document.selectSingleNode
                         ("catalog/journal"));
short elementRemove =catalogElement.canRemoveChild(journalNode);
```

```
    if (elementRemove == NodeEditVAL.VAL_TRUE)
        System.out.println("Element Removal is VALID_TRUE");
    if (elementRemove == NodeEditVAL.VAL_FALSE)
        System.out.println("Element Removal is VALID_FALSE");
    if (elementRemove == NodeEditVAL.VAL_UNKNOWN)
        System.out.println("Element Removal is VALID_UNKNOWN");
```

11. Retrieve the required and allowed attributes for the `journal` element.

```
attrRequired = journalNode.getRequiredAttributes();
System.out.println("The required attributes of the journal
element are: ");
for (int i = 0; i < attrRequired.getLength(); i++)
    System.out.println(attrRequired.getName(i) + " ");
attr = journalNode.getAllowedAttributes();
System.out.println("The allowed attributes of the journal element
are: ");
for (int i = 0; i < attr.getLength(); i++)
    System.out.println(attr.getName(i) + " ");
```

12. Test the validity of setting a `date` attribute on the `journal` element and set the `date` attribute.

```
short setAttr = journalNode.canSetAttribute
                ("date", "March-April 2008");
if (setAttr == NodeEditVAL.VAL_TRUE){
    journalNode.setAttribute("date", "March-April 2008");
    System.out.println("Attribute Addition is VALID_TRUE");
}
if (attrSet == NodeEditVAL.VAL_FALSE)
    System.out.println("Attribute Addition is VALID_FALSE");
if (attrSet == NodeEditVAL.VAL_UNKNOWN)
    System.out.println("Attribute Addition is VALID_UNKNOWN");
```

13. Select the `article` node using XPath. Retrieve the required and allowed attributes of the `article` node.

```
XMLElement articleNode = (XMLElement)(document.selectSingleNode
                        ("catalog/journal/article"));
attrRequired = articleNode.getRequiredAttributes();
System.out.println("The required attributes of the article element
are: ");
for (int i = 0; i < attrRequired.getLength(); i++)
    System.out.println(attrRequired.getName(i) + " ");
attr = articleNode.getAllowedAttributes();
System.out.println("The allowed attributes of the article element
are: ");
for (int i = 0; i < attr.getLength(); i++)
    System.out.println(attr.getName(i) + " ");
```

14. Test the validity of setting a `section` attribute on the `article` element and set the `section` attribute.

```
setAttr =articleNode.canSetAttribute("section", "ORACLE
DEVELOPER");
 if (setAttr == NodeEditVAL.VAL_TRUE)
   articleNode.setAttribute("section", "ORACLE DEVELOPER");

 setAttr = articleNode.canSetAttribute("section", "XSLT");
 if (attrSet == NodeEditVAL.VAL_TRUE)
   System.out.println("Attribute Addition is VALID_TRUE");
 if (attrSet == NodeEditVAL.VAL_FALSE)
   System.out.println("Attribute Addition is VALID_FALSE");
 if (attrSet == NodeEditVAL.VAL_UNKNOWN)
   System.out.println("Attribute Addition is VALID_UNKNOWN");

 short contentType = articleNode.getContentType();
 if (contentType == ElementEditVAL.VAL_ANY_CONTENTTYPE)
   System.out.println("Content type of article element is  VAL_
ANY_CONTENTTYPE");
 if (contentType == ElementEditVAL.VAL_ELEMENTS_CONTENTTYPE)
   System.out.println("Content type of article element is  VAL_
ELEMENTS_CONTENTTYPE");
 if (contentType == ElementEditVAL.VAL_SIMPLE_CONTENTTYPE)
    System.out.println("Content type of article element is  VAL_
SIMPLE_CONTENTTYPE");
 if (contentType == ElementEditVAL.VAL_EMPTY_CONTENTTYPE)
    System.out.println("Content type of article element is  VAL_
EMPTY_CONTENTTYPE");
 if (contentType == ElementEditVAL.VAL_MIXED_CONTENTTYPE)
System.out.println("Content type of article element is  VAL_MIXED_
CONTENTTYPE");
```

15. Retrieve a list of the allowed children of the `article` element. Create and add the sub-elements of the `article` element.

```
elementList = articleNode.getAllowedChildren();
  System.out.println("Elements which may be specified in an
article element are: ");
for (int i = 0; i < elementList.getLength(); i++)
System.out.println(elementList.getName(i) + " ");

XMLElement titleElement =(XMLElement)document.
createElement("title");
short editVal =articleNode.canAppendChild(titleElement);

if (editVal == NodeEditVAL.VAL_TRUE) {
   System.out.println("Element addition VALID_TRUE");
articleNode.appendChild(titleElement);
```

```
          }
   if (editVal == NodeEditVAL.VAL_FALSE)
      System.out.println("Element addition is VALID_FALSE");
   if (editVal == NodeEditVAL.VAL_UNKNOWN)
      System.out.println("Element addition is VALID_UNKNOWN");

   XMLElement authorElement =
        (XMLElement)document.createElement("author");
   editVal =articleNode.canAppendChild(authorElement);

   if (editVal == NodeEditVAL.VAL_TRUE) {
      System.out.println("Element addition VALID_TRUE");
   articleNode.appendChild(authorElement);
          }
   if (editVal == NodeEditVAL.VAL_FALSE)
      System.out.println("Element addition is VALID_FALSE");
   if (editVal == NodeEditVAL.VAL_UNKNOWN)
      System.out.println("Element addition is VALID_UNKNOWN");
   XMLText title = (XMLText)document.createTextNode("Declarative Data
   Filtering");
      titleElement.appendChild(title);
      XMLText author = (XMLText)document.createTextNode("Steve
   Muench");
      authorElement.appendChild(author);
```

16. Test the validity of the `journal` node.

```
   short nodeValid = journalNode.nodeValidity(ElementEditVAL.VAL_
   SCHEMA);
   if (nodeValid == NodeEditVAL.VAL_TRUE)
      System.out.println("Node Valid VALID_TRUE");
   if (nodeValid == NodeEditVAL.VAL_FALSE)
      System.out.println("Node Valid VALID_FALSE");
   if (nodeValid == NodeEditVAL.VAL_UNKNOWN)
      System.out.println("Node Valid VALID_UNKNOWN");
```

17. Test if the `title` element is defined in the `catalog` element.

```
   short elementDefined =catalogElement.isElementDefined("title");
   if (elementDefined == NodeEditVAL.VAL_TRUE)
      System.out.println("Element is defined VALID_TRUE");
   if (elementDefined == NodeEditVAL.VAL_FALSE)
      System.out.println("Element is defined VALID_FALSE");
   if (elementDefined == NodeEditVAL.VAL_UNKNOWN)
      System.out.println("Element is defined VALID_UNKNOWN");

   editVal =catalogElement.canAppendChild(titleElement);
```

```
if (editVal == NodeEditVAL.VAL_TRUE)
  System.out.println("Element addition VALID_TRUE");
if (editVal == NodeEditVAL.VAL_FALSE)
  System.out.println("Element addition is VALID_FALSE");
if (editVal == NodeEditVAL.VAL_UNKNOWN)
  System.out.println("Element addition is VALID_UNKNOWN");
```

18. Retrieve a list of the allowed sub nodes of the `catalog` element.

```
elementList = catalogElement.getAllowedChildren();
System.out.println("Elements which may be specified in the
catalog element are: ");
    for (int i = 0; i < elementList.getLength(); i++)
      System.out.println(elementList.getName(i) + " ");
```

19. Create a `journal` element.

```
XMLElement journalElement =
    (XMLElement)document.createElement("journal");
journalElement.setAttribute("date", "May-June 2008");

XMLElement articleElement = (XMLElement)document.createElement
                              ("article");
journalElement.appendChild(articleElement);
articleElement.setAttribute("section", "ORACLE DEVELOPER");
                titleElement=(XMLElement)document.
                        createElement("title");
                articleElement.appendChild(titleElement);
                authorElement=(XMLElement)document.
createElement("author");
articleElement.appendChild(authorElement);

title = (XMLText)document.createTextNode("On the PGA and Indexing
Collections");
titleElement.appendChild(title);
author = (XMLText)document.createTextNode("Steven Feuerstein");
authorElement.appendChild(author);
```

20. Test the validity of adding the `journal` element to the `catalog` element and add the `journal` element to the `catalog` element.

```
editVal =catalogElement.canAppendChild(journalElement);

if (editVal == NodeEditVAL.VAL_TRUE) {
  System.out.println("Element addition VALID_TRUE");
catalogElement.appendChild(journalElement);

            }
if (editVal == NodeEditVAL.VAL_FALSE)
  System.out.println("Element addition is VALID_FALSE");
if (editVal == NodeEditVAL.VAL_UNKNOWN)
  System.out.println("Element addition is VALID_UNKNOWN");
```

21. Test the validity of the XML document constructed.

```
short valid = document.validateDocument();
 if (valid == NodeEditVAL.VAL_TRUE)
   System.out.println("Document is VALID_TRUE");
 if (valid == NodeEditVAL.VAL_FALSE)
   System.out.println("Document is VALID_FALSE");
 if (valid == NodeEditVAL.VAL_UNKNOWN)
   System.out.println("Document is VALID_UNKNOWN");
```

22. Output the XML document constructed using an LSSerializer, which was discussed in Chapter 7.

```
LSSerializer domWriter =impl.createLSSerializer();
LSOutput output= impl.createLSOutput();
OutputStream outputStream=new FileOutputStream(new File
("catalog.xml"));
output.setByteStream(outputStream);
output.setEncoding("UTF-8");
domWriter.write(document, output);

} catch (MalformedURLException e) {
System.err.println(e.getMessage());
} catch (XSDException e) {
System.err.println(e.getMessage());
} catch (XSLException e) {
System.err.println(e.getMessage());
} catch (FileNotFoundException e) {
System.err.println(e.getMessage());
}
}
```

23. Finally add the main method in which to create an instance of the DOM3Validation class and invoke the validate method.

```
public static void main(String[] args) {
    DOM3Validation dom3Validation = new DOM3Validation();
    dom3Validation.validate();
}
}
```

Copy the `DOM3Validation.java` listing to the `DOM3Validation.java` class in the JDeveloper project `DOM3Validation`. To run the `DOM3Validation.java` application right-click on the **DOM3Validation.java** class and select **Run**.

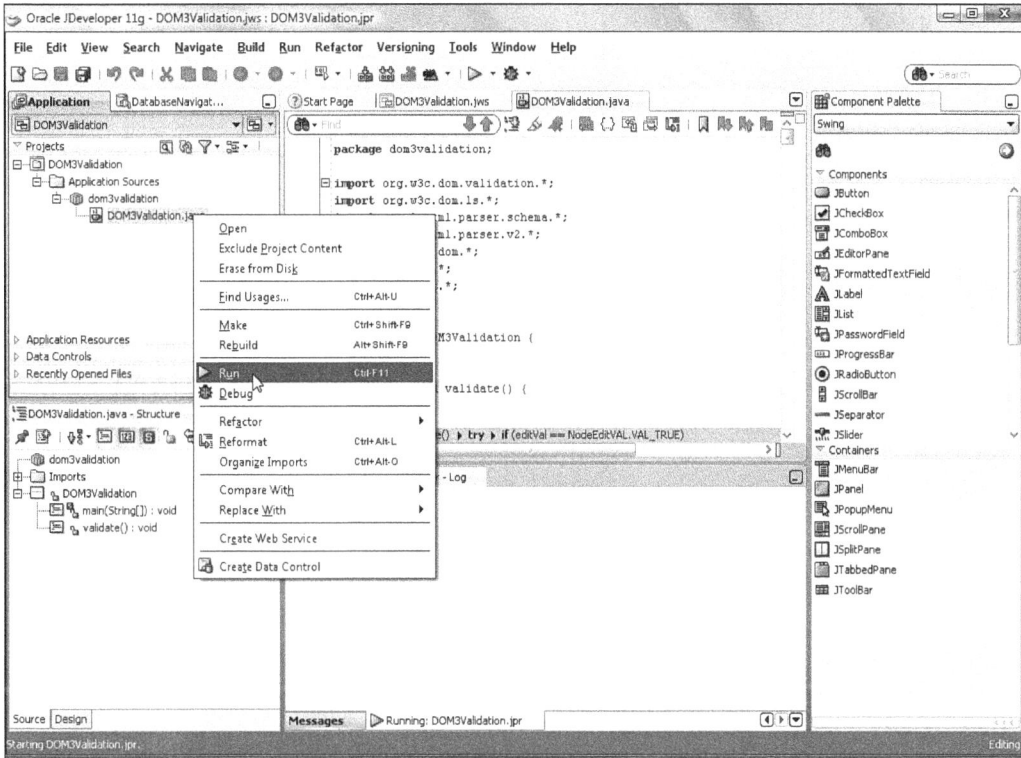

The catalog.xml XML document gets constructed. The output from the DOM3Validation application shows the validity of adding/removing elements and attributes in catalog.xml. Snippets from the output were also listed in the different method sections earlier.

```
Running: DOM3Validation.jpr - Log
domsvalidation.DOMSValidation
Element at index 0 is catalog
Element at index 1 is journal
Element at index 2 is article
The required attributes of the catalog element are:
publisher
The allowed attributes of the catalog element are:
title
publisher
Attribute Addition is VALID_FALSE
Attribute Removal is VALID_TRUE
Attribute Removal is VALID_FALSE
Element Removal is VALID_TRUE
The required attributes of the journal element are:
The allowed attributes of the journal element are:
date
Attribute Addition is VALID_TRUE
Attribute Addition is VALID_FALSE
The required attributes of the article element are:
The allowed attributes of the article element are:
section
Attribute Addition is VALID_FALSE
Content type of article element is  VAL_ELEMENTS_CONTENTTYPE
Elements which may be specified in an article element are:
title
author
Element addition VALID_TRUE
Element addition VALID_TRUE
Node Valid VALID_TRUE
Element is defined VALID_FALSE
Element addition is VALID_FALSE
Elements which may be specified in the catalog element are:
journal
Element addition VALID_TRUE
Document is VALID_TRUE
Process exited with exit code 0.
```

Select **View | Refresh** to add the completely constructed XML document,
`catalog.xml`, to the **Application Navigator**.

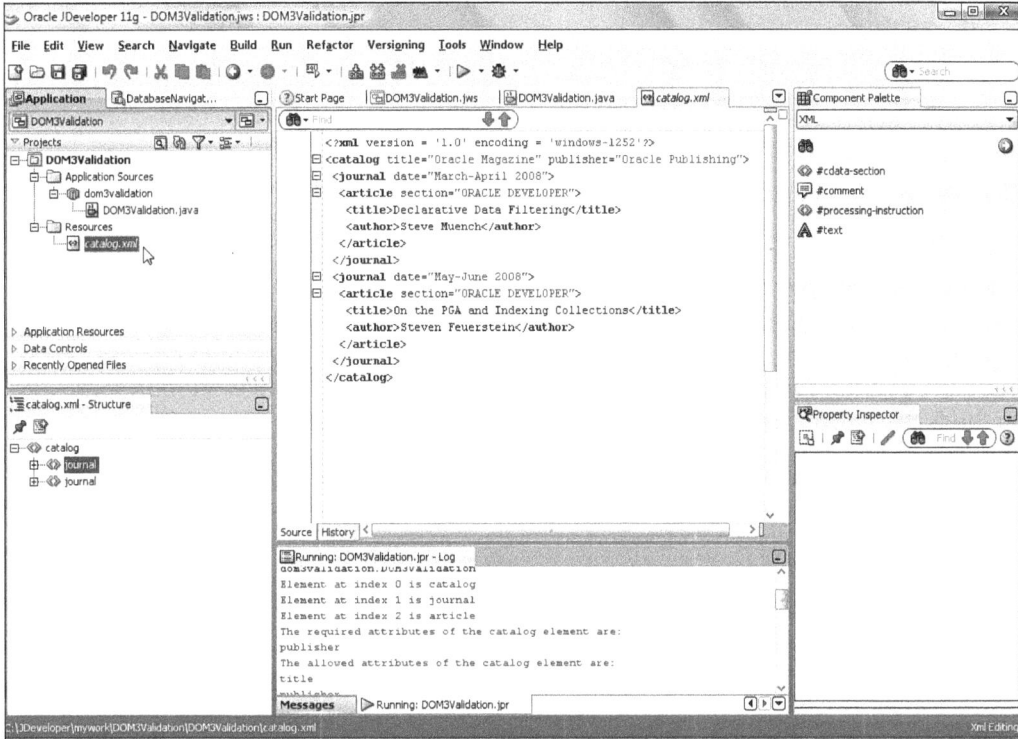

XDK 11g limitations

The DOM 3 Validation specification implementation in Oracle XDK 11g has some
limitations, which are listed as follows:

1. The root element in an XML document is required to make the document
   valid. The DOM 3 Validation specification implementation in XDK 11g
   permits the removal of the root element. The validity test for the removal
   of root element, `catalog`, returns `VAL_TRUE`, whereas it should return
   `VAL_FALSE`.

2. The cardinality of an element is not taken into consideration. In the
   example schema, `catalog.xsd`, even if the `journal` element is defined with
   `minOccurs` cardinality of 1, its removal, which makes number of `journal`
   elements less than 1, is valid as indicated by the return value `VAL_TRUE` for
   the `canRemoveChild` validity test.

3. The canAppendChild method returns VAL_UNKNOWN for the validity test to add an XMLText node to an XMLElement node even with the xs:element construct in the schema defined as of the type xs:string.

4. The setContinuousValidityChecking(boolean continuousValidityChecking) method of XMLDocument class generates an error if continuous validity checking is set to true.

Summary

The methods you've used in this chapter cover DOM Level 3.0 Validation, letting you test whether you can add or remove elements and attributes from an XML document according to a given schema. We constructed and dynamically validated an example XML document catalog.xml with an XML schema catalog.xsd. The DOM 3 Validation implementation in XDK 11g does have a limitation in that not all methods are supported.

In the next chapter we will discuss the **Java API** for **XML Binding (JAXB)** to bind an XML schema to Java classes.

9
JAXB 2.0

Java Architecture for **XML Binding (JAXB)** is an API/framework that binds XML schemas to Java representations. JAXB consists of two components: a compiler that compiles an XML schema into an equivalent Java model, and an API that may be used for basic operations such as marshalling and unmarshalling of XML documents. Marshalling an XML document means creating an XML document from Java objects. Unmarshalling means creating a Java representation of an XML document (or, in effect, the reverse of marshalling). JAXB unmarshalling is similar to parsing an XML document using a SAX or a DOM parser, but is easier than parsing. In parsing, first a parser has to be created and subsequently a content handler (for SAX) or a Document Object Model (for DOM) has to be created. JAXB provides a simpler API for accessing an XML document. You may retrieve the element and attribute values of the XML document from the Java representation. JAXB marshalling is similar to serializing a DOM structure to an XML document using the **TrAX (Transformation API** for **XML)**, but is simpler than the Transformation API as a Transformer does not need to be created. JAXB is effectively a form of highly controlled, structured serialization.

JAXB was introduced as JAXB version 1.0. The new Web Services stack in Java EE 5.0 includes support for **Java API** for **XML web services (JAX-WS)** 2.0 and JAXB 2.0. A practical use of JAXB 2.0 is in implementing Web Services and **Service Oriented Architecture (SOA)**. In the JAX-WS and JAXB 2.0 integration, JAX-WS delegates all data binding to JAXB. During development time JAXB generates Java types from a WSDL schema, and generates the WSDL schema from Java types. During runtime JAXB marshals/unmarshals the SOAP message and the payload. This chapter discusses the most common application of JAXB 2.0 in marshalling and unmarshalling XML documents.

Java Specification Request (JSR) 222 specifies the Java Architecture for XML Binding (JAXB) 2.0. JAXB 2.0 has some new features, which facilitate the marshalling and unmarshalling of an XML document. JAXB 2.0 also allows you to map a Java object to an XML document or an XML schema. Some of the new features in JAXB 2.0 include:

- JAXB 2.0 requires J2SE 5.0 or later as it uses some of the new language features such as annotations and generic types.

- Smaller runtime libraries are required for JAXB 2.0, which require lesser runtime memory.

- Significantly fewer Java classes are generated from a schema by the binding compiler, compared to JAXB 1.0. For each top-level `complexType`, 2.0 generates a value class instead of an interface and an implementation class with JAXB 1.0. A value class is a Java class that consists of attributes defined as variables and getter and setter methods for the attributes. For each top-level `element`, JAXB 2.0 generates a `Factory` class method instead of an interface and an implementation class with JAXB 1.0.

- Support for all W3C XML schema constructs. JAXB 1.0 does not support key XML schema components such as `any`, `anyAttribute`, `key`, `keyref`, and `unique`. It also does not support attributes such as `complexType. abstract`, `element.abstract`, `element.substitutionGroup`, `xsi:type`, `complexType.block`, `complexType.final`, `element.block`, `element. final`, `schema.blockDefault`, and `schema.finalDefault`. JAXB 2.0 provides support for all the XML schema constructs in the schema, allowing you to bind a wider range of XML schemas.

- Support for generic/parameterized types (refer to `http://java.sun.com/ j2se/1.5/pdf/generics-tutorial.pdf`). With generic types, casts are not required and type checking is performed at compile time. Using casts (as in JAXB 1.0) runs the risk of incurring a runtime exception if an object is cast to a type of which is not an instance.

- Support for JAXP 1.3 validation. The `UnMarshaller` interface method `setValidating()` has been deprecated and replaced with JAXP 1.3 validation. Validation is the process of confirming that an XML document conforms to an XML schema. JAXB 2.0 Validation's additional features make it much more flexible than JAXB 1.0's. In JAXB 1.0 validation is available only during the unmarshalling operation, and it is terminated if an error is found. In JAXB 2.0, validation is also available during the marshalling operation, which continues even if a validation error occurs when a custom `ValidationEventHandler` is used.

- Support for binding Java to XML with the `javax.xml.bind.annotation` package. JAXB 2.0 provides bi-directional mapping with which an annotated Java class may be mapped to an XML schema.

JDeveloper 11g supports JAXB 2.0 through TopLink. JAXB 2.0 provides a XML schema compiler to bind an XML schema to Java classes. We shall use the JAXB 2.0 XML schema compiler to bind an XML schema to Java objects. Subsequently, we shall marshal an XML document from the Java classes, and unmarshal an XML document, using the JAXB 2.0 API. We shall also bind a Java class containing JAXB annotations to an XML document.

Setting the environment

In JDeveloper 11g, create an application and a project. Select **File | New**, and in the **New Gallery** window select **Categories | General** and **Items | Generic Application**, and click on **OK**. In the **Create Generic Application** window specify an **Application Name**, JAXB, and click on **Next**. In the **Name your Generic project** window specify a **Project Name**, JAXB, and click on **Finish**.

An application and a project get added to the **Application Navigator**. In the project, create an XML schema with **File | New**. In the **New Gallery** window select **Categories | General | XML** and **Items | XML Schema**, and click on **OK**.

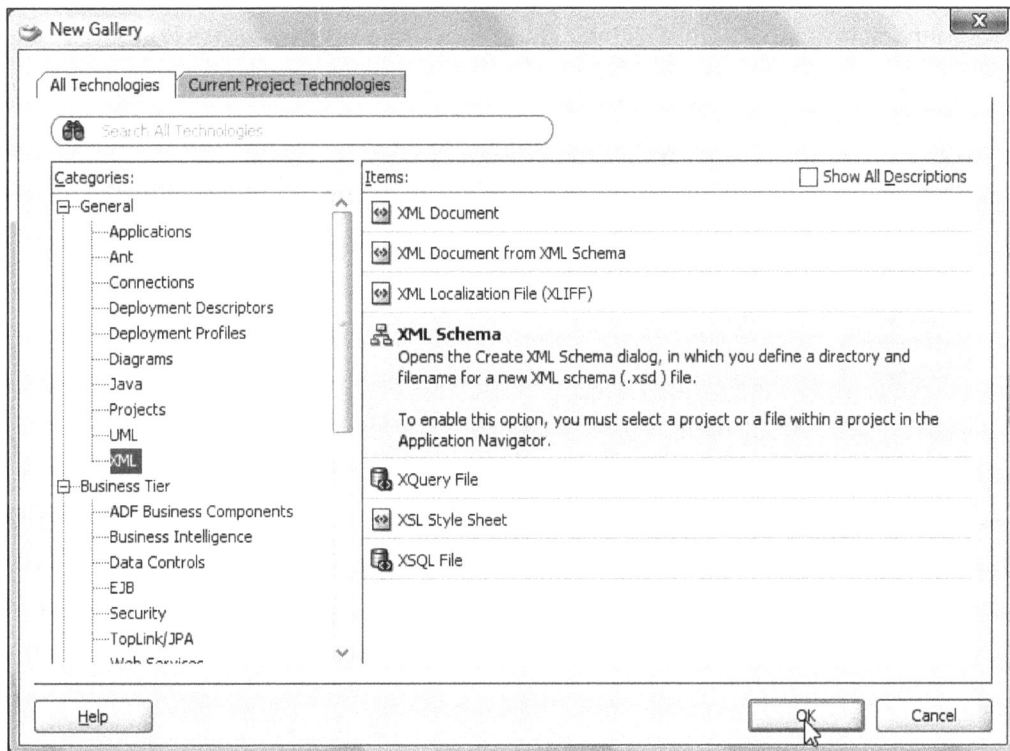

In the **Create XML Schema** window specify a **File Name**, catalog.xsd, and click on **OK**. An XML schema gets added to the JAXB project.

We need to add the **Oracle XML Parser v2** library, which contains the **Java API for XML Processing (JAXP)** and the XML parsers. Also add the **Xml.jar** JAR file, which contains the javax.xml.bind package API. To add the **Oracle XML Parser v2** library select **Tools | Project Properties**. In the **Project Properties** window select **Libraries and Classpath** and select **Add Library**. In the **Add Library** window select the **Oracle XML Parser v2** library and click on **OK**. To add the **Xml.jar** JAR select **Add JAR/ Directory**. In the **Add Archive or Directory** window select the **Xml.jar** JAR file from the C:\Oracle\Middleware\jdeveloper\modules\oracle.xdk_11.1.1 directory and click on **Select**. The libraries and JAR file in the JAXB project are shown as follows:

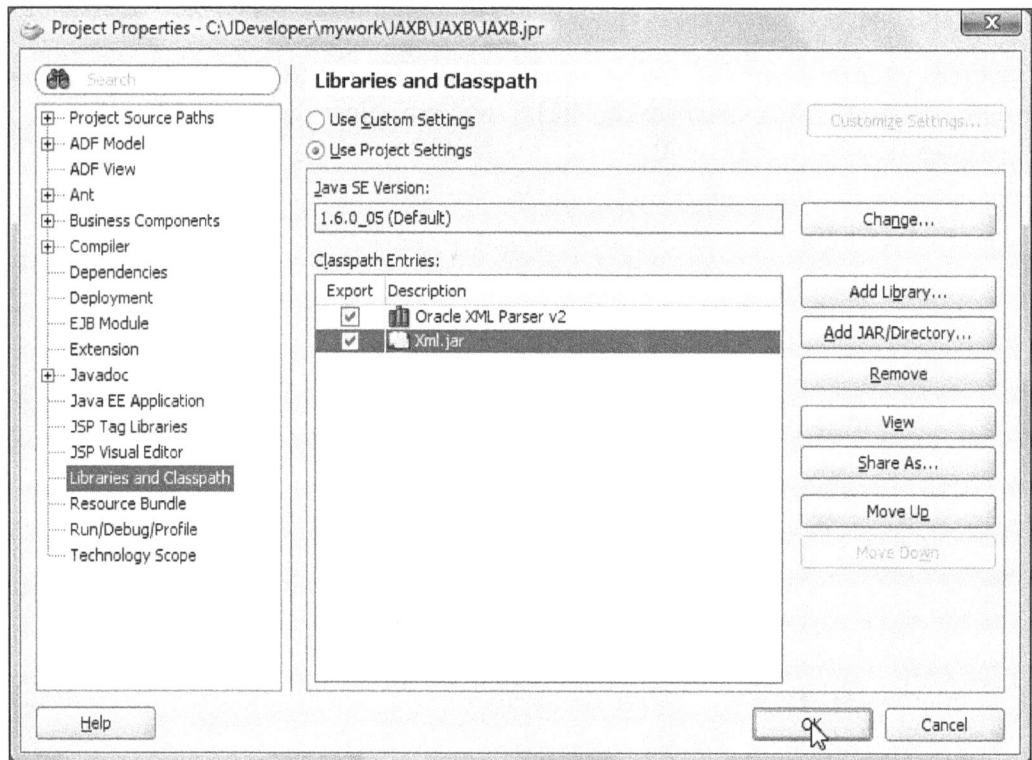

The JAXB compiler generates Java classes corresponding to the top-level complexTypes. The XML schema was introduced in Chapter 2. In an XML schema an element is represented with `<xs:element/>`, and a `complexType` is represented by `<xs:complexType/>`. The example XML schema, `catalog.xsd`, which we shall compile using the JAXB compiler is listed as follows:

```
<xsd:schema xmlns:xsd="http://www.w3.org/2001/XMLSchema">
  <xsd:element name="catalog" type="catalogType"/>
  <xsd:complexType name="catalogType">
    <xsd:sequence>
      <xsd:element name="journal" type="journalType" minOccurs="0"
      maxOccurs="unbounded"/>
    </xsd:sequence>
    <xsd:attribute name="title" type="xsd:string"/>
    <xsd:attribute name="publisher"  type="xsd:string"/>
  </xsd:complexType>

  <xsd:complexType name="journalType">
    <xsd:sequence>
      <xsd:element name="article" type="articleType" minOccurs="0"
      maxOccurs="unbounded"/>
    </xsd:sequence>
    <xsd:attribute name="date" type="xsd:string"/>
  </xsd:complexType>
  <xsd:complexType name="articleType">
    <xsd:sequence>
      <xsd:element name="title" type="xsd:string"/>
      <xsd:element name="author" type="xsd:string"/>
    </xsd:sequence>
    <xsd:attribute name="section" type="xsd:string"/>
  </xsd:complexType>
</xsd:schema>
```

Copy the `catalog.xsd` listing to the `catalog.xsd` file in **Application Navigator**. In the next section, we shall compile the example XML schema into Java classes representation. Subsequently, we shall marshal a Java representation to an XML document. Also, we shall unmarshal an XML document using the JAXB API.

Compiling an XML schema

In this section, we shall compile the example XML schema using the JAXB compiler in JDeveloper 11g. To compile the example XML schema, select the schema node in **Application Navigator** and select **File | New**. In the **New Gallery** window select **Categories | Business Tier | TopLink/JPA** and **Items | JAXB 2.0 Content Model from XML Schema**, and click on **OK**.

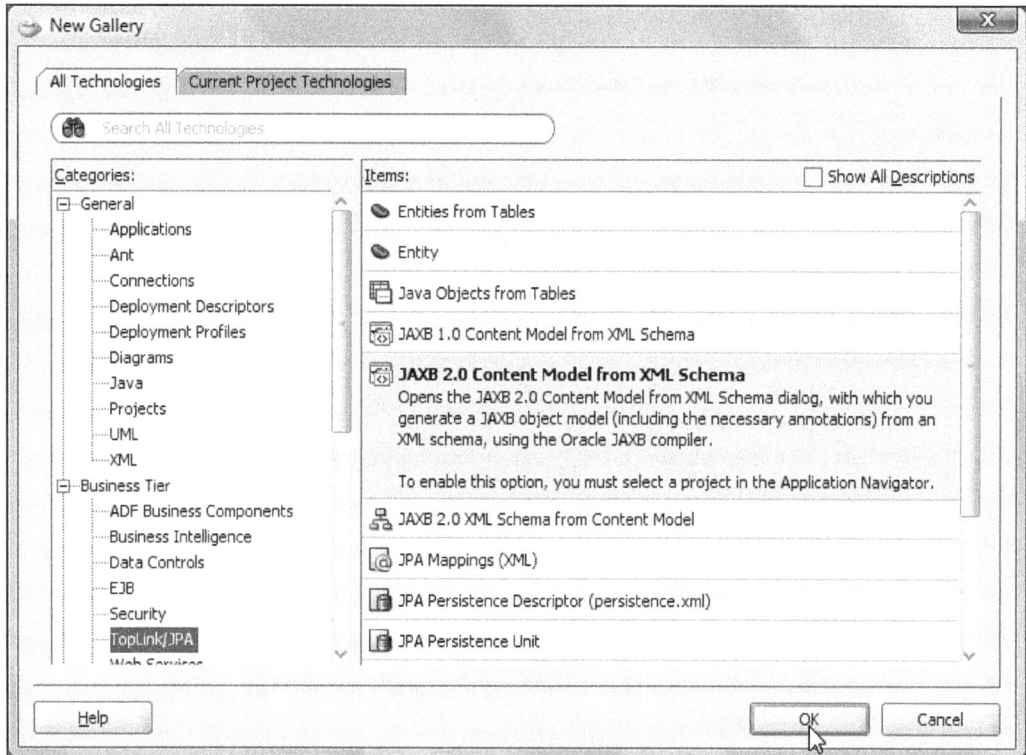

In the **JAXB 2.0 Content Model from XML Schema** window select the **Schema File** as `catalog.xsd`, if not already selected. Select the **Output Source Directory** as **src** (the default). Specify **Package Name for Generated Classes** as **jaxb** and click on **OK**.

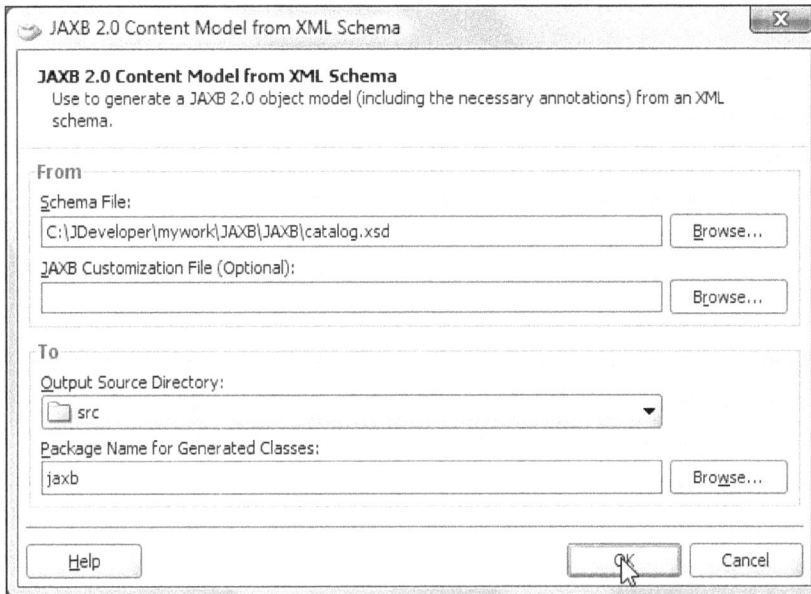

The schema gets compiled and the Java classes get generated in the specified package. A Java class gets generated for each of the `complexType` definitions. The value class `CatalogType.java` gets generated for `complexType catalogType`. `CatalogType.java` consists of accessor methods for the `journal`, `title`, and `publisher` properties and is listed as follows:

```
package jaxb;

import java.util.ArrayList;
import java.util.List;
import javax.xml.bind.annotation.XmlAccessType;
import javax.xml.bind.annotation.XmlAccessorType;
import javax.xml.bind.annotation.XmlAttribute;
import javax.xml.bind.annotation.XmlType;
/**
 * <p>Java class for catalogType complex type.
 *
 * <p>The following schema fragment specifies the expected content
contained within this class.
 *
 * <pre>
```

```
 *   &lt;complexType name="catalogType">
 *     &lt;complexContent>
 *       &lt;restriction base="{http://www.w3.org/2001/
XMLSchema}anyType">
 *         &lt;sequence>
 *           &lt;element name="journal" type="{}journalType"
maxOccurs="unbounded" minOccurs="0"/>
 *         &lt;/sequence>
 *         &lt;attribute name="title" type="{http://www.w3.org/2001/
XMLSchema}string" />
 *         &lt;attribute name="publisher" type="{http://www.w3.org/2001/
XMLSchema}string" />
 *       &lt;/restriction>
 *     &lt;/complexContent>
 *   &lt;/complexType>
 * </pre>
 *
 *
 */
@XmlAccessorType(XmlAccessType.FIELD)
@XmlType(name = "catalogType", propOrder = { "journal" })
public class CatalogType {

    protected List<JournalType> journal;
    @XmlAttribute
    protected String title;
    @XmlAttribute
    protected String publisher;

    /**
     * Gets the value of the journal property.
     *
     * <p>
     * This accessor method returns a reference to the live list,
     * not a snapshot. Therefore any modification you make to the
     * returned list will be present inside the JAXB object.
     * This is why there is not a <CODE>set</CODE> method for the
       journal property.
     *
     * <p>
     * For example, to add a new item, do as follows:
     * <pre>
     *    getJournal().add(newItem);
     * </pre>
     *
```

```
 *
 * <p>
 * Objects of the following type(s) are allowed in the list
 * {@link JournalType }
 *
 *
 */
public List<JournalType> getJournal() {
    if (journal == null) {
        journal = new ArrayList<JournalType>();
    }
    return this.journal;
}

/**
 * Gets the value of the title property.
 *
 * @return
 *     possible object is
 *     {@link String }
 *
 */
public String getTitle() {
    return title;
}

/**
 * Sets the value of the title property.
 *
 * @param value
 *     allowed object is
 *     {@link String }
 *
 */
public void setTitle(String value) {
    this.title = value;
}

/**
 * Gets the value of the publisher property.
 *
 * @return
 *     possible object is
 *     {@link String }
 *
 */
```

```
        public String getPublisher() {
            return publisher;
        }

        /**
         * Sets the value of the publisher property.
         *
         * @param value
         *     allowed object is
         *     {@link String }
         *
         */
        public void setPublisher(String value) {
            this.publisher = value;
        }

    }
```

Java class `JournalType.java` gets generated from the `journalType complexType`. The `JournalType` class consists of accessor methods for the `article` and `date` properties, and is listed as follows:

```
package jaxb;
import java.util.ArrayList;
import java.util.List;
import javax.xml.bind.annotation.XmlAccessType;
import javax.xml.bind.annotation.XmlAccessorType;
import javax.xml.bind.annotation.XmlAttribute;
import javax.xml.bind.annotation.XmlType;
/**
 * <p>Java class for journalType complex type.
 *
 * <p>The following schema fragment specifies the expected content
contained within this class.
 *
 * <pre>
 * &lt;complexType name="journalType">
 *   &lt;complexContent>
 *     &lt;restriction base="{http://www.w3.org/2001/
XMLSchema}anyType">
 *       &lt;sequence>
 *         &lt;element name="article" type="{}articleType"
maxOccurs="unbounded" minOccurs="0"/>
 *       &lt;/sequence>
```

```
 *          &lt;attribute name="date" type="{http://www.w3.org/2001/
XMLSchema}string" />
 *      &lt;/restriction>
 *    &lt;/complexContent>
 * &lt;/complexType>
 * </pre>
 */
@XmlAccessorType(XmlAccessType.FIELD)
@XmlType(name = "journalType", propOrder = { "article" })
public class JournalType {
    protected List<ArticleType> article;
    @XmlAttribute
    protected String date;
    /**
     * Gets the value of the article property.
     *
     * <p>
     * This accessor method returns a reference to the live list,
     * not a snapshot. Therefore any modification you make to the
     * returned list will be present inside the JAXB object.
     * This is why there is not a <CODE>set</CODE> method for the
       article property.
     *
     * <p>
     * For example, to add a new item, do as follows:
     * <pre>
     *    getArticle().add(newItem);
     * </pre>
     * <p>
     * Objects of the following type(s) are allowed in the list
     * {@link ArticleType }
     */
    public List<ArticleType> getArticle() {
        if (article == null) {
            article = new ArrayList<ArticleType>();
        }
        return this.article;
    }

    /**
     * Gets the value of the date property.
     * @return
     *     possible object is
     *     {@link String }
     */
```

```
    public String getDate() {
        return date;
    }
    /**
     * Sets the value of the date property.
     * @param value
     *      allowed object is
     *      {@link String }
     */
    public void setDate(String value) {
        this.date = value;
    }
}
```

Java class `ArticleType.java` gets generated corresponding to `complexType`
`articleType`. `ArticleType.java` consists of accessor methods for `title`, `author`,
and `section` properties and is listed as follows:

```
package jaxb;
import javax.xml.bind.annotation.XmlAccessType;
import javax.xml.bind.annotation.XmlAccessorType;
import javax.xml.bind.annotation.XmlAttribute;
import javax.xml.bind.annotation.XmlElement;
import javax.xml.bind.annotation.XmlType;
/**
 * <p>Java class for articleType complex type.
 * <p>The following schema fragment specifies the expected content
contained within this class.
 * <pre>
 * &lt;complexType name="articleType">
 *   &lt;complexContent>
 *     &lt;restriction base="{http://www.w3.org/2001/
XMLSchema}anyType">
 *       &lt;sequence>
 *         &lt;element name="title" type="{http://www.w3.org/2001/
XMLSchema}string"/>
 *         &lt;element name="author" type="{http://www.w3.org/2001/
XMLSchema}string"/>
 *       &lt;/sequence>
 *       &lt;attribute name="section" type="{http://www.w3.org/2001/
XMLSchema}string" />
 *     &lt;/restriction>
 *   &lt;/complexContent>
 * &lt;/complexType>
 * </pre>
```

```
 */
@XmlAccessorType(XmlAccessType.FIELD)
@XmlType(name = "articleType", propOrder = { "title", "author" })
public class ArticleType {
    @XmlElement(required = true)
    protected String title;
    @XmlElement(required = true)
    protected String author;
    @XmlAttribute
    protected String section
    /**
     * Gets the value of the title property.
     * @return
     *     possible object is
     *     {@link String }
     */
    public String getTitle() {
        return title;
    }
    /**
     * Sets the value of the title property.
     * @param value
     *     allowed object is
     *     {@link String }
     */
    public void setTitle(String value) {
        this.title = value;
    }
    /**
     * Gets the value of the author property.
     * @return
     *     possible object is
     *     {@link String }
     */
    public String getAuthor() {
        return author;
    }
    /**
     * Sets the value of the author property.
     * @param value
     *     allowed object is
     *     {@link String }
     */
    public void setAuthor(String value) {
```

```
            this.author = value;
    }
    /**
     * Gets the value of the section property.
     * @return
     *     possible object is
     *     {@link String }
     */
    public String getSection() {
        return section;
    }
    /**
     * Sets the value of the section property.
     * @param value
     *     allowed object is
     *     {@link String }
     */
    public void setSection(String value) {
        this.section = value;
    }
}
```

An ObjectFactory.java factory class also gets generated. The factory class consists of create<> methods to create instances of Java value classes CatalogType.java, JournalType.java, and ArticleType.java, the Java classes corresponding to the complexType definitions. The ObjectFactory.java class also consists of a create method, createCatalog, for the top-level element catalog. ObjectFactory.java class is listed as follows:

```
package jaxb;
import javax.xml.bind.JAXBElement;
import javax.xml.bind.annotation.XmlElementDecl;
import javax.xml.bind.annotation.XmlRegistry;
import javax.xml.namespace.QName;
/**
 * This object contains factory methods for each
 * Java content interface and Java element interface
 * generated in the jaxb package.
 * <p>An ObjectFactory allows you to programatically
 * construct new instances of the Java representation
 * for XML content. The Java representation of XML
 * content can consist of schema derived interfaces
 * and classes representing the binding of schema
 * type definitions, element declarations and model
```

```
 * groups.  Factory methods for each of these are
 * provided in this class.
 */
@XmlRegistry
public class ObjectFactory {
    private final static QName _Catalog_QNAME = new QName("",
"catalog");

    /**
     * Create a new ObjectFactory that can be used to create new
instances of schema derived classes for package: jaxb
     */
    public ObjectFactory() {
    }
    /**
     * Create an instance of {@link JournalType }
     */
    public JournalType createJournalType() {
        return new JournalType();
    }
    /**
     * Create an instance of {@link CatalogType }
     */
    public CatalogType createCatalogType() {
        return new CatalogType();
    }
    /**
     * Create an instance of {@link ArticleType }
     */
    public ArticleType createArticleType() {
        return new ArticleType();
    }
    /**
     * Create an instance of {@link JAXBElement }{@code <}{@link
CatalogType }{@code >}}
     *
     */
    @XmlElementDecl(namespace = "", name = "catalog")
    public JAXBElement<CatalogType> createCatalog(CatalogType value) {
        return new JAXBElement<CatalogType>(_Catalog_QNAME,
CatalogType.class,null, value);
    }
}
```

The Java classes and the `ObjectFactory.java` class generated from compiling the XML schema, `catalog.xsd`, are shown in the **Application Navigator** as follows:

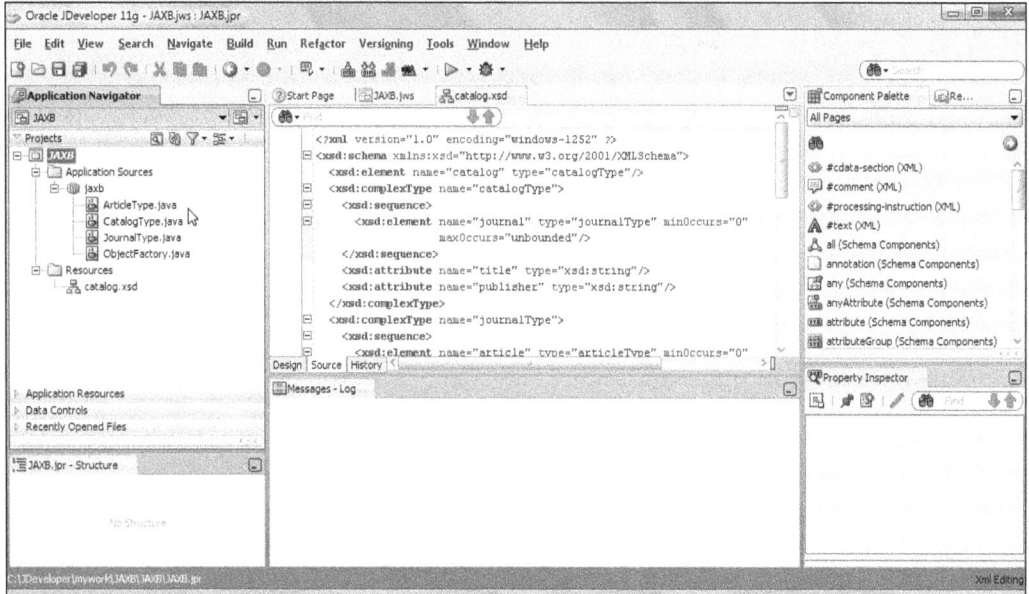

Marshalling an XML document

Marshalling is the construction of an XML document from a Java representation of the document, from the equivalent Java model. In this section, we shall marshal an XML document. The XML document that will be marshalled is listed as follows:

```xml
<?xml version="1.0" encoding = 'UTF-8'?>
<catalog title="Oracle Magazine" publisher="Oracle Publishing">
  <journal date="September-October 2008">
    <article section="FEATURES">
      <title>Share 2.0</title>
      <author>Alan Joch</author>
    </article>
  </journal>
  <journal date="March-April 2008">
    <article section="ORACLE DEVELOPER">
      <title>Declarative Data Filtering</title>
      <author>Steve Muench</author>
    </article>
  </journal>
</catalog>
```

We need to create a Java application to marshal an XML document. Select the project node in the **Application Navigator** and select **File | New**. In the **New Gallery** window select **Categories | General** and **Items | Java Class** and click on **OK**. In the **Create Java Class** window, specify the class name (**JAXBMarshaller**) in the **Name** field and package name (**jaxb**) in the **Package** field and click on **OK**. Java class JAXBMarshaller.java gets added to package jaxb in the **Application Navigator**. In the marshaller application, import the JAXB API package.

```
import javax.xml.bind.*;
```

Create a JAXBContext object, which provides a JAXB context for implementing JAXB binding framework operations. A JAXBContext object is initialized with a colon-separated list of Java package names, which consist of schema-derived classes and user-annotated classes. A user-annotated class is just a Java class containing JAXB annotations.

```
JAXBContext jaxbContext = JAXBContext.newInstance("jaxb");
```

Create a Marshaller object from the JAXBContext object. The Marshaller object is used to marshal a Java object to an XML document.

```
Marshaller marshaller = jaxbContext.createMarshaller();
```

For a formatted output set the Marshaller property jaxb.formatted.output to true.

```
marshaller.setProperty("jaxb.formatted.output",new Boolean(true));
```

Create an ObjectFactory object, which is used to initialize the Java object representation of the XML document to be marshalled. Create a CatalogType object, which represents the root element catalog using the createCatalogType() method of the ObjectFactory class.

```
jaxb.ObjectFactory factory = new jaxb.ObjectFactory();
CatalogType catalog = factory.createCatalogType();
```

Set the title and publisher attributes of the root element catalog.

```
catalog.setTitle("Oracle Magazine");
catalog.setPublisher("Oracle Publishing");
```

Create a JournalType object, which represents a journal element. Set the date attribute of the journal element using the setDate method.

```
JournalType journal = factory.createJournalType();
journal.setDate("September-October 2008");
```

Get a `List` of parameter type `JournalType` from the `CatalogType` object, and add the `JournalType` object to the `List` object.

```
List<JournalType> journalList = catalog.getJournal();
journalList.add(journal);
```

Create an `ArticleType` object, which represents an `article` element. Set the `edition`, `title`, and `author` values.

```
ArticleType article = factory.createArticleType();
article.setSection("FEATURES");
article.setTitle("Share 2.0");
article.setAuthor("Alan Joch");
```

Obtain a `List` object of parameter type `ArticleType` and add the `ArticleType` object to the `List`.

```
List<ArticleType> articleList = journal.getArticle();
articleList.add(article);
```

Similarly, add another `JournalType` object to the `JournalType` parametrized `List` obtained from the `CatalogType` object. Next, obtain a `JAXBElement` object of parameter type `CatalogType` using a factory object. A `JAXBElement` object is a JAXB representation of an XML element.

```
JAXBElement<CatalogType> catalogElement=factory.
createCatalog(catalog);
```

The `Marshaller` interface provides overloaded `marshal()` methods to marshal a Java object to either a `ContentHandler` object, a `Node`, an `OutputStream`, a `Result` object, or a `Writer` object. In the example application a Java object is marshalled to an XML document using an `OutputStream`.

```
String xmlDocument = "catalog.xml";
marshaller.marshal(catalogElement, new FileOutputStream(xmlDocument));
```

`JAXBMarshaller.java` is listed as follows with explanations:

1. First, we specify the package and import statements.
    ```
    package jaxb;
    import javax.xml.bind.*;
    import java.io.File;
    import java.io.FileOutputStream;
    import java.io.IOException;
    import java.util.List;
    ```

2. Define Java class `JAXBMarshaller` for marshalling an XML document.
    ```
    public class JAXBMarshaller {
    ```

3. Define method `generateXMLDocument` to generate an XML document using JAXB marshalling.

```
public void generateXMLDocument(File xmlDocument) {
    try {
```

4. Create a `Marshaller` object and a `ObjectFactory` object.

```
JAXBContext jaxbContext = JAXBContext.newInstance("jaxb");
Marshaller marshaller = jaxbContext.createMarshaller();
marshaller.setProperty("jaxb.formatted.output",new Boolean(true));
jaxb.ObjectFactory factory = new jaxb.ObjectFactory();
```

5. Construct the DOM tree to be marshalled to an XML document.

```
CatalogType catalog = factory.createCatalogType();
catalog.setTitle("Oracle Magazine");
catalog.setPublisher("Oracle Publishing");
JournalType journal = factory.createJournalType();
journal.setDate("September-October 2008");
List<JournalType> journalList =  catalog.getJournal();
journalList.add(journal);
ArticleType article = factory.createArticleType();
article.setSection("FEATURES");
article.setTitle("Share 2.0");
article.setAuthor("Alan Joch");
List<ArticleType> articleList = journal.getArticle();
articleList.add(article);
journal = factory.createJournalType();
journal.setDate("March-April 2008");

journalList.add(journal);
article = factory.createArticleType();
article.setSection("ORACLE DEVELOPER");
article.setTitle("Declarative Data Filtering");
article.setAuthor("Steve Muench");
articleList = journal.getArticle();
articleList.add(article);
```

6. Marshal the DOM tree Java object to an XML document.

```
JAXBElement<CatalogType> catalogElement=factory.
createCatalog(catalog);
    marshaller.marshal(catalogElement, new FileOutputStream(xmlDocu
ment));

    } catch (IOException e) {
        System.err.println(e.toString());
```

```
        } catch (JAXBException e) {
            System.err.println(e.toString());

        }

    }
```

7. Finally, add the `main` method, in which create an instance of the
    `JAXBMarshaller` class and invoke the `generateXMLDocument` method.

```
    public static void main(String[] argv) {
        String xmlDocument = "catalog.xml";
        JAXBMarshaller jaxbMarshaller = new JAXBMarshaller();
        jaxbMarshaller.generateXMLDocument(new File(xmlDocument));
    }
}
```

Copy the `JAXBMarshaller.java` listing to the `JAXBMarshaller` class in the `JAXB`
project in the **Application Navigator**. To run the `JAXBMarshaller` application,
right-click on **JAXBMarshaller.java** in **Application Navigator** and select **Run**.

The DOM tree Java object constructed using the JAXB compiler generated classes
gets marshalled to an XML document. Select **View | Refresh** to add the `catalog.xml`
document to the **Application Navigator**.

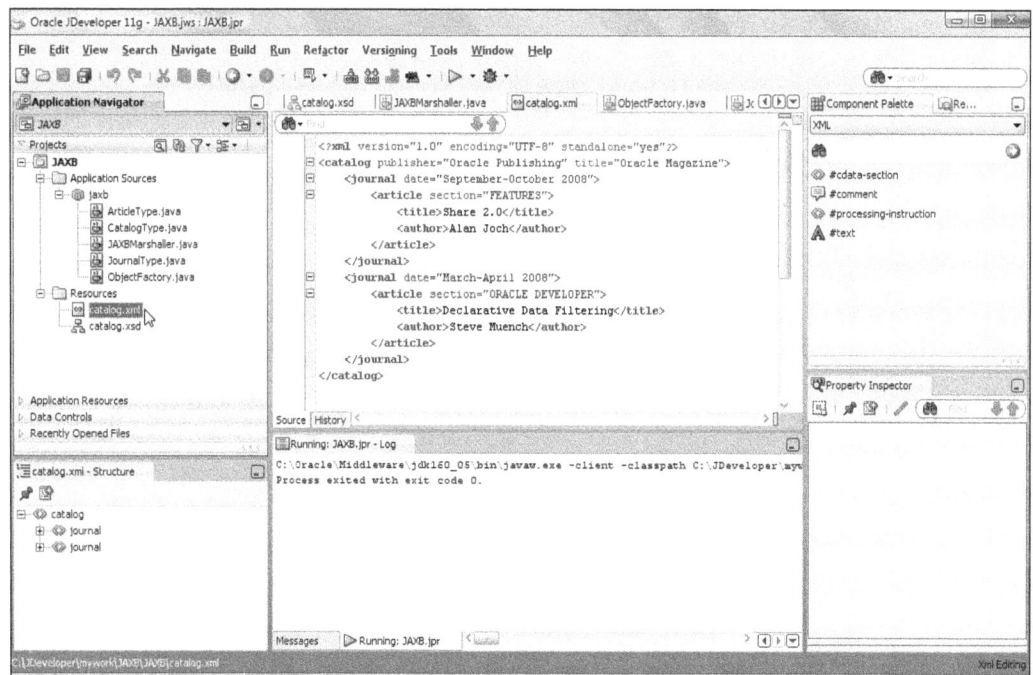

Unmarshalling an XML document

In this section, we shall unmarshal an XML document using the JAXB API and the Java classes generated by compiling the example XML schema. A prerequisite for unmarshalling is that the XML document should conform to the XML schema from which the binding classes are generated. The XML document that we shall unmarshal is the same that is marshalled in the previous section. Create a Java application, `JAXBUnMarshaller.java`, in JDeveloper project JAXB similar to the `JAXBMarshaller` application. In the `JAXBUnMarshaller` class import the JAXB API package. As `JAXBUnMarshaller.java` is created in the same package as the binding classes, the binding classes do not need to be imported.

```
import javax.xml.bind.*;
```

Create a `JAXBContext` object using static method `newInstance(String contextPath)`. `ContextPath` is a colon-separated list of packages that contain the schema-derived binding classes.

```
JAXBContext jaxbContext=JAXBContext.newInstance("jaxb");
```

Create an `Unmarshaller` object, which is used to convert an XML document to a Java object, from the `JAXBContext` object.

```
Unmarshaller unMarshaller = jaxbContext.createUnmarshaller();
```

If the application were a JAXB 1.0 application, we would have set the `Unmarshaller` to be validating using the `setValidating()` method. The `setValidating()` method has been deprecated in JAXB 2.0. Schema validation in JAXB 2.0 is performed using the JAXP 1.3 Validation API. Create a `SchemaFactory` object and create a `Schema` object from the `SchemaFactory` object. Set the schema on the `Unmarshaller` object using the `setSchema` method.

```
SchemaFactory schemaFactory = SchemaFactory.newInstance("http://www.
w3.org/2001/XMLSchema");
Schema schema = schemaFactory.newSchema(new File("catalog.xsd"));
unMarshaller.setSchema(schema);
```

Error handling in JAXB 2.0 may be customized using a custom `ValidationEventHandler` that overrides the default event handler. To add error handling to the example application, create a class `CustomValidationEventHandler` that implements the `ValidatonEventHandler` interface. In the implementation class implement the `handleEvent` method, in which output an error message including the line number at which the error is generated. The Boolean value returned by the `handleEvent` method indicates if the `unmarshal` operation should continue. If the value returned is `true`, the `unmarshal` operation continues. If the value returned is `false`, the `unmarshal` operation is terminated. The provision to continue with the `unmarshal` operation even after an error is generated is not available in JAXB 1.0, which uses "structural unmarshalling" in which if a structural error is found in the XML document the unmarshalling is terminated and an `UnmarshalException` is generated. The `CustomValidationEventHandler` will return `true` if a warning is generated, and return `false` if an error is generated.

```
class CustomValidationEventHandler implements ValidationEventHandler {
    public boolean handleEvent(ValidationEvent event) {
        if (event.getSeverity() == ValidationEvent.WARNING) {
            return true;
        }
        if ((event.getSeverity() == ValidationEvent.ERROR)
                || (event.getSeverity() ==
            ValidationEvent.FATAL_ERROR)) {
    System.err.println("Validation Error:" + event.getMessage());

    ValidationEventLocator locator = event.getLocator();
    System.err.println("at line number:" +
    locator.getLineNumber());
            System.err.println("Unmarshalling Terminated");
            return false;
        }
        return true;
    }
}
```

A custom `ValidationEventHandler` may also be used during the marshalling operation.

The `Unmarshaller` interface provides overloaded `unmarshal` methods to unmarshal an XML document from a `File`, `InputSource`, `InputStream`, `Node`, `Source`, or `URL` object. Unmarshal using the `unmarshal(File)` method, which returns a parameterized `JAXBElement` object. The parameter type is `CatalogType`.

```
File xmlDocument = new File("catalog.xml");
JAXBElement<CatalogType> catalogElement = (JAXBElement<CatalogType>)
unMarshaller.unmarshal(xmlDocument);
```

Obtain a `CatalogType` object from the `JAXBElement` object using the `getValue()` method.

```
CatalogType catalog = catalogElement.getValue();
```

Output the `title` and `publisher` attribute values using getter methods for these attributes.

```
System.out.println("Journal Title: " + catalog.getTitle());
System.out.println("Publisher: " + catalog.getPublisher());
```

Obtain a parameterized list of parameter type `JournalType`. Iterate over the `JournalType List` object. Output the `jounal date` value using the getter method `getDate`. Obtain a parameterized `List` of parameter type `ArticleType` for each of the `JournalType` objects. Iterate over the parameterized `List` of parameter type `ArticleType` and output values for `section`, `title`, and `author` using the getter methods `getSection`, `getTitle`, and `getAuthor`.

```
List<JournalType> journalList = catalog.getJournal();
for (int i = 0; i < journalList.size(); i++) {
   JournalType journal =  journalList.get(i);
   System.out.println("Journal Date: "+ journal.getDate());
   List<ArticleType> articleList = journal.getArticle();

   for (int j = 0; j < articleList.size(); j++) {
      ArticleType article =  articleList.get(j);
      System.out.println("Section: "+ article.getSection());
      System.out.println("Title: " + article.getTitle());
      System.out.println("Author: " + article.getAuthor());
         }
      }
```

Java class `JAXBUnMarshaller.java` is listed as follows with explanations:

1. First, we add the `package` and `import` statements.

   ```
   package jaxb;
   import javax.xml.bind.*;
   import javax.xml.validation.SchemaFactory;
   import javax.xml.validation.Schema;
   import org.xml.sax.SAXException;
   import java.io.*;
   import java.util.List;
   ```

2. Define the Java class `JAXBUnMarshaller` to unmarshal an XML document.

   ```
   public class JAXBUnMarshaller {
   ```

3. Define a method `unMarshall` to unmarshal an XML document.

   ```
   public void unMarshall(File xmlDocument) {
      try {
   ```

4. Create an `Unmarshaller` object and set an XML schema for validation on the `Unmarshaller` object. Also set a `CustomValidationEventHandler` on the `Unmarshaller` object.

```
JAXBContext jaxbContext = JAXBContext.newInstance("jaxb");
Unmarshaller unMarshaller = jaxbContext.createUnmarshaller();
SchemaFactory schemaFactory = SchemaFactory.newInstance("http://
www.w3.org/2001/XMLSchema");
Schema schema = schemaFactory.newSchema(new File("catalog.xsd"));
unMarshaller.setSchema(schema);
CustomValidationEventHandler validationEventHandler = new
CustomValidationEventHandler();
unMarshaller.setEventHandler(validationEventHandler);
```

5. Unmarshal the XML document `catalog.xml` and output the element and attribute values.

```
JAXBElement<CatalogType> catalogElement = (JAXBElement<CatalogType
>) unMarshaller.unmarshal(xmlDocument);
CatalogType catalog = catalogElement.getValue();
System.out.println("Journal Title: " + catalog.getTitle());
System.out.println("Publisher: " + catalog.getPublisher());
List<JournalType> journalList = catalog.getJournal();
    for (int i = 0; i < journalList.size(); i++) {

    JournalType journal =  journalList.get(i);
     System.out.println("Journal Date: "+ journal.getDate());
     List<ArticleType> articleList = journal.getArticle();
      for (int j = 0; j < articleList.size(); j++) {
      ArticleType article = articleList.get(j);

      System.out.println("Section: "+ article.getSection());
      System.out.println("Title: " + article.getTitle());
      System.out.println("Author: " + article.getAuthor());
              }
           }
        } catch (JAXBException e) {
          System.err.println(e.getMessage());
        } catch (SAXException e) {
          System.err.println(e.getMessage());
        }
     }
```

6. Add the `main` method, in which create an instance of the `JAXBUnMarshaller` class and invoke the `unMarshall` method.

```java
public static void main(String[] argv) {
    File xmlDocument = new File("catalog.xml");
    JAXBUnMarshaller jaxbUnmarshaller = new JAXBUnMarshaller();

    jaxbUnmarshaller.unMarshall(xmlDocument);

}
```

7. Finally, define the `CustomValidationEventHandler` class.

```java
class CustomValidationEventHandler implements
ValidationEventHandler {
    public boolean handleEvent(ValidationEvent event) {
      if (event.getSeverity() == ValidationEvent.WARNING) {
            return true;
      }
      if ((event.getSeverity() == ValidationEvent.ERROR)
|| (event.getSeverity() == ValidationEvent.FATAL_ERROR))  {

System.err.println("Validation Error:" +   event.getMessage());

        ValidationEventLocator locator = event.getLocator();
System.err.println("at line number:" + locator.getLineNumber());
        System.err.println("Unmarshalling Terminated");
            return false;
        }
        return true;
    }

  }
}
```

Copy the JAXBUnMarshaller listing to the JAXBUnMarshaller.java class in the JAXB project in the **Application Navigator**. To unmarshal the example XML document, catalog.xml, right-click on **JAXBUnMarshaller.java** and select **Run**. The output from JAXBUnMarshaller.java lists the values of the different attributes and elements in the example XML document.

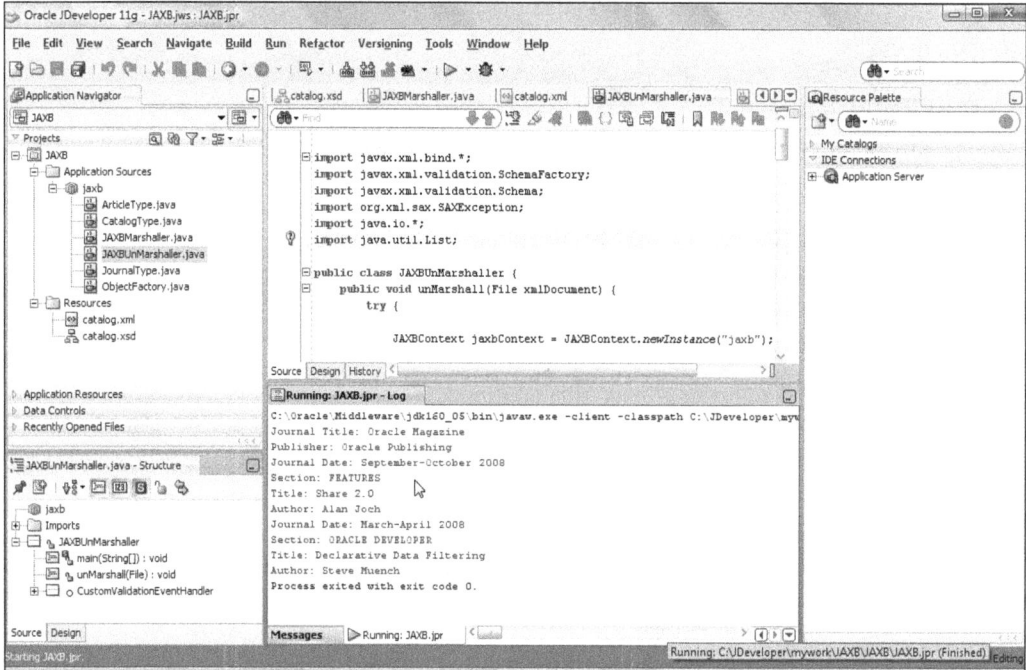

Mapping Java to XML using annotations

The JAXB compiler binds an XML schema to Java objects. JAXB 2.0 has added the provision to bi-directionally marshal a Java object to an XML schema or an XML document using annotations. The annotations are defined in the javax.xml.bind. annotation package. The following table shows some of the most commonly used annotations, as defined in the javax.xml.bind.annotation package.

Annotation Type	Description	Annotation Elements
XmlValue	Maps a class to an XML schema complex type with simpleContent or an XML schema simple type.	-
XmlType	Maps a class or an enum type to an XML schema type, which may be a simple type or a complex type.	name — Name of XML schema type. namespace — Target namespace of XML schema type. propOrder — Specifies order of XML schema elements when a class is mapped to a complex type.
XmlSchema	Maps a package name to a XML namespace.	attributeFormDefault — Specifies value of attributeFormDefault attribute. elementFormDefault — Specifies value of attribute elementFormDefault. namespace — XML namespace. xmlns — Maps namespace prefixes to namespace URIs.
XmlRootElement	Maps a class to root element.	name — Local name of root element. namespace — Namespace of root element.
XmlList	Maps a property to a list simple type.	-
XmlEnum	Maps an enum to simple type with enumeration.	value — Enumeration value.
XmlElement	Maps a JavaBean property to an element.	defaultValue — Default value of element. name — Element name. namespace — Target namespace of element. nillable — Specifies if element is nillable. Default is false. Type — Element type.
XmlAttribute	Maps a JavaBean property to an attribute.	name — Attribute name. namespace — Attribute namespace. required — Specifies if attribute is required. Default is false.

In this section we shall generate the following example XML document from a Java object using JAXB 2.0 annotations.

```
<?xml version="1.0" encoding="UTF-8" standalone="yes"?>
<catalog journal="Oracle Magazine">
    <publisher>Oracle Publishing</publisher>
    <edition>March-April 2008</edition>
    <title>Declarative Data Filtering</title>
    <author>Steve Muench</author>
</catalog>
```

The XML schema on which the XML document is based is listed as follows:

```
<xsd:schema xmlns:xsd="http://www.w3.org/2001/XMLSchema">
<xsd:element name="catalog">
<xsd:complexType>
<xsd:sequence>
<xsd:element name="publisher" type="xsd:string"/>
<xsd:element name="edition" type="xsd:string"/>
<xsd:element name="title" type="xsd:string"/>
<xsd:element name="author" type="xsd:string"/>
</xsd:sequence>
<xsd:attribute name="journal" type="xsd:string"/>
</xsd:complexType>
</xsd:element>
</xsd:schema>
```

To create the XML document, create an annotated class, `Catalog.java`, using **File | New**. Create the root element of the XML document with `@XmlRootElement` annotation. Create a `complexType` using `@XmlType` annotation.

```
@XmlRootElement
@XmlType(name="", propOrder={"publisher", "edition", "title",
"author"})
```

The annotation element `name` is specified as an empty string, because the `complexType` is defined within an element. The element order is specified using the `propOrder` annotation element. In the `Catalog` class define constructors for the class, and define the different JavaBean properties (`publisher`, `edition`, `title`, `author`). The root element `catalog` has an attribute `journal`. Define the `journal` attribute using `@XmlAttribute` annotation.

```
@XmlAttribute
protected String journal;
```

Define getter and setter methods for the different properties and the `journal` attribute. The `Catalog.java` class is listed as follows:

```java
package jaxb;
import javax.xml.bind.annotation.XmlRootElement;
import javax.xml.bind.annotation.XmlAttribute;
import javax.xml.bind.annotation.XmlType;

@XmlRootElement
@XmlType(name = "", propOrder = { "publisher", "edition", "title",
"author" })
public class Catalog {
    private String publisher;
    private String edition;
    private String title;
    private String author;
    public Catalog() {
    }
    public Catalog(String journal, String publisher, String edition,
            String title, String author) {
        this.journal = journal;
        this.publisher = publisher;
        this.edition = edition;
        this.title = title;
        this.author = author;
    }
    @XmlAttribute
    public String journal;
    private String getJournal() {
        return this.journal;
    }
    public void setJournal(String journal) {
        this.journal = journal;
    }
    public String getPublisher() {
        return this.publisher;
    }
    public void setPublisher(String publisher) {
        this.publisher = publisher;
    }
    public String getEdition() {
        return this.edition;
    }
    public void setEdition(String edition) {
        this.edition = edition;
```

```
    }
    public String getTitle() {
        return this.title;
    }
    public void setTitle(String title) {
        this.title = title;
    }
    public String getAuthor() {
        return this.author;
    }

    public void setAuthor(String author) {
        this.author = author;
    }
}
```

Copy the `Catalog.java` listing to the `Catalog.java` class in the JAXB project in **Application Navigator**. We also need a JAXB marshalling class to marshal the Java class `Catalog.java` to an XML document. Create a Java class `JavaToXML.java` in the JAXB project `jaxb` package with **File | New**. In the marshalling class `JavaToXML.java` create a JAXBContext using the `newInstance()` method with `Catalog.class` as argument to the method.

```
JAXBContext jaxbContext = JAXBContext.newInstance(Catalog.class);
```

Create a `Marshaller` object and set the output formatting to `true`.

```
Marshaller marshaller = jaxbContext.createMarshaller();
 marshaller.setProperty("jaxb.formatted.output", Boolean.
valueOf(true));
```

Create a `Catalog` class object and set the values of elements and attributes using the setter methods defined in the `Catalog` class.

```
Catalog catalog = new Catalog();
catalog.setJournal("Oracle Magazine");
catalog.setPublisher("Oracle Publishing");
catalog.setEdition("March-April 2008");
catalog.setTitle("Declarative Data Filtering");
catalog.setAuthor("Steve Muench");
```

Marshal the `Catalog` object with the `Marshaller` object using the `marshal(Object, OutputStream)` method.

```
String xmlDocument = "catalog.xml";
marshaller.marshal(catalog, new FileOutputStream(xmlDocument));
```

The `JavaToXML.java` class is listed as follows:

```
package jaxb;
import javax.xml.bind.*;
import java.io.File;
import java.io.FileOutputStream;
import java.io.IOException;

public class JavaToXML {
    public void marshalXMLDocument(File xmlDocument) {
        try {
JAXBContext jaxbContext = JAXBContext.newInstance(Catalog.class);
Marshaller marshaller = jaxbContext.createMarshaller();
marshaller.setProperty("jaxb.formatted.output", Boolean.
valueOf(true));
            Catalog catalog = new Catalog();
            catalog.setJournal("Oracle Magazine");
            catalog.setPublisher("Oracle Publishing");
            catalog.setEdition("March-April 2008");
            catalog.setTitle("Declarative Data Filtering");
            catalog.setAuthor("Steve Muench");
            marshaller.marshal(catalog, new FileOutputStream
            (xmlDocument));
        } catch (IOException e) {
            System.err.println(e.toString());
        } catch (PropertyException e) {
            System.err.println(e.toString());
        } catch (JAXBException e) {
            System.err.println(e.toString());
        }
    }
    public static void main(String[] argv) {
        String xmlDocument = "catalog.xml";
        JavaToXML javaToXML = new JavaToXML();
        javaToXML.marshalXMLDocument(new File(xmlDocument));
    }
}
```

Copy the `JavaToXML.java` listing to the `JavaToXML.java` file in the JAXB project in the **Application Navigator**. Before running the `JavaToXML.java` application, delete the `catalog.xml` document from the JAXB project in the **Application Navigator**. To run the `JavaToXML.java` application, right-click on the class node in the **Application Navigator** and select **Run**.

The XML document gets created. To add the `catalog.xml` generated to the JAXB project in the **Application Navigator** select **View | Refresh**. Java classes may also be mapped to XML schemas using annotations.

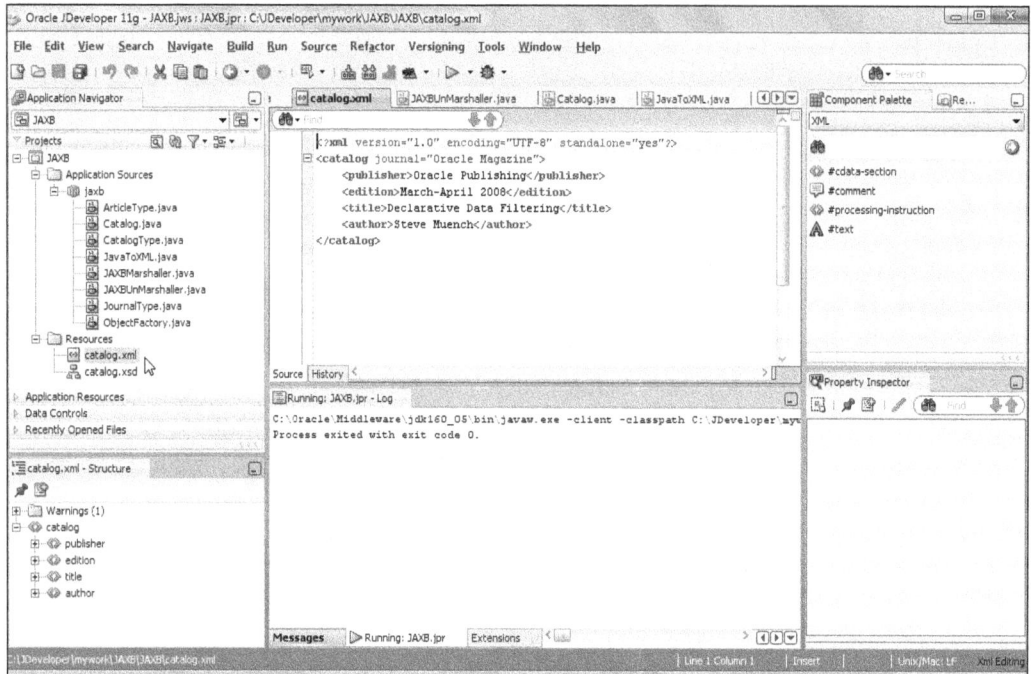

Summary

JDeveloper 11g provides a JAXB 2.0 compiler with which an XML schema may be compiled to its Java representation containing annotations. In this chapter we compiled an XML schema to Java classes using the JAXB compiler. Subsequently, we marshalled the Java classes to an XML document and also unmarshalled an XML document. JAXB 2.0's new features reduce the code generated from a schema with the schema binding compiler and make use of JDK 5.0 features such as annotations and parameterized types. With its support for annotations, JAXB 2.0 provides bi-directional mapping between XML schema, and Java objects; an annotated class hierarchy may be mapped to an XML schema. Generic types provide compile-time type checking, which means that runtime exceptions do not get generated. In the next chapter we will compare XML documents using the XDK 11g API.

10
Comparing XML Documents

As an XML developer, you might sometimes be interested in comparing a modified XML document with the pre-modified version of that document. Or you might want to compare two XML documents that are based on the same DTD or XML schema. This chapter is designed to give you the information you need to answer the following questions:

- Is one XML document the same as another?
- What are the differences between two XML documents?
- How to transform one XML document to the other?

Various tools are available to compare XML documents. In the following table we discuss some of the commonly used XML tools to compare XML documents and their features:

XML Comparison Tool	Description
Microsoft XML Diff and Patch Tool	XML Diff compares only the XML-based features and ignores the following features: • Order of attributes • Insignificant whitespaces • Document encoding XML Diff does not differentiate between an empty element, `<elementA/>`, and an element with no content, `<elementA></elementA>`. XML Diff creates a diffgram that represents the differences between two XML documents. The XML Patch Tool may be used to patch the original document. The Microsoft XML Diff and Patch Tool can be downloaded from `http://msdn.microsoft.com/en-us/xml/bb190622.aspx`.

XML Comparison Tool	Description
IBM's XML Diff and Merge Tool	The XML Diff and Merge Tool is a Java application to represent changes made to an XML document. The XML Diff Tool highlights the changes between the original document (base file) and the modified document using symbols and colors. A developer may choose to include the changes in the modified document on a per-modification basis. Using the Merge Tool, a developer may optionally create a final file that has some of the elements from the base file and some from the modified file. The XML Diff and Merge Tool may be downloaded from `http://www.alphaworks.ibm.com/tech/xmldiffmerge/download`.
Stylus Studio XML Differencing Tool	Stylus Studio displays differences between two XML files using icons and colors. You may compare the text of two XML files using the XML text view or you may display the differences in two XML files in a tree structure using the XML tree view. The XML Differencing Tool has the option to display only the nodes that are different between two XML files. The tool also has the provision to display a merged view of the differences between two XML files in the same XML tree view. The tool has the provision to optionally compare or ignore the different XML components such as comments, entities, whitespaces, processing instruction, and attributes. The Stylus Studio XML Differencing Tool may be downloaded from `http://www.stylusstudio.com/xml_differencing.html`.
XMLSpy 2008 XML Differencing Utility	The XMLSpy 2008 XML Differencing Utility compares two XML files and displays the differences using colors in a Text view or Grid view. The tool may be used to create a merged XML document that has components from the two XML files being compared. The tool has the provision to optionally include or ignore namespaces, namespace prefixes, entities, attributes, CDATA, comments, processing instructions, DOCTYPE, whitespaces, and order of child nodes in the XML document comparison. The XMLSpy 2008 XML Differencing Tool may be downloaded from `http://www.altova.com/products/xmlspy/xml_differencing.html`.

In addition to the commonly used XML comparison tools discussed in the table, some other XML comparison tools such as XyDiff and DeltaXML are also available.

XDK 11g provides an API with which you can reduce the complex process of comparing XML documents to a simple set of library calls that lets you determine if the documents are the same, see what the differences are, or use the comparison information to generate other documents. In this chapter, we will discuss the procedure to compare two XML documents and list their differences using the XDK 11g API.

XDK 11g provides an API in the `oracle.xml.differ` package to compare XML documents. The `oracle.xml.differ` package is included in the `xml.jar` JAR file, which is included in the `lib` directory of the JDeveloper installation. The `oracle.xml.differ.XMLDiff` class defines an interface for comparing XML documents. Two XML files are equivalent if all the nodes, including empty space nodes, are the same. The differences between two XML files may be represented as an XSL stylesheet. The first XML file may be transformed into the second using the XSL stylesheet. In this chapter, we will compare two XML files and generate an XSL stylesheet that represents the differences between the XML files.

Setting the environment

We need to create an application (**XMLDiff**) and a project (**XMLDiff**) in JDeveloper to compare two XML documents. In the project, create the XML documents `catalog1.xml` and `catalog2.xml` that are to be compared with **File | New**. In the **New Gallery** window select **Categories | General | XML** and **Items | XML Document**. In the **Create XML File** window specify the **File Name** and click on **OK**. Add a Java class **XMLCompare.java** to the project with **File | New**. In the **New Gallery** window select **Categories | General** and **Items | Java Class**. In the **Create Java Class** window specify the **File Name** and click on **OK**. The directory structure of the application to compare two XML documents is shown in the following illustration:

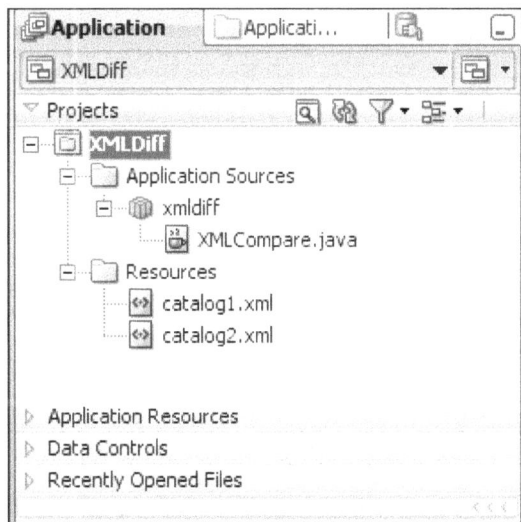

We need to add the **Oracle XML Parser v2** library and the `C:/Oracle/Middleware/jdeveloper/modules/oracle.xdk_11.1.1/xml.jar` JAR file to the project with **Tools | Project Properties**. In the **Project Properties** window select **Libraries and Classpath**. Select **Add Library** to add the **Oracle XML Parser v2** library, and select **Add JAR/Directory** to add the **xml.jar** JAR file. Click on **OK** in the **Project Properties** window.

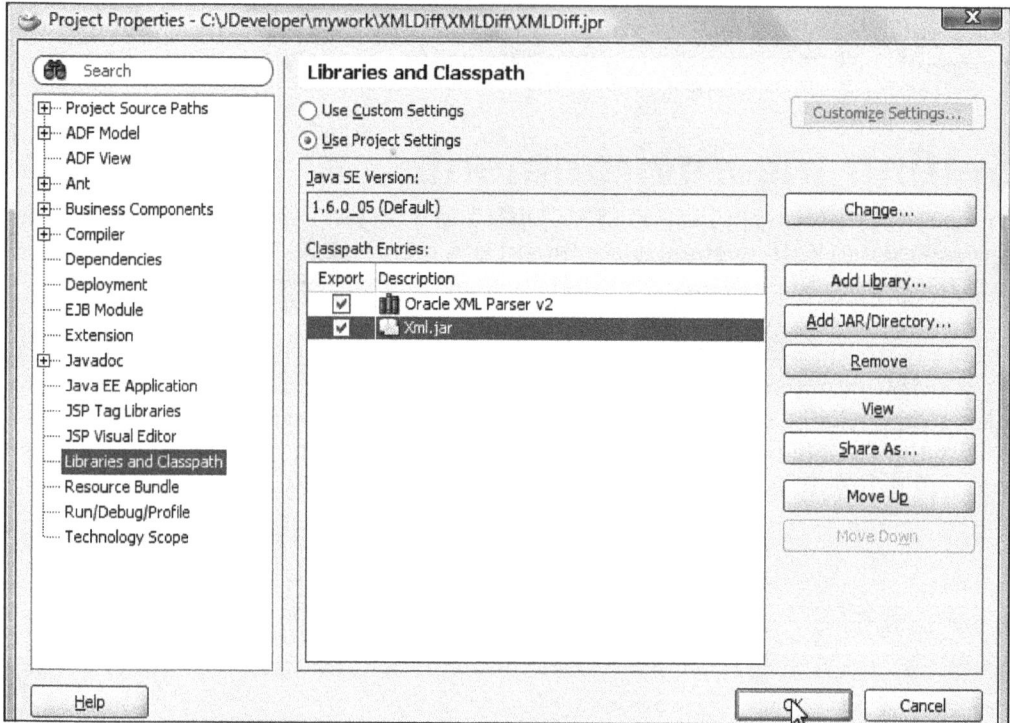

Comparing XML documents with the XMLDiff class

You use the `XMLDiff` class in the `oracle.xml.differ` package to compare two XML documents. The class contains methods to compare two XML documents and enumerate the differences between them. In addition, you can choose to generate an XSLT stylesheet consisting of the differences between the two XML documents. You can then use the stylesheet to convert one of the compared XML documents into the other. This section compares an example XML document named `catalog1.xml` with another XML document called `catalog2.xml`. `Catalog1.xml` is listed as follows:

```
<?xml version="1.0" encoding="windows-1252" ?>
<catalog>
<journal title="Oracle Magazine" publisher="Oracle
Publishing" edition="September-October 2008">
  <article section="FEATURES">
    <title>Share 2.0</title>
    <author>Alan Joch</author>
  </article>
</journal>
<journal title="Oracle Magazine" publisher="Oracle Publishing"
  edition="September-October 2008">
  <article section="ORACLE DEVELOPER">
    <title>Task and You Shall Receive</title>
    <author>Steve Muench</author>
  </article>
</journal>
</catalog>
```

`catalog2.xml` is listed as follows:

```
<?xml version="1.0" encoding="windows-1252" ?>
<catalog>
<journal edition="March-April 2008">
  <article section="Technology">
    <title>Oracle Database 11g Redux</title>
    <author>Tom Kyte</author>
  </article>
</journal>
<journal edition="March-April 2008">
  <article section="ORACLE DEVELOPER">
    <title>Declarative Data Filtering</title>
    <author>Steve Muench</author>
  </article>
</journal>
<journal></journal>
</catalog>
```

Copy the `catalog1.xml` and `catalog2.xml` listings to the `catalog1.xml` and `catalog2.xml` files in the `XMLDiff` project in JDeveloper. In comparing the two XML documents, the empty (white) spaces in the XML document are also considered as nodes. You should remove whitespace in XML documents that you want to compare if the whitespaces are not required for comparison.

Next, we develop the Java application, `XMLCompare.java`, to compare the two example XML documents. To compare the two documents you first import the `XMLDiff` class package `oracle.xml.differ` into the Java application, shown as follows:

```
import oracle.xml.differ.*;
```

Parsing the XML files

Next, create a DOMParser to parse the XML documents to be compared. The DOMParser class extends the oracle.xml.parser.v2.XMLParser class.

```
DOMParser parser=new DOMParser();
```

You have to load and parse the documents, using one of the parse() methods in the XMLParser class. You can load and parse an XML document from an InputSource, InputStream, Reader, String, or URL. We've used an InputStream in this chapter. Create an InputStream object from the XML document catalog1.xml and parse the document with the parse(InputStream) method.

```
InputStream catalog1=new FileInputStream(new File("catalog1.xml"));
parser.parse(catalog1);
```

Obtain the XMLDocument object corresponding to the XML document parsed.

```
XMLDocument xmlDocument1=parser.getDocument();
```

Similarly, create an InputStream for the XML document catalog2.xml and parse the XML document. Next, obtain an XMLDocument object for the XML document catalog2.xml as follows:

```
InputStream catalog2=new FileInputStream(new File("catalog2.xml"));
parser.parse(catalog2);
XMLDocument xmlDocument2=parser.getDocument();
```

Comparing the XML files

The XMLDiff class is an interface for comparing two XML documents. You'll need to create an XMLDiff class object. The example class XMLCompare extends the XMLDiff class to compare the two sample XML documents. Here's how you create an XMLCompare class object, which is also an XMLDiff class object.

```
XMLCompare  xmlDiff=new XMLCompare();
```

Specify the XML documents to be compared, either as oracle.xml.parser. v2.XMLDocument class objects, or as java.io.File objects. You can set them as XMLDocument objects with the setDocuments(XMLDocument, XMLDocument) method or (using two calls) setInput1(XMLDocument) and setInput2(XMLDocument) methods. Alternatively, you can set them as File objects using the setFiles(File, File) method, or the two setInput1(File) and setInput2(File) method calls. The sample code uses the setDocuments(XMLDocument, XMLDocument) method shown as follows:

```
xmlDiff.setDocuments(xmlDocument1, xmlDocument2);
```

You can compare the two example XML documents with the `diff()` method, which returns a `boolean`.

```
boolean diff=xmlDiff.diff();
```

If the value of the `diff` variable is `false`, the two XML documents are the same, while if `diff` is `true`, the documents are different. For comparison purposes `<elem />` is the same as `<elem></elem>`. Using the example documents, you'll get a value of `true` for the `diff` variable, which indicates that the documents are different. You can also compare nodes, including the complete subtree, using the `equals(Node, Node)` method, which also returns a `boolean`.

Now that you know the documents are different, you might be interested in listing the actual differences. You can generate a listing of the differences using the `printDiffTree(int, BufferedWriter)` method. The `int` parameter specifies which XML document to use as the base document when evaluating the differences. In other words, if the `int` parameter value is 1, the `printDiffTree()` method outputs the additions/deletions/modifications in XML document 1 as compared to XML document 2, while if `int` is 2, the method outputs the differences for document 2 as compared to document 1. The `BufferedWriter` parameter specifies the output file. To obtain the results, specify the `int` parameter value as 1 and create a `BufferedWriter` to output the differences between the XML documents, shown as follows:

```
BufferedWriter bufferedWriter=new BufferedWriter
(new FileWriter(new File("diff.txt")));
xmlDiff.printDiffTree(1, bufferedWriter);
bufferedWriter.flush();
```

The `BufferedWriter` outputs the set of features that are different between the two XML documents. The sample output file, `diff.txt`, containing the differences between the two example documents is listed here:

```
            [DOCUMENT]
            catalog
            "       "
            journal
ADDED    -- title="Oracle Magazine"
ADDED    -- publisher="Oracle  Publishing"
MODIFIED -- edition="September-October 2008"
            "       "
            article
MODIFIED -- section="FEATURES"
            "       "
            title
```

```
       MODIFIED -- "Share 2.0"
                    "        "

                    author
       MODIFIED -- "Alan Joch"
                    "      "

                    "    "

                    "    "

                    journal
       ADDED     -- title="Oracle Magazine"
       ADDED     -- publisher="Oracle Publishing"
       MODIFIED -- edition="September-October 2008"
                    "      "

                    article
                    section="ORACLE DEVELOPER"
                    "        "

                    title
       MODIFIED -- "Task and You Shall Receive"
                    "        "

                    author
                    "Steve Muench"
                    "      "

                    "    "

       DELETED   -- "    "
       DELETED   -- journal
                    "  "
```

The output is fairly straightforward. The MODIFIED keyword indicates elements that are present in both the XML documents, but differ (are modified) from each other. Added elements are indicated by the keyword ADDED, and deleted elements by DELETED.

> The elements that are marked DELETED would be marked ADDED, and elements marked ADDED would be marked DELETED if the int value in printDiffTree() method were modified from 1 to 2.

Generating an XSLT stylesheet

You can generate an XSLT stylesheet from the element/attribute differences between the example XML documents. To create an XSLDocument object, use the generateXSLDoc() method. To create it as a file, use the generateXSLFile(java.lang.String filename) method.

```
xmlDiff.generateXSLFile("diff.xslt");
```

The XSLT file generated, `diff.xslt`, is listed as follows; although some of the whitespaces have been omitted for readability:

```
<xsl:stylesheet version="1.0" xmlns:xsl=
"http://www.w3.org/1999/XSL/Transform">
<xsl:output encoding="utf-8"/>
<!--Select all nodes-->
<xsl:template match="node()|@*">
  <xsl:copy>
    <xsl:apply-templates select="node()|@*"/>
  </xsl:copy>
</xsl:template>
<xsl:template match="/catalog[1]/journal[1]/@title"/>
<xsl:template match="/catalog[1]/journal[1]/@publisher"/>
<xsl:template match="/catalog[1]/journal[1]/@edition">
  <xsl:attribute name="edition">March-April 2008</xsl:attribute>
</xsl:template>
<xsl:template match="/catalog[1]/journal[1]/article[1]/@section">
  <xsl:attribute name="section">Technology</xsl:attribute>
</xsl:template>
<xsl:template match="/catalog[1]/journal[1]/article[1]/title[1]">
  <xsl:element name="{name()}">
    <xsl:apply-templates select="@*"/>
    Oracle Database 11g Redux
  </xsl:element>
</xsl:template>
<xsl:template match="/catalog[1]/journal[1]/article[1]/author[1]">
  <xsl:element name="{name()}">
    <xsl:apply-templates select="@*"/>
    Tom Kyte
  </xsl:element>
</xsl:template>
<xsl:template match="/catalog[1]/journal[2]/@title"/>
<xsl:template match="/catalog[1]/journal[2]/@publisher"/>
<xsl:template match="/catalog[1]/journal[2]/@edition">
  <xsl:attribute name="edition">March-April 2008</xsl:attribute>
</xsl:template>
<xsl:template match="/catalog[1]/journal[2]/article[1]/title[1]">
  <xsl:element name="{name()}">
    <xsl:apply-templates select="@*"/>
    Declarative Data Filtering
  </xsl:element>
</xsl:template>
<xsl:template match="/catalog[1]/journal[2]">
```

```
      <xsl:copy>
        <xsl:apply-templates select="node()|@*"/>
      </xsl:copy>
      <journal></journal>
    </xsl:template>
  </xsl:stylesheet>
```

You can use the XSLT document generated from the differences between the two example documents to update the first document to the second document. For example, to apply the `diff.xslt` file to the XML document `catalog1.xml`, run the `XSLTTransform.java` application (seen in Chapter 5) with `catalog1.xml` and `diff.xslt`. That transformation generates the XML document `catalog2.xml`.

Alternatively, you can apply the XSLT stylesheet to some other document that may have additional differences from the second example document. For example, applying the stylesheet `diff.xslt` would update only the modified elements/ attributes (including those added or removed) between `catalog1.xml` and `catalog2.xml`.

Additionally, you can use the generated XSLT stylesheet to generate an XML document that consists only of the modified attribute and element values between the two input XML documents. To do that, apply the XSLT to an XML document, `catalog-null.xml`, that does not specify values for any of the attributes and elements. It is shown as follows:

```
<?xml version="1.0" encoding="utf-8"?>
<catalog>
<journal title="" publisher="" edition="">
  <article section="">
    <title></title>
    <author></author>
  </article>
</journal>
<journal  title=""  publisher=""  edition="">
  <article section="">
    <title></title>
    <author></author>
  </article>
</journal>

</catalog>
```

To apply `diff.xslt` to the preceding XML document with null values, run the `XSLTTransform.java` application in the XSLT chapter with `diff.xslt` and `catalog-null.xml`. The preceding transformation generates an XML document containing only the modified attributes and elements, not the added or deleted elements/attributes, as shown in the following listing:

```xml
<?xml version = '1.0' encoding = 'UTF-8'?>
<catalog>
  <journal edition="March-April 2008">
    <article section="Technology">
      <title>Oracle Database 11g Redux</title>
      <author>Tom Kyte</author>
    </article>
  </journal>
  <journal edition="March-April 2008">
    <article section="">
      <title>Declarative Data Filtering</title>
      <author/>
    </article>
  </journal>
   <journal/>
</catalog>
```

Running the Java application

The following listing is the sample `XMLCompare.java` program used to compare the two example XML documents. The listing is divided into segments with code explanations.

1. First, we declare the `package` and `import` statements.

```java
package xmldiff;
import oracle.xml.parser.v2.*;
import oracle.xml.differ.*;
import java.io.*;
import org.xml.sax.SAXException;
```

2. We define the Java class `XMLCompare` that extends the `XMLDiff` class.

```java
public class XMLCompare extends XMLDiff {
    protected static XMLCompare xmlDiff;
```

3. We define the method `xmlCompare` to compare two XML documents.

```java
public void xmlCompare(XMLDocument document1, XMLDocument
  document2) {
    try {
```

```
            xmlDiff.setDocuments(document1, document2);
            boolean diff = xmlDiff.diff();
            if (diff == false)
                System.out.println("The XML documents are the same");
            else
                System.out.println("The XML documents are different");
            BufferedWriter bufferedWriter = new BufferedWriter
            (new FileWriter (newFile ("diff.txt")));
            xmlDiff.printDiffTree(1, bufferedWriter);
            bufferedWriter.flush();
            xmlDiff.generateXSLFile("diff.xslt");
                } catch (IOException e) { System.err.println(e.
                getMessage());
        }
    }
```

4. We define the `main` method in which we parse the XML files to be compared. We create an instance of the `XMLCompare` class and invoke the `xmlCompare` method.

```
        public static void main(String[] args) {
            try {
                DOMParser parser = new DOMParser();
                InputStream catalog1 =
                    new FileInputStream(new File("catalog1.xml"));
                parser.parse(catalog1);
                XMLDocument xmlDocument1 = parser.getDocument();
                InputStream catalog2 =
                    new FileInputStream(new File("catalog2.xml"));
                parser.parse(catalog2);
                XMLDocument xmlDocument2 = parser.getDocument();
                xmlDiff = new XMLCompare();
                xmlDiff.xmlCompare(xmlDocument1, xmlDocument2);
    } catch (XMLParseException e) { System.err.println(e.
getMessage());

    } catch (SAXException e) { System.err.println(e.getMessage());

    } catch (IOException e) { System.err.println(e.getMessage());

            }
        }
    }
```

Copy the XMLCompare.java listing to the XMLCompare.java class in the **XMLDiff** project in JDeveloper. To run the XMLCompare.java application in JDeveloper, right-click on the **Application** node, and select **Run**.

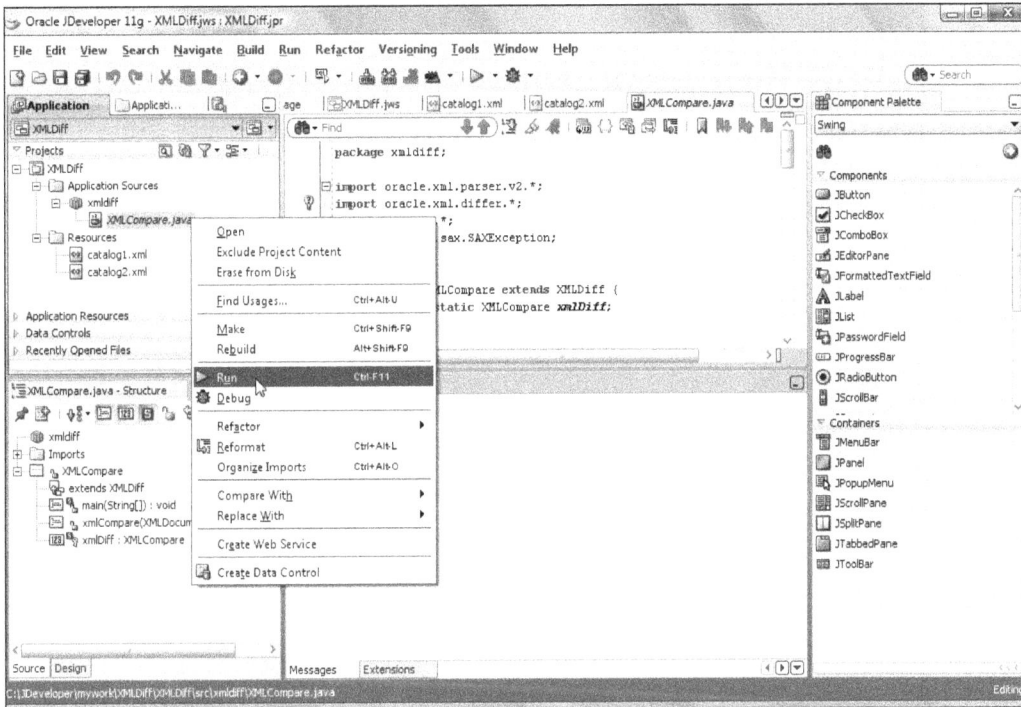

The output indicates that the files catalog1.xml and catalog2.xml are different.

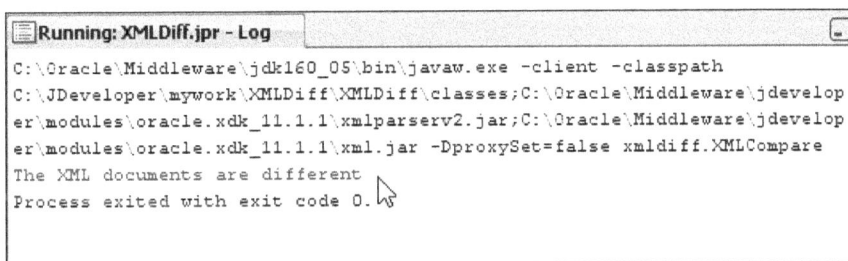

A file containing the differences in the XML documents gets generated. An XSLT stylesheet that represents the differences in the XML files also gets generated. Select the project node in the **Application Navigator** and select **View | Refresh** to display the generated files in the **Application Navigator**.

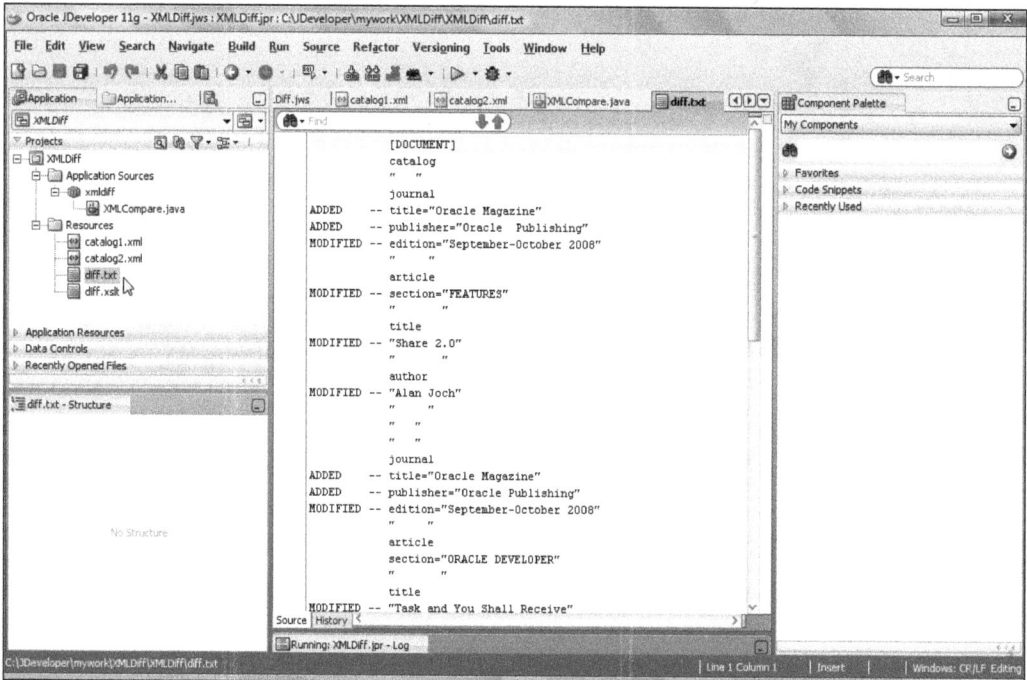

Summary

As you have learned, the `oracle.xml.differ` package contains everything you need to compare two XML documents in Java, list the differences between them, make one document match the other, or create a new document containing only attributes and elements that differ. In the next chapter, we will convert an XML document to a PDF document.

11
Converting XML to PDF

XML is the most suitable format for data exchange, but not for data presentation. Adobe's PDF and Microsoft Excel's spreadsheet are the commonly used formats for data presentation. If you receive an XML file containing data that needs to be included in a PDF or Excel spreadsheet file, you need to convert the XML file to the relevant format. Some of the commonly used XML-to-PDF conversion tools/APIs are discussed in the following table:

Tool/API	Description
iText	iText is a Java library for generating a PDF document. iText may be downloaded from http://www.lowagie.com/iText/.
Stylus Studio XML Publisher	XML Publisher is a report designer, which supports many data sources, including XML, to generate PDF reports.
Stylus Studio XML Editor	XML Editor supports XML conversion to PDF.
Apache FOP	The Apache project provides an open source FO processor called Apache FOP to render an XSL-FO document as a PDF document. We will discuss the Apache FOP processor in this chapter.
XMLMill for Java	XMLMill may be used to generate PDF documents from XML data combined with XSL and XSLT. XMLMill may be downloaded from http://www.xmlmill.com/.
RenderX XEP	RenderX provides an XSL-FO processor called XEP that may be used to generate a PDF document.

We can convert an XML file data to a PDF document using any of these tools/APIs in JDeveloper 11g. In this chapter, we will use the Apache FOP API.

The XSL specification consists of two components: a language for transforming XML documents (XSLT), and an XML syntax for specifying formatting objects (XSL-FO). Using XSL-FO, the layout, fonts, and representations of the data may be formatted. Apache **FOP (Formatting Objects Processor)** is a print formatter for converting XSL formatting objects (XSL-FO) to an output format such as PDF, PCL, PS, SVG, XML, Print, AWT, MIF, or TXT. In this chapter, we will convert an XML document to PDF using XSL-FO and the FOP processor in Oracle JDeveloper 11g. The procedure to create a PDF document from an XML file using the Apache FOP processor in JDeveloper is as follows:

1. Create an XML document.
2. Create an XSL stylesheet.
3. Convert the XML document to an XSL-FO document.
4. Convert the XSL-FO document to a PDF file.

Setting the environment

We need to download the FOP JAR file `fop-0.20.5-bin.zip` (or a later version) from `http://archive.apache.org/dist/xmlgraphics/fop/binaries/` and extract the ZIP file to a directory. To develop an XML-to-PDF conversion application, we need to create an application (`ApacheFOP` for example) and a project (`ApacheFOP` for example) in JDeveloper. In the project add an XML document, `catalog.xml`, with **File | New**. In the **New Gallery** window select **Categories | General | XML** and **Items | XML Document**. Click on **OK**. In the **Create XML File** window specify a **File Name**, `catalog.xml`, and click on **OK**. A **catalog.xml** file gets added to the **ApacheFOP** project. Copy the following `catalog.xml` listing to **catalog.xml**:

```xml
<?xml version="1.0" encoding="UTF-8"?>
<catalog  title="Oracle Magazine" publisher="Oracle Publishing">
  <journal edition="September-October 2008">
  <article>
    <title>Share 2.0</title>
    <author>Alan Joch</author>
   </article>
  <article>
    <title>Restrictions Apply</title>
    <author>Alan Joch</author>
   </article>

  </journal>
  <journal edition="March-April 2008">
  <article>
    <title>Oracle Database 11g Redux</title>
```

```
      <author>Tom Kyte</author>
    </article>
    <article>
      <title>Declarative Data Filtering</title>
      <author>Steve Muench</author>
    </article>

  </journal>
</catalog>
```

We also need to add an XSL stylesheet to convert the XML document to an XSL-FO document. Create an XSL stylesheet with **File | New**. In the **New Gallery** window, select **Categories | General | XML** and **Items | XSL Stylesheet**. Click on **OK**. In the **Create XSL File** window specify a **File Name** (**catalog.xsl**) and click on **OK**. A **catalog.xsl** file gets added to the **ApacheFOP** project. To convert the XML document to an XSL-FO document and subsequently create a PDF file from the XSL-FO file, we need a Java application. Add a Java class, **XMLToPDF.java**, with **File | New**. In the **New Gallery** window select **Categories | General** and **Items | Java Class**. Click on **OK**. In the **Create Java Class** window specify a class **Name** (**XMLToPDF** for example) and click on **OK**. A Java class gets added to the **ApacheFOP** project. The directory structure of the FOP application is shown in the following illustration:

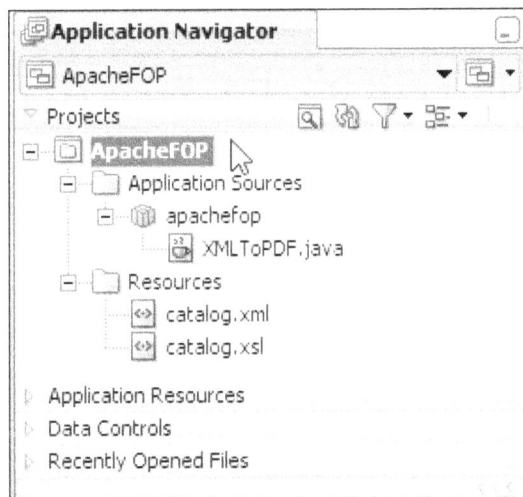

Next, add the FOP JAR files to the project. Select the project node (**ApacheFOP** node) and then **Tools | Project Properties**. In the **Project Properties** window, select **Libraries and Classpath**. Add the **Oracle XML Parser v2** library with the **Add Library** button. The JAR files required to develop an FOP application are listed in the following table:

JAR File	Description
`<FOP>/fop-0.20.5/build/fop.jar`	Apache FOP API
`<FOP>/fop-0.20.5/lib/batik.jar`	Graphics classes
`<FOP>/fop-0.20.5/lib/ avalon-framework-cvs-20020806.jar`	Logger classes
`<FOP>/fop-0.20.5/lib/ xercesImpl-2.2.1.jar`	The DOMParser and the SAXParser classes

The variable `<FOP>` is the directory in which Apache FOP is installed. Add the JAR files with the **Add JAR/Directory** button. Click on **OK** in the **Project Properties** window.

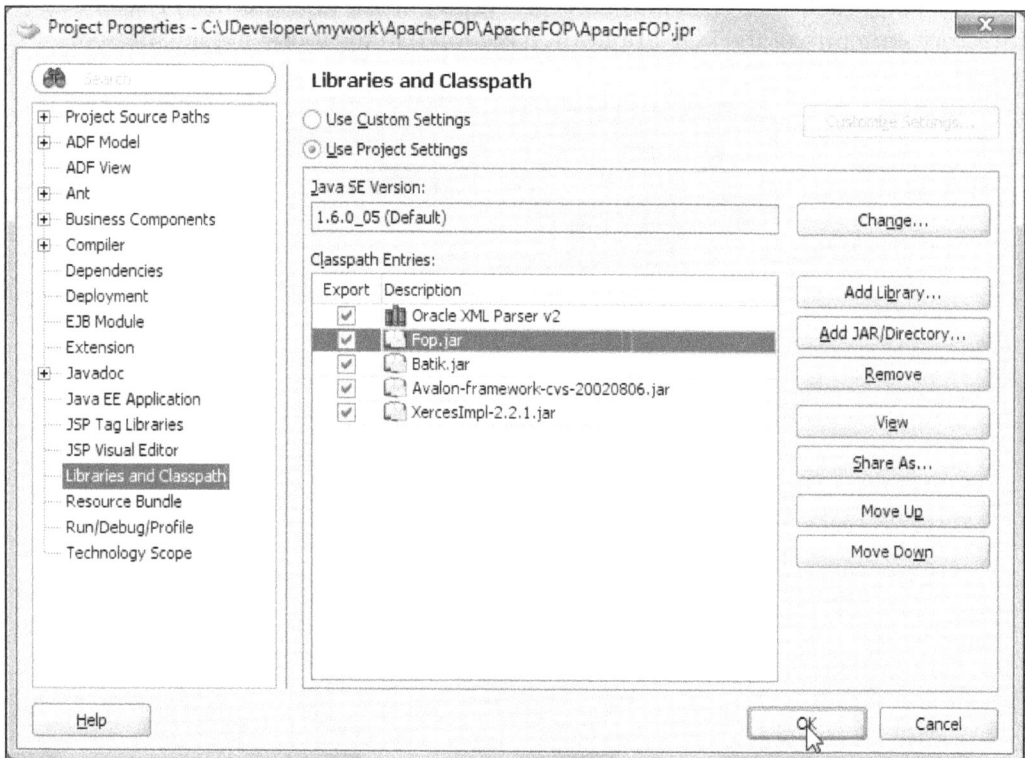

Converting XML to XSL-FO

In this section, we will convert the example XML document (`catalog.xml`) to an XSL-FO document. An XSL-FO document includes formatting information about the data to be presented. It includes the layout, fonts, and tables in the document. An XSL-FO document is created in the `fo` prefix namespace using the namespace declaration `xmlns:fo=http://www.w3.org/1999/XSL/Format`. The root element of the XSL-FO document is `fo:root`. The XSL-FO document elements are based on the `fo.dtd` DTD, which may be downloaded from `http://www.syntext.com/products/dtd2xs/doc/fo.dtd`. Some of the commonly used elements in an XSL-FO document are listed here:

Element	Attributes	Sub-Elements	Description
`fo:root`	xmlns:fo	`fo-layout-master-set`, `fo-page-sequence`	Root element
`fo:layout-master-set`	-	`fo:simple-page-master`	
`fo:simple-page-master`	margin-right, margin-left, margin-bottom, margin-top, page-width, page-height, master-name	`fo:region-body`	Page layout
`fo:page-sequence`	master-reference	`fo:title`, `fo:static-content`, `fo:flow`	Additional page layout
`fo:flow`	flow-name	`fo:block`	Page content
`fo:block`	space-before, space-after, font-weight, font-size	`fo:table`, `fo:list-block`	Block content
`fo:list-block`	provisional-distance-between-starts, provisional-label-separation	`fo:list-item`	List in a page
`fo:list-item`	text-indent	`fo:list-item-label`, `fo:list-item-body`	List item
`fo:table`	border-spacing, table-layout	`fo:table-column`, `fo:table-header`, `fo:table-body`	Table in a page
`fo:table-column`	column-number, column-width	-	Column in a table

Element	Attributes	Sub-Elements	Description
`fo:table-header`	-	`fo:table-row`	Table header
`fo:table-body`	table-layout	`fo:table-row`	Table rows
`fo:table-row`	font-weight	`fo:table-cell`	Row in a table
`table:cell`	column-number	`fo:block`	Row cell that has the text of a row cell

The example XML document to be converted to a PDF document consists of a journal catalog. The XSLT stylesheet `catalog.xsl`, from which the example XML document is converted to an XSL-FO document, is listed as follows:

```
<?xml version="1.0" encoding="UTF-8"?>
<xsl:stylesheet version="1.1" xmlns:xsl="http://www.w3.org/1999/XSL/
Transform"
    xmlns:fo="http://www.w3.org/1999/XSL/Format" exclude-result-
    prefixes="fo">
  <xsl:output method="xml" version="1.0" omit-xml-declaration="no"
  indent="yes"/>
  <!-- ========================= -->
  <!-- root element: catalog -->
  <!-- ========================= -->
  <xsl:template match="/catalog">
    <fo:root xmlns:fo="http://www.w3.org/1999/XSL/Format">
      <fo:layout-master-set>
        <fo:simple-page-master master-name="simpleA4" page-
        height="29.7cm"
             page-width="21cm" margin-top="2cm" margin-bottom="2cm"
          margin-left="2cm" margin-right="2cm">
          <fo:region-body/>
        </fo:simple-page-master>
      </fo:layout-master-set>
      <fo:page-sequence master-reference="simpleA4">
        <fo:flow flow-name="xsl-region-body">
          <fo:block font-size="16pt" font-weight="bold" space-
          after="5mm">
            Catalog:  <xsl:value-of select="@title"/>
          </fo:block>
        <fo:block font-size="16pt" font-weight="bold" space-after="5mm">
            Publisher:  <xsl:value-of select="@publisher"/>
          </fo:block>
          <fo:block font-size="10pt">
```

```
<fo:table table-layout="fixed">
    <fo:table-column column-width="4cm"/>
    <fo:table-column column-width="4cm"/>
    <fo:table-column column-width="5cm"/>
  <fo:table-header>
  <fo:table-row font-weight="bold"><fo:table-cell>
<fo:block>
  <xsl:text>Edition</xsl:text>
</fo:block>
</fo:table-cell>
    <fo:table-cell>
    <fo:block>
      <xsl:text>Title</xsl:text>
    </fo:block>
</fo:table-cell>
    <fo:table-cell>
    <fo:block>
      <xsl:text>Author</xsl:text>
    </fo:block>
</fo:table-cell>
  </fo:table-row>

</fo:table-header>

  <fo:table-body>
            <xsl:apply-templates select="journal"/>
            </fo:table-body>
          </fo:table>
        </fo:block>
      </fo:flow>
    </fo:page-sequence>
  </fo:root>
  </xsl:template>

 <xsl:template match="journal">

<xsl:for-each select="article">
 <fo:table-row>
      <fo:table-cell>
      <fo:block>
        <xsl:value-of select="../@edition"/>
      </fo:block>
    </fo:table-cell>
    <fo:table-cell>
      <fo:block>
        <xsl:value-of select="title"/>
      </fo:block>
```

```
        </fo:table-cell>
        <fo:table-cell>
          <fo:block>
            <xsl:value-of select="author"/>
          </fo:block>
        </fo:table-cell>
      </fo:table-row>
    </xsl:for-each>

    </xsl:template>
  </xsl:stylesheet>
```

Copy the `catalog.xsl` listing to the **catalog.xsl** file in the JDeveloper project in the **Application Navigator**. Next, we will convert the example XML document to an XSL-FO document in the Java application `XMLToPDF.java`.

Parsing the XML document

Create a `DocumentBuilderFactory` object using the static method `newInstance()`. The factory class is used to create a `DocumentBuilder` parser.

```
DocumentBuilderFactory factory =DocumentBuilderFactory.newInstance();
```

Create a `DocumentBuilder` parser from the `DocumentBuilderFactory` object using the `newDocumentBuilder()` method.

```
DocumentBuilder builder = factory.newDocumentBuilder();
```

Parse the example XML document using one of the overloaded `parse()` methods.

```
File xmlFile = new File("catalog.xml");
Document document = builder.parse(xmlFile);
```

Generating the XSL-FO document

Create a `TransformerFactory` object using the static method `newInstance()`. The factory class is used to create a `Transformer` object.

```
TransformerFactory transformerFactory = TransformerFactory.
newInstance();
```

Create a `Transformer` object from the `TransformerFactory` object using the `newTransformer()` method.

```
File stylesheet = new File("catalog.xsl");
Transformer transformer = transformerFactory.newTransformer(new Stream
Source(stylesheet));
```

Transform the `Document` object obtained from the example XML document using the method `transform(Source, Result)`. The input XML document may be specified as a `DOMSource`, `SAXSource`, or `StreamSource` object. The transformation output may be specified as `DOMResult`, `SAXResult`, or `StreamResult`.

```
DOMSource source = new DOMSource(document);
    StreamResult  result = new StreamResult(new File("catalog.fo"));
    transformer.transform(source, result);
```

The XSL-FO document, `catalog.fo`, generated from the example XML document is listed as follows:

```
<?xml version = '1.0' encoding = 'UTF-8'?>
<fo:root xmlns:fo="http://www.w3.org/1999/XSL/Format">
   <fo:layout-master-set>
      <fo:simple-page-master master-name="simpleA4" page-
      height="29.7cm" page-width="21cm" margin-top="2cm"
      margin-bottom="2cm" margin-left="2cm" margin-right="2cm">
         <fo:region-body/>
      </fo:simple-page-master>
   </fo:layout-master-set>
   <fo:page-sequence master-reference="simpleA4">
      <fo:flow flow-name="xsl-region-body">
         <fo:block font-size="16pt" font-weight="bold" space-
         after="5mm">
            Catalog:  Oracle Magazine</fo:block>
         <fo:block font-size="16pt" font-weight="bold" space-
         after="5mm">
            Publisher:  Oracle Publishing</fo:block>
         <fo:block font-size="10pt">
            <fo:table table-layout="fixed">
               <fo:table-column column-width="4cm"/>
               <fo:table-column column-width="4cm"/>
               <fo:table-column column-width="5cm"/>
               <fo:table-header>
                  <fo:table-row font-weight="bold">
                     <fo:table-cell>
                        <fo:block>Edition</fo:block>
                     </fo:table-cell>
                     <fo:table-cell>
                        <fo:block>Title</fo:block>
                     </fo:table-cell>
                     <fo:table-cell>
                        <fo:block>Author</fo:block>
                     </fo:table-cell>
```

```
                    </fo:table-row>
                </fo:table-header>
                <fo:table-body>
                    <fo:table-row>
                        <fo:table-cell>
                            <fo:block>July-August 2005</fo:block>
                        </fo:table-cell>
                        <fo:table-cell>
            <fo:block>Tuning Undo Tablespace </fo:block>
                        </fo:table-cell>
                        <fo:table-cell>
                        <fo:block>
                            Kimberly Floss
                        </fo:block>
                        </fo:table-cell>
                    </fo:table-row>
                    <fo:table-row>
                        <fo:table-cell>
                            <fo:block>July-August 2005</fo:block>
                        </fo:table-cell>
                        <fo:table-cell>
              <fo:block>Browsing and Editing Data</fo:block>
                        </fo:table-cell>
                        <fo:table-cell>
                            <fo:block>
                                Steve Muench
                            </fo:block>
                        </fo:table-cell>
                    </fo:table-row>
                    <fo:table-row>
                        <fo:table-cell>
               <fo:block>September-October 2005</fo:block>
                        </fo:table-cell>
                        <fo:table-cell>
            <fo:block>Sharing Memory—Automatically</fo:block>
                        </fo:table-cell>
                        <fo:table-cell>
                            <fo:block>Kimberly Floss </fo:block>
                        </fo:table-cell>
                    </fo:table-row>
                    <fo:table-row>
                        <fo:table-cell>
              <fo:block>September-October 2005</fo:block>
                        </fo:table-cell>
```

```
            <fo:table-cell>
        <fo:block>Creating Search Pages </fo:block>
          </fo:table-cell>
          <fo:table-cell>
        <fo:block>
            Steve Muench
        </fo:block>
          </fo:table-cell>
        </fo:table-row>
      </fo:table-body>
    </fo:table>
  </fo:block>
</fo:flow>
</fo:page-sequence>
</fo:root>
```

Converting XSL-FO to PDF

In this section, we will convert the XSL-FO document generated in the previous section to a PDF document using the FOP driver. In the Java application `XMLToPDF.java`, import the FOP Driver class and the logger classes required to convert an XML document to a PDF document.

```
import org.apache.fop.apps.Driver;
import org.apache.avalon.framework.logger.Logger;
import org.apache.avalon.framework.logger.ConsoleLogger;
```

Creating the FOP driver

Create an FOP driver object using the constructor for the `Driver` class.

```
Driver driver=new Driver();
```

Create a logger with level setting `LEVEL_INFO` using the `ConsoleLogger` constructor.

```
Logger logger=new ConsoleLogger(ConsoleLogger.LEVEL_INFO);
```

Set the logger on the FOP driver using the `setLogger` method, and set the logger on the `MessageHandler` using the `setScreenLogger` method.

```
driver.setLogger(logger);
org.apache.fop.messaging.MessageHandler.setScreenLogger(logger);
```

Set the renderer for the FOP driver using the `setRenderer` method. For conversion to a PDF file, specify `Driver.RENDER_PDF` as the renderer.

```
driver.setRenderer(Driver.RENDER_PDF);
```

Generating the PDF document

Specify the XSL-FO document that is to be converted to a PDF document. The XSL-FO document, which was generated from an XML document previously in this chapter, is used to generate a PDF document. An XSL-FO object is set on a `Driver` object using the `setInputSource(InputSource)` method.

```
File xslFOFile=new File("catalog.fo");
InputStream input=new FileInputStream(xslFOFile);
driver.setInputSource(new InputSource(input));
```

Specify an output PDF document using the `setOutputStream(OutputStream)` method.

```
File pdfFile=new File("catalog.pdf");
OutputStream output=new FileOutputStream(pdfFile);
driver.setOutputStream(output);
```

Run the FOP driver to generate a PDF document using the `run` method.

```
driver.run();
```

Running the Java application

The Java application, `XMLToPDF.java`, used for converting an XML document to a PDF document is listed here with explanations:

1. First, we add the `package` and `import` statements.

```
package apachefop;

import org.apache.fop.apps.Driver;
import java.io.*;
import org.apache.avalon.framework.logger.ConsoleLogger;
import org.apache.avalon.framework.logger.Logger;
import org.apache.fop.apps.FOPException;
import org.xml.sax.InputSource;
import javax.xml.transform.*;
import javax.xml.transform.stream.StreamSource;
import javax.xml.transform.stream.StreamResult;
import javax.xml.parsers.DocumentBuilder;
import javax.xml.parsers.DocumentBuilderFactory;
import javax.xml.parsers.ParserConfigurationException;
import javax.xml.transform.dom.DOMSource;

import org.xml.sax.SAXException;
import org.w3c.dom.Document;
```

2. We define the Java class XMLToPDF.

```
public class XMLToPDF
{
  public XMLToPDF()
  {
  }
}
```

3. Next, we add the Java method xmlToFO to convert an XML document to an XSL-FO document.

```
    public void xmlToFO(){
    try{
       DocumentBuilderFactory factory =
               DocumentBuilderFactory.newInstance();

           File stylesheet = new File("catalog.xsl");
           File xmlFile   = new File("catalog.xml");

           DocumentBuilder builder = factory.
newDocumentBuilder();
          Document   document = builder.parse(xmlFile);

       TransformerFactory transformerFactory = TransformerFactory.
newInstance();

       Transformer transformer = transformerFactory.
newTransformer(new StreamSource(stylesheet));


       DOMSource source = new DOMSource(document);
       StreamResult  result = new StreamResult(new File("catalog.
fo"));
       transformer.transform(source, result);

    }catch(TransformerConfigurationException e)
{System.err.println("TransformerConfigurationException: "+e.
getMessage());}
     catch(TransformerException e)
{System.err.println("TransformerException: "+e.getMessage());}
      catch(ParserConfigurationException e)
{System.err.println("TransformerConfigurationException: "+e.
getMessage());}
         catch(IOException e){System.err.println("TransformerExcepti
on: "+e.getMessage());}
      catch(SAXException e){System.err.println("TransformerException
: "+e.getMessage());}

    }
```

4. We add the Java method `foToPDF` to convert a XSL-FO document to a
    PDF document.

```
public void foToPDF(){
try{
   Driver driver=new Driver();
   Logger logger=new ConsoleLogger(ConsoleLogger.LEVEL_INFO);
   driver.setLogger(logger);
   org.apache.fop.messaging.MessageHandler
   .setScreenLogger(logger);
   driver.setRenderer(Driver.RENDER_PDF);
   File xslFOFile=new File("catalog.fo");
   File pdfFile=new File("catalog.pdf");
   InputStream input=new FileInputStream(xslFOFile);
   driver.setInputSource(new InputSource(input));
   OutputStream output=new FileOutputStream(pdfFile);
   driver.setOutputStream(output);

   driver.run();
   output.flush();
   output.close();
  }catch(IOException e){System.err.println("IOException: "+e.
getMessage());}
   catch(FOPException e){System.err.println("FOPException: "+e.
getMessage());}

  }
```

5. Finally, we add the main method in which we create an instance of the
    XMLToPDF class and invoke the `xmlToFO` and `fopToPDF` methods.

```
public static void main(String[] argv){
   XMLToPDF   fop=new XMLToPDF();
   fop.xmlToFO();
   fop.foToPDF();

  }
}
```

Copy the XMLToPDF.java listing to the **XMLToPDF.java** class in the JDeveloper project **ApacheFOP**. To run the Java application, right-click on the Java application node in the **Application Navigator**, and select **Run**.

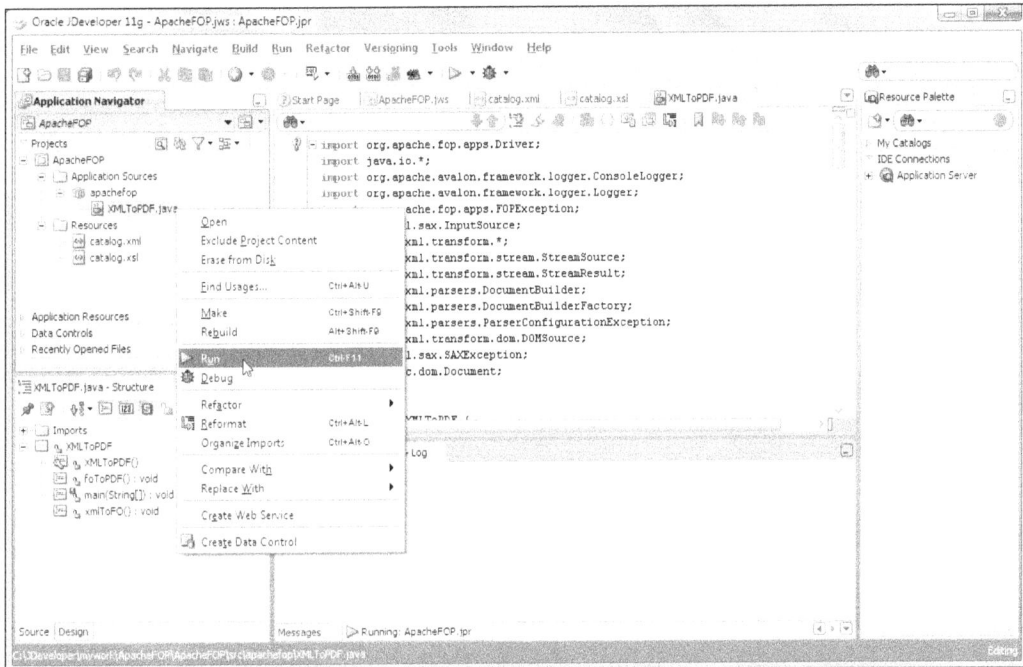

The output from the application run indicates that org.pache.xerces.parsers. SAXParser is used to parse the XML document. A formatting object gets built, the fonts get set, and a PDF document gets generated. Select **View | Refresh** to add the **catalog.pdf** document generated from the example XML document **catalog.xml** to the **ApacheFOP** project.

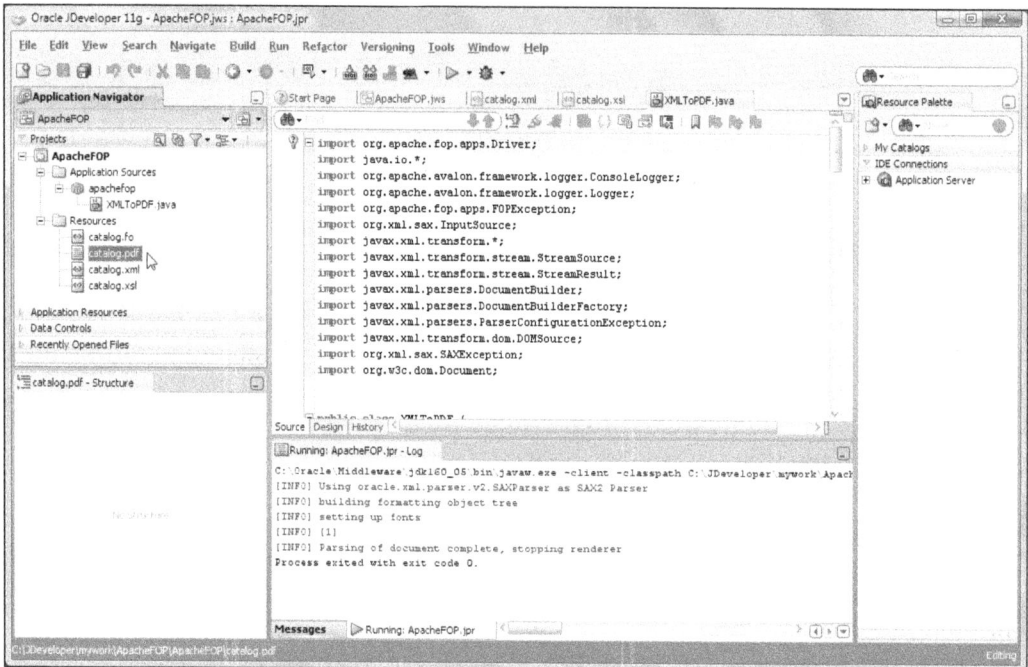

The `catalog.pdf` document generated is shown as follows:

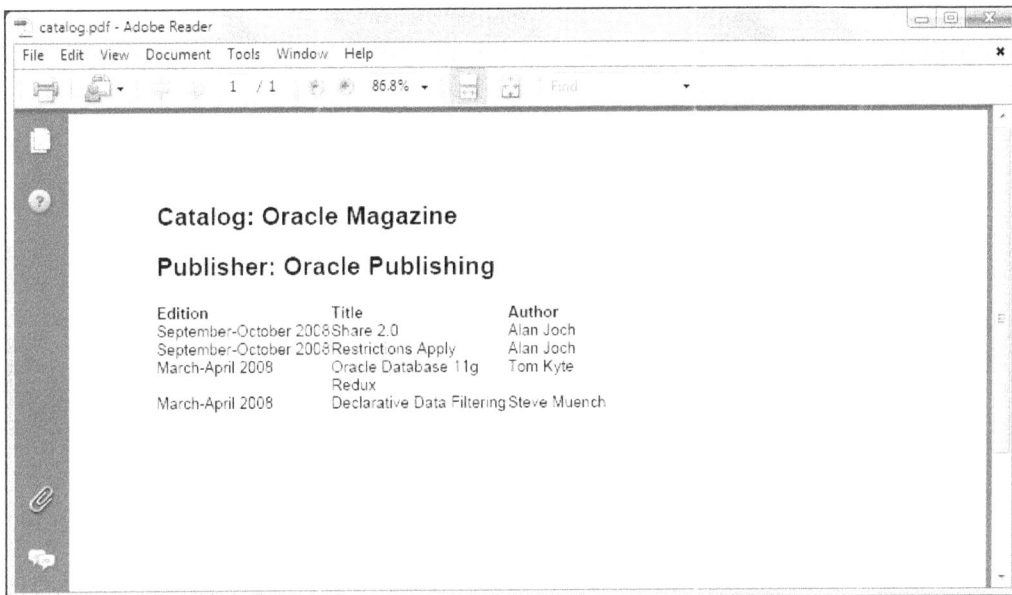

We did not include any graphics within the PDF generated, but Apache FOP supports the inclusion of graphics within PDF documents. Refer to `http://xmlgraphics.apache.org/fop/0.94/graphics.html` for graphics support in Apache FOP.

Summary

In this chapter we converted an example XML document, `catalog.xml`, to a PDF document, `catalog.pdf`, using the Apache FOP driver in JDeveloper 11g. In the next chapter we will convert an example XML document to an Excel spreadsheet.

12
Converting XML to MS Excel

As explained in the previous chapter, while XML is the standard format for data exchange, Adobe PDF and Microsoft Excel are better suited for data presentation. Using the Java API for XML Processing or the XPath API, data may be retrieved from an XML document and then presented in an Excel spreadsheet using a Java API for Excel spreadsheet. Various Java APIs are available for processing an Excel spreadsheet. Some of the more commonly used are discussed in the following table:

Java API	Description
Apache POI-HSSF	Apache POI Project's HSSF API is an open source Java API to create, modify, read, and write XLS spreadsheets. It supports graphics and images.
JExcel	JExcel is an open source Java API to read, write, and modify Microsoft Excel spreadsheets. It supports charts and images. JExcel may be downloaded from `http://sourceforge.net/project/showfiles.php?group_id=79926`.
Java e.Spreadsheet Engine and Excel API	e.Spreadsheet Engine and Excel API is a commercial tool to create, read, and modify spreadsheets in a Java application and may be downloaded from `http://www.birt-exchange.com/products/spreadsheet-engine/`.
jXLS	jXLS is a Java library to create complex Excel reports using XLS templates. jXLS may be downloaded from `http://jxls.sourceforge.net/`.

As touched upon in the table, the Apache POI project's HSSF API may be used to create an Excel spreadsheet. The POI HSSF API may also be used to parse an Excel spreadsheet and convert to another format such as XML. The HSSF API has the provision to set the layout, border settings, and fonts of an Excel document. In this chapter, an example Excel spreadsheet is generated by parsing an XML document and adding data from the XML document to the spreadsheet. Subsequently, the Excel spreadsheet is converted to an XML document.

The Jakarta POI HSSF API has classes to create an Excel workbook and add spreadsheets to the workbook. In the POI API, a workbook is represented by the HSSFWorkbook class. Spreadsheet fonts, sheet order, and cell styles are set in the HSSFWorkbook class. A spreadsheet is represented with the HSSFSheet class, where sheet layout, including column widths, margins, header, footer, and print setup is set. A spreadsheet row is represented with the HSSFRow class, where the row height is set. The HSSFCell class represents a cell in a spreadsheet row, and the style is set there. The indexing of spreadsheets in a workbook, rows in a spreadsheet, and cells in a row is 0-based.

Setting the environment

An Excel spreadsheet is created and parsed using the Apache POI HSSF API. Download the Apache POI ZIP file (poi-bin-3.2-FINAL-20081019 or a later version) from http://poi.apache.org/ and extract the ZIP file to an installation directory. The example XML document is parsed with the XPath API, the support for which was added in JDK 5.0. Therefore, JDK 5.0 or a later version is required. JDeveloper 11g is pre-configured with JDK 6.0. The Excel spreadsheet generated from the example XML document is opened with the Excel Viewer 2003. Therefore, download and install the Excel Viewer 2003 from http://www.microsoft.com/ downloads/details.aspx?FamilyId=C8378BF4-996C-4569-B547-75EDBD03A AF0&displaylang=en. The Excel document may also be displayed in MS Excel, which may be obtained from http://office.microsoft.com/en-us/excel/ FX100487621033.aspx.

First, we need to create an application and a project in JDeveloper 11g. Select **File | New**, and in the **New Gallery** window select **Categories | General** and **Items | Generic Application**. Click on **OK**. In the **Create Generic Application** window specify an application name (**XMLExcel** for example) and click on **Next**. In the **Name your Generic project** window specify a project name (**XMLExcel** for example), and click on **Finish**. An application and a project get created.

Next, we need to add the XML document that is to be converted to an Excel spreadsheet. Select **File | New**, and in the **New Gallery** window select **Categories | General |XML** and **Items | XML Document**. Click on **OK**. In the **Create XML File** window specify a file name (**catalog.xml** for example) and click on **OK**. An XML file gets added to the **XMLExcel** project. We also need to add a Java class (**XMLToExcel. java**) to convert the XML document to an Excel spreadsheet and another Java class, (**ExcelToXML.java**) to convert the Excel spreadsheet to an XML document. To add a Java class select **File | New**, and in the **New Gallery** window select **Categories | General** and **Items | Java Class**. Click on the **OK** button. In the **Create Java Class** window specify a file name and click on the **OK** button. A Java class gets added.

The directory structure of the **XMLExcel** application is shown in the following illustration:

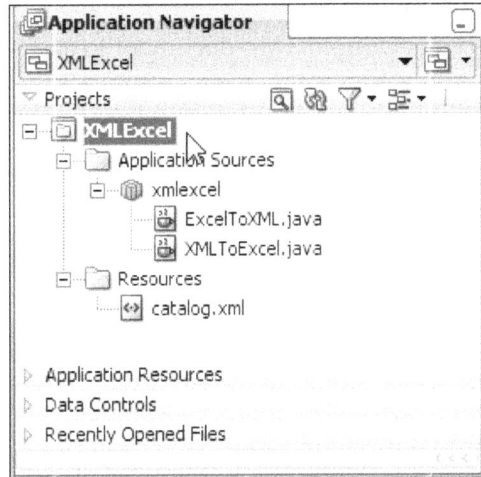

Next, add the Apache POI JAR file to the project classpath. Select **Tools | Project Properties**, and in the **Project Properties** window select **Libraries and Classpath**. Add the **poi-3.0.2-FINAL-20080204.jar** JAR file with the **Add JAR/Directory** button. Click on the **OK** button in the **Project Properties** window.

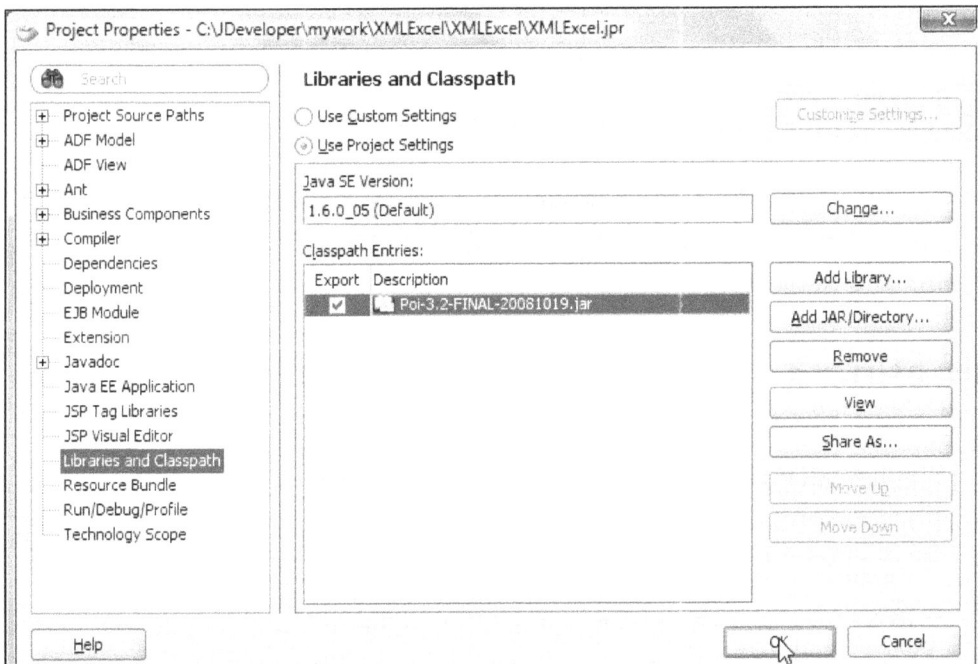

Converting an XML document to an Excel spreadsheet

In this section we convert an example XML document to an Excel document with the Apache HSSF API in the `XMLToExcel.java` application. The example document, `catalog.xml`, is listed as follows:

```
<?xml version="1.0" encoding="UTF-8"?>
<catalog>
    <journal>
        <journal-title>Oracle Magazine</journal-title>
        <publisher>Oracle Publishing</publisher>
        <section>COMMENT</section>
        <edition>November-December 2008</edition>
        <title>Application Server Convergence</title>
        <author>David Baum</author>
    </journal>
    <journal>
        <journal-title>Oracle Magazine</journal-title>
        <publisher>Oracle Publishing</publisher>
        <section>Technology</section>
        <edition>March-April 2008</edition>
        <title>Oracle Database 11g Redux</title>
        <author>Tom Kyte</author>
    </journal>
</catalog>
```

Copy the `catalog.xml` listing to the **catalog.xml** file in the **XMLExcel** project in JDeveloper 11g. We shall parse the XML document with the XPath API and add the values retrieved to an Excel spreadsheet. First, import the Apache POI HSSF package:

```
import org.apache.poi.hssf.usermodel.*;
```

Creating a spreadsheet

To create a spreadsheet, follow these steps:

1. Create an Excel workbook with the `HSSFWorkbook` constructor.

   ```
   HSSFWorkbook wb=new HSSFWorkbook();
   ```

2. Create a spreadsheet from the workbook using the `createSheet` method.

   ```
   HSSFSheet spreadSheet=wb.createSheet("spreadSheet");
   ```

3. Create a cell style object for the spreadsheet from the workbook using the `createCellStyle` method.

   ```
   HSSFCellStyle cellStyle=wb.createCellStyle();
   ```

4. Specify the border settings for the `HSSFCellStyle` object using the `setBorderRight` and `setBorderTop` methods. Set the border to `BORDER_MEDIUM`, which is a medium-size border.

   ```
   cellStyle.setBorderRight(HSSFCellStyle.BORDER_MEDIUM);
   cellStyle.setBorderTop(HSSFCellStyle.BORDER_MEDIUM);
   ```

A row in the spreadsheet has cells corresponding to each of the elements in a `journal` tag of the example XML document. Set the column width of each of the columns in the spreadsheet using the `setColumnWidth(int columnIndex,int width)` method. The width is specified in units of 1/256th of a character width. For example, the column width of the first cell (index 0) of a row is specified as follows:

```
spreadSheet.setColumnWidth(0, (256*25));
```

Parsing the XML document

The XML document can be parsed with the following steps:

1. Create an `InputSource` object for the XML document that is to be converted to an Excel spreadsheet.

   ```
   InputSource inputSource = new InputSource(new FileInputStream
                               (new File("catalog.xml")));
   ```

2. Create an `XPath` object to parse the example XML document. To create an `XPath` object, first create an `XPathFactory` instance using the static method `newInstance`. Subsequently, create the `XPath` object using the `newXPath` method.

   ```
   XPathFactory  factory=XPathFactory.newInstance();
   XPath xPath=factory.newXPath();
   ```

3. Specify the XPath expression for which a node list is to be obtained. The XPath expression for selecting the `journal` nodes in the example document is specified as follows:

   ```
   String expression="/catalog/journal";
   ```

4. Obtain a node list for the specified XPath expression using the `evaluate` method. The node list consists of nodes corresponding to the `journal` elements in the example XML document.

   ```
   com.sun.org.apache.xml.internal.dtm.ref.DTMNodeList nodeList =
       (com.sun.org.apache.xml.internal.dtm.ref.DTMNodeList) (xPath.
   evaluate(expression, inputSource, XPathConstants.NODESET));
   ```

Adding XML data to the spreadsheet

Follow these steps to add XML data to the spreadsheet:

1. Iterate over the node list and add a row to the spreadsheet corresponding to each of the `journal` nodes in the node list. A spreadsheet row is added with the `createRow(int rownum)` method of the `HSSFRow` object.

   ```
   for(int i=0; i<nodeList.getLength(); i++){
   HSSFRow row=spreadSheet.createRow(i);
   }
   ```

2. Create a cell in a spreadsheet row for each of the elements in the `journal` element. A cell is created with the `createCell(int columnIndex)` method of the `HSSFRow` object. The row cells have 0-based indices.

   ```
   HSSFCell cell=row.createCell(0);
   ```

3. Retrieve the element values from the node list using the JAXP API and set the values of row cells with the `setCellValue(HSSFRichTextString value)` method. For example, the value of the cell for the `section` element is set as follows:

   ```
   cell.setCellValue(new HSSFRichTextString. (((Element)(nodeList.
   item(i)))getElementsByTagName("section").item(0).getFirstChild().
   getNodeValue()));
   ```

4. The first cell in a row has index 0. Set the cell style of the cell with the `setCellStyle` method of the `HSSFCell` object.

   ```
   cell.setCellStyle(cellStyle);
   ```

5. Similarly, set the values of the columns for the other cells in a row.

Outputting the spreadsheet

Follow these steps to get the output of the spreadsheet:

1. Create a `FileOutputStream` to output the Excel workbook to an XLS file.

   ```
   FileOutputStream output=new FileOutputStream
                          (new File("catalog.xls"));
   ```

2. Output the Excel workbook to an XLS file using the `write` method, and close the `FileOutputStream`.

   ```
   wb.write(output);
    output.flush();
    output.close();
   ```

Running the Java application

The Java application XMLToExcel.java that is used to convert an XML document to an Excel spreadsheet is listed as follows with additional explanations:

1. First, we declare the package and the import statements.

```
package xmlexcel;

import org.apache.poi.hssf.usermodel.*;
import javax.xml.xpath.*;
import java.io.*;
import org.w3c.dom.*;
import org.xml.sax.InputSource;
```

2. We add the Java class XMLToExcel.

```
public class XMLToExcel {
```

3. We add the Java method generateExcel.

```
public void generateExcel(File xmlDocument) {
    try {
```

4. Next, we create a spreadsheet workbook and add a spreadsheet to it. We also set the cell style and the spreadsheet column width.

```
HSSFWorkbook wb = new HSSFWorkbook();
HSSFSheet spreadSheet = wb.createSheet("spreadSheet");
HSSFCellStyle cellStyle = wb.createCellStyle();
cellStyle.setBorderRight(HSSFCellStyle.BORDER_MEDIUM);
cellStyle.setBorderTop(HSSFCellStyle.BORDER_MEDIUM);
/*cellStyle.setFillForegroundColor(org.apache.poi.
hssf.util.HSSFColor.BLUE.index);
cellStyle.setFillPattern(HSSFCellStyle.SOLID_FOREGROUND);*/
spreadSheet.setColumnWidth(0, (256 * 25));
spreadSheet.setColumnWidth(1, (256 * 25));
spreadSheet.setColumnWidth(2, (256 * 25));
spreadSheet.setColumnWidth(3, (256 * 25));
spreadSheet.setColumnWidth(4, (256 * 75));
spreadSheet.setColumnWidth(5, (256 * 25));
```

5. Next, we select nodes from the XML document and add node values to the spreadsheet.

```
InputSource inputSource =
new InputSource(new FileInputStream(xmlDocument));
XPathFactory factory = XPathFactory.newInstance();
XPath xPath = factory.newXPath();
String expression = "/catalog/journal";
```

```
                    com.sun.org.apache.xml.internal.dtm.ref.DTMNodeList
nodeList = (com.sun.org.apache.xml.internal.dtm.ref.DTMNodeList)
(xPath.evaluate(expression,inputSource, XPathConstants.NODESET));
                    HSSFRow row=spreadSheet.createRow(0);
                    row.createCell(0).setCellValue("Journal");
                    row.createCell(1).setCellValue("Publisher");
                    row.createCell(2).setCellValue("Section");
                    row.createCell(3).setCellValue("Edition");
                    row.createCell(4).setCellValue("Title");
                    row.createCell(5).setCellValue("Author");
                    for (int i = 0; i < nodeList.getLength(); i++) {
                        row = spreadSheet.createRow(i+1);

                    HSSFCell cell = row.createCell(0);
                    cell.setCellValue(new HSSFRichTextString
(((Element)(nodeList.item(i))).getElementsByTagName("journal-
title").item(0).getFirstChild().getNodeValue()));
                    cell.setCellStyle(cellStyle);
                    cell = row.createCell(1);

                    cell.setCellValue(new HSSFRichTextString
(((Element)(nodeList.item(i))).getElementsByTagName("publisher").
item(0).getFirstChild().getNodeValue()));
                    cell.setCellStyle(cellStyle);
                    cell = row.createCell(2);
                  cell.setCellValue(new HSSFRichTextString
(((Element)(nodeList.item(i))).getElementsByTagName("section").
item(0).getFirstChild().getNodeValue());)
                    cell.setCellStyle(cellStyle);
                    cell = row.createCell(3);
                  cell.setCellValue(new HSSFRichTextString
(((Element)(nodeList.item(i))).getElementsByTagName("edition").
item(0).getFirstChild().getNodeValue()));
                    cell.setCellStyle(cellStyle);
                    cell = row.createCell(4);
                    cell.setCellValue(new HSSFRichTextString
((Element)(nodeList.item(i))).getElementsByTagName("title").
item(0).getFirstChild().getNodeValue()));
                    cell.setCellStyle(cellStyle);
                    cell = row.createCell(5);
                    cell.setCellValue(new HSSFRichTextString
(((Element)(nodeList.item(i))).getElementsByTagName("author").
item(0).getFirstChild().getNodeValue()));
                    cell.setCellStyle(cellStyle);
                }
```

6. We output the spreadsheet `catalog.xls`.

```
            FileOutputStream output =
                new FileOutputStream(new File("catalog.xls"));
```

```
        wb.write(output);
        output.flush();
        output.close();
    } catch (IOException e) { System.err.println(e.getMessage());
    } catch (XPathExpressionException e) { System.err.println(e.
getMessage());
    }
}
```

7. Finally, we define the `main` method in which we create an instance of the class `XMLToExcel` and invoke the `generateExcel` method.

```
public static void main(String[] argv) {
    File xmlDocument = new File("catalog.xml");
    XMLToExcel excel = new XMLToExcel();
    excel.generateExcel(xmlDocument);
}
```

Copy the `XMLToExcel.java` listing to the **XMLToExcel** class in the **XMLExcel** project in JDeveloper. To run the **XMLToExcel.java** application, right-click on the application node in the **Application Navigator** and select **Run**.

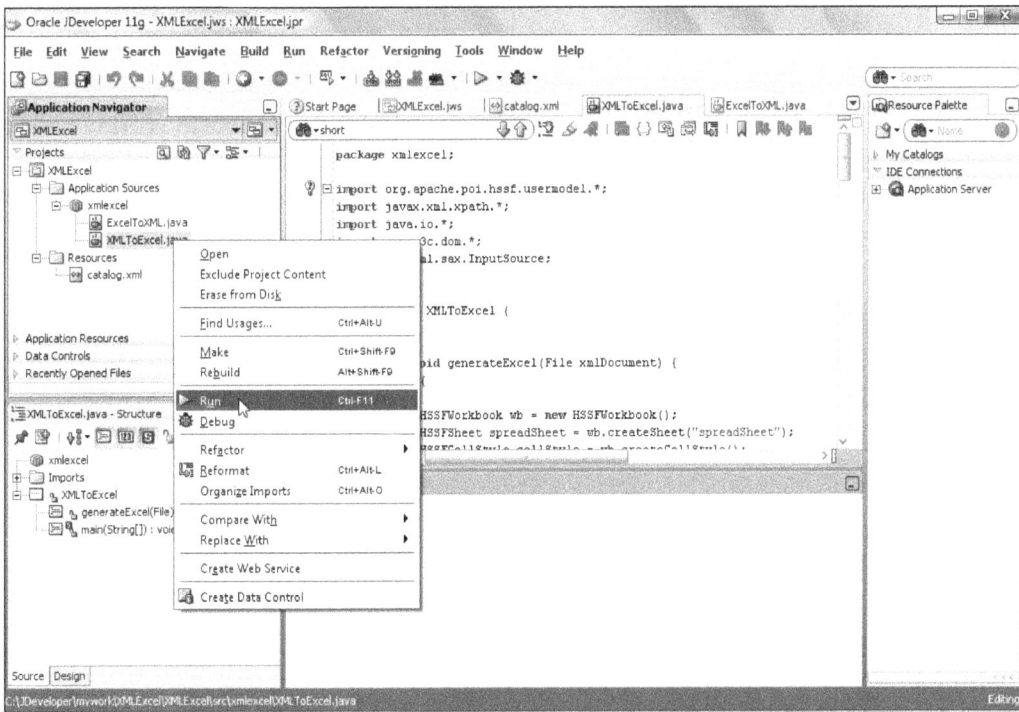

An Excel spreadsheet gets generated. Select the **XMLExcel** project node in the **Application Navigator** and select **View | Refresh** to add the **catalog.xls** spreadsheet file to the project.

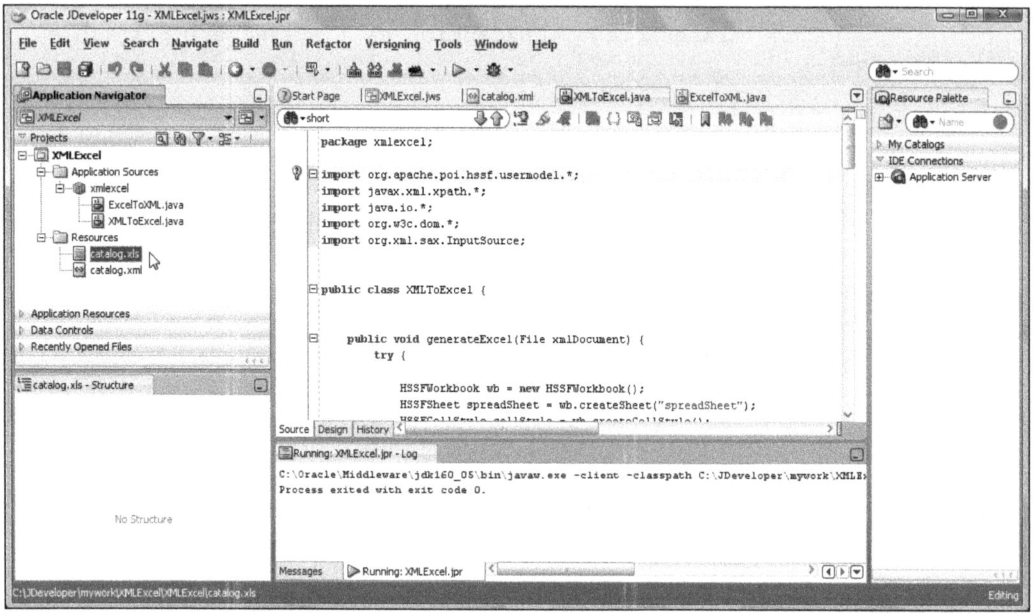

The `catalog.xls` spreadsheet, which may be opened in Excel Viewer 2003 or MS Excel, is shown in the following illustration:

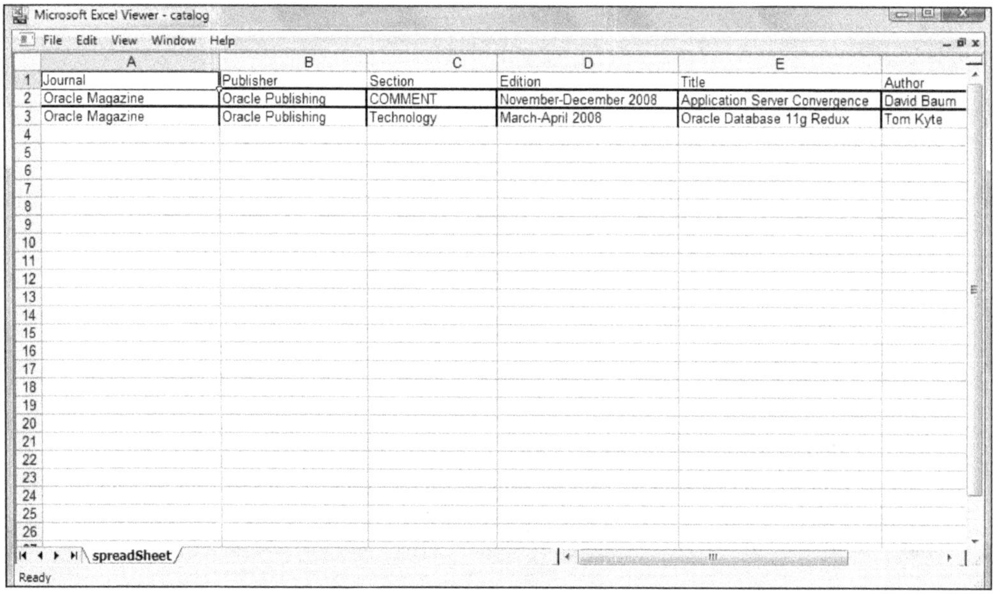

Converting an Excel spreadsheet to an XML document

In the previous section an Excel document was generated from an XML document. In this section the Excel document is converted back to an XML document. The Apache POI HSSF API may also be used to parse an Excel spreadsheet and retrieve the cell values from the spreadsheet.

In the **ExcelToXML.java** application in the **XMLExcel** project in JDeveloper, import the Apache POI HSSF API.

```
import  org.apache.poi.hssf.usermodel.*;
```

Creating the XML document

The root element of the XML document that we shall generate is `catalog`. We shall add a `journal` element to the root element corresponding to each of the rows of the Excel spreadsheet. First, generate an XML document and specify the root element of the document using the JAXP API, which was discussed in Chapter 1.

```
DocumentBuilderFactory factory =DocumentBuilderFactory.newInstance();
DocumentBuilder builder = factory.newDocumentBuilder();
Document document = builder.newDocument();
Element catalogElement=document.createElement("catalog");
document.appendChild(catalogElement);
```

Parsing the Excel spreadsheet

To parse the Excel spreadsheet follow these steps:

1. Create an `InputStream` object for the Excel spreadsheet that is to be converted to an XML document.

   ```
   InputStream input=new FileInputStream(excelFile);
   ```

2. Obtain the workbook for the `InputStream` object using the `HSSFWorkbook` constructor.

   ```
   HSSFWorkbook workbook=new HSSFWorkbook(input);
   ```

3. Obtain the spreadsheet for the Excel workbook. A spreadsheet is represented by an `HSSFSheet` object and is obtained from a workbook using the `getSheetAt(int index)` method. The first spreadsheet in the workbook is at index 0.

   ```
   HSSFSheet spreadsheet=workbook.getSheetAt(0);
   ```

Constructing the XML DOM tree

Iterate over the rows in the spreadsheet and add a `journal` element to the XML document for each of the rows. A row is retrieved from a spreadsheet using the `getRow(int rowIndex)` method. The rows in a spreadsheet have 0-based indices. The XML document is constructed using the JAXP API, which was discussed in Chapter 1.

```
for(int i=0; i<=spreadsheet.getLastRowNum(); i++)
{
HSSFRow row=spreadsheet.getRow(i);
Element journalElement=document.createElement("journal");
catalogElement.appendChild(journalElement);
}
```

A cell in a spreadsheet row is retrieved with the `getCell(int cellnum)` method. A cell value is retrieved with the `getRichStringCellValue()` method, which returns an `HSSFRichTextString` object that may be converted to a `String` using the `getString()` method. For example, the `section` cell value is retrieved from the spreadsheet and set in the XML document as follows:

```
Element sectionElement=document.createElement("section");
journalElement.appendChild(sectionElement);
sectionElement.appendChild(document.createTextNode(row.getCell(0).
getRichStringCellValue().getString()));
```

Similarly, retrieve the other cell values from the spreadsheet using the Apache POI API and specify the values in the XML document using the JAXP API. The XML document generated is outputted using the Transformation API for XML (TrAX) that was discussed in Chapter 5.

Running the Java application

The Java application used to convert an Excel spreadsheet to an XML document, `ExcelToXML.java`, is listed as follows with explanations about the different sections of the application:

1. First, we declare the `package` and the `import` statements.

    ```
    package xmlexcel;
    import org.apache.poi.hssf.usermodel.*;
    import org.w3c.dom.*;
    import javax.xml.parsers.*;
    import javax.xml.transform.*;
    import javax.xml.transform.dom.DOMSource;

    import javax.xml.transform.stream.StreamResult;
    import java.io.*;
    ```

2. We add the Java class `ExcelToXML`.

    ```
    public class ExcelToXML {
    ```

3. We add the Java method `generateXML`.

    ```
    public void generateXML(File excelFile) {

        try {
    ```

4. We create a `Document` object, which represents an XML document.

    ```
            DocumentBuilderFactory factory =
                DocumentBuilderFactory.newInstance();
            DocumentBuilder builder =
            factory.newDocumentBuilder();
            Document document = builder.newDocument();
            Element catalogElement = document.createElement
            ("catalog");
            document.appendChild(catalogElement);
    ```

5. We get the spreadsheet values and add corresponding elements to the `Document` object.

    ```
            InputStream input = new FileInputStream(excelFile);
            HSSFWorkbook workbook = new HSSFWorkbook(input);
            HSSFSheet spreadsheet = workbook.getSheetAt(0);

            for (int i = 1; i <= spreadsheet.getLastRowNum(); i++)

            {
                HSSFRow row = spreadsheet.getRow(i);

                Element journalElement = document.createElement(
    "journal");
                catalogElement.appendChild(journalElement);

                Element journalTitleElement = document.
    createElement("journal-title");
                journalElement.appendChild(journalTitleElement);
                journalTitleElement.appendChild(document.
    createTextNode(row.getCell(0).getRichStringCellValue().
    getString()));

                Element publisherElement = document.createElement(
    "publisher");
                journalElement.appendChild(publisherElement);
                publisherElement.appendChild(document.
    createTextNode(row.getCell(1).getRichStringCellValue().
    getString()));

                Element sectionElement = document.createElement(
    "section");
    ```

```
                journalElement.appendChild(sectionElement);
                sectionElement.appendChild(document.
createTextNode(row.getCell(2).getRichStringCellValue().
getString())));

                Element editionElement = document.createElement(
"edition");
                journalElement.appendChild(editionElement);
                editionElement.appendChild(document.
createTextNode(row.getCell(3).getRichStringCellValue().
getString())));

                Element titleElement = document.
createElement("title");
                journalElement.appendChild(titleElement);
                titleElement.appendChild(document.
createTextNode(row.getCell(4).getRichStringCellValue().
getString())));

                Element authorElement = document.
createElement("author");
                journalElement.appendChild(authorElement);
                authorElement.appendChild(document.
createTextNode(row.getCell(5).getRichStringCellValue().
getString())));
            }
```

6. We output the XML document that is generated from the spreadsheet.

```
            TransformerFactory tFactory = TransformerFactory.
newInstance();

            Transformer transformer = tFactory.newTransformer();

            DOMSource source = new DOMSource(document);
            StreamResult result = new StreamResult(new
File("catalog.xml"));
            transformer.transform(source, result);

        } catch (IOException e) {System.err.println(e.
getMessage());
        } catch (ParserConfigurationException e) { System.err.
println(e.getMessage());
        } catch (TransformerConfigurationException e) { System.
err.println(e.getMessage());
        } catch (TransformerException e) { System.err.println(e.
getMessage());
        }
    }
```

7. Finally, we add the `main` method in which we create an instance of the `ExcelToXML` class and invoke the `generateXML` method.

```
public static void main(String[] argv) {
    ExcelToXML excel = new ExcelToXML();
    File input = new File("catalog.xls");
    excel.generateXML(input);
}

}
```

Copy the `ExcelToXML.java` listing to the **ExcelToXML.java** class in the **XMLExcel** project in JDeveloper. Before running the `ExcelToXML.java` application, delete the `catalog.xml` file from the `XMLExcel` project. To run the **ExcelToXML.java** application, right-click on the **ExcelToXML.java** application node and select **Run**.

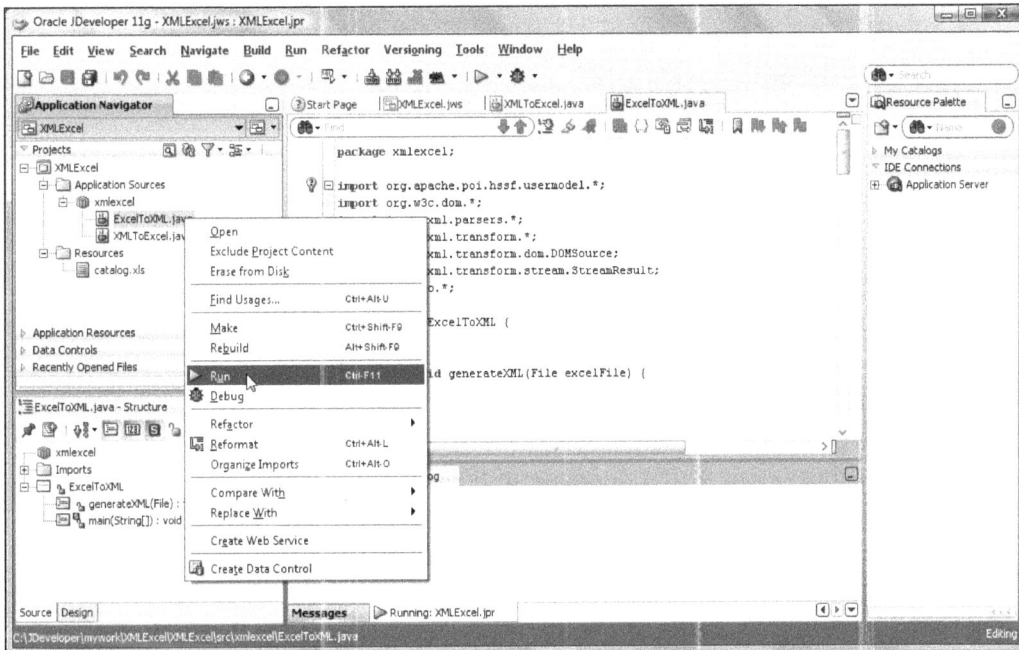

An XML document, `catalog.xml`, gets generated. Add the **catalog.xml** document to the **XMLExcel** project by selecting the project node in the **Application Navigator** and subsequently selecting **View | Refresh**. You should notice that the `catalog.xml` document is the same as the XML document that we started with.

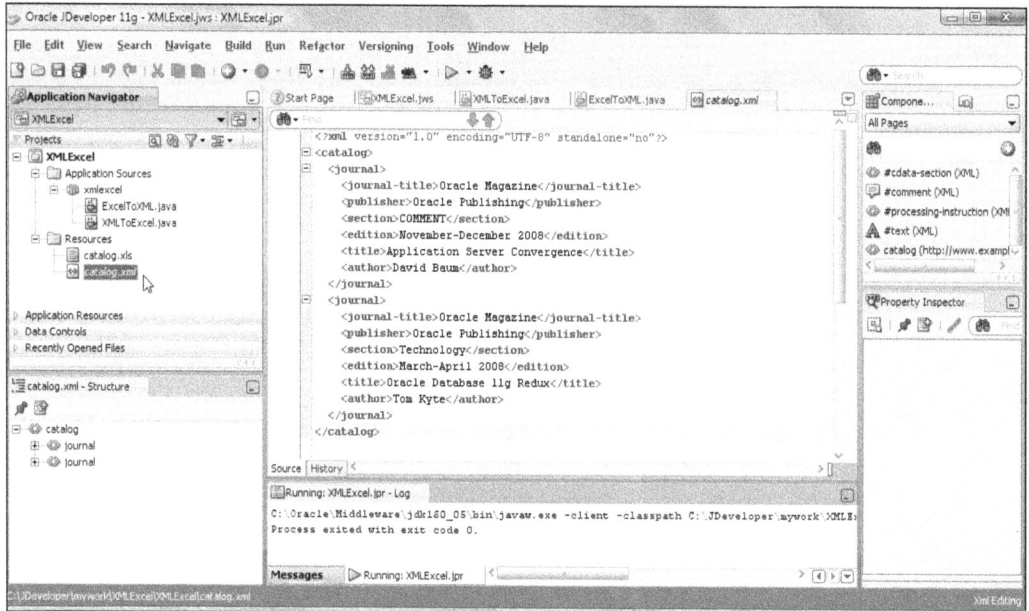

Summary

In this chapter you learned to convert an XML document to an MS Excel spreadsheet, and the spreadsheet to an XML document in JDeveloper 11g, all using the Apache POI API. However, we had to use some other APIs such as the JAXP and the TrAX APIs for XML document processing. In the next chapter you will learn to store an XML document in the Oracle Berkeley DB XML database, a native XML database.

13
Storing XML in Oracle Berkeley DB XML

Traditionally, XML has been stored in a relational database by mapping the XML document structures to the rows and columns of a database table. Storing an XML document in a relational database has its limitations. XML's hierarchical structures of elements and element attributes do not map well to relational database structures. An XML document has a top-level element, element attributes, and may have 'n' levels of elements within the top-level element. In comparison, a relational database has tables, which have a grid of columns and rows. That's where an embeddable XML database with its support for hierarchical data structures has advantages over a relational one. "Embedded" does not imply it is embedded in embedded devices such as mobile phones and PDAs. For embedded databases, "embedded" implies integrated with an application from which the database data is accessed. Oracle database (since Oracle 9*i* database R2) provides the Oracle XML DB feature to store and query XML documents in an `XMLType` data type column, but you still need a DBA to manage the Oracle database. The Oracle Berkeley DB XML database may be used in parallel to an Oracle relational database. The Oracle Berkely DB XML database may be used for both XML document management and transactional data.

Oracle **Berkeley DB XML (BDB XML)** is an embeddable XML database for storing and retrieving XML documents. Oracle Berkeley DB XML provides efficient querying of XML documents using **XQuery**. For an introduction to XQuery, refer to: `http://www.w3.org/TR/xquery/`. Oracle Berkeley DB XML is built on the embeddable Oracle Berkeley DB database and inherits all the features of the database. For a comparison of Oracle Berkeley DB and relational database systems, refer to *A Comparison of Oracle Berkeley DB and Relational Database Management Systems* (`http://www.oracle.com/database/docs/Berkeley-DB-v-Relational.pdf`).

Oracle Berkeley DB XML database stores XML data in a container. A container is a .dbxml file and we will discuss the different types of containers in a later section. A container is managed with an XmlManager object. XML documents may be stored in an Oracle BDB XML database as whole documents or as a set of nodes. It's recommended to store whole documents if the documents are relatively small, and loading performance is more important than query performance. Storing in nodes is recommended if query performance is more important than loading performance and documents are relatively large. BDB XML supports XQuery 1.0 and XPath 2.0 specifications to query an XML document in the database. XML documents in a BDB XML database may be modified, updated, and deleted.

Installing Oracle Berkeley DB XML

We need to download Oracle Berkeley DB XML 2.4.13 or a later version. Download the Oracle Berkeley DB XML Windows Installer .msi file from http://www.oracle. com/technology/software/products/berkeley-db/xml/index.html. Berkeley DB XML 2.4.13 is not supported on Windows Vista. Install an earlier version 2.3.10 for Windows Vista. To install Oracle BDB XML, double-click on the dbxml-2.4.13. msi file. The installer gets started. Click on **Next**.

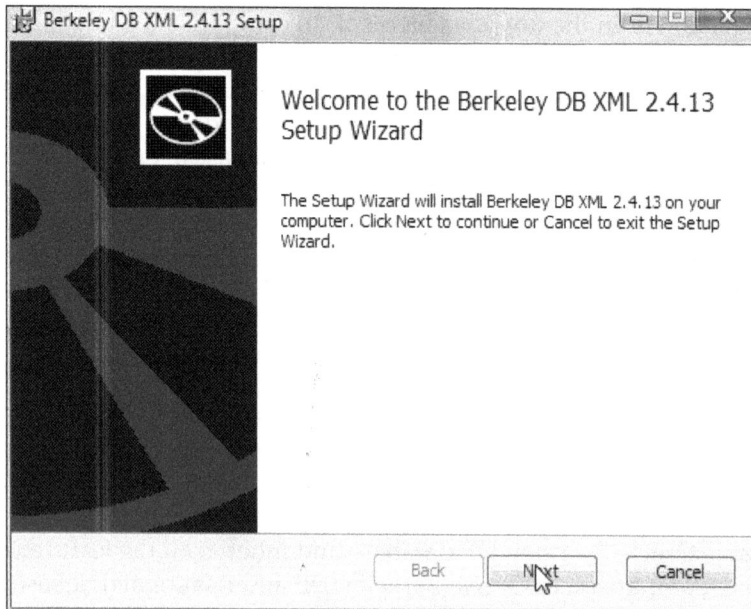

Accept the **End User License** and click on **Next**. Select the default features to install. Select the default installation folder, **C:\Program Files\Oracle\Berkeley DB XML 2.4.13**, and click on **Next**.

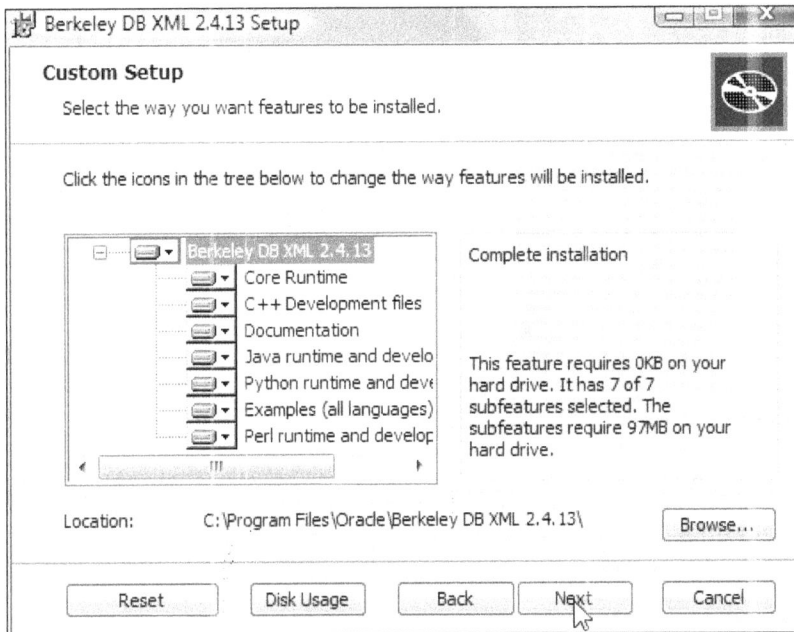

Click on **Install** to install Oracle Berkeley DB XML.

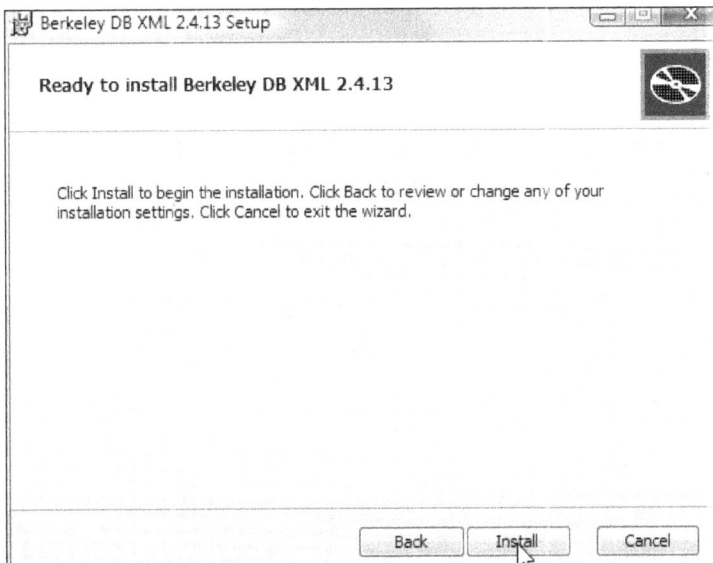

Berkeley DB XML 2.4.13 gets installed. Click on **Finish**.

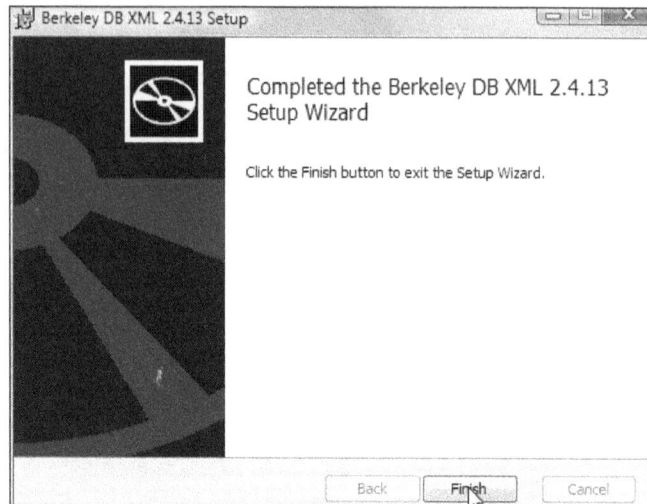

Berkeley DB XML requires some Windows environment variables (CLASSPATH and PATH) to be modified. The following Oracle Berkeley DB XML JAR files get added to the CLASSPATH environment variable:

```
C:\Program Files\Oracle\Berkeley DB XML 2.4.13\jar\dbxmlexamples.
jar;C:\Program Files\Oracle\Berkeley DB XML 2.4.13\jar\dbxml.
jar;C:\Program Files\Oracle\Berkeley DB XML 2.4.13\jar\db.jar
```

The following bin directory gets added to the PATH environment variable:

```
C:\Program Files\Oracle\Berkeley DB XML 2.4.13\bin
```

Berkeley DB XML may be accessed from a command-line shell or with a Java API. We will discuss each of these methods in the following sections.

Using the command shell

The dbxml shell may be started with the following command from a command line:

C:/>dbxml

The command shell gets started and the following prompt is displayed:

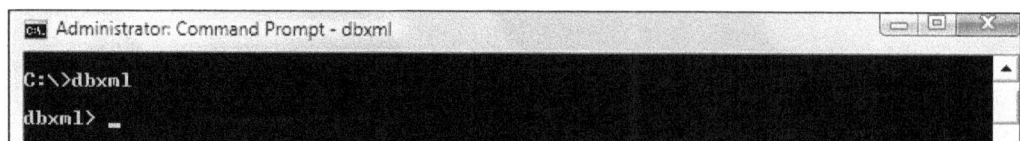

Berkeley DB XML commands may be specified at the dbxml command prompt. Some of the commonly used commands are discussed in the following table:

Command	Description
append <queryExpr> <objectType> <objectName> <objectContent>	Appends an object of type element, attribute, comment, or processes instruction to node(s) selected by a query expression.
createContainer <containerName> [n|in|d|id] [[no]validate]	Creates a container. The first argument specifies the container name. The second argument specifies the container type. Default value is in, which creates a node storage container with node indexes. Value d creates a Wholedoc container. Value n creates a node storage container. Value id creates a document storage container with node indexes. The third argument specifies if documents are to be validated on insertion.
getDocuments [<docName>]	Gets all the documents in the default container, or, if the docName is specified, gets the specified document.
insertAfter <queryExpr> <objectType> <objectName> <objectContent>	Inserts new content after the nodes specified by the query expression. The new content may be element, attribute, comment, or PI. Content type is specified with the <objectType> argument and content value is specified with the <objectContent> argument.
insertBefore <queryExpr> <objectType> <objectName> <objectContent>	Similar to insertAfter, except that the content is inserted before the specified nodes.
openContainer <container> [[no]validate]	Opens a container and sets the container as the default container. The validate / novalidate option specifies if documents are to be validated on insertion.
print [n <number>] [pathToFile]	Prints the most recent results to stdout. Results may be printed to a file by specifying the path to a file. A specified number of results may be output with the n argument.
putDocument <namePrefix> <string> [f|s|q]	Adds an XML document to the default container. The <namePrefix> argument specifies the document name. The <string> parameter specifies the XML document string. The third argument specifies the content of the second argument. If the value is f the string specifies a filename. If the value is s (the default), the string is the XML document to be added. If the value is q, the string specifies an XQuery expression.
query <queryExpression>	Evaluates an XQuery expression.

Command	Description
`removeContainer` `<containerName>`	Removes a container. The `.dbxml` file corresponding to the container gets deleted.
`removeDocument <docName>`	Removes a document from the default container.
`removeNodes` `<queryExpression>`	Removes the nodes specified by the XQuery expression.

`renameNodes`
`<queryExpression>`
`<newName>`
	Renames the nodes specified by the XQuery expression.

`run`	Runs the specified file as a script.

`updateNodes`
`<queryExpression>`
`<newContent>`
	Replaces the content of the nodes specified by the query expression with new content.

Let's first create a container to store XML documents. For example, create a container `catalog` to store catalog entries for journals.

```
dbxml>createContainer catalog.dbxml
```

A node storage container with indexed nodes gets created and opened.

The BDB XML database is just a `.dbxml` file created in the directory in which the `dbxml` command was issued.

Adding XML documents

Next, we will add XML documents to the BDB XML database using the `putDocument` command. For example, add an XML document that represents a catalog entry to the database. The `dbxml` command to add an XML document to a BDB XML container is as follows:

```
dbxml>putDocument catalog1 '<catalog title="Oracle Magazine"
publisher="Oracle Publishing">
 <journal date="November-December 2008">
  <article>
   <title>Application Server Convergence</title>
```

```
      <author>David Baum</author>
    </article>
  </journal>
</catalog>' s
```

Single quotes are used for any command parameters that span multiple lines or contain spaces. The character s, used to terminate the command, indicates that the XML document is added using a string. The XML document gets added and the output from the command is as follows:

```
Administrator: Command Prompt - dbxml

dbxml> putDocument catalog1 '<catalog title="Oracle Magazine" publisher="Oracle
Publishing">
 <journal date="November-December 2008">
  <article>
   <title>Application Server Convergence</title>
   <author>David Baum</author>
  </article>
 </journal>
</catalog>' s
Document added, name = catalog1

dbxml> _
```

As discussed in the putDocument method description in the previous table, an XML document may be stored from a string, a file, or an XQuery expression. Next, we will add an XML document from a file. Store the following listing to a file catalog.xml in the directory from which the dbxml command was made:

```
<catalog title="Oracle Magazine" publisher="Oracle Publishing">
  <journal date="March-April 2008">
   <article>
    <title> Oracle Database 11g Redux</title>
    <author> Tom Kyte</author>
   </article>
  </journal>
</catalog>
```

With the putDocument command, store the XML document in the catalog.xml file in the catalog.dbxml container. The character f at the end of the command indicates that the XML document is stored from a file.

```
dbxml>putDocument catalog2 catalog.xml f
```

Unlike in a relational database, the XML document storage transactions do not have to be committed. The XML documents added during all the preceding transactions may be retrieved with the getDocuments command.

The documents retrieved may be outputted to stdout with the print command.

Querying XML documents with XQuery

In this section we will query the XML documents added to the Berkeley DB XML database using XQuery. XQuery is an XPath-based SQL-like language for XML. XQuery queries retrieve subsets of data similar to the SELECT statement in SQL. Each query has two components. The first component identifies the set of documents to be queried using an XQuery navigation function such as collection() or doc(). The collection() function is used to navigate to a container. For example, container container1.dbxml may be navigated to with the following XQuery expression:

```
collection("container1.dbxml")
```

Multiple containers may be queried using the '|' operator. For example, containers `container1.dbxml` and `container2.dbxml` may be queried using the following expression:

```
collection(("collection1.dbxml")|("collection2.dbxml"))
```

The `doc()` function may be used to navigate to a specified XML document in a container. The `doc()` function takes a base URI (`dbxml:` by default), a container name, and an XML document name in the XQuery expression. For example, the XML document `xmldocument1.xml` in container `container1.dbxml` may be navigated to with the following expression:

```
doc("dbxml:/container1.dbxml/xmldocument1.xml")
```

As an example of a query, select all the article titles in the `catalog.dbxml` container. If Berkeley DB XML 2.3.8 is used, before we may query an XML document in a container, we need to set the base URI.

```
dbxml> setBaseUri dbxml:/
```

The query command, including the XQuery Expression to select all the titles, is as follows:

```
query collection('catalog.dbxml')/catalog/journal/article/title/text()
```

The `text()` function in the XQuery expression selects the text nodes within the title elements. For an introduction to XQuery, refer to `http://www.w3.org/TR/xquery/`. To output the results of the query use the `print` command.

As another example, retrieve the `author` of the article with the title **Application Server Convergence**. The query command including the XQuery expression for retrieving the author is as follows:

```
query collection('catalog.dbxml')/catalog/journal/article[title=
"Application Server Convergence"]/author/text()
```

Output the results with the `print` command.

```
Administrator: Command Prompt - dbxml

dbxml> query collection('catalog.dbxml')/catalog/journal/article[title="Applicat
ion Server Convergence"]/author/text()
1 objects returned for eager expression 'collection('catalog.dbxml')/catalog/jou
rnal/article[title="Application Server Convergence"]/author/text()'

dbxml> print
David Baum

dbxml> _
```

Modifying XML documents

The Oracle BDB XML command shell provides various commands such as `append`, `insertAfter`, and `insertBefore` to modify an XML document in the database. For example, append the `section` attribute to the article elements in the XML documents in the `catalog.dbxml` container. The command to append a `section` attribute with value `Developer` is as follows:

```
dbxml>append './catalog/journal/article' 'attribute' 'section'
'Developer'
```

The `append` command in the example won't append an attribute if the context has not been set. The query expression for modifying nodes should be relative. It should navigate from the context item (".") rather than evaluating an expression with the `collection()` or the `doc()` function. The context is set prior to the modifications with the `query` command. For example, set the context to the `catalog.dbxml` container. We will use the `catalog1` container context for the subsequent modification examples.

```
dbxml> query 'collection("catalog.dbxml")'
```

Having set the context we may run an `append` command. The syntax for the `append` command is as follows:

```
append <queryExpr>  <objectType> <objectName> <objectContent>
```

In the `append` command, `<queryExpr>` is the XQuery expression to select an XML document node to which another node is to be added. `<objectType>` is the type of the node to be added, such as an attribute or an element; `<objectName>` is name of the node to be added, and `<objectContent>` is the content of the node to be added. As an example, add a `section` attribute to the `article` node with title `Application Server Convergence`. The `dbxml` shell command to append the `attribute` node is as follows:

```
dbxml>append './catalog/journal/article[title="Application Server
Convergence"]' 'attribute' 'section' 'COMMENT'
```

An attribute node section gets added to the article element and the output from the append command is shown as follows:

As another example, add a journal element to the first catalog element, which has its journal element's date attribute value as November-December 2008. The append command to add the journal element is as follows:

```
dbxml>append './catalog[journal[@date="November-December 2008"]]'
'element' 'journal' '<article>
   <title>Instant ODP.NET Deployment</title>
   <author>Mark A. Williams</author>
</article>'
```

Output the modified `catalog1` document with the `getDocuments` command. The
output from the `print` command shows that a `section` attribute and a `journal`
element have been added.

We have used the `append` command to add an attribute and an element, but the
`append` command may also be used to add a comment or a processing instruction.

Replacing/deleting XML document nodes

Using the Oracle BDB XML command shell, nodes in an XML document in the
database may be replaced, renamed, and removed. For example, replace the article
title `Oracle Database 11g Redux` with `Oracle Database 11g Redux-Feature
Review`. The shell command to replace the `title` is as follows:

```
dbxml> updateNodes  './catalog/journal/article[title="Oracle Database 11g
Redux"]/title'   'Oracle Database 11g Redux-Feature Review'
```

As another example, rename the `journal` nodes to `magazine`. The shell command to rename the `journal` nodes to `magazine` is as follows:

```
dbxml>renameNodes  './catalog/journal'   'magazine'
```

Next, remove the `magazine` node with `date` attribute `March-April 2008`. The shell command to remove the `magazine` node is as follows:

```
dbxml>removeNodes './catalog/magazine[@date="March-April 2008"]'
```

After updating, renaming, and removing nodes, retrieve the XML documents using `getDocuments` and output the XML documents using `print`. As shown in the output, the `journal` nodes have been renamed to `magazine` and one of the renamed `magazine` nodes has been removed. The output from the `updateNodes` command shows that the title **Oracle Database 11g Redux** was updated to **Oracle Database 11g Redux-Feature Review**.

An XML document may be deleted from the database with the `removeDocument` command. For example, remove the `catalog1` document.

```
dbxml>removeDocument catalog1
```

A database container may be removed with the `removeContainer` command. For example, remove the `catalog.dbxml` container.

```
dbxml>removeContainer catalog.dbxml
```

The output shows that the `catalog1` document has been deleted and the `catalog.dbxml` container has been removed.

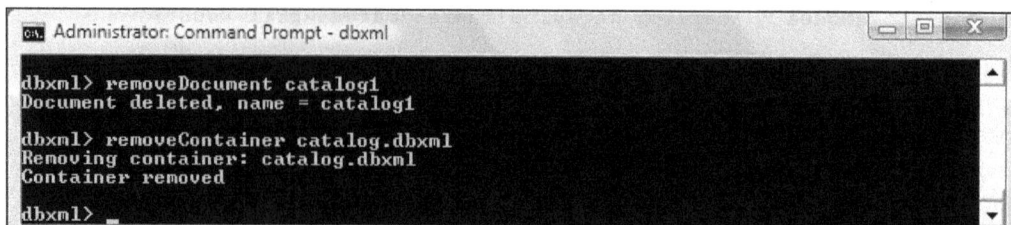

```
Administrator: Command Prompt - dbxml

dbxml> removeDocument catalog1
Document deleted, name = catalog1

dbxml> removeContainer catalog.dbxml
Removing container: catalog.dbxml
Container removed

dbxml>
```

Using the Berkeley DB XML API in JDeveloper

In BDB XML, documents are stored in containers. Containers are of two types: **Wholedoc** containers and **Node** containers. A Wholedoc container stores the complete XML document without any modifications to line breaks or whitespaces. In a Node container, XML documents are stored as nodes. Each element in an XML document is stored as a node in the database along with the element attributes, attribute values, and text nodes. BDB XML also stores information about reassembling an XML document from the nodes stored in the database. The Node container is the preferred type and is the default type. A comparison of Node container and Wholedoc container is discussed in the following table:

Container Type	Storage Mode	Query Performance	Load Performance	Application
Node Container	XML document stored in nodes	Faster to query	Lower load performance	Use Node container if faster query performance is required, or if document size is more than 1MB.
Wholedoc Container	Whole XML document stored	Lower query performance because complete document has to be navigated	Faster document loading because an XML document does not have to be deconstructed into nodes	Use Wholedoc container if load performance is more important than query performance, or if document is relatively small and requires to be frequently retrieved.

A container is represented with the class com.sleepycat.dbxml.XmlContainer. Configuration settings for a container are specified in the XmlContainerConfig object. An XmlManager object is used to manage many of the objects used in a BDB XML application, including managing an XmlContainer, and preparing and running XQuery queries. XmlManager is the main class in a BDB XML application. Before we may get started with using the Berkeley DB XML database with the Berkeley DB XML API, we need to set the application environment in JDeveloper 11g.

Setting the environment

Create an application and a project in JDeveloper 11g. Select **File|New**, and in the **New Gallery** window select **Categories | General** and **Items | Generic Application**. Click on **OK**. In the **Create Generic Application** window specify an application name (**BerkeleyDBXML** for example) and click on the **Next** button. In the **Name your Generic Project** window, specify a project name (**BerkeleyDBXML** for example) and click on the **Finish** button. An application and a project get added to the **Application Navigator**. Next, we need to add a Java class to create the Java application for Berkeley DB XML. Create a Java class with **File | New**. In the **New Gallery** window select **Categories | General** and **Items | Java Class**. Click on the **OK** button. In the **Create Java Class** window specify a class Name (**BDBXML.java** for example) and click on the **OK** button. A Java class gets added to the **BerkeleyDBXML** project.

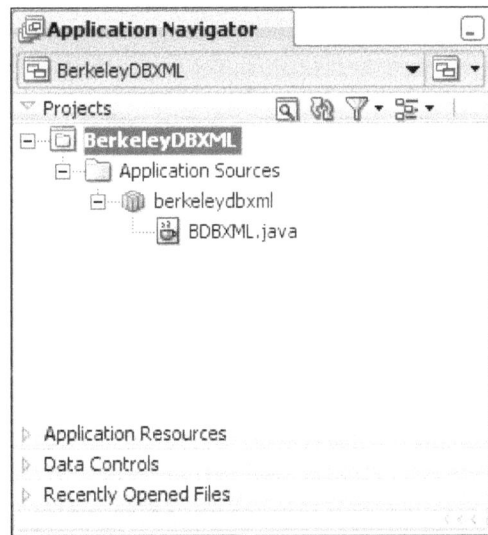

We also need to add some Berkeley DB XML JAR files to the project classpath. Select the project node in the **Application Navigator** and select **Tools | Project Properties**. In the **Project Properties** window select **Libraries and Classpath**, and add the JAR files shown in the following illustration from the `jar` directory of the Berkeley DB XML installation using the **Add JAR/Directory** button. Click on the **OK** button.

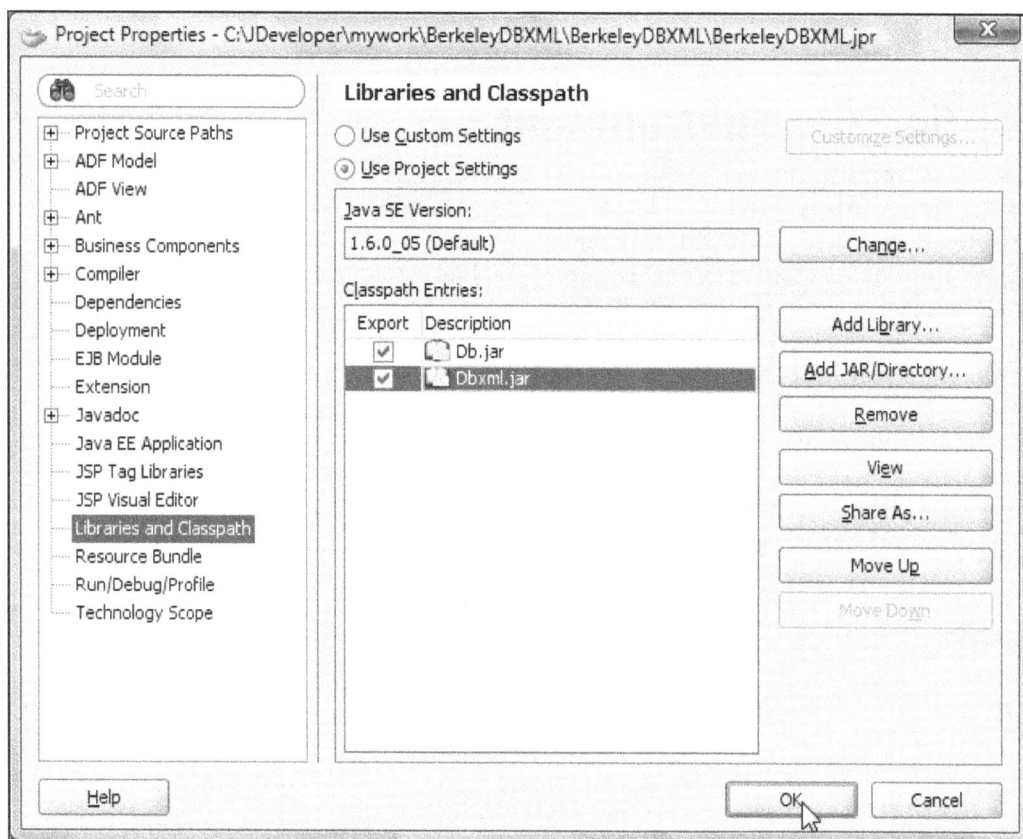

Next, we will create a container, add XML documents to the container, query the XML documents with XQuery, modify the XML documents, and update the XML documents—all with the BDB XML API in the `com.sleepycat.dbxml` package classes in the Java application `BDBXML.java`.

Creating a container

1. Create an `XmlManager` object and set the default container type to be `NodeContainer`.

```
XmlManager xmlManager = new XmlManager();
xmlManager.setDefaultContainerType(XmlContainer.NodeContainer);
```

2. Now, create a container `catalog.dbxml`. The container is the equivalent of a table in a relational database.

```
XmlContainer xmlContainer = xmlManager.createContainer(
"catalog.dbxml");
```

Adding XML documents

Next, we will add XML documents to the BDB XML database. Similar to the `putDocument` shell command, the BDB XML API provides the method `putDocument()` to store an XML document in a database. Create a `String` object that represents an XML document and specify a document name.

```
String docString = "<catalog title='Oracle Magazine' publisher='Oracle
Publishing'>" +
        "<journal date='November-December 2008'>" + "<article>" +
            "<title>Application Server Convergence</title>" +
            "<author>David Baum</author>" + "</article>" +
            "</journal>" + "</catalog>";
            String docName = "catalog1";
```

Instantiate a new, default `XmlUpdateContext` object. An `XmlUpdateContext` object represents the context within which update operations are performed in a container. Presently, the `XmlUpdateContext` class is a no-op, which implies that creating and setting the `XmlUpdateContext` object is just a programming statement that effectively does nothing.

```
XmlUpdateContext updateContext = xmlManager.createUpdateContext();
```

Store the XML document using the `putDocument(String name, String content, XmlUpdateContext context, XmlDocumentConfig config)` method.

```
xmlContainer.putDocument(docName, docString, updateContext, null);
```

The `putDocument` method is overloaded to add an XML document from various sources including a `String`, an `InputStream`, or an `XMLDocument` object. Next, add another XML document, but add the document from a file instead of a string.

Create an XML document in the JDeveloper project BerkeleyDBXML with **File | New**. In the **New Gallery** window select **Categories | General | XML** and **Items | XML Document**, and click on **OK**. In the **Create XML File** window specify **File Name** as **catalog.xml** and click on **OK**. A **catalog.xml** XML document gets added to the JDeveloper project **BerkeleyDBXML**. Copy the following XML document listing to the `catalog.xml` file:

```
<catalog title="Oracle Magazine" publisher="Oracle Publishing">
 <journal date="March-April 2008">
  <article>
   <title>Oracle Database 11g Redux</title>
   <author>Tom Kyte</author>
  </article>
 </journal>
</catalog>
```

We will add the XML document from the `catalog.xml` file using the `putDocument(String name, XmlInputStream input, XmlUpdateContext context, XmlDocumentConfig config)` method of class `XmlContainer`. Create an `InputStream` object from the `catalog.xml` file, and subsequently create an `XmlInputStream` object from the `InputStream` object using the `createInputStream` method. Specify the XML document name in the `catalog.dbxml` container as `catalog2`, and add the XML document to the container using the `putDocument` method.

```
InputStream inputStream =
                new FileInputStream(new File("catalog.xml"));
XmlInputStream xmlInputStream =
                xmlManager.createInputStream(inputStream);
docName = "catalog2";
            xmlContainer.putDocument(docName, xmlInputStream,
updateContext,null);
```

Querying XML documents with XQuery

Next, we will query the XML documents in the `catalog.dbxml` BDXML database using XQuery. XQuery is an SQL-like query language for XML and is based on XPath. First, create an `XmlQueryContext` object. An `XmlQueryContext` object represents the context within which an XML document in a container is queried.

```
XmlQueryContext context = xmlManager.createQueryContext();
```

As an example query, retrieve the values of all the titles in the BDB XML database. Specify the query string that represents the XQuery expression for the query.

```
String query = "collection('catalog.dbxml')/catalog/journal/article/
title/text()";
```

Compile the XQuery expression into an `XmlQueryExpression` object using the `prepare(String query, XmlQueryContext context)` method of the `XmlManager` class.

```
XmlQueryExpression qe = xmlManager.prepare(query, context);
```

Next, evaluate the XQuery expression using the `execute(XmlQueryContext context)` method of the `XmlQueryExpression` object. When the XQuery query is run, the results are represented by the `XmlResults` object.

```
XmlResults results = qe.execute(context);
```

Iterate over the results and output the titles retrieved.

```
while (results.hasNext()) {
            XmlValue xmlValue = results.next();
            System.out.println(xmlValue.asString());
        }
```

The output from the query is as follows:

```
Application Server Convergence

Oracle Database 11g Redux
```

Modifying XML documents

Next, we will modify an XML document in the database. The BDB XML API provides the `XmlModify` class to modify an XML document. The procedure to modify an XML document is as follows:

1. Create an `XmlModify` object.
2. Select the nodes to be modified.
3. Specify the modification steps. Modifications are performed in the order specified.
4. Run the modifications in the context of an XML document or a set of XML documents.

First, create an `XmlModify` object.

```
XmlModify mod = xmlManager.createModify();
```

Additionally, create an `XmlQueryContext` object, which represents the context in which an XQuery query is performed to select nodes for modification. Also create an `XmlUpdateContext` object, which represents the context within which update operations are performed.

```
XmlQueryContext qc = xmlManager.createQueryContext();
XmlUpdateContext uc = xmlManager.createUpdateContext();
```

The `XmlModify` class provides various methods to modify an XML document. What these methods really do is add commands to the `XMLModify` class, which implements the Interpreter pattern; it's basically a composition of commands. Thus, the `XMLModify` object allows you to assemble a sequence of modifications and then run them in a batch. These methods are discussed in the following table:

Method	Description
`addAppendStep(XmlQueryExpression selectionExpr, int type, String name, String content)`	Appends the provided data to a specified node's child nodes as an element, attribute, comment, text, or processing instruction.
`addInsertAfterStep(XmlQueryExpression selectionExpr, int type, String name, String content)`	Inserts the provided data after a specified node as an element, attribute, comment, text, or a processing instruction.
`addInsertBeforeStep(XmlQueryExpression selectionExpr, int type, String name, String content)`	Inserts the provided data before a specified node.
`addRemoveStep(XmlQueryExpression selectionExpr)`	Removes a specified node.
`addRenameStep(XmlQueryExpression selectionExpr, String newName)`	Renames a specified node.
`addUpdateStep(XmlQueryExpression selectionExpr, String content)`	Updates a specified node.

As an example, add a `section` attribute to the article element in `catalog1` document. Select the `article` node using an XQuery expression.

```
XmlQueryExpression select =
        xmlManager.prepare("/catalog/journal/article[title='Application
Server Convergence']",qc);
```

Use the `addAppendStep()` method to append the `section` attribute to the `article` element. The type of an object to be added may be an element (represented with `XmlModify.Element`), an attribute (`XmlModify.Attribute`), a comment (`XmlModify.Comment`), text (`XmlModify.Text`), or a processing instruction (`XmlModify.ProcessingInstruction`). In the example we will add a `section` attribute with value COMMENT:

```
mod.addAppendStep(select, XmlModify.Attribute,
"section","COMMENT");
```

Next, add a `journal` element after the `journal` element in the `catalog1` document. Select the `journal` node in the `catalog1` document.

```
select =xmlManager.prepare("/catalog/journal",qc);
```

Specify the element content to be added.

```
String objectContent ="<article>"+"<title>Declarative Data Filtering
</title>"+"<author>Steve Muench</author>"+"</article>";
```

Add the `journal` element using the `addInsertAfterStep()` method.

```
mod.addInsertAfterStep(select, XmlModify.Element, "journal",objectCon
tent);
```

The modification is not complete yet. Obtain the XML document in which the modification is to be performed.

```
XmlDocument xmlDocument = xmlContainer.getDocument("catalog1");
```

Obtain the `XmlValue` object for the XML document and run the modifications.

```
XmlValue xmlValue = new XmlValue(xmlDocument);
  mod.execute(xmlValue, qc, uc);
```

A `section` attribute gets added to the `article` element, and a `journal` element gets added after the `journal` element in `catalog1` document.

Updating/renaming in XML documents

Next, we will update and rename elements in the `catalog1` XML document. As an example, we will update the title Oracle Database 11g Redux to Oracle Database 11g Redux-Feature Review. We will rename the `journal` element to magazine.

1. First, create `XmlModify`, `XmlQueryContext`, and `XmlUpdateContext` objects.

```
XmlModify mod = xmlManager.createModify();
XmlQueryContext qc = xmlManager.createQueryContext();
XmlUpdateContext uc = xmlManager.createUpdateContext();
```

2. Select the `title` text node to be updated.

```
XmlQueryExpression select =xmlManager.prepare
("/catalog/journal/article[title='Oracle Database 11g Redux']/
title/text()",qc);
```

3. Specify the update content.

```
String updateContent = "Oracle Database 11g Redux-Feature Review";
```

4. Add a update modification to the `XmlModify` object using the `addUpdateStep()` method.

```
mod.addUpdateStep(select, updateContent);
```

5. Next, rename the `journal` nodes to `magazine`. Select the `journal` nodes with an XQuery expression.

```
select = xmlManager.prepare("/catalog/journal", qc);
```

6. Add a renaming modification to the `XmlModify` object using the `addRenameStep()` method.

```
mod.addRenameStep(select,"magazine");
```

7. Obtain the `catalog2` document from the BDB XML database and run the modifications on the document.

```
XmlDocument xmlDocument = xmlContainer.getDocument("catalog2");
XmlValue xmlValue = new XmlValue(xmlDocument);
 mod.execute(xmlValue, qc, uc);
```

The title text gets updated, and the `journal` node gets renamed to `magazine`. The `BDBXML.java` application used to access the BDB XML database is listed with explanations as follows:

1. First, we add the package and import statements.

```
package berkeleydbxml;

import com.sleepycat.dbxml.XmlContainer;
import com.sleepycat.dbxml.XmlDocument;
import com.sleepycat.dbxml.XmlException;
import com.sleepycat.dbxml.XmlInputStream;
import com.sleepycat.dbxml.XmlManager;
import com.sleepycat.dbxml.XmlModify;
import com.sleepycat.dbxml.XmlQueryContext;
import com.sleepycat.dbxml.XmlQueryExpression;
import com.sleepycat.dbxml.XmlResults;
import com.sleepycat.dbxml.XmlUpdateContext;
import com.sleepycat.dbxml.XmlValue;
```

```
import java.io.File;
import java.io.FileInputStream;
import java.io.FileNotFoundException;
import java.io.InputStream;
```

2. We define the Java class `BDBXML`.

```
public class BDBXML {
```

3. We declare the instance variables.

```
XmlManager xmlManager = null;
XmlContainer xmlContainer = null;
```

4. We add Java method `createContainer` to create a container.

```
public void createContainer() {
    try {
        xmlManager = new XmlManager();
xmlManager.setDefaultContainerType(XmlContainer.NodeContainer);
        xmlContainer = xmlManager.createContainer(
"catalog.dbxml");
    } catch (XmlException e) {
        System.err.println("XmlException" + e.getMessage());
    } catch (java.io.FileNotFoundException e) {
        System.err.println("FileNotFoundException" +
        e.getMessage());
    }
}
```

5. Next, we define Java method `addDocument` to add XML documents to the container.

```
public void addDocument() {
    try {
        String docString =
            "<catalog title='Oracle Magazine' publisher='Oracle
            Publishing'>" +
            "<journal date='November-December 2008'>" +
            "<article>" +
            "<title>Application Server Convergence</title>" +
            "<author>David Baum</author>" + "</article>" +
            "</journal>" +
            "</catalog>";
        String docName = "catalog1";

        XmlUpdateContext updateContext =
        xmlManager.createUpdateContext();
        xmlContainer.putDocument(docName, docString,
```

```
                updateContext, null);

                InputStream inputStream =
                    new FileInputStream(new File("catalog.xml"));
                XmlInputStream xmlInputStream =
                    xmlManager.createInputStream(inputStream);

                docName = "catalog2";
                xmlContainer.putDocument(docName, xmlInputStream,
                updateContext, null);

                XmlResults results = xmlContainer.getAllDocuments(null);

                while (results.hasNext()) {
                    XmlValue xmlValue = results.next();
                    System.out.println(xmlValue.asString());
                }
            } catch (XmlException e) {
                System.err.println("XmlException" + e.getMessage());
            } catch (FileNotFoundException e) {
                System.err.println("XmlException" + e.getMessage());
            }
        }
```

6. We define the Java method `queryMethod` to query the documents added.

```
        public void queryDocument() {
            try {
                XmlQueryContext context = xmlManager.createQueryContext();

                String query ="collection('catalog.dbxml')
                /catalog/journal/article/title/text()";
                XmlQueryExpression qe = xmlManager.prepare
                (query, context);
                XmlResults results = qe.execute(context);

                while (results.hasNext()) {
                    XmlValue xmlValue = results.next();
                    System.out.println(xmlValue.asString());
                }
            } catch (XmlException e) {
                System.err.println("XmlException" + e.getMessage());
            }
        }
```

7. Next, we define the Java method `modifyDocument` to modify the documents in the container.

```
public void modifyDocument() {
    try {
        XmlQueryContext qc = xmlManager.createQueryContext();
        XmlUpdateContext uc = xmlManager.createUpdateContext();
        XmlModify mod = xmlManager.createModify();
        XmlQueryExpression select = xmlManager.prepare
        ("/catalog/journal/article[title='Application Server
        Convergence']", qc);
        mod.addAppendStep(select, XmlModify.Attribute, "section",
                        "COMMENT");

        String objectContent ="<article>"+"<title>Declarative Data
        Filtering</title>"+"<author>Steve Muench</author>"+"
        </article>";

        select =xmlManager.prepare("/catalog/journal",qc);
        mod.addInsertAfterStep(select, XmlModify.Element,
        "journal",objectContent);
        XmlDocument xmlDocument =
        xmlContainer.getDocument("catalog1");
        XmlValue xmlValue = new XmlValue(xmlDocument);
        mod.execute(xmlValue, qc, uc);

        System.out.println("XML Documents after modification");

        XmlResults results = xmlContainer.getAllDocuments(null);

        while (results.hasNext()) {
            xmlValue = results.next();
            System.out.println(xmlValue.asString()+"\n");
        }
    } catch (XmlException e) {
        System.err.println("XmlException" + e.getMessage());
    }
}
```

8. We define the Java method `updateDocument` to update the documents in the container.

```
public void updateDocument() {
    try {
        XmlQueryContext qc = xmlManager.createQueryContext();
        XmlUpdateContext uc = xmlManager.createUpdateContext();
        XmlModify mod = xmlManager.createModify();

        String updateContent = "Oracle Database 11g Redux-Feature
        Review";
```

```
            XmlQueryExpression select = xmlManager.prepare
            ("/catalog/journal/article[title='Oracle Database 11g
             Redux']/title/text()", qc);
            mod.addUpdateStep(select, updateContent);

            select = xmlManager.prepare("/catalog/journal", qc);
            mod.addRenameStep(select, "magazine");

            System.out.println("XML Documents after Update");

            XmlDocument xmlDocument =
            xmlContainer.getDocument("catalog2");
            XmlValue xmlValue = new XmlValue(xmlDocument);
            mod.execute(xmlValue, qc, uc);

            XmlResults results = xmlContainer.getAllDocuments(null);

            while (results.hasNext()) {
                xmlValue = results.next();
                System.out.println(xmlValue.asString());
            }
        } catch (XmlException e) {
            System.err.println("XmlException" + e.getMessage());
        }

    }
```

9. Finally, we add the `main` method in which we create an instance of the
    BDBXML class. Then we invoke different methods to create a Berkeley DB
    XML container and add, modify, update, and query XML documents in
    the container.

```
public static void main(String[] argv) {
    BDBXML bdbXML = new BDBXML();

  bdbXML.createContainer();
    bdbXML.addDocument();
  bdbXML.queryDocument();
  bdbXML.modifyDocument();
    bdbXML.updateDocument();
  }
}
```

Copy the BDBXML.java listing to the **BDBXML.java** class in the JDeveloper project **BerkeleyDBXML**. To run the BDBXML.java application, right-click on the application node and select **Run**. First, we will run the application after commenting out the invocations of the modifyDocument and updateDocument methods.

The output from **BDBXML.java** is shown in the following illustration. The output shows the result of creating a container, adding documents to the container, and querying the documents.

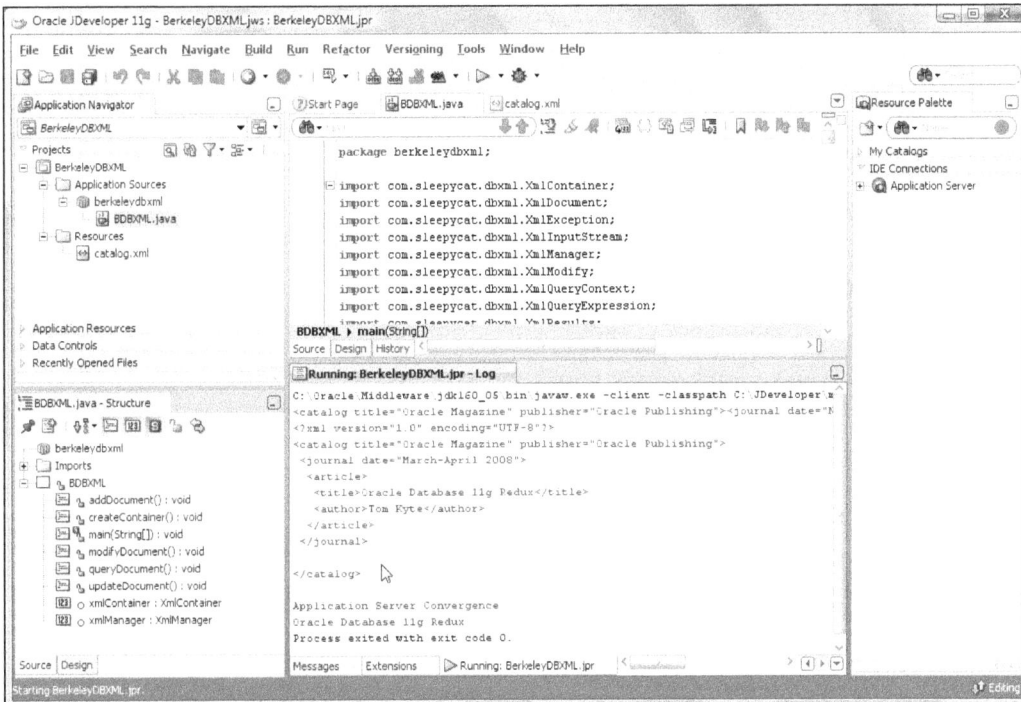

Next, we run the `BDBXML.java` application again after uncommenting all the methods. Delete the `catalog.dbxml` file from the BerkeleyDBXML project directory before re-running the application. The output shows that a `section` attribute and a `journal` element get added after modifying the `catalog1` document in the `catalog.dbxml` container. After updating the `catalog2` document in the Berkeley DB XML container, the `journal` node gets renamed to `magazine` and a `title` element gets updated.

```
Running: BerkeleyDBXML.jpr - Log
XML Documents after modification
<catalog title="Oracle Magazine" publisher="Oracle Publishing"><journal
date="November-December 2008"><article
section="COMMENT"><title>Application Server
Convergence</title><author>David
Baum</author></article></journal><journal><article><title>Declarative
Data Filtering</title><author>Steve
Muench</author></article></journal></catalog>

<?xml version="1.0" encoding="UTF-8"?>
<catalog title="Oracle Magazine" publisher="Oracle Publishing">
  <journal date="March-April 2008">
   <article>
    <title>Oracle Database 11g Redux</title>
    <author>Tom Kyte</author>
   </article>
  </journal>

</catalog>


XML Documents after Update
<catalog title="Oracle Magazine" publisher="Oracle Publishing"><journal
date="November-December 2008"><article
section="COMMENT"><title>Application Server
Convergence</title><author>David
Baum</author></article></journal><journal><article><title>Declarative
Data Filtering</title><author>Steve
Muench</author></article></journal></catalog>
<?xml version="1.0" encoding="UTF-8"?>
<catalog title="Oracle Magazine" publisher="Oracle Publishing">
  <magazine date="March-April 2008">
   <article>
    <title>Oracle Database 11g Redux-Feature Review</title>
    <author>Tom Kyte</author>
   </article>
  </magazine>

</catalog>


Process exited with exit code 0.
Messages    Extensions    ▷ Running: BerkeleyDBXML.jpr
```

Summary

A relational database has its limitations when it comes to storing XML documents. The Berkeley DB XML database stores all XML documents and provides the provision to query, modify, and update documents without having to retrieve the documents from the database. In this chapter you learned to use the Berkeley DB XML database from the command shell and with the Berkeley DB XML API in JDeveloper 11g.

In the next chapter we will create PDF and XML reports using the Oracle XML Publisher API in JDeveloper.

14
Oracle XML Publisher

In Chapter 11 we generated a PDF report using the Apache FOP API, and in Chapter 12 we generated an Excel spreadsheet using the Apache POI API. Oracle also provides a reporting tool to generate reports. Oracle provides the Oracle XML Publisher to generate AWR, Excel spreadsheet, HTML, PDF, RTF, and UIX reports. Oracle XML Publisher is available as a GUI tool as well as a set of core API components. The Oracle XML Publisher has many advantages over the Apache FOP/Apache POI APIs, some of which are discussed as follows:

- Reports may be generated from multiple input XML files
- XML documents are not required to be parsed using the JAXP/XPath API
- PDF documents may be merged
- XML Publisher supports other formats such as HTML and RTF in addition to PDF and Excel spreadsheet

The following core APIs may be integrated with Oracle JDeveloper 11g to generate PDF, Excel, HTML, or RTF reports:

- **PDF Form Processing Engine API**: This merges a PDF template with XML data to generate a PDF document
- **RTF Processor**: This converts an RTF template to an **Extensible Style Language-Formatting Objects** (**XSL-FO**) file, which may then be used as an input to an FO Processor Engine
- **FO Processor Engine**: This merges an XML file (data source file) and an XSLT file (template) to generate PDF, Excel, HTML, and RTF reports
- **XSL-FO Utility**: This generates an XSL-FO file from an XML file and an XSLT file, or from a set of XML and XSLT files
- **PDF Document Merger**: This combines PDF documents and adds page numbering

- **PDF Book Binder Processor**: This merges a set of PDF documents into a single document with chapters, sections, subsections, and a table of contents

- **Document Processor Engine**: This batch-processes the above APIs with a single XML document that specifies templates, data sources, and outputs

In this chapter you'll learn how to use the FO Processor Engine, the XSL-FO Utility, and the PDF Document Merger. You'll also get an overview of the Data Engine API, which generates an XML document from a database. This API uses an XML template to specify the SQL queries to the database as well as the structure of the generated XML document.

Some of the Oracle XML Publisher conversions require RTF and PDF templates as inputs. To create an RTF template you'll need Oracle XML Publisher Desktop, an add-in to Microsoft Word. To create a PDF template, simply define a layout in a Word document and then convert it to PDF with Adobe Acrobat Distiller. Although this chapter doesn't discuss the APIs that need RTF and PDF templates, generating reports with them is similar to the procedure used for the Oracle XML Publisher APIs that are discussed in the chapter.

Setting the environment

1. Download Oracle XML Publisher Enterprise 5.6.2 for Microsoft Windows from `http://www.oracle.com/technology/software/products/publishing/index.html`, and extract the ZIP file `XMLP562_WIN.zip` to a directory.

2. In Oracle JDeveloper 11g, select **File | New** to open the **New Gallery** Wizard.

3. Create a new application by selecting **Categories | General** and **Items | Generic Application**, and then click the **OK** button.

4. In the **Create Generic Application** window, specify an application name (for example **XMLPublisher**) and click **Next**.

5. In the **Name your Generic project** window, specify a project name (for example **XMLPublisher**) and click **Finish**. An application and a project will be added to the **Application Navigator**.

6. Next, add a Java class to the project by selecting **File | New**, and **Categories | General**, and **Items | Java Class** in the **New Gallery** window. Click on **OK**.

7. In the **Create Java Class** window, specify a class name (for example **XMLPublisher**) and a package name (for example `xmlpublisher`).

8. Click on the **OK** button. A Java class will be added to the **XMLPublisher** project.

9. We will be generating PDF reports from input XML documents. Therefore, add XML documents **catalog.xml**, **catalog2.xml**, and **catalog3.xml** by selecting **Categories | General|XML** and **Items | XML Document** in the **New Gallery** window. We also need to add an XSL stylesheet, **catalog.xsl**, by selecting **Categories | General | XML** and **Items | XSL Stylesheet** in the **New Gallery** window.

10. In this chapter, you'll also create a XML report from an Oracle database table using an XML template. So, add an XML document, **catalogDataTemplate. xml**, to the project by selecting **Categories | General | XML** and **Items | XML Document** in the **New Gallery** window.

11. The directory structure of the Oracle XML Publisher project is shown in the following illustration.

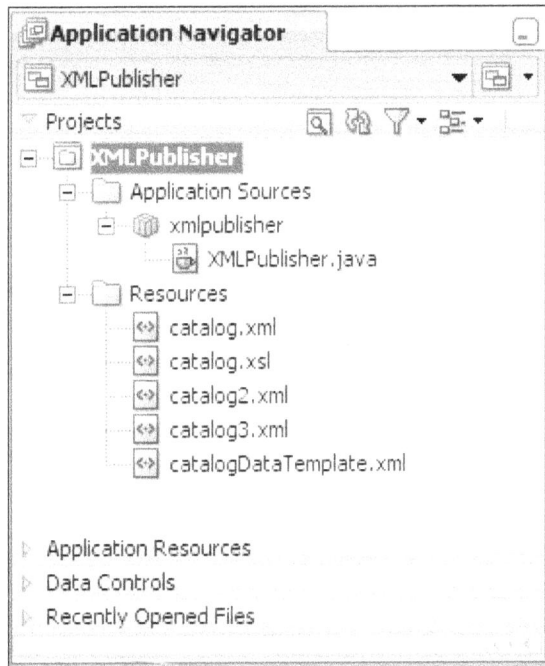

12. Next, add the Oracle XML Publisher API's JAR files to the Oracle XML Publisher project by selecting **Tools | Project Properties**.

13. In the **Project Properties** window, select **Libraries and Classpath**.

14. Add JAR files with the **Add JAR/Directory** button. The Oracle XML Publisher JAR files are in the `<XMLP562_WIN>\manual\lib` directory. `<XMLP562_WIN>` is the directory where the Oracle XML Publisher ZIP file is installed.

15. We also need to add the **Oracle JDBC** library, which you'll need to establish a JDBC connection with Oracle database for the Data Engine API. The **Oracle JDBC** library included with JDeveloper 11g generates an error with the Oracle XML Publisher Data Engine API. Therefore, we need to import the Oracle JDBC library definition from JDeveloper 10.1.3, for which you must install JDeveloper 10.1.3 Studio edition. Use the **Add Library** button to create a new **Oracle JDBC** library in JDeveloper 11g. In the **Add Library** window, select the **Project** node and click on **New**.

16. In the **Create Library** window specify a **Library Name**, for example **OracleJDBC** (**Oracle JDBC** library is already defined in JDeveloper 11g) and add the JDeveloper 10g JAR files shown in the following illustration using the **Add Entry** button. Click on **OK** in the **Create Library** window.

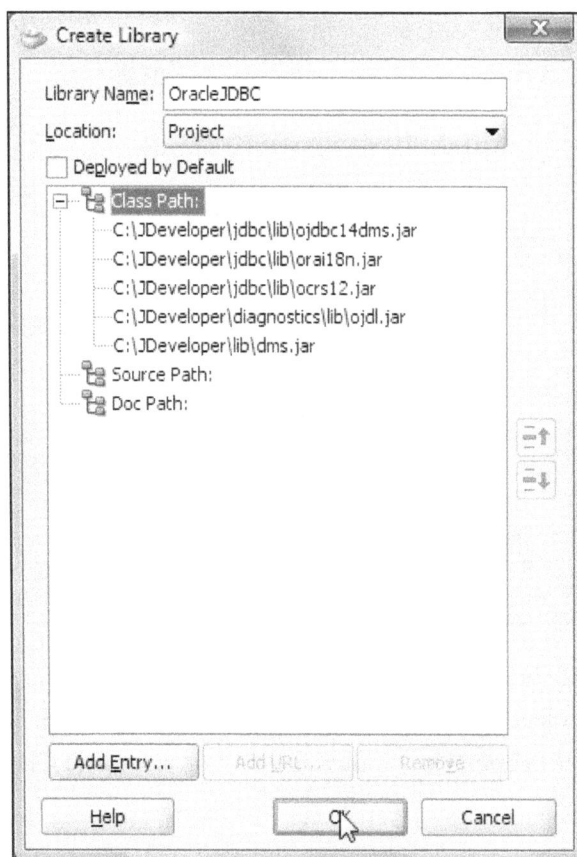

17. The **OracleJDBC** library gets added to the **Project** node in the **Add Library** window. Click on **OK** in the **Add Library** window.

18. The following illustration shows the JAR files or libraries in the Oracle XML Publisher project.

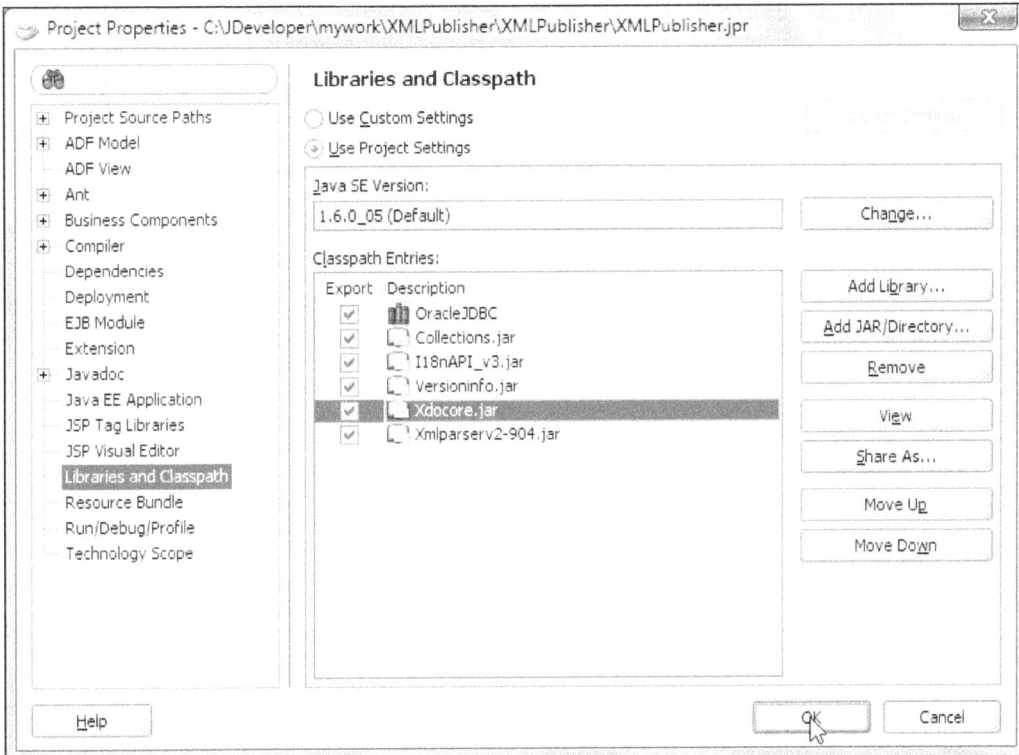

We need the Oracle database for the Data Engine API. Download and install Oracle Database 10g or 11g from `http://www.oracle.com/technology/software/products/database/index.html`, and create a database instance including the sample schemas. Then, create an example database table in the OE schema with the SQL script shown here:

```
CREATE TABLE OE.Catalog(CatalogId VARCHAR(25) PRIMARY KEY,
Journal VARCHAR(25), Publisher VARCHAR(25),
Edition VARCHAR(25), Title Varchar(45), Author Varchar(25));

INSERT INTO OE.Catalog VALUES('catalog1', 'Oracle Magazine', 'Oracle
Publishing',
'November-December 2008', 'Application Server Convergence', 'David
Baum');
```

```
INSERT INTO OE.Catalog VALUES('catalog2', 'Oracle Magazine', 'Oracle
Publishing',
'September-October 2008', 'Share 2.0', 'Alan Joch');

INSERT INTO OE.Catalog VALUES('catalog3', 'Oracle Magazine', 'Oracle
Publishing',
'March-April 2008', 'Oracle Database 11g Redux', 'Tom Kyte');
```

FO Processor Engine

The FO Processor Engine API is used to generate a PDF, Excel, HTML, or RTF
report from an XML document and an XSLT stylesheet. In this section, we'll create
a PDF document. The input XML document, catalog.xml, for the PDF report is
shown here:

```xml
<?xml version="1.0" encoding="UTF-8"?>
<!--A Oracle Magazine Catalog-->
<catalog  title="Oracle Magazine" publisher="Oracle Publishing">

  <magazine date="September-October 2008">
  <article>
    <title>Share 2.0</title>
    <author>Alan Joch</author>
   </article>
  <article>
    <title>Task and You Shall Receive</title>
    <author>Steve Muench</author>
   </article>

  </magazine>
  <magazine date="March-April 2008">
  <article>
    <title>Oracle Database 11g Redux</title>
    <author>Tom Kyte</author>
   </article>
  <article>
    <title>Declarative Data Filtering</title>
    <author>Steve Muench</author>
   </article>

  </magazine>
</catalog>
```

Copy `catalog.xml` to the **catalog.xml** file in the **XMLPublisher** project in JDeveloper 11g. To generate a PDF report, you'll need an XSL-FO file. XSL-FO is a W3C specification and is a subcomponent of the W3C **XSL** (**Extensible Stylesheet Language**) specification. Formatting objects are explained in the XSL specification (`http://www.w3.org/TR/xsl/#fo-section`). Here you'll define an XSL stylesheet, using which the FO Processor Engine will convert the XML file to an XSL-FO file. The XSL-FO file is created internally by the FO Processor Engine, and is not output. The FO Processor Engine then converts that file to a report.

An XSL-FO file specifies how data will be formatted in a report, including layout, fonts, and tables. Elements in an XSL-FO file are in the `fo` prefix namespace, which is specified with the namespace declaration `xmlns:fo=http://www.w3.org/1999/XSL/Format`. The DTD for an XSL-FO file is available in `fo.zip` from `http://www.renderx.com/Tests/validator/fo.zip`.

You can validate an XSL-FO file with an XML schema by converting the DTD for an XSL-FO file to an XML schema. Oracle JDeveloper can register the XML schema for XSL-FO files and generate or validate instances of XSL-FO files. Validating an XSL-FO file implies checking the format of the XSL-FO file. Schema Validation was discussed in Chapter 3. Some of the elements in the XSL-FO file are shown in the following table:

Element	Description
`fo:root`	Root element in an XSL-FO document
`fo:layout-master-set`	Specifies a set of page masters
`fo:simple-page-master`	Page layout
`fo:page-sequence`	Specifies the order of page masters
`fo:flow`	Page content
`fo:block`	Block content
`fo:list-block`	Specifies a list
`fo:list-item`	List item
`fo:table`	Table
`fo:table-column`	Table column
`fo:table-header`	Table header
`fo:table-body`	Table body
`fo:table-row`	Table row
`fo:table-cell`	Table cell

The example XSL stylesheet, `catalog.xsl` (listed as follows), is used to generate an XSL-FO file from the input XML file, `catalog.xml`. This may be created using the XSL **Component Palette** in JDeveloper.

```
<?xml version="1.0" encoding="UTF-8"?>
<xsl:stylesheet version="1.1"
xmlns:xsl="http://www.w3.org/1999/XSL/Transform"
    xmlns:fo="http://www.w3.org/1999/XSL/Format">
  <xsl:output method="xml" version="1.0"
  omit-xml-declaration="no" indent="yes"/>
  <!-- ========================= -->
  <!-- root element: catalog -->
  <!-- ========================= -->
  <xsl:template match="/catalog">
    <fo:root xmlns:fo="http://www.w3.org/1999/XSL/Format">
      <fo:layout-master-set>
        <fo:simple-page-master master-name="simpleA4" page-
height="29.7cm"
              page-width="21cm" margin-top="2cm" margin-bottom="2cm"
          margin-left="2cm" margin-right="2cm">
          <fo:region-body/>
        </fo:simple-page-master>
      </fo:layout-master-set>
      <fo:page-sequence master-reference="simpleA4">
        <fo:flow flow-name="xsl-region-body">
          <fo:block font-size="16pt" font-weight="bold" space-
after="5mm">
            Catalog:  <xsl:value-of select="@title"/>
          </fo:block>
 <fo:block font-size="16pt" font-weight="bold" space-after="5mm">
            Publisher:  <xsl:value-of select="@publisher"/>
          </fo:block>
          <fo:block font-size="10pt">

  <fo:table table-layout="fixed">
              <fo:table-column column-width="4cm"/>
              <fo:table-column column-width="4cm"/>
              <fo:table-column column-width="5cm"/>
            <fo:table-header>
 <fo:table-row font-weight="bold"><fo:table-cell>
        <fo:block>
          <xsl:text>Date</xsl:text>
        </fo:block>
      </fo:table-cell>
  <fo:table-cell>
```

```
            <fo:block>
              <xsl:text>Title</xsl:text>
            </fo:block>
        </fo:table-cell>
<fo:table-cell>
          <fo:block>
            <xsl:text>Author</xsl:text>
          </fo:block>
        </fo:table-cell>
   </fo:table-row>

</fo:table-header>

  <fo:table-body>
              <xsl:apply-templates select="magazine"/>
              </fo:table-body>
            </fo:table>
          </fo:block>
        </fo:flow>
      </fo:page-sequence>
    </fo:root>
  </xsl:template>

<xsl:template match="magazine">

<xsl:for-each select="article">
<fo:table-row>
        <fo:table-cell>
        <fo:block>
          <xsl:value-of select="../@date"/>
        </fo:block>
      </fo:table-cell>
      <fo:table-cell>
        <fo:block>
          <xsl:value-of select="title"/>
        </fo:block>
      </fo:table-cell>
      <fo:table-cell>
        <fo:block>
          <xsl:value-of select="author"/>
        </fo:block>
      </fo:table-cell>
    </fo:table-row>

</xsl:for-each>
  </xsl:template>
</xsl:stylesheet>
```

The `catalog.xsl` document provides the XSL-FO document elements: the `fo:root` element creates the root of an XSL-FO document, the `fo:layout-master-set` element creates layout page masters, the `fo:block` element creates block content, and the `fo:table` element creates a table. Copy `catalog.xsl` to the `catalog.xsl` file in the JDeveloper 11g project **XMLPublisher**. Next, develop a Java application to generate reports with the Oracle XML Publisher APIs.

1. In the `XMLPublisher.java` class, import the Oracle XML Publisher classes.

   ```
   import oracle.apps.xdo.template.FOProcessor;
   import oracle.apps.xdo.template.fo.util.FOUtility;
   import oracle.apps.xdo.common.pdf.util.PDFDocMerger;
   import oracle.apps.xdo.dataengine.DataProcessor;
   import oracle.apps.xdo.XDOException;
   ```

2. Create an `FOProcessor` object. The `FOProcessor` class is the main class for using the FO Processing Engine.

   ```
   FOProcessor processor = new FOProcessor();
   ```

3. Set the input XML file using the `setData` method of the `FOProcessor` object. The `setData` method is overloaded so that the input data may be set from an `InputStream`, a `Reader`, or an XML file specified as a `String`. We will set data from an XML file, `catalog.xml`, specified as a `String`.

   ```
   processor.setData("catalog.xml");
   ```

4. Set the XSL template using the `setTemplate` method.

   ```
   processor.setTemplate("catalog.xsl");
   ```

5. Set the output file and the output format for a PDF document using the `setOutput` and `setOutputFormat` methods.

   ```
   processor.setOutput("catalog.pdf");
   processor.setOutputFormat(FOProcessor.FORMAT_PDF);
   ```

The following table lists the supported output formats:

Output Format	Description
FORMAT_AWT	AWT format constant
FORMAT_EXCEL	Excel spreadsheet format constant
FORMAT_EXCEL_MHTML	MHTML constant for Excel charts
FORMAT_HTML	HTML format constant
FORMAT_PDF	PDF format constant
FORMAT_RTF	RTF format constant

Output Format	Description
FORMAT_UIX	UIX format constant. UIX output is not supported. An HTML file gets generated
FORMAT_FO	FO format constant
FORMAT_MHTML	MHTML format constant
FORMAT_PPTMHT	PowerPoint constant
FORMAT_PPTX	PowerPoint 2007 constant

If an HTML output is required, specify an HTML output file and an HTML output format.

```
processor.setOutput("catalog.html");
processor.setOutputFormat(FOProcessor.FORMAT_HTML);
```

When creating the XSL-FO for a report, specify only the properties that are supported by the report format to be generated. For example, specifying page height and page width would not be relevant when creating an HTML format report. Run the FO Processor Engine using the generate method.

```
processor.generate();
```

When the XMLPublisher.java application is run, which we will see later in the chapter, the PDF report, catalog.pdf (shown as follows), is generated:

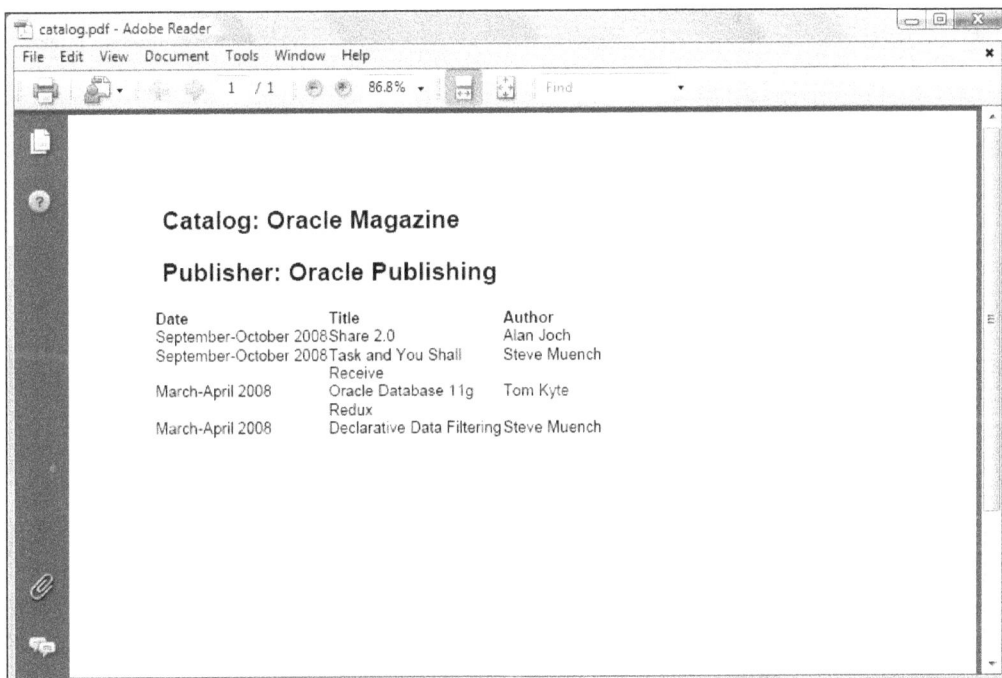

XSL-FO Utility

In the previous section, you generated an Oracle XML Publisher report from an XML file and an XSLT file. The input can also be a set of XML files and XSLT files. The XSL-FO Utility generates an XSL-FO file from a set of input XML and XSLT files.

For example, let's create an XSL-FO file from two input XML files, `catalog2.xml` and `catalog3.xml`.

1. Copy `catalog2.xml` (listed as follows) to the **catalog2.xml** file in the JDeveloper 11g project **XMLPublisher**.

```
<?xml version="1.0" encoding="UTF-8"?>
<!--A Oracle Magazine Catalog-->
<catalog title="Oracle Magazine" publisher="Oracle Publishing">

  <magazine date="March-April 2008">
  <article>
    <title>Declarative Data Filtering</title>
    <author>Steve Muench</author>
  </article>
  </magazine>
</catalog>
```

2. Also copy `catalog3.xml` (listed as follows) to **catalog3.xml** in the JDeveloper 11g project **XMLPublisher**.

```
<?xml version="1.0" encoding="UTF-8"?>
<!--A Oracle Magazine Catalog-->
<catalog title="Oracle Magazine" publisher="Oracle Publishing">
  <magazine date="September-October 2008">
  <article>
    <title>Task and You Shall Receive</title>
    <author>Steve Muench</author>
  </article>

  </magazine>
  <magazine date="March-April 2008">
  <article>
    <title>Oracle Database 11g Redux</title>
    <author>Tom Kyte</author>
  </article>
  </magazine>
</catalog>
```

3. We'll use the XSL stylesheet, `catalog.xsl`, to generate XSL-FO files for the input XML files, and then merge the XSL-FO files to generate a single XSL-FO file.

4. Create an array of `InputStream` objects for the XSL-FO files to be generated from the input XML and XSLT files.

```
InputStream[] input = new  InputStream[2];
```

5. Create XSL-FO files from the input XML and XSLT files with the XSL-FO Utility's main class `FOUtility`. Use the static method `createFO(java.lang.String xmlFile,java.lang.String xslFile)` to create the XSL-FO files.

```
InputStream firstFOStream = FOUtility.createFO("catalog2.xml",
"catalog.xsl");
InputStream secondFOStream = FOUtility.createFO("catalog3.xml",
"catalog.xsl");
```

6. Set the XSL-FO `InputStream` objects in the `InputStream` array using the `set` method.

```
Array.set(input, 0,  firstFOStream);
Array.set(input, 1, secondFOStream);
```

7. Merge the XSL-FO `InputStream` objects using the static method `mergeFOs()`.

```
InputStream mergedFOStream = FOUtility.mergeFOs(input, null);
```

8. Create an `FOProcessor` object to generate a PDF report from the merged XSL-FO file.

```
FOProcessor processor = new FOProcessor();
```

9. Set the merged XSL-FO `InputStream` on the `FOProcessor` object using the `setData` method.

```
processor.setData(mergedFOStream);
```

10. If an XSL-FO file is specified as the datasource to an `FOProcessor`, you don't need to set an XSL document. Set the XSL template to null.

```
processor.setTemplate((String)null);
```

11. Set the output PDF file using the `setOutput` method, then set the output format using the `setOutputFormat` method, and then generate a PDF report using the `generate` method.

```
processor.setOutput("catalog2.pdf");
processor.setOutputFormat(FOProcessor.FORMAT_PDF);
processor.generate();
```

12. You'll find the PDF report, `catalog2.pdf` (shown below as two illustrations, because the PDF has two pages), in the output when the `XMLPublisher.java` application is run.

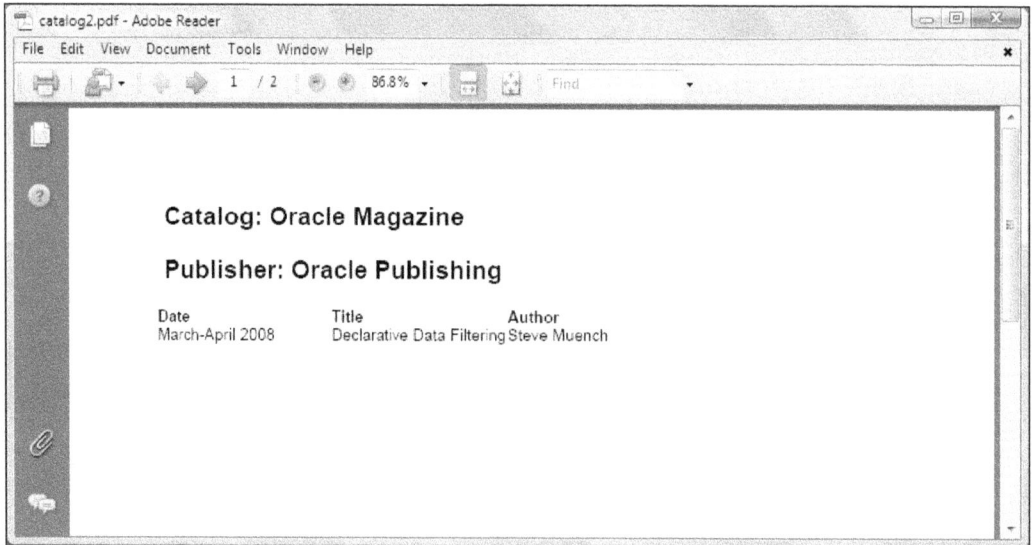

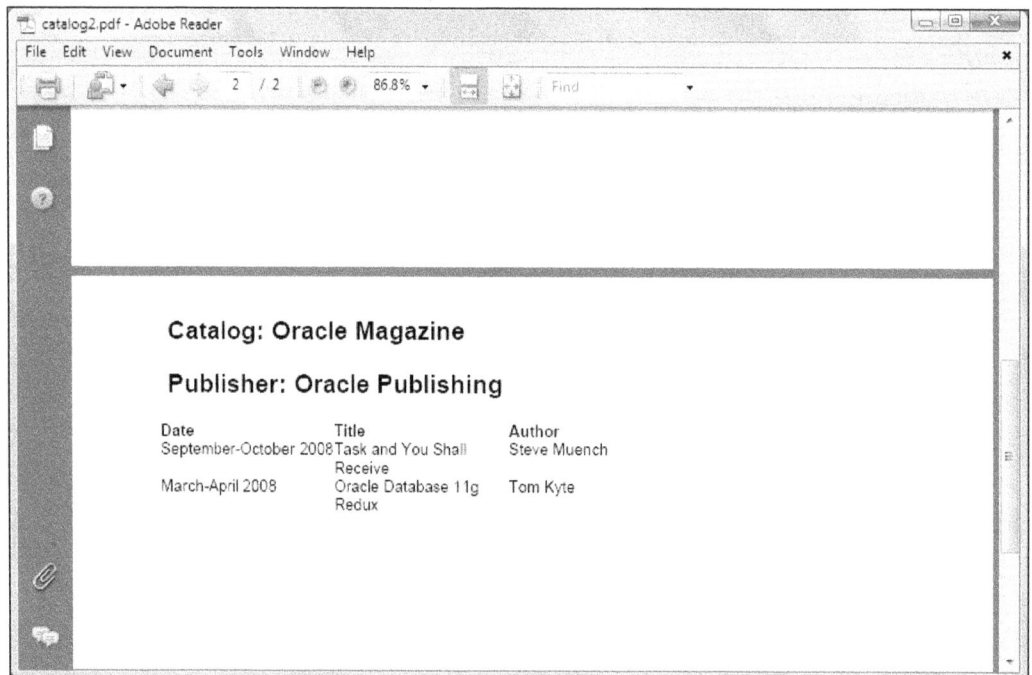

PDF Document Merger

Sometimes, you have to merge PDF documents. The PDF Document Merger combines PDF documents and optionally adds page numbering to the merged document. In this section we'll merge `catalog.pdf` and `catalog2.pdf`, which we generated in the previous sections.

1. First, create an `InputStream` array from the `catalog.pdf` and `catalog2.pdf` reports.

   ```
   FileInputStream[] inputStreams = new FileInputStream[2];
   inputStreams[0] = new FileInputStream("catalog.pdf");
   inputStreams[1] = new  FileInputStream("catalog2.pdf");
   ```

2. Create a `FileOutputStream` object for the merged PDF document.

   ```
   FileOutputStream  outputStream = new FileOutputStream(
   "catalog3.pdf");
   ```

3. Merge the PDF documents with the `PDFDocMerger` class.

   ```
   PDFDocMerger pdfMerger = new PDFDocMerger(inputStreams,
   outputStream);
   ```

4. To add page numbering, specify the page numbering coordinates using the `setPageNumberCoordinates` method, and set the page numbering font using the `setPagNumberFontInfo` method.

   ```
   pdfMerger.setPageNumberCoordinates(300, 20);
   pdfMerger.setPageNumberFontInfo("Courier", 10);
   ```

5. Set the page numbering value with the `setPageNumberValue(int initialValue, int startPageIndex)` method. The `initialValue` specifies the initial value of page numbering. The `startPageIndex` specifies the page from which numbering should start.

   ```
   pdfMerger.setPageNumberValue(1, 1);
   ```

> The PDF Document Merger has the provision to add an image watermark to the merged PDF document. The image watermark is added to each page of the merged PDF document. The image watermark may be used to set a background image or add a logo image.

6. We will add an image watermark as a header. Create an `InputStream` for the image to be set as an image watermark.

   ```
   FileInputStream imgStream = new FileInputStream
   ("C:\\XMLPublisher\\pdfwatermark.jpg");
   ```

7. Specify the coordinates of the rectangle in which the image watermark is to be added.

```
float[] rct = {10f, 800f, -1f, -1f};
```

8. Set the image watermark with the `setImageWatermark` method.

```
pdfMerger.setImageWatermark(imgStream, rct);
```

9. Run the PDF Document Merger using the `process` method.

```
pdfMerger.process();
```

You'll find the merged PDF document, `catalog3.pdf` (shown in the following three illustrations), in the output files when the `XMLPublisher.java` application is run. The image watermark is shown added as a header to each of the PDF document pages.

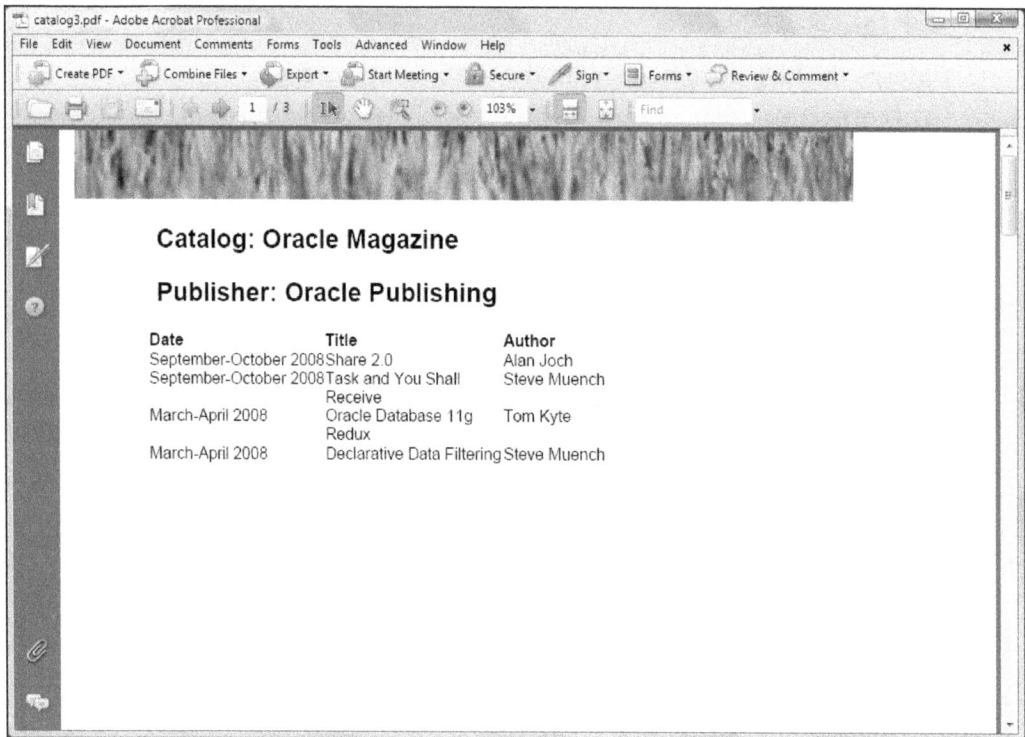

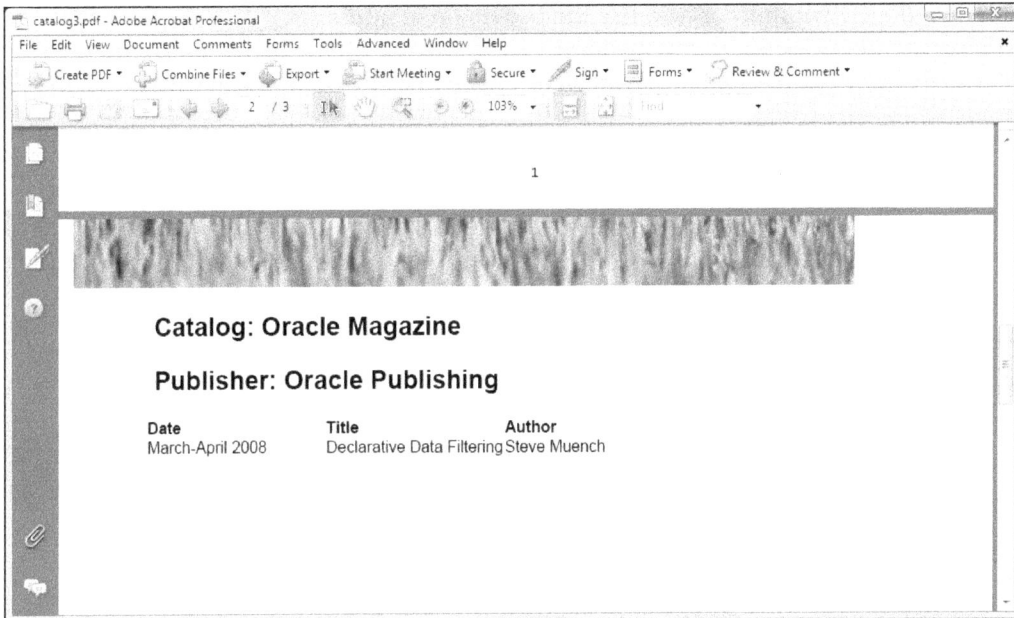

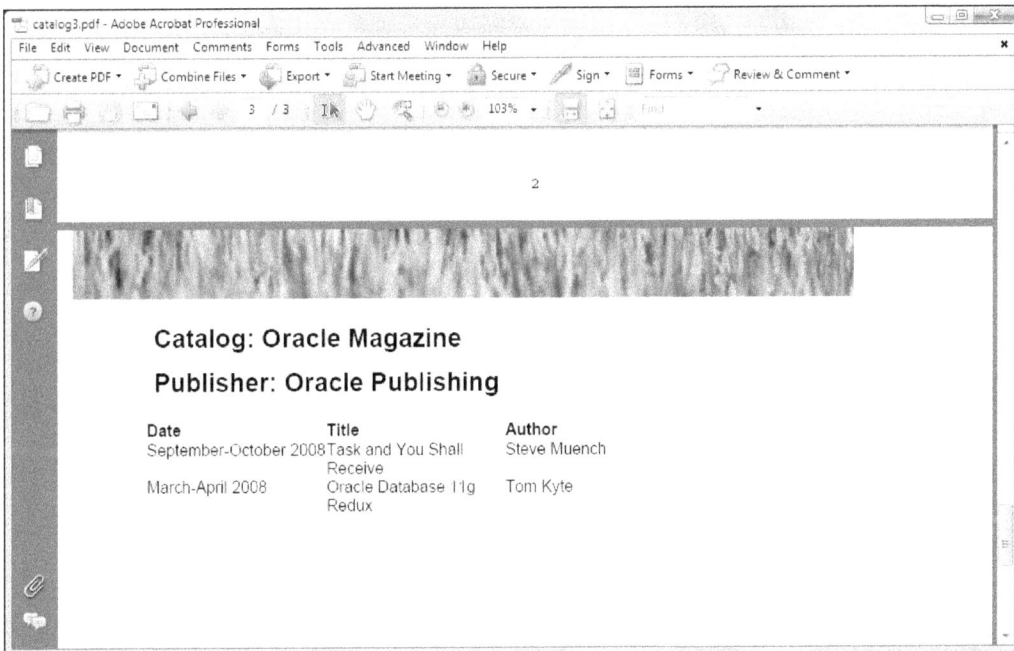

The PDF document merger also has the provision to add a text watermark. If both an image watermark and a text watermark are set, only the image watermark gets added. Next, we will add a text watermark instead of the image watermark.

1. Set the text watermark using the `setTextWatermark(java.lang.String watermarkText, float startX, float startY)` method.

    ```
    pdfMerger.setTextWatermark("Oracle XML Publisher", 50f, 450f);
    ```

2. Set the angle of the text watermark using the `setTextWatermarkAngle( int angDeg)` method.

    ```
    pdfMerger.setTextWatermarkAngle(45);
    ```

3. Set the color of the text watermark using the `setTextWatermarkColor( float red, float green, float blue)` method.

    ```
    pdfMerger.setTextWatermarkColor(0.3f, 0.3f, 1.0f);
    ```

If a text watermark is set, do not set an image watermark. When the `XMLPublisher.java` application is run with text watermark option, a the text watermark gets added to each of the pages in the merged PDF document as shown in following figure:

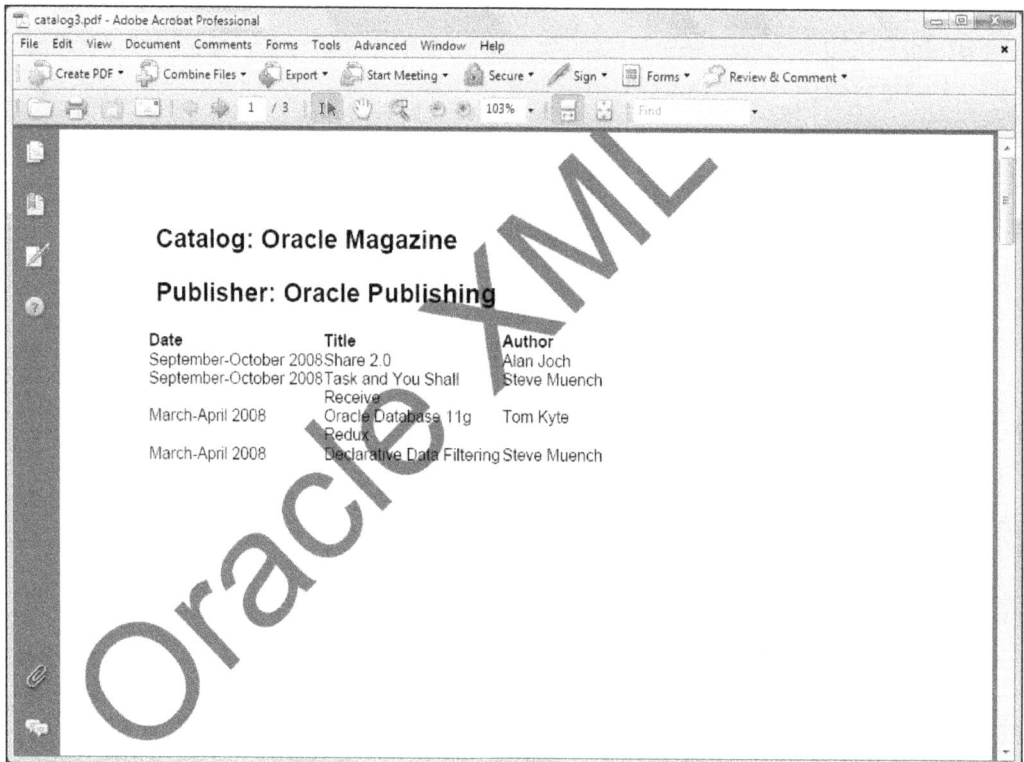

Data Engine

The Data Engine API creates an XML document from database data. The `DataProcessor` class is used to generate an XML document from a data template. This template is an XML file that specifies the input parameters, the SQL query to retrieve data from the database, and the data structure of the XML document to be generated. One advantage of the Data Engine API over the XML SQL Utility (which also generates an XML document from a database) is that it lets you generate a hierarchy of elements in an XML document. The following table shows some of the commonly used elements and attributes in the data template with the required elements/attributes indicated with "(required)":

Element	Description	Attributes
dataTemplate (required)	Root element.	name (required) version (required)
parameters	Specifies input parameters to the SQL query. Consists of <parameter> elements. Parameter values may be set at runtime.	name (required) dataType – values may be "character", "date" or "number"; default value is "character".
dataQuery (required)	Specifies the SQL queries to retrieve data from the database. Consists of <sqlstatement> elements.	-
sqlstatement (required)	Specifies the SQL statement.	name (required)
dataStructure (required for multiple queries)	Defines structure of output XML. Consists of <group> and <element> elements. If not specified for a single query, the output XML consists of elements corresponding to the columns in the SQL query.	-
group	Specifies a group of elements and subgroups. Hierarchies of elements may be specified with subgroup elements.	name (required) source (required) – specifies the query identifier for the corresponding SQL statement from which the group's elements are derived.
element (required)	Specifies an element in output XML document	name (required) value (required) – specifies the column name for the SQL statement.

The following example data template, `catalogDataTemplate.xml`, is used to generate an XML document from the database table:

```xml
<?xml version="1.0" encoding="WINDOWS-1252" ?>
<dataTemplate name="catalogDataTemplate" description="Magazine
Catalog" defaultPackage="" Version="1.0">
<parameters>
<parameter name="id" dataType="character" />
</parameters>
<dataQuery>
<sqlStatement name="Q1">
<![CDATA[
  SELECT CatalogId, Journal, Publisher, Edition, Title,
  Author from OE.CATALOG WHERE CatalogId=:id]]>
</sqlStatement>
</dataQuery>
<dataStructure>
<group name="G_Catalog" source="Q1">
<element name="CATALOGID" value="CatalogId" />
<element name="JOURNAL" value="Journal" />
<element name="PUBLISHER" value="Publisher"/>
<element name="EDITION" value="Edition" />
<element name="TITLE" value="Title"/>
<element name="AUTHOR" value="Author" />
</group>
</dataStructure>
</dataTemplate>
```

Copy the `catalogDataTemplate.xml` file to the **catalogDataTemplate.xml** file in JDeveloper 11g project **XMLPublisher**. The example data template specifies a parameter `id` of type `character`. Bind variable is used in the SQL query to set the value of the `CatalogId` column with the `id` parameter. The value of the `CatalogId` column is set at runtime. All the columns in the example query are of type VARCHAR. The following column type may be specified in a SQL query: VARCHAR2, CHAR, NUMBER, DATE, TIMESTAMP, BLOB, CLOB, and XMLType.

1. Next, we'll generate an XML document from database data with the Data Engine API. First, create a `DataProcessor` object.

   ```java
   DataProcessor dataProcessor = new DataProcessor();
   ```

2. Set the data template on the `DataProcessor` object using the `setTemplate` method.

   ```java
   dataProcessor.setDataTemplate("catalogDataTemplate.xml");
   ```

3. Create a `HashTable` of input parameters and specify a value for the `id` parameter using the `put` method. Set the parameters on the `DataProcessor` object using the `setParameters` method.

```
Hashtable parameters = new Hashtable();
parameters.put("id","catalog1");
dataProcessor.setParameters(parameters);
```

4. Create a JDBC connection with Oracle Database and set the connection on the `DataProcessor` object using the `setConnection` object.

```
Class.forName("oracle.jdbc.OracleDriver");
String url="jdbc:oracle:thin:@localhost:1521:ORCL";
java.sql.Connection jdbcConnection = DriverManager.
getConnection(url, "OE", "password");
dataProcessor.setConnection(jdbcConnection);
```

5. Set the output XML document using the `setOutput` method and run the data processor using the `processData` method.

```
dataProcessor.setOutput("catalogData.xml");
dataProcessor.processData();
```

6. The database generates an XML document, `catalogData.xml`, as here.

```
<?xml version="1.0" encoding="UTF-8"?>

<catalogDataTemplate>
<id>catalog1</id>
<LIST_G_CATALOG>
<G_CATALOG>
<CATALOGID>catalog1</CATALOGID>
<JOURNAL>Oracle Magazine</JOURNAL>
<PUBLISHER>Oracle Publishing</PUBLISHER>
<EDITION>November-December 2008</EDITION>
<TITLE>Application Server Convergence</TITLE>
<AUTHOR>David Baum</AUTHOR>
</G_CATALOG>
</LIST_G_CATALOG>
</catalogDataTemplate>
```

The Java class `XMLPublisher.java` with code explanations is listed as follows:

1. First, define the `package` and `import` statements.

    ```
    package xmlpublisher;

    import com.sun.java.util.collections.Hashtable;

    import oracle.apps.xdo.XDOException;
    import oracle.apps.xdo.common.pdf.util.PDFDocMerger;
    import oracle.apps.xdo.dataengine.DataProcessor;
    import oracle.apps.xdo.template.FOProcessor;
    import oracle.apps.xdo.template.fo.util.FOUtility;


    import java.io.FileInputStream;
    import java.io.FileNotFoundException;
    import java.io.FileOutputStream;
    import java.io.InputStream;

    import java.lang.reflect.Array;

    import java.sql.DriverManager;
    import java.sql.SQLException;
    ```

2. Define Java class `XMLPublisher`.

    ```
    public class XMLPublisher {
        public XMLPublisher() {
        }
    ```

3. Add Java method `foProcessorEngine` to convert an XML file and an XSL file to a PDF document using the `FOProcessor`.

    ```
    public void foProcessorEngine() {
        try {
            FOProcessor processor = new FOProcessor();
            processor.setData("catalog.xml");
            processor.setTemplate("catalog.xsl");
            processor.setOutput("catalog.pdf");
            processor.setOutputFormat(FOProcessor.FORMAT_PDF);

            processor.generate();
        } catch (XDOException e) {
            System.err.println("XDOException " + e.getMessage());
        }
    }
    ```

4. Add a Java method `xslFoUtility` to generate a PDF report from sets of input XML and XSL files.

```
public void xslFoUtility() {
    try {
        InputStream[] input = new InputStream[2];
        InputStream firstFOStream = FOUtility.createFO
        ("catalog2.xml", "catalog.xsl");
        InputStream secondFOStream = FOUtility.createFO
        ("catalog3.xml", "catalog.xsl");
        Array.set(input, 0, firstFOStream);
        Array.set(input, 1, secondFOStream);

        InputStream mergedFOStream = FOUtility.mergeFOs
        (input, null);

        if (mergedFOStream == null) {
            System.err.println("Merge failed.");
        }

        FOProcessor processor = new FOProcessor();
        processor.setData(mergedFOStream);
        processor.setTemplate((String) null);
        processor.setOutput("catalog2.pdf");
        processor.setOutputFormat(FOProcessor.FORMAT_PDF);
        processor.generate();
    } catch (XDOException e) {
        System.err.println("XDOException" + e.getMessage());
    }
}
```

5. Define a Java method `pdfDocumentMerger` to merge PDF documents.

```
public void pdfDocumentMerger() {
    try {
        FileInputStream[] inputStreams = new FileInputStream[2];
        inputStreams[0] = new FileInputStream("catalog.pdf");
        inputStreams[1] = new FileInputStream("catalog2.pdf");

        FileOutputStream outputStream = new FileOutputStream(
        "catalog3.pdf");
        PDFDocMerger pdfMerger = new PDFDocMerger(inputStreams,
        outputStream);

        pdfMerger.setPageNumberCoordinates(300, 20);
        pdfMerger.setPageNumberFontInfo("Courier", 10);
        pdfMerger.setPageNumberValue(1, 1);

pdfMerger.setTextWatermark("Oracle XML Publisher", 50f, 450f);
```

```
            pdfMerger.setTextWatermarkAngle(45);
            pdfMerger.setTextWatermarkColor(0.3f, 0.3f, 1.0f);

        /*  FileInputStream imgStream = new FileInputStream
            ("C:\\XMLPublisher\\pdfwatermark.jpg");
            float[] rct = {10f, 800f, -1f, -1f};
            pdfMerger.setImageWatermark(imgStream, rct);*/
            pdfMerger.process();
            pdfMerger = null;
        } catch (XDOException e) {
            System.err.println("XDOException" + e.getMessage());
        } catch (FileNotFoundException e) {
            System.err.println("FileNotFoundException " +
            e.getMessage());
        }
    }
```

6. Define a Java method `dataEngine` to generate an XML document from a database.

```
public void dataEngine() {
    try {
        Class.forName("oracle.jdbc.OracleDriver");

        String url = "jdbc:oracle:thin:@localhost:1521:ORCL";
        java.sql.Connection jdbcConnection = DriverManager.
        getConnection(url,
                "OE", "password");

        DataProcessor dataProcessor = new DataProcessor();
        dataProcessor.setDataTemplate("catalogDataTemplate.xml");

        Hashtable parameters = new Hashtable();
        parameters.put("id", "catalog1");
        dataProcessor.setParameters(parameters);
        dataProcessor.setConnection(jdbcConnection);

        dataProcessor.setOutput("catalogData.xml");
        dataProcessor.processData();
    } catch (SQLException e) {
        System.err.println("SQLException " + e.getMessage());
    } catch (ClassNotFoundException e) {
        System.err.println("ClassNotFoundException " +
        e.getMessage());
    } catch (XDOException e) {
        System.err.println("XDOException" + e.getMessage());
    } finally{try { jdbcConnection.close();}catch(
        SQLException e){ System.err.println("SQLException in closing
        connection" + e.getMessage());
    }}
    }
```

7. Finally, define the `main` method in which you create an instance of the `XMLPublisher` class and invoke the instance methods to generate reports.

```
public static void main(String[] argv) {
    XMLPublisher xmlPublisher = new XMLPublisher();
    xmlPublisher.foProcessorEngine();
    xmlPublisher.xslFoUtility();
    xmlPublisher.pdfDocumentMerger();
    xmlPublisher.dataEngine();
    }
}
```

Next, run the Oracle XML Publisher application. Right-click on the **XMLPublisher. java** class and select **Run**.

This will generate PDF and XML reports. Select **View | Refresh** to add the PDF and XML reports to the **XMLPublisher** project. The XML report **catalogData.xml** is shown in the following illustration:

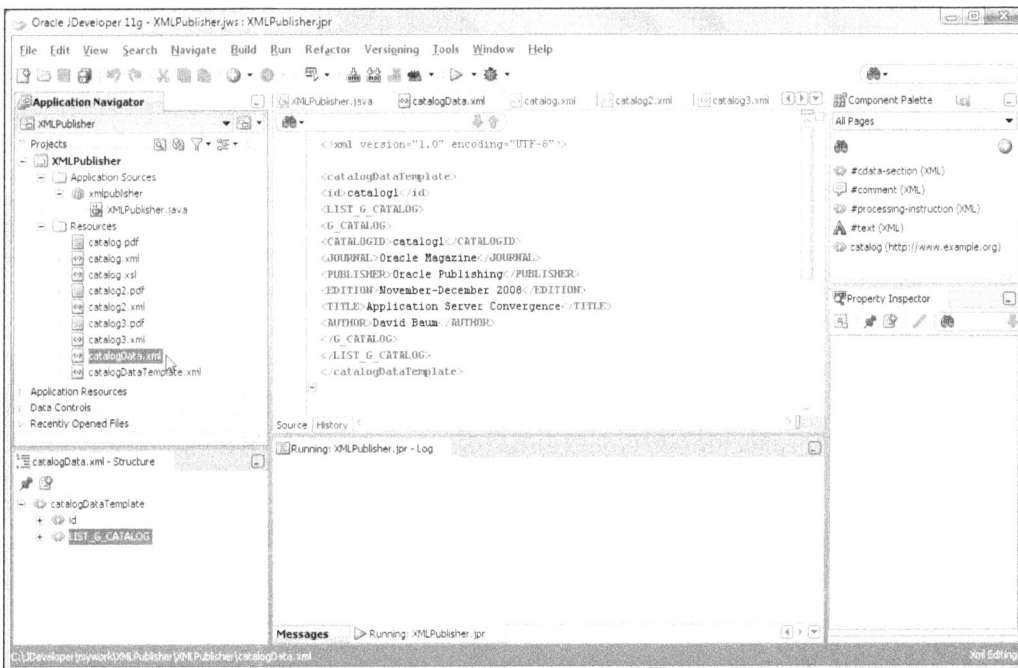

If the output format in the FO Processor Engine section is set to HTML in the
`foProcessorEngine` method, as explained earlier, it will generate an output
HTML report. This is shown in the following screenshot:

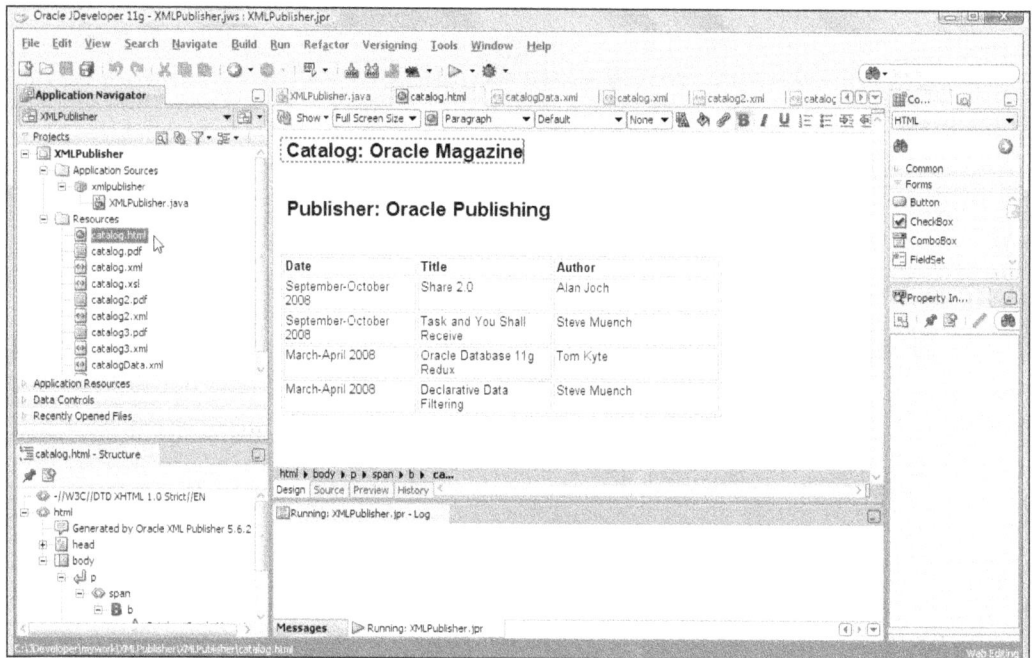

The XML Publisher APIs, which are not discussed, may also be integrated with a
similar procedure.

- The XML Publisher class for **PDF Form Processing Engine** is
  `oracle.apps.xdo.template.FormProcessor`
- The class for **RTF Processor** is `oracle.apps.xdo.template.RTFProcessor`
- The class for **Document Processor** is `oracle.apps.xdo.batch.`
  `DocumentProcessor`
- The class for **PDF Book Binder Processor** is `oracle.apps.xdo.template.`
  `pdf.book.PDFBookBinder`

Summary

The Oracle XML Publisher is available as a set of core component APIs that may be
integrated with JDeveloper 11g. We generated a PDF report using the FO Processor
Engine. We also generated a PDF report using multiple input XML and XSL files
with the XSL-FO Utility. Subsequently, we merged the PDF reports generated using
the PDF Document Merge API. We also created an XML report from Oracle database
using the Data Engine API.

Index

E

element, XML schema
  attribute construct, attributes 48
  attributeGroup 49
  element declaration example 48
  maxOccurs attribute 48
  minOccurs attribute 48
  name attribute 48
  type attribute 48
embedded database 307
Excel to XML conversion
  Excel spreadsheet, parsing 301
  Java application, running 301-306
  XML document, creating 301
  XML DOM tree, constructing 302
Extensible Style Language-Formatting
      Objects (XSL-FO) file 337
Extensible Stylesheet Language. *See* **XSL**
Extensible Stylesheet Language
      Transformation. *See* **XSLT**

F

FO Processor Engine
  about 337, 342-347
  Java application, developing 346
  output formats 346
  PDF document, creating 342, 343
  XSL-FO file 343
  XSL-FO file, elements 343
  XSL Component Palette used 344-346
FO Processor Engine, output formats
  FORMAT_AWT 346
  FORMAT_EXCEL 346
  FORMAT_EXCEL_MHTML 346
  FORMAT_FO 347
  FORMAT_HTML 346
  FORMAT_MHTML 347
  FORMAT_PDF 346
  FORMAT_PPTMHT 347
  FORMAT_PPTX 347
  FORMAT_RTF 346
  FORMAT_UIX 347

G

generate method 347
getDocuments command 314

I

if tag, JSTL XML tag library 159
input filter, values returning
  SHOW_ALL value 194
  SHOW_CDATA_SECTION value 194
  SHOW_COMMENT value 194
  SHOW_ELEMENTvalue 194
  SHOW_ENTITY_REFERENCE value 194
  SHOW_PROCESSING_INSTRUCTION
      value 194
  SHOW_TEXT value 194
installing
  Oracle BDB XML 308-310
iText 273

J

Java API for XML Processing *See* **JAXP**
Java API for XML web services (JAX-WS)
      2.0 227
Java application, XML document
  runing 18, 20, 22
Java Architecture for XML Binding.
      See **JAXB**
Java objects
  binding with XML schema, annotations
      used 252-257
Java Server Pages Standard Tag Library. *See*
      JSTL
Java Specification Request (JSR) 228
JAXB
  about 227
  compiler 227
  XML document, marshalling 227
  XML document, unmarshalling 227
JAXB 2.0
  annotations 253
  features 228, 229

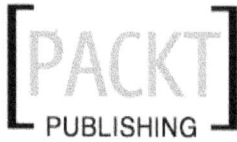

Thank you for buying
Processing XML documents with Oracle JDeveloper 11g

About Packt Publishing

Packt, pronounced 'packed', published its first book "*Mastering phpMyAdmin for Effective MySQL Management*" in April 2004 and subsequently continued to specialize in publishing highly focused books on specific technologies and solutions.

Our books and publications share the experiences of your fellow IT professionals in adapting and customizing today's systems, applications, and frameworks. Our solution based books give you the knowledge and power to customize the software and technologies you're using to get the job done. Packt books are more specific and less general than the IT books you have seen in the past. Our unique business model allows us to bring you more focused information, giving you more of what you need to know, and less of what you don't.

Packt is a modern, yet unique publishing company, which focuses on producing quality, cutting-edge books for communities of developers, administrators, and newbies alike. For more information, please visit our website: www.packtpub.com.

Writing for Packt

We welcome all inquiries from people who are interested in authoring. Book proposals should be sent to authors@packtpub.com. If your book idea is still at an early stage and you would like to discuss it first before writing a formal book proposal, contact us; one of our commissioning editors will get in touch with you.

We're not just looking for published authors; if you have strong technical skills but no writing experience, our experienced editors can help you develop a writing career, or simply get some additional reward for your expertise.

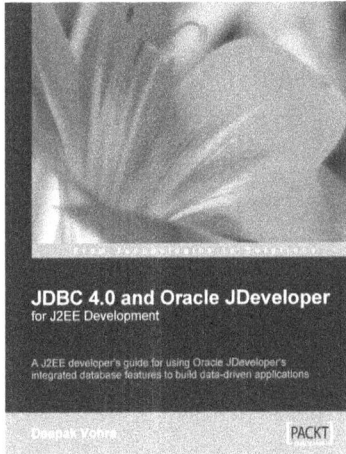

JDBC 4.0 and Oracle JDeveloper for J2EE Development

ISBN: 978-1-847194-30-5   Paperback: 431 pages

A J2EE developer's guide to using Oracle JDeveloper's integrated database features to build data-driven applications

1. Develop your Java applications using JDBC and Oracle JDeveloper

2. Explore the new features of JDBC 4.0

3. Use JDBC and the data tools in Oracle JDeveloper

4. Configure JDBC with various application servers

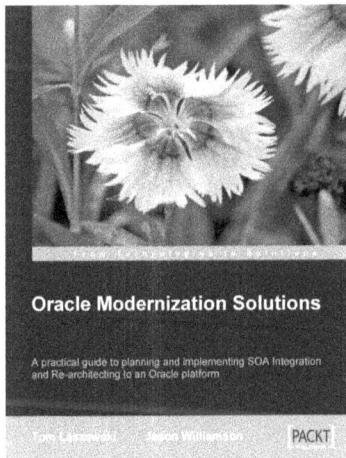

Oracle Modernization Solutions

ISBN: 978-1-847194-64-0   Paperback: 432 pages

A practical guide to planning and implementing SOA Integration and Re-architecting to an Oracle platform

1. Complete, practical guide to legacy modernization using SOA Integration and Re-architecture

2. Understand when and why to choose the non-invasive SOA Integration approach to reuse and integrate legacy components quickly and safely

3. Understand when and why to choose Re-architecture to reverse engineer legacy components and preserve business knowledge in a modern open and extensible architecture

4. Modernize to a process-driven SOA architecture based on Java EE, Oracle Database, and Fusion Middleware

Please visit **www.PacktPub.com** for information on our titles

www.ingramcontent.com/pod-product-compliance
Lightning Source LLC
Chambersburg PA
CBHW080709220326
41598CB00033B/5361